SHAKESPEARE'S
COMEDIES

Oxford University Press, Amen House, London E.C.4

GLASGOW NEW YORK TORONTO MELBOURNE WELLINGTON
BOMBAY CALCUTTA MADRAS KARACHI LAHORE DACCA
CAPE TOWN SALISBURY NAIROBI IBADAN ACCRA
KUALA LUMPUR HONG KONG

SHAKESPEARE'S COMEDIES

BY

BERTRAND EVANS

OXFORD
AT THE CLARENDON PRESS

FIRST PUBLISHED 1960
REPRINTED LITHOGRAPHICALLY IN GREAT BRITAIN
BY D. R. HILLMAN & SONS LTD., FROME
1961

TO MARGARET

No, I do not know you; nor I am not sent to you by my lady, to bid you come speak with her; nor your name is not Master Cesario; nor this is not my nose neither. Nothing that is so is so.

Twelfth Night, IV. i. 5–9

Tell your piteous heart
There's no harm done.

Tempest, I. ii. 14–15

Preface

'O, what men dare do!' cries Claudio of *Much Ado about Nothing*: 'What men may do! What men daily do, not knowing what they do!' When he exclaims thus on the ignorance of men in general, Claudio's own good sense has been overcome by false report and false show, and he is ready to denounce his intended bride at the altar. He does indeed accuse the innocent and gentle Hero, in terrible language, before friends, family, and priest:

> Give not this rotten orange to your friend;
> She's but the sign and semblance of her honour.
> Behold how like a maid she blushes here!
> O, what authority and show of truth
> Can cunning sin cover itself withal!
> Comes not that blood as modest evidence
> To witness simple virtue? Would you not swear,
> All you that see her, that she were a maid,
> By these exterior shows? But she is none.
> She knows the heat of a luxurious bed;
> Her blush is guiltiness, not modesty.

It is a potent moment, simultaneously demanding multiple, equally urgent, and mutually contradictory responses. The finest of its effects, without which the scene would certainly be forceful but hardly distinguished, rise not from our simple perception of the action itself but from what occupies our minds as we perceive it. With the outer eye we see only what is shown; with the inner eye, by the light of special knowledge placed in our minds at just the right time, we review and reconstruct what is shown. Between the awareness that packs our minds and the ignorance that afflicts the participants lies a crucial—and highly exploitable—discrepancy.

This book attempts an approach to the comedies through one of Shakespeare's notable dramaturgical characteristics—his uses of awareness and control.

The world's dramatists—indeed, the world's story-tellers—might be classified in a rather fundamental way according to their preferences in the handling of the relative awarenesses of audience and participants. Three possibilities are available to a dramatist: he can keep the audience less informed than the participants, equally aware with them, or more aware than they. The first way, of course, has always been a favourite of mystery writers—including the Gothic novelists and dramatists of the late eighteenth and early nineteenth centuries, who chose to represent a villain or a hero-villain as bearing in his bosom some dark and agonizing secret that is kept from us until its potential of suspense has been exhausted. The second, if one were to make a statistical survey, would doubt-less be found the most prevalent way for both dramatic and narra-tive story-tellers past and present; it might be considered the 'normal' or standard way.

But the third way is Shakespeare's. It is a way of other great dramatists also—of Sophocles, Jonson, Ibsen, Goldsmith, Sheridan, Oscar Wilde—but it is not so consistently *the* way of any other dramatist.

The degree of Shakespeare's devotion to a dramatic method that gives the audience an advantage in awareness, and thus opens ex-ploitable gaps both between audience and participants and between participant and participant, can be partially suggested through some simple but extraordinary statistics. The seventeen comedies and romances include 297 scenes, in 170 of which an arrangement of discrepant awarenesses is the indispensable condition of dramatic effect; that is to say, we hold significant advantage over participants during these scenes. Further, the comedies include 277 named persons (and unnamed ones whose roles have some importance), of whom 151 stand occasionally, frequently, or steadily in a con-dition of exploitable ignorance; that is to say, we hold significant advantage at some time over these persons.

Or to put these general facts in another way: more than half the persons in the comedies and romances are shown as speaking and acting 'not knowing what they do' in about two-thirds of the scenes in which they appear. When only principal persons and scenes (omitting, for example, the many mainly expository scenes) are counted, the proportion is far higher: then roughly four of five persons are shown acting ignorantly in four of five scenes. Or to put the matter in yet another way: if a comedy requires two hours and a half to perform, attention is centred for nearly two hours on persons whose vision is less complete than ours, whose sense of the facts of situations most pertinent to themselves is either quite mis-taken or quite lacking, and whose words and actions would be very different if the truth known to us were known to them.

Though these figures barely hint the story, they do suggest that Shakespeare's dramatic method relied heavily on arrangements of discrepant awarenesses, and that examination of his management of

these can shed light on some fundamental principles of his dramaturgy. My first concern in the following pages has been to present
a faithful account of the dramatist's means and ends in the creation,
maintenance, and exploitation of differences in the awarenesses of
participants and of differences between participants' awarenesses
and ours as audience.

I hope, of course, that I have succeeded in doing more. I wished
not just to describe a principle of dramatic practice, but to find
what general illumination of individual plays could result from
this approach. Accordingly, I have arranged my account so that
the play itself is always the primary object, and the management of
awarenesses only an approach. Especially in the chapters given to
single plays, I have kept one question constantly in mind: *How
does this play, its action, its people, and its world, look from this
single point of view?* In proceeding chronologically, I have inevitably paid much attention to change and development in Shakespeare's handling of the awarenesses; before moving on I have often
looked far ahead, and having moved ahead have regularly looked
back. Thus, although I have sought primarily to make my method
throw what light it could on plays as distinct, whole works, I have
also been mindful of the temporal relations of plays and trust that
the total account presents something of a history of the subject.

In pursuing the uses of awareness, I have necessarily employed
most of the terms that are conventional in Shakespeare criticism—
irony, disguise, mistaken identity, deception, soliloquy, aside, exposition, denouement, and many others. I have never sought to give
my study a look of originality by avoiding these. But I would like
to make clear that my study places some of them in a perspective
very different from the usual ones. 'Disguise', for example, is here
treated as but *one of several means by which Shakespeare creates
a structure of discrepant awarenesses.* 'Irony' appears as *one of the
effects that result from exploitation of discrepant awarenesses.* The
study is not, in any sense, 'about' any or all of these familiar terms,
but centres on the condition itself to which each bears a special
relation.

On the other hand, 'awareness' itself stands as one of the means of
'control', both control in the world that is represented by the play
and control of the dramatist's representation of that world. Increasingly, as the early comedies yield to the mature ones, the
mature ones to the darkly uncertain ones, and these to the romances,
the problems of awareness and control become inextricably bound
up with one another.

Every reader will be conscious of large omissions. Perhaps I should cite A. C. Bradley in the Preface to *Shakespearian Tragedy*, for his words are pertinent: 'Nothing will be said of Shakespeare's place in the history either of English literature or of the drama in general. No attempt will be made to compare him with other writers. I shall leave untouched . . . questions regarding his life and character . . . the genuineness, sources, texts, interrelations of his various works. Even what may be called, in a restricted sense, the "poetry" . . . the beauties of style, diction, versification—I shall pass by in silence.' I must confess that I have many times been sorely tempted to comment on matters that my particular kind of study seemed to light up from a new angle—questions of Shakespeare's adaptation of source materials, questions of chronology, questions of authorship. I am convinced that analysis of the particular dramaturgical practices here studied will, when applied to such problems, add significantly to knowledge that we have gained by historical and other approaches. I have resisted even the strongest of my temptations in this respect, because there was even more than enough to do if I did no more than hew to the line that I had set. The size of this volume is the best proof that I was right.

For the same reason, the present volume deals only with the comedies and romances. A similar account of the management of awarenesses in the histories and tragedies is nearly finished at the present time. I should like to say that though it seemed desirable to include at least the two parts of *Henry IV* in the study of the comedies, it seemed even more desirable to leave them for the study of the histories. On the other hand, if some readers are disturbed that I have included *Troilus and Cressida* with the comedies, I can say only that I was unable to imagine including it with either the histories or the tragedies; and as a matter of fact my examination of the play has convinced me that it is best placed just where it is.

To my own mind, what most emerges from the present study is a view of Shakespeare as the shrewdest of dramatic engineers. True, shrewdness in the management of awarenesses is not all there is to dramatic shrewdness, nor is dramatic shrewdness all there is to Shakespeare. But I offer this study as one more item in the enormous and swiftly growing body of evidence that Shakespeare as dramatist (like Shakespeare as poet) was about as remote from that warbler of 'native woodnotes wild' of Milton's as it is possible to get. I, for one, have never believed in that warbler, and this study of but one facet of Shakespeare's dramaturgy has made me even surer that his deliberateness was anything but that of Fancy's child. Several of his habits as dramatist are set in relief when the plays are examined from the point of view of the uses of awareness: his habit of making assurance doubly sure that we *cannot* miss an effect that he has been at pains to prepare—and he is *always* at pains to prepare; his habit of advising us *before* rather than *after* the event; his habit of requiring climactic scenes to demand multiple responses; his habit of squeezing each prepared situation for its last drop of dramatic effect before releasing it. These are samples only; but they and other habits to which this study draws attention evince the quality of an art that is deliberate, calculated, infinitely shrewd.

Finally, I hope that this book will be read as a humble—if minutely detailed—chapter in the great and lasting search for the deep secrets of Shakespeare's incredible hold upon the mind that comes near enough to be seized.

All references are to *The Complete Plays and Poems of William Shakespeare*, edited by Neilson and Hill, Houghton Mifflin Company, 1942. My examination of *Pericles* rests in part on my essay, 'The Poem of *Pericles*', in *The Image of the Work*, by B. H. Lehman and Others, University of California Press, 1955, and my general approach here was first tried in an essay on *Romeo and Juliet*, 'The Brevity of Friar Lawrence', *P.M.L.A.*, September 1950.

It is of course quite impossible to compute one's whole debt to writers and lecturers on Shakespeare; probably something of all that I have read and heard about these plays is included here—however much 'translated', to use Bottom's word. But I want particularly to thank several of my colleagues in the University of California who have helped me in various ways, all generously: Travis M. Bogard, James M. Cline, Willard E. Farnham, James D. Hart, James J. Lynch, and Alain Renoir. I am grateful to the Regents of the University of California for making available both the time and the money needed to prepare the manuscript. Finally, I should like to name three men who, in successive periods over many years, have given me help and encouragement of such magnitude that I must account the contribution of each indispensable not only to this book but to what else I have written and will write: George Van de Wetering, John M. Kierzek, and Benjamin H. Lehman; to the last-named of these I am even further indebted for the unfailingly generous and illuminating criticism which has left its imprint on every page of the present volume. The only greater debt that I can acknowledge is implied in the Dedication.

B. E.

Berkeley, California
20 *March* 1960

Table of Contents

potential, here serves chiefly to keep us advised of situation. Here are no malapropisms, dialectal oddities, few quirks and twists of phrase: the very pun, hereafter ubiquitous, is scanted. With neither character nor language making notable comic contribution, then, the great resource of laughter is the exploitable gulf spread between the participants' understanding and ours.

This gap is held open from beginning to end: it is available for exploitation and is exploited during ten of the éleven scenes. In the course of the action we hold an advantage in awareness over fifteen of the sixteen persons—Aemilia alone never being exhibited on a level beneath ours. Not until *The Tempest* (in the comedies) did Shakespeare again hold one gap open so long for exploitation; never again did he place so great a responsibility on a single gap.

As in most later plays, Shakespeare here opens the gap—that is to say, raises our vantage póint above that of the participants—as soon as possible. After forty lines in Scene ii (at the entrance of Dromio of Ephesus) the facts of the enveloping situation are fixed in our minds: a father, facing death unless he can raise money by sunset, his twin sons, long separated, and their twin servants are all in the city of Ephesus. But the key fact that is quickly revealed to us is denied them: they are ignorant that all are in the same city. On our side, thus, is complete vision, and on theirs none at all. This condition, kept essentially unchanged, is made to yield virtually all of the comic effects during ten scenes.

In that the secret committed to our keeping is both simple and single, *The Comedy of Errors* is unique among the comedies. In later ones our awareness is packed, often even burdened, with multiple, complex, interrelated secrets, and the many circles of individual participants' visions, though they cross and recross one another, do not wholly coincide. In *Twelfth Night*, thus, certain but not all facts of the intricate situation are known to both Sir Toby and Sir Andrew, and some are known to Sir Toby but not to Sir Andrew; a few, but only a few, are shared by Viola and Sir Toby; some are known to Viola alone of the participants; and one fact of enormous significance, known to us alone, is hidden even from Viola. In *The Comedy of Errors* only a single great secret exists, which is ours alone; the participants, therefore, stand all on one footing of ignorance. Shakespeare never again used so simple an arrangement of the awarenesses.

The enveloping situation which makes both action and comic effects possible is itself static; it remains unchanged, until the last 100 lines, by the bustling incidents that fill up the scenes between beginning and end. Between the point midway in the second scene,

CHAPTER I

Here Sit I in the Sky: First Explorations

In *The Comedy of Errors, The Two Gentlemen of Verona, Love's Labour's Lost*, and *The Taming of the Shrew*, overlooking nothing in his quest of the way, Shakespeare tried four basic modes: the Roman, the romantic, the satiric, and the farcical—and, as he would continue to do right down to *The Tempest*, mixed some of all in each. To create comic effects he exploited in multiple ways the resources of language, situation, and character, using puns, parody, quibbles, caricature, slapstick and horseplay, local allusion, elaborate nonsense, pedantry, high language and low—all in profusion, like wild growth. Variety thus characterizes the first approaches and the first results.

Yet even here, amid the diversity of what at times seems random experiment, certain predilections are evident, and among these the one that best forecasts the future is the reliance upon exploitable gaps or discrepancies among the awarenesses of participants and between the awarenesses of participants and audience. Passing review of these first comedies may serve to introduce the subject of these gaps, which were to become and to remain for Shakespeare an indispensable condition of comedy—indeed, an indispensable condition of drama.

1. *The Comedy of Errors*

To describe the creation, maintenance, and exploitation of the gaps that separate the participants' awarenesses and ours in *The Comedy of Errors* is almost to describe the entire play, for in his first comedy Shakespeare came nearer than ever afterward to placing his whole reliance upon an arrangement of discrepant awarenesses. This comedy has no Falstaff, Toby Belch, Dogberry— not even an Armado. Comic effect emerges not once from character as such. If the Dromios prove laughable, it is not in themselves but in the incompleteness of their vision of situation that they prove so. Language, which regularly afterwards is squeezed for its comic at which all relevant facts have been put into our minds, and the ending, we neither need nor get additional information in order to hold our one great advantage over the participants. The many expository devices by which Shakespeare was later to sustain the advantage given us in the initial exposition—as soliloquies and asides strategically placed, scene-introductions which shed special light on following action, confidential dialogue of persons perpetrating some 'practice' on their unwitting fellows—are here absent because they would be superfluous. For whereas in later comedies situations emerge, swell, and multiply, generating new ones to replace the old, so that repeated injections of fact are needed to keep our vision clearer and wider than the participants', in *The Comedy of Errors* the first situation holds firm, unaffected by the frantic activity which it contains. The play has not one 'aside', and though there are brief soliloquies they exist not to advise us of what we had been ignorant but to exploit the speaker's ignorance of what we already know.

The Comedy of Errors is unique also in that its exploitable gap between awarenesses is created and sustained throughout the play without the use of a 'practiser'. No one here wilfully deceives another or even passively withholds a secret—for none here knows enough of the situation to deceive others about it, and none has a secret to withhold. In later comedies, some 'practice', some form of deliberate deception, is foremost among the means by which Shakespeare creates discrepancies in awareness and is prominent also among the means by which he maintains or widens these. Moreover, in all the later plays in which exploitation of discrepancies is of primary importance, the role of the deceiver is also of primary importance; that is to say, in plays that show a high proportion of scenes in which most participants perceive the situation less clearly than we do, this high proportion is typically the result of the presence and activity of one or more wilful practisers. Many of these practisers—in the histories and the tragedies especially—are of a villainous turn, or are outright villains, whose practices on their fellows are wicked. In *Richard III* the huge proportion of scenes which exploit participants' ignorance of their situations owes largely to Richard's secret machinations; in *Titus Andronicus*, to those of Aaron and Tamora; in *Othello*, to those of Iago; in *Much Ado about Nothing*, to those of Don John; in *Cymbeline*, to those of Iachimo. But not all the practisers who serve the dramatist well by opening exploitable gaps between the awarenesses of participants and audience are vicious. There are far, far more 'good' than 'bad' practisers in Shakespeare's plays, and accordingly more scenes of unawareness are acted under a benign light than under a sinister shadow. For Rosalind is no less a 'practiser' than Iago; and Bassanio's Portia, Viola, Helena, and Imogen deceive even as do Edmund and Iachimo, and by deceiving open gaps between other participants' awarenesses and ours. Hamlet stands high among the notable benevolent practisers, along with Oberon, Duke Vincentio, and many others, all looking ultimately to Prospero.

With the roles of 'practisers' it will be necessary to be much concerned hereafter—and with the differences in dramatic effect when, on the one hand, the highest point of awareness among the participants is occupied by a benevolent or, at worst, a sportive practiser and, on the other, when it is held by a vicious one. Frequently the truth that is hidden from the persons of a scene is worse than they suspect; often it is better than they dream. Nearly always, it is the nature of the practiser that determines. Nevertheless, though his role is conspicuous in most plays, the practiser is but one of several means used by the dramatist to create differences between awarenesses. And the fullest evidence that a play can rely for its effects almost exclusively on exploitation of such differences and yet get along without any deceiver, either benevolent or wicked, is presented by *The Comedy of Errors*. If Antipholus of Syracuse deceives Adriana by looking like his brother, yet he does not do so deliberately, and he is himself deceived by Dromio of Ephesus, who looks like Dromio of Syracuse. And if Dromio of Syracuse deceives by resembling his brother, yet he is simultaneously deceived because Antipholus of Ephesus looks like Antipholus of Syracuse. None who deceives in this play is aware that he deceives. None perceives the truth clearly enough to try to deceive another about it.

In fact, none sees the truth at all, or guesses anywhere near it. The third distinguishing mark of *The Comedy of Errors*, seen from the point of view of its uses of awareness, is the universal depth of the participants' ignorance. In later plays persons ignorant of a situation occasionally glimpse the truth, even though dimly and obliquely, and the effect is an instant flash of irony. So, for example, in *Twelfth Night*, the Duke at once sees and sees not when, speaking to the loving 'Cesario', he asserts that 'thine eye / Hath stay'd upon some favour that it loves'. And, in tragedy, Romeo, entering the Capulet house, expresses misgivings of 'some consequence yet hanging in the stars'—and his hit on the truth told us in the Prologue is recorded by a flash. But no person in *The Comedy of Errors* ever rises enough from the bottom of oblivion to glimpse the truth that we see steadily. In the first lines of Scene ii, the First Merchant

4

mentions a fact which—if he but knew—would be enormously significant to Antipholus of Syracuse: 'This very day a Syracusian merchant / Is apprehended for arrival here.' And he goes on:

> And, not being able to buy out his life
> According to the statute of the town,
> Dies ere the weary sun set in the west.
> There is your money that I had to keep.
>
> (I. ii. 5–8.)

Without a word about the plight of the 'Syracusian merchant', Antipholus takes the money—the very sum that would buy his father's life—and turns to instruct his servant. The intellectual remoteness of Antipholus from a truth that physically brushes against him at the outset of the action is matched constantly thereafter by the remoteness of other participants from truth that assaults their eyes and ears, and escapes detection. In his first use of the method, Shakespeare risks no dialogue that strikes the unsuspected truth. Nor, certainly, does he allow any participant to come close to guessing the truth. In *Twelfth Night*, after her encounter with the officers taking Antonio to jail, Viola's quick mind accurately interprets the incident: 'Prove true, imagination, O, prove true, / That I, dear brother, be now ta'en for you!' There are no such moments in *The Comedy of Errors*; here Shakespeare keeps all persons safely oblivious. Though truth beats at them incessantly, it beats in vain.

The severest problem of the dramatist, accordingly, was to make it credible—at least sufficiently credible for farce—that such steady hammering, without which nothing would be comic, would never break in upon that obliviousness, without which action itself would cease. A partial solution was to emphasize the Ephesian reputation as a seat of the black arts. Antipholus of Syracuse, after his first encounter with the wrong Dromio, emphasizes this: 'They say this town is full of cozenage. . . .' The same explanation is accepted by Dromio of Syracuse after the pair, wrong servant and wrong master, are ordered home to dinner by Adriana:

> This is the fairy land. O spite of spites!
> We talk with goblins, owls, and sprites.
>
> (II. ii. 191–2.)

Such comments at once exploit the gap, creating comic effect, and justify its continuation. After dining with Adriana and Luciana, the visitors express rising fear of the seemingly bewitched city; says Antipholus:

5

An if the wind blow any way from shore,
I will not harbour in this town to-night.
(III. ii. 152–3.)

'There's none but witches do inhabit here', he concludes, and heads for the port, eager to board the first ship that puts out, whatever its destination. When next we see him, additional experiences of the same sort have heightened his alarm: 'Lapland sorcerers inhabit here!'

A second way of solving the problem of credibility was to emphasize the Syracusian brother's distrust of his own sanity. At first the master had suspected that his servant was merely in a 'merry fit', and had beaten him. Next, he questioned his own wits, which seemed unable to distinguish dream from reality:

What, was I married to her in my dream?
Or sleep I now and think I hear all this?
What error drives our eyes and ears amiss?
(II. ii. 184–6.)

Finally, after other baffling encounters, he distrusts both his own and Dromio's sanity, and the witchery of the city, all in a breath:

The fellow is distract, and so am I;
And here we wander in illusions.
(IV. iii. 42–43.)

In this condition, believing both himself and Dromio 'transformed', he grows hysterical when the Courtezan hails him as an old friend. 'Avaunt, thou witch!' he shouts, and runs off. When we see him again, it is with rapier drawn, ready, if necessary, to hack a path to the port. Though Dromio could 'find in my heart to stay here still and turn witch', Antipholus will bear no more: 'I will not stay to-night for all the town.'

It is, then, chiefly by concentrating on the mounting fears of Antipholus that he is losing his wits in a bewitched city that Shakespeare attacks the problem of making credible the continued unawareness of participants. It is clearly proper that the main effort should be spent on keeping the visiting Antipholus's ignorance plausible, since it is he who is searching for his brother and whom we might expect to be first to perceive that the search has ended when 'everyone knows us and we know none'. Little care is needed to make credible the obliviousness of Antipholus of Ephesus, since, separated from his family as an infant and lacking knowledge that any relative exists, he would be unlikely to guess the truth under any circumstances. As for Adriana—in whom, alone among these persons, Shakespeare designs character specifically appropriate to

6

action—her special bent leads her to assume that her husband has tired of her; hence it is plausible that she should believe the report of his conduct toward Dromio of Ephesus and his refusal to come home to dinner. The tense relations of husband and wife, resulting from her shrewishness, thus help also to make it credible that error should become general and should prevail so long. The existing state of their affairs is enough to explain why Adriana is not simply astonished at the extraordinary conduct of her 'husband' when she meets the wrong Antipholus on the street and orders him home, and why the real husband readily accepts the situation when he comes home to find the door locked against him. And here, again, his recollection of the Courtezan helps conveniently to make his acquiescence plausible. Further, as one inexplicable incident follows another, his fury itself comes to be blinding, and as his irrationality waxes it becomes less and less likely that he would guess the truth; in turn, because his fury comes to look more and more like lunacy, it also helps to prevent others from guessing the truth.

In these various ways, then, Shakespeare worked to make it credible that the participants should continue, throughout the bustling action, to be abused by error; that is to say, thus he kept open for his uses the exploitable gap from which rise the comic effects.

The participants' unawareness, however, is always but one side of the gap: the other is our awareness, which, with a few noteworthy exceptions in plays between *Henry VI* and *The Tempest*, Shakespeare always kept well informed. In this first try at comedy, he succeeded better in maintaining the participants' condition of plausible ignorance than in keeping our vantage point at the most effective height. Although our view of the incidents which are contained by the frame is perfect, our view of the frame itself is not.

His addition of the frame story of Aegeon and Aemilia greatly complicated for Shakespeare the system of awarenesses which prevails throughout the play. It also profoundly affects our view of the farcical scenes. In the opening scene, with Aegeon's speech and the dialogue that immediately follows it, the dramatist strikes a tragic note—indeed, strikes it very hard, as though he meant the tones to vibrate in our memories during the succession of explosions that make the hilarity of all the middle scenes. Says the Duke after hearing Aegeon:

> Hapless Aegeon, whom the fates have mark'd
> To bear the extremity of dire mishap!
> Now, trust me, were it not against our laws,
> Against my crown, my oath, my dignity,
> Which princes, would they, may not disannul,

My soul should sue as advocate for thee.
But though thou art adjudged to the death,
And passed sentence may not be recall'd,
But to our honour's great disparagement,
Yet I will favour thee in what I can.
Therefore, merchant, I'll limit thee this day
To seek thy life by beneficial help.

(I. i. 141–52.)

Expressing the Duke's own pity, these words are contagious; they urge us to be as deeply moved. The last words of the scene, just before the hilarity starts, are Aegeon's sad ones:

Hopeless and helpless doth Aegeon wend,
But to procrastinate his lifeless end.

(Ibid. 158–9.)

This same note, of pity demanding our pity, is struck a third time, in the remarks of the First Merchant to Antipholus of Syracuse at the opening of the second scene, just before the fun starts. If the heavy emphasis given it is indicative of intention, Shakespeare meant the painful sound to be carried in our memories through all the fun until we meet Aegeon again, on his way to execution.

We are thus obliged to observe the comic action—which is the entire action except for the containing frame itself—while our minds hold a spot of anxiety for Aegeon. The method here first used, or its converse, Shakespeare would repeat in every comedy after this, and not only in the comedies, but also in the tragedies and the mature histories. It becomes a regular formula: we are required to look sometimes on hilarious scenes with a troubled awareness that shadows them, sometimes on dark and dangerous scenes with a secret and comforting assurance that lightens them. Because of the management of our awareness, scenes that would otherwise ask only a single, simple response demand instead conflicting responses simultaneously. In adding the frame story, then, fixing in our minds the tragic plight of Aegeon, Shakespeare was trying a dramatic method that at once became a principle of his dramaturgy.

At the same time, the handling of the frame story contrasts significantly with his later habitual method. Just this once, he withholds not only from the participants *but from us also* an all-important fact: he hides a key, that is to say, which exists all the while but of which we are denied knowledge. When we learn that there is an Abbess in Ephesus and that this Abbess is no other than old Aegeon's lost wife, the play is within eighty lines of the end. Had we been told of her existence at the outset, we would have been assured, even while recollection of Aegeon's desperate plight shadowed the hilarious scenes, that all would finally be well. As the play stands,

8

with only half of the frame—Aegeon's plight—presented to us at the outset, it is plain that the dramatist has simply deceived us. He makes us believe our view complete when it is only partial. Except for the quite dishonest report of Hermione's death in *The Winter's Tale*, Shakespeare never again deals so crookedly with our awareness by holding back vital secrets while making us think that we know everything. There are a very great many 'Aemilias' in the comedies—keys, or key elements essential to the solution of problems—the identities or existences of which are hidden from participants until the denouement; but they are not hidden from us as audience. Shakespeare's regular practice after *The Comedy of Errors* is to expose to us at the outset the existence of the potential solvent. Thus, for example, in *Twelfth Night* he brings Viola's brother Sebastian within our range of vision at the earliest possible moment, to show us that he has escaped drowning and is at hand; then, while greater and lesser trials distress Viola in her dealings with the households of Orsino and Olivia, we know that all will nevertheless be well, because we have perceived the means. By introducing Aemilia early in the action, Shakespeare could have added another level to the structure of awarenesses and thus have increased the complexity of our responses. Though we should then, as now, have observed the hilarity while our minds are troubled by recollection of Aegeon's plight, yet overlying our anxiety would have been the comforting assurance that, after all, all must be well. By denying us an early view of Aemilia, the dramatist did intensify the force of our anxiety; but the way of the mature comedies is to contain anxieties within a frame of warm reassurance.

2. *The Two Gentlemen of Verona*

Most immediately, this is the way of *The Two Gentlemen of Verona*. Whereas *The Comedy of Errors* afforded for exploitation only one discrepancy in awareness, all Ephesus being denied and ourselves provided with one all-important fact, *The Two Gentlemen of Verona* exploits multiple gaps that involve no fewer than six notable secrets. The first comedy used no deliberate 'practisers'; the second has almost as many as it has participants. In *The Comedy of Errors* a single, initial expository scene sufficed to establish the single, static situation, open the single gap between awarenesses, and sustain our single advantage over participants for all of five acts; in *The Two Gentlemen of Verona* the first two acts are used to create the principal situation and open the main gaps, and thereafter repeated expository passages, including asides and soliloquies, are

9

added to keep the circle of our vision complete. Whereas in the earlier play the participants remained equally ignorant of the situation, here we share with one participant our advantage over others with respect to one part of the situation, and with another participant our advantage with respect to another part of it. In *The Comedy of Errors* the single exploitable gap lay between all the participants on the one side and ourselves on the other. But in *The Two Gentlemen* Shakespeare makes use of differences in awareness between participant and participant, besides those between participants and ourselves: the fact represents a great step from the earlier comedy toward the mature ones.

All the named persons of *The Two Gentlemen* except the clowns —who here as hereafter, like the heroines of comedy and the villains of tragedy, are commonly immune to the condition of unawareness —stand at one time or another ignorant of some relevant fact. On the other hand, each of these persons except Thurio sometime holds advantage over another participant; each, that is to say, serves either as a secret-holder or as a perpetrator of practices on others. We are provided with advantage over some participant or other during nine of nineteen scenes—a much lower proportion than in *The Comedy of Errors*.

In summary, although alike in that both make large use of exploitable discrepancies in awareness, the two plays contrast markedly in the complexity which characterizes their paraphernalia of exploitation. The first is Roman in this respect, the second Elizabethan, elaborate. *The Two Gentlemen* is clearly on the high road to *Twelfth Night*.

Although Shakespeare does not begin until the third act to exploit the main discrepancies, two scenes in Act II deserve notice as the first in which we hold advantage over participants and also as prophetic of greater scenes in later plays. In ii. i we share with Silvia and Speed an advantage over Valentine. 'Last night', says Valentine to his servant, 'she enjoin'd me to write some lines to one she loves.' Since we have not yet seen Silvia or otherwise been prepared, we cannot know just yet that her request is in fact a way of hinting her interest in Valentine and of inviting him to woo her. Indeed, it is uncertain at what exact point in the ensuing dialogue the dramatist intends us to catch on:

> *Val.* As you enjoin'd me, I have writ your letter
> Unto the secret nameless friend of yours;
> Which I was much unwilling to proceed in
> But for my duty to your ladyship.
> *Sil.* I thank you, gentle servant. 'Tis very clerkly done.

Val. Now trust me, madam, it came hardly off;
For being ignorant to whom it goes
I writ at random, very doubtfully.
Sil. Perchance you think too much of so much pains?
Val. No, madam; so it stead you, I will write,
Please you command, a thousand times as much;
And yet—　　　　　•
Sil. A pretty period! Well, I guess the sequel;
And yet I will not name it; and yet I care not;
And yet take this again; and yet I thank you,
Meaning henceforth to trouble you no more.
                                                    (II. i. 110–25.)

By the time of Silvia's final speech, certainly, we have gained advantage over Valentine; even Speed, by this time, perceives the truth, for he remarks, aside, 'And yet you will; and yet another "yet"'. But Valentine—true prototype of heroes and secondary heroes of comedies to come, of Orlando, Orsino, Claudio, Bassanio, some better, some worse, but all essentially obtuse, less aware than heroines—does not glimpse it, either here or during the next eighty lines, though Speed exhausts himself with pointing out the truth:

My master sues to her, and she hath taught her suitor,
He being her pupil, to become her tutor.
O excellent device! was there ever heard a better,
That my master, being scribe, to himself should write the letter?
                                                    (Ibid. 143–6.)

With this device Silvia becomes the first practiser in the play, Valentine the first victim whose ignorance is exploited for comic effect.

The second scene in which we hold advantage ends Act II. Here the discrepancy in awareness is exploited not for loud laughter, as in the scene just noted and as throughout *The Comedy of Errors*, but for subtler effect of a kind Shakespeare would seek again and again by means of adroit manipulation of the awarenesses. It will be well, therefore, to examine in detail this first of a frequent kind.

This is a scene of ninety lines between Julia and her waiting woman, Lucetta. It is primarily expository, existing to inform us of Julia's intention to dress in weeds 'As may beseem some well-reputed page' and seek out Proteus in Milan. As an expository scene announcing this purpose, it is forerunner of many: of Portia and Nerissa, leaving Belmont for the Venetian Court-room; of Rosalind and Celia, fleeing to the forest of Arden; of Viola and her sea captain, as she prepares to invade Orsino's court; of Helena, leaving the palace of the Countess to track down Bertram; of Imogen, with Pisanio, setting off for Milford-Haven to find Posthumus. Like some of these, it is a gay scene:

Luc. What fashion, Madam, shall I make your breeches?
Jul. That fits as well as, 'Tell me, good my lord,
What compass will you wear your farthingale?'
Why even what fashion thou best likes, Lucetta.
Luc. You must needs have them with a codpiece, madam.
Jul. Out, out, Lucetta!

(II. vii. 49–54.)

The vein is richer than mere jest, however; it is a fresh, lyrical scene, in which Julia's eager youth and beauty, and her love for Proteus, shine out:

Then let me go, and hinder not my course.
I'll be as patient as a gentle stream,
And make a pastime of each weary step,
Till the last step have brought me to my love;
And there I'll rest, as after much turmoil
A blessed soul doth in Elysium.

(Ibid. 33–38.)

Viewed only in its own light, with nothing before or after, it would be a sparkling scene, its qualities of love, youth, wit, and lyricism rendering it pleasing and dramatic. But it is not to be viewed only in its own light.

Shakespeare has equipped our minds with special knowledge just before he shows this scene. The scene just preceding it, set in Milan, is all composed of a sharply pointed soliloquy uttered by Proteus, in which he expresses determination to commit 'three fold perjury', by leaving Julia, loving Silvia, and betraying Valentine. The lines of this soliloquy are emphatic, as though the dramatist meant their impression to be indelible:

I to myself am dearer than a friend,
For love is still most precious in itself;
And Silvia—witness Heaven, that made her fair!—
Shows Julia but a swarthy Ethiope.
I will forget that Julia is alive,
Rememb'ring that my love to her is dead;
And Valentine I'll hold an enemy,
Aiming at Silvia as a sweeter friend.

(II. vi. 23–30.)

Immediately the scene shifts to Verona, where we hear Julia asking Lucetta to tell her 'How, with my honour, I may undertake / A journey to my loving Proteus'. Proteus's soliloquy inevitably casts a special light over what follows—a light which is surely as much a part of the total scene as the dialogue itself. Julia's expression of devotion to Proteus, the merriment as the girls plan her costume, Lucetta's doubts and Julia's certainties—our view of all this is conditioned by Proteus's soliloquy; seen by a double light, its own and

12

that from Proteus's soliloquy, the whole takes on a richness which, though inferior to that of the great scenes of later comedies, is yet precious enough. It is not merely for the bold flashes of irony that starkly outline the gap between Julia's awareness and ours—

> But truer stars did govern Proteus' birth;
> His words are bonds, his oaths are oracles,
> His love sincere, his thoughts immaculate,
> His tears pure messengers sent from his heart,
> His heart as far from fraud as heaven from earth.
>   (II. vii. 74–78.)

—that the dramatic effect is notable; flashes of irony are the most spectacular but not always the richest effects produced by exploitation of discrepant awarenesses. In the fuller scenes of mature comedies it will be appropriate to distinguish the subtler, pervasive effects from the flashier surface manifestations. It may suffice to say here only that the Julia–Lucetta scene, exhibited under the special light of Proteus's soliloquy, anticipates these finer effects of later scenes.

In the scene just reviewed our advantage owes simply to the device of scene-placement, the dramatist having immediately preceded the particular action by a speech calculated to cast a transforming light on it. The deliberateness of this placement is itself noteworthy. The soliloquy spoken by Proteus could easily have been placed not to precede but to follow the Julia–Lucetta scene. It would then have occurred at the opening of Act III, and the action which at present opens Act III could then have gone straight ahead, with no interruption, directly after the soliloquy. Again, the soliloquy could readily have been incorporated in Proteus's earlier soliloquy which closes II. iv, where it would have joined on smoothly. Either of these placements would have been less awkward than that which in fact Shakespeare chose. But had he placed the soliloquy after rather than before the Julia–Lucetta scene, we should have lacked its special light as we watched that scene; coming afterward, it would of course have cast some light back upon the scene already played, and in retrospect we might have caught a little of the irony of Julia's lines. *But almost invariably Shakespeare preferred to project light forward upon a scene to be played rather than to cast it backward on action already past.* On the other hand, he regularly avoided setting his light-casting scene too far in advance of the action it should illuminate, lest intervening action blur the effect. In this instance, had the second Proteus soliloquy been incorporated in the first, which ends II. iv, the Speed–Launce dialogue of II. v would have intervened before the Julia–Lucetta scene. It is a mark of Shakespeare's method from the first

13

that he took no risks with effects he intended: when he provided us with a special advantage over participants, he took care to make this advantage active in our awareness at the moment of its greatest usefulness. Since, thus, Julia was to say 'tell me some good means / How, with my honour, I may undertake / A journey to my loving Proteus', Shakespeare's method required that we hear Proteus say —neither afterwards, nor several scenes before, but immediately before—'I will forget that Julia is alive'.

Dramatically the most significant speech in the play, Proteus's light-casting second soliloquy is indispensable both to our view of the Julia–Lucetta scene and to our view of the three subsequent acts. It contributes greatly to the disposition of awarenesses with which Act III opens—the first truly complex disposition that Shakespeare had attempted in comedy. Excepting the clowns, all persons who take part in Act III are ignorant of one or another crucial fact of the situation. Moreover, the participants are stationed on different levels of awareness, some higher, some lower, rising from Thurio at the bottom to Proteus at the top. Excepting Thurio, every principal person attempts deception, with Proteus as the out-topping practiser. It is the Duke who stands on the lowest level when the act opens, as Proteus, feigning reluctance, exposes Valentine's elopement plan:

> Know, noble lord, they have devis'd a mean
> How he her chamber-window will ascend
> And with a corded ladder fetch her down.
> (III. i. 38–40.)

Proteus speaks truthfully in that Valentine does intend to carry off Silvia—but the Duke is nevertheless deceived because he knows nothing of the motives which Proteus exhibited to us in that same indispensable soliloquy which earlier gave us advantage over Julia. So the Duke thanks Proteus, and, himself unwitting, lays a trap for the unsuspecting Valentine, who, being practised on by one who is himself ignorant, accordingly replaces the Duke on the lowest level of awareness. Yet Valentine, entering immediately after Proteus has exposed the elopement plan, supposes himself to occupy a vantage point above the Duke's, and, knowing nothing of Proteus's practices, supposes that no point higher than his own exists. Hiding beneath his coat the corded ladder he expects to use, he is privileged, as he imagines, to relish his advantage. With Silvia's image in his mind and the ladder under his cloak, being asked how one may woo, win, and wed 'a lady of Verona here' whom the Duke pretends to affect, he replies boldly, describing the details of reaching her chamber 'aloft, far from the ground, / And built so shelving that one cannot climb it / Without apparent hazard of his life'—

> Why then, a ladder, quaintly made of cords,
> To cast up, with a pair of anchoring hooks,
> Would serve to scale another Hero's tower.
> (Ibid. 117–19.)

Such a ladder, he brazenly suggests, might be hidden under just such a cloak as his own. The cat-and-mouse game here played between Proteus's two mice, each supposing himself the cat, extends through eighty-five lines, until the Duke snatches off Valentine's cloak and exposes the ladder and a sonnet to Silvia. With that act, of course, which equalizes the awarenesses of the two, the main exploitable discrepancy on which depend the effects of the scene vanishes, leaving only Proteus's unsuspected vantage-point above them, and above all others.

Or so Proteus supposes. Throughout Act III, like a minor Iago, he overpeers, deceives, and manipulates Valentine, the Duke, and Thurio. In the dialogue that follows the Duke's banishment of Valentine, Proteus consoles his friend, brings him the latest news, advises him, seems solicitous for his safety, offers to escort him to the city-gate, and, with Valentine gone, he turns his attention to stealing Silvia under the very auspices of the Duke and Thurio. As though reluctant, he promises to slander Valentine, and, as he 'unwinds' Silvia's former love, promises 'to bottom it' on Thurio. The Duke and Thurio urge him on in perfect confidence, for, as the Duke says,

> ... we know, on Valentine's report,
> You are already Love's firm votary
> And cannot soon revolt and change your mind.
> (Ibid. 257–9.)

Thus throughout Act III Proteus rides high over the others, exulting in his position, practising on them all. But even as the Julia–Lucetta scene which ends Act II is changed by Proteus's soliloquy which immediately precedes it, so the effect of Act III is transformed by the Julia–Lucetta scene. For while we watch Proteus's confident manipulation of Valentine, the Duke, and Thurio, we hold an advantage that makes his villainy laughable rather than dangerous: we know that as he is making his triply treacherous play for Silvia, Julia, habited like 'some well-reputed page', is on the road to Milan. Though still ignorant of Proteus's duplicity, she must surely discover it before Proteus learns that all his passes are observed. *The heroines of Shakespeare's comedies either hold from the outset, or very shortly gain, the highest vantage-point in their worlds.* Julia is the first of these heroines, and Proteus, from our point of view, can appear only a somewhat taller mouse than his own dupes, Valentine, the Duke, and Thurio.

In Act IV, still working his imagined advantage, Proteus continues his successful practice on the dull Thurio, but fails miserably in his attempts to deceive the heroines. From any point of view, perhaps, but certainly from that of the management of awarenesses, the finest scene of this act is the serenade of Silvia, ostensibly for Thurio's but in reality for Proteus's own purposes. The song to Silvia, exquisite in itself, certainly unmatched by any earlier lyric of Shakespeare's and possibly by any afterwards, is at the same time transformed by its context, which exists, as the scene progresses, only in our own minds. In our perspective, the song is itself a practice by Proteus directly upon Thurio, indirectly upon the Duke, Valentine, Julia, and Silvia herself. Moreover, with great shrewdness, Shakespeare has made it virtually impossible for us to lay aside our awareness of the total situation while we hear the song, for he has opened the scene with a new soliloquy which prods our recollection of Proteus's perfidy. We are thus prompted to hear the song not in itself alone, but in its special meanings for the participants who hear it, and particularly we are kept mindful of Valentine, who, though absent, has with Julia the keenest interest in any wooing of Silvia by Proteus. To Thurio, quite oblivious, nothing is apparent in the situation or the song itself except what is obvious—and quite wrong: it seems to him that his own suit to Silvia is being forwarded. To Proteus, gloating in his sense that he alone comprehends all that is happening, the song is a device for betraying everyone and winning Silvia for himself. To the Host, to whom the details of the situation are quite irrelevant, it is only a lovely song in the night. To Silvia, while the music plays, it is hardly more than a flattering serenade for which she thanks the unknown musicians. But when she hears Proteus speak, her quick wit catches the full import:

> Thou subtle, perjur'd, false, disloyal man!
> Think'st thou I am so shallow, so conceitless,
> To be seduced by thy flattery,
> That hast deceiv'd so many with thy vows?
> (IV. ii. 95–98.)

But what, now, is it to Julia? It is her presence, 'unobserved, in boy's clothes', that most transforms the scene. Like Silvia, she catches the significance of the song, which advises her of Proteus's treachery with jolting abruptness. Entering with the Host just before the music began, she had had no more doubts of Proteus than the intuitive ones that had inspired her journey to Milan. But when the song is done, she has caught on, and our realization of the effect of the song upon Julia is, then, the key factor in its effect upon ourselves. The effect is complex in character, bearing the forces of both pleasure and pain. The song is a thing of exquisite beauty; yet it pierces the heart of Julia—but, again, Julia is resilient, capable of swift recovery, and, besides, her position is actually improved by this experience. She had left Verona in ignorance, and now, having heard the serenade and the conversation of Proteus and Silvia, she knows all. Her discovery raises her abruptly to our level of awareness. Unobserved, she has observed Proteus's passes, heard his lies, recognized Silvia's integrity, and at the end of the scene is quite ready—like her very capable heroinely successors—to use her advantage for victory: 'Pray you, where lies Sir Proteus?' It is not she, but Proteus, suddenly the hunted rather than the hunter, who is now to be pitied. Fallen from top place in the scheme of awarenesses, he is lost and does not know it.

The inferiority of his position is conspicuous in IV. ii, when, oblivious, he dispatches his disguised and watchful mistress to woo Silvia for him—sending a ring that Julia had once given him. If Julia's situation is hardly a happy one, yet neither is it desperate. Her vision has full sweep; she is perfect mistress of her situation, and knows it. So absolute is her advantage that she can pity her prodigal lover, who, in confident obliviousness, has chosen an inappropriate love-emissary.

In his relation to Julia, then, Proteus the practiser has become the practisee, she the practiser: he is under her eye, his waywardness observed, his duplicity exposed. In relation to Silvia he is no better off. She has recognized and castigated his hypocrisy from the first. And now, immediately before the scene in which Proteus sends Julia to woo Silvia, Shakespeare has set a scene which lights the latter and displays a further depth in Proteus's unawareness. For in the preceding scene Silvia tells us that she will go to find Valentine in Mantua, 'where I hear he makes abode'. The true position of Proteus, then, is hardly enviable: supposing himself the master practiser with all strings in hand, he sends as love-envoy his own mistress, who can cross him at need; and she to whom the messenger is sent has already arranged to leave the city. The case of Proteus, hero bent on making a villain of himself, is typical: in the comedies, villainy can but peep at what it would, for it is circumscribed and rendered impotent, if not ridiculous, by the bright-eyed heroines who with their superior awareness control everything in this woman's world.

The gap between Proteus's awareness and ours continues as the principal exploitable condition during Act V. Here not only is Julia constantly at his elbow, her disguised presence reminding us of the true state of things, but, within this situation, Shakespeare contrives to set him at a further disadvantage in relation to both Silvia and Valentine. Act V, ii, when Proteus and Thurio discuss Silvia while Julia speaks 'asides', is noteworthy as showing Shakespeare's first use of four simultaneous levels of awareness. At the top is our own awareness, packed with all the facts of the situation: that Silvia has fled the court (as the dramatist, taking no chances with our forgetfulness, has just reminded us in the preceding scene); that Proteus's page, 'Sebastian', is in fact his betrothed Julia; that Proteus supposes himself to have deceived Julia, the Duke, Valentine, and Thurio in his wooing of Silvia and that he is now in the act of deceiving Thurio by reporting his progress with Thurio's love suit. On the level just below ours stands Julia, possessed of all our facts but one: that Silvia has fled the court. Below Julia is Proteus, who is ignorant that Silvia has gone, ignorant that Julia is beside him, and aware only that Thurio is deceived. And at the bottom is Thurio, who here as before and after is wrong about everything. The dialogue which exploits the gaps between these levels is itself not so remarkable as is this first appearance of the stair-stepped structure of awarenesses which becomes a fixture in the climactic scenes of subsequent comedies.

In the final scene of the play the disposition and uses of awareness again significantly mark the direction of Shakespeare's development. The preparation of our minds for this scene was begun far, far back—when Julia first took up her boy's masquerade. It continued through to Act IV, when Valentine became the outlaws' captain on his own terms:

> I take your offer and will live with you,
> Provided that you do no outrages
> On silly women or poor passengers.
> (IV. i. 70–72.)

When in IV. iii, therefore, fleeing the court to seek Valentine in Mantua, Silvia fears for her safety—'And, for the ways are dangerous to pass, / I do desire thy worthy company'—we have had reason enough to know that this forest is safe for her. Even so, in the third scene of Act V, when she is caught by outlaws, the dramatist—making doubly sure that we shall feel no alarm for Silvia's safety—again reminds us that no harm can befall her; for in the first line of the scene the First Outlaw, struggling with his captive, commands her, 'Be patient; we must bring you to our captain'—who, of course, can be none but Valentine. When Proteus snatches Silvia from the outlaws, it is noteworthy that Shakespeare neither shows her in his company—more dangerous to her than the outlaws—nor even lets us know that he has taken her, until we have again been assured that all is well. The final scene opens with Valentine's brief soliloquy which ends abruptly at the approach of Proteus, Silvia, and Julia: 'Withdraw thee, Valentine; who's this comes here?' And thereafter, lest the excitement of threatened violence to Silvia make us forget Valentine's comforting presence, Shakespeare has him speak an 'aside' to remind us that he is at hand, hearing, observing, armed, and ready to act.

Once more, then, in this final moment, it is this comedy's eager but thwarted representative of villainy who stands in the inferior place, unwittingly circumscribed and impotent. Proteus is doubly, pitifully unaware: for not only is Valentine, Silvia's betrothed, hidden within a sword's length of him, but also, at his side, disguised, is his own betrothed. When, therefore, rebuffed, he turns savage and seizes Silvia with 'I'll force thee yield to my desire', we perceive that any real peril in the situation is his, not hers. For Silvia, knowing no more than Proteus of the presence of Julia and Valentine and accordingly in mortal terror, the truth apparent to us is much better than she imagines; for Proteus it is far worse. Hemmed in, he can only expose himself to humiliation. Such is always the plight of the villain in the comedies: as Proteus in *The Two Gentlemen of Verona*, so also Shylock in *The Merchant of Venice*, Don John in *Much Ado about Nothing*, and Angelo in *Measure for Measure*. Not only cannot villainy harm innocence; it is even prevented from doing irreparable harm to itself.

3. *Love's Labour's Lost*

In the third experiment, *Love's Labour's Lost*, Shakespeare tried exploitation of the comic potentialities in language and eccentric humanity. No later comedy relies so much on language as a source of laughter, or exhibits such a collection of human oddities as Armado, Sir Nathaniel, Holofernes, Dull, Costard, Jaquenetta, and Moth. Nor, for that matter, does a later play exhibit so many courtly wits: the King with his lords and the Princess with her ladies make eight, and Boyet, as sharp as any, nine. To the potentialities of language, wit, and eccentric character, add those of satiric allusion to contemporary affairs, and the main resources of fun in *Love's Labour's Lost* are accounted for. In the range of its comic devices, the play differs most from its predecessors.

Since these sources are the primary subjects of experiment, this comedy inevitably relies less for effect on exploitation of discrepant awarenesses. Such exploitation, in fact, is confined to two of the nine scenes, and—excepting some persons who are afflicted with some form of congenital unawareness—only four of the seventeen named characters ever occupy levels below ours. In terms of such statistics, no comedy, but only *Henry VI*, shows a lower proportion. But of greater import is the fact that the two scenes which *do* exploit discrepant awarenesses are the climactic portions of the play, are the most satisfying dramatically and comically, and, if one excepts the songs of Summer and Winter, are the most memorable artistic moments of *Love's Labour's Lost*.

The first of these scenes is particularly prophetic of Shakespeare's way in its elaboration of a stair-step structure of awarenesses, the first version of which was erected in *The Two Gentlemen of Verona* (III. i) when Thurio, the Duke, and Proteus stood on ascending levels—with ours above all. In the present scene, it is Biron who occupies the level next below ours. Entering 'with a paper in his hand', he tells us that he has broken his oath to the King by falling in love. The King enters 'with a paper', and Biron withdraws. The King reads a sonnet—and we, with Biron, perceive that he, too, has fallen. Next Longaville enters and reads a sonnet while we, Biron, and the King look on. Finally Dumain approaches and reads the lyric 'On a day—alack the day!— / Love, whose month is ever May', and we, with Biron, the King, and Longaville, perceive that he, too, is fallen and foresworn. The King and his three gentlemen make four steps of a stair, Dumain at the bottom, overpeering none, and Biron at the top, crowing above all:

> 'All hid, all hid;' an old infant play.
> Like a demigod here sit I in the sky,
> And wretched fools' secrets heedfully o'er-eye.
> (IV. iii. 78-80.)

Never one to abandon an exploitable situation while possibilities of its exploitation remain, Shakespeare next unbuilds the stair, step by step. First Longaville comes out of hiding to shame Dumain:

> You may look pale, but I should blush, I know,
> To be o'erheard and taken napping so.
> (Ibid. 29-30.)

After him, in order, come the others. Throughout the process of unbuilding, the boldest effects are the flashes of irony which illuminate the gap between the speaker's ignorance and our knowledge; thus the King, stepping forward to shame both Dumain and Longaville:

> What will Biron say when that he shall hear
> Faith infringed, which such zeal did swear?
> How will he scorn! how will he spend his wit!
> How will he triumph, leap, and laugh at it!
> For all the wealth that ever I did see,
> I would not have him know so much by me.
>
> (Ibid. 145–50.)

The flashes grow ever more spectacular as each man descends; the flashiest of all comes last. Biron descends: 'Now step I forth to whip hypocrisy.'

> *King.* Are we betray'd thus to thy over-view?
> *Bir.* Not you to me, but I betray'd by you,
> I, that am honest; I that hold it sin
> To break the vow I am engaged in;
> I am betray'd by keeping company
> With men like you, men of inconstancy.
> When shall you see me write a thing in rhyme,
> Or groan for love, or spend a minute's time
> In pruning me? When shall you hear that I
> Will praise a hand, a foot, a face, an eye,
> A gait, a state, a brow, a breast, a waist,
> A leg, a limb?
>
> (Ibid. 174–86.)

The words have barely left his mouth when the Clown and Jaquenetta rush in, bringing—as we knew they would—Biron's sonnet addressed to Rosaline.

The perfection of the jest, of course, is that we overpeer the topmost overpeerer. The scene uses five levels of awareness, from Dumain's upward to ours. The preparation of our advantage was begun in III. i, when Biron ordered Costard to deliver 'This seal'd-up counsel' into the white hands of Rosaline; but, indeed, preparation had begun even earlier, for Costard had previously been ordered to deliver Armado's letter to Jaquenetta. When the Clown, mistaking, brings this letter to the Princess, it becomes apparent that Biron's sonnet must go wrong, too. In IV. ii it reaches Sir Nathaniel, who reads it aloud for Jaquenetta, and thereafter Holofernes orders wench and clown to 'deliver this paper into the royal hand of the King; it may concern much'. Characteristically, Shakespeare has placed this final instruction immediately before Biron's entrance at the start of the stair-stepped scene, so that it is impossible for us to forget, all the while the stairs are building up and then down again, that Jaquenetta and Costard, sonnet in hand, are running

21

through the park seeking the King. But merely to assure our remembrance of so crucial a point was not enough for Shakespeare. To make assurance doubly sure that we will not forget and thus lose the advantage which is indispensable to the full force of the scene, he gives our awareness repeated sharp prods by means of Biron's repetition of the relevant facts—as far as he knows them—at the opening of the scene:"Well, she hath one o' my sonnets already; the clown bore it, the fool sent it, and the lady hath it: sweet clown, sweeter fool, sweetest lady!' Thereafter, each crowing word of Biron's on his lofty perch reminds us also of our advantage and exploits the space between his vantage-point and ours: 'Like a demigod here sit I in the sky, / And wretched fools' secrets heedfully o'er-eye.'

Though obviously contrived, Lyly-mannered in balance and movement, this scene is of enormous significance, for here Shakespeare worked out in detail a structure for the exploitation of discrepancies in awareness: with greater complexity but no essential changes, this structure was to become a central fixture in the comedies.

Similarly artificial in its balance and movement and also featuring a complex pattern of awarenesses is v. ii, the second climactic point of the play. Two episodes compose the heart of this scene, the first running through 100 lines (160–260) from the entrance of the King's party 'like Muscovites or Russians' to their departure; the second extending through 115 lines (335–450) from the second meeting of the ladies and their wooers up to the moment of Biron's perception that the gentlemen have twice been the ladies' dupes. The grace and charm of this portion of the scene are remarkable; the wit of the lines and the balanced precision of the physical action make it a treat for eye and ear. But it would hardly excel similar arrangements by Lyly if its effectiveness depended wholly on these qualities. What makes it superior is that more is going on than merely that which directly strikes the eye and the ear. 'There's no such sport', says the Princess to her ladies just before the entrance of the masqueraders, 'as sport by sport o'erthrown.' As in the earlier stair-stepped scene, it is not the decorative effects but the maintenance of exploitable gaps between the awarenesses of the participants and between the participants' awarenesses and ours that makes the scene dramatic.

Here, as usually in the comedies, it is the ladies who hold the advantage; the gentlemen, supposing themselves overpeerers, are from the outset overpeered. Boyet betrays his own sex, revealing to the ladies that the King's men will come

> Like Muscovites or Russians, as I guess;
> Their purpose is to parle, to court, and dance.
> And every one his love-feat will advance
> Unto his several mistress, which they'll know
> By favours several which they did bestow.
> (v. ii. 121-5.)

Forewarned, the ladies exchange favours; says the Princess, justifying the counter-practice and characterizing the spirit in which it is undertaken:

> The effect of my intent is to cross theirs.
> They do it but in mocking merriment,
> And mock for mock is only my intent.
> (Ibid. 138-40.)

When the gentlemen enter, then, they are twice deceived, being unaware that they are known and their purpose marked and unaware of the identities of their respective mistresses. Each courts the wrong lady and is, as Biron puts it, 'all dry-beaten with pure scoff!' 'The tongues of mocking wenches are as keen', observes Boyet, 'As is the razor's edge invisible.' The retreat ending the first movement is like a rout. Still, the unwitting gentlemen suppose that, though dry-beaten as Russians, they have passed unrecognized; but Boyet, again traitor, tells the ladies that the King's party will return 'In their own shapes', and Rosaline—who might be arguing for Shakespeare's own dramatic method—at once insists that no such fine advantage should be surrendered until its potentialities have been exhausted:

> Let's mock them still, as well known as disguis'd.
> Let us complain to them what fools were here,
> Disguis'd like Muscovites, in shapeless gear.
> (Ibid. 301-3.)

Re-entering, the gentlemen are still doubly ignorant, being unaware that they were known before and that each had courted and been mocked by the wrong mistress; absurdly clinging to their illusion, they are again dry-beaten one by one—for example, Biron:

> *Ros.* We four indeed confronted were with four
> In Russian habit; here they stay'd an hour,
> And talk'd apace; and in that hour, my lord,
> They did not bless us with one happy word.
> I dare not call them fools; but this I think,
> When they are thirsty, fools would fain have drink.
> *Bir.* This jest is dry to me.
> (Ibid. 367-73.)

Not until each gentleman's condition has been exploited does the dramatist begin to close the gap that has made all the fun. First the gentlemen learn that their masquerade had fooled no one. Next their ignorance that they had unbosomed themselves 'To loves mistook' is dispelled, but less abruptly, for the ladies want to relish their advantage to the last moment. The denouement, here as usually in the comedies, amounts to a closing of gaps, an equalizing of awarenesses:

> *Bir.* I see the trick on't; here was a consent,
> Knowing aforehand of our merriment,
> To dash it like a christmas comedy. -
> (v. ii. 460–2.)

Boyet last strikes the key of this and of many such bouts between man and woman to come in the later comedies: 'Full merrily / Hath this brave manage, this career, been run.'

4. *The Taming of the Shrew*

Last of the four widely divergent experiments, *The Taming of the Shrew* stands apart, in its own ways, as does each of the others. When it is examined from the point of view of the disposition and uses of awareness, its most conspicuous feature looms up at once: it is the profound contrast in the dramatic management of the two plots. One of these is developed on the lines of later romantic comedies, the other in a way that Shakespeare never used again.

Counting those of the Induction, *The Taming of the Shrew* has fourteen scenes, in nine of which our view of the situation is superior to that of some participants. Seven of the sixteen named persons (again including the Induction) stand occasionally in a condition of exploitable unawareness. Action and effects alike depend mainly upon the existence of multiple secrets, upon multiple discrepancies in awareness, and upon a remarkable throng of practisers, practices, and practisees. The stair-step structure of awarenesses, reared in several scenes, is once composed of three levels, once of five—with Baptista Minola, like Thurio of *The Two Gentlemen of Verona*—always at the bottom and Tranio–Lucentio at the top. Multiple blind spots afflict some persons occasionally, some frequently, some continuously: Baptista is wrong about everything that most concerns him—that 'Lucentio' is Tranio; that 'Cambio' is Lucentio; that 'Licio' is Hortensio; that both 'Tutors' are wooers; that 'Vincentio' is a Pedant; that Vincentio is in very fact Vincentio.

But it is most noteworthy that excepting one scene of the Induction all of the scenes that exploit discrepancies in awareness are in the sub-plot, none in the main plot of the taming of Kate. Though Petruchio is incidentally ignorant (I. ii), along with Gremio, Grumio, and Hortensio, of the right identities of Lucentio and Tranio, his unawareness is relevant only to the minor plot. So also, at the moment before the denouement begins (v. i), both Kate and Petruchio, returning to Padua to marvel at the mad confusion over the supposed Vincentio and the right Vincentio, the supposed Lucentio and the right Lucentio, are as much in the dark as Baptista and others who are directly concerned—but here, too, their unawareness is unrelated to the shrew story. Indeed, their separation from the frantic Padua situation is carefully marked: 'Prithee, Kate, let's follow, to see the end of this ado.' Petruchio and Kate, like ourselves, are spectators, though with less than our advantage. *The Taming of the Shrew*, then, is unique among Shakespeare's comedies in that it has two distinct plots, one relying mainly on discrepant awarenesses, the other using them not at all. Moreover, the shrew plot is the only plot ever developed by Shakespeare without use of gaps between awarenesses, with the result that, in their dramatic character, its scenes are remote from the great body of his works. However successful was the comic action of the taming of Kate on Shakespeare's own stage, the dramatist never tried that dramatic way again.

But in this one trial he proceeded without compromise to unfold a comic plot in which no participant stands in a position of unawareness, none has a fuller view of the situation than another, and we ourselves occupy a vantage-point equal to that of the actors. The principal persons have no illusions about each other. Shakespeare appears to have taken pains not only to have each of the mad pair recognize the other's character, but to make it unmistakable to us that each does so. It is significant that none of the persons centrally involved—Hortensio, Gremio, Baptista—attempts to deceive Petruchio about Katherina, even though Hortensio and Gremio, as suitors of Bianca, would gain much by fooling him into marrying the older sister. Rather, far from practising on him, suitors and father alike seem determined that Petruchio shall know the worst. 'Katherine the curst', Hortensio begins, and goes on:

> Her only fault, and that is faults enough
> Is that she is intolerable curst
> And shrewd and froward, so beyond all measure
> That, were my state far worser than it is,
> I would not wed her for a mine of gold.
> (I. ii. 88–96.)

'Thou know'st not gold's effect', replies Petruchio, and assures

Hortensio that he 'will board her, though she chide as loud / As thunder when the clouds in autumn crack'. Gremio, like Hortensio, and without his cause of friendship, goes out of his way in honesty, demanding at once on learning that Petruchio seeks Kate for wife, 'Hortensio, have you told him all her faults?' So also Baptista, long-suffering father with even more interest in getting Kate married off than have Bianca's suitors: 'But for my daughter Katherine, this I know, / She is not for your turn, the more my grief.' And more pointedly still:

> *Pet.* Pray, have you not a daughter
> Call'd Katherina, fair and virtuous?
> *Bap.* I have a daughter, sir, call'd Katherina.
> (II. i. 41–43.)

Surely in the world of Shakespearian comedy, where the normal condition is to delight in deception, where almost everyone finds or makes occasion to practise on others, the villains for wicked purposes, the pranksters for the prank's sake, the heroines for the love of mockery and ultimate matrimony—in such a world the excessive concern of Hortensio, Gremio, and Baptista to see that Petruchio is not deceived about Kate is unique—is, in fact, curiously un-Shakespearian. And the dramatist's concern to have us understand that Petruchio knows all is curiously insistent also: he does not bring Katherina and Petruchio face to face until both we and Petruchio have had—besides the several verbal characterizations of Kate's shrewishness—an actual demonstration: *Re-enter* HORTENSIO *with his head broke.*

Nor is Kate allowed to mistake the nature of Petruchio. If her awareness of his quality lags briefly behind ours at first—since we hear much of him and see him in action before Kate even knows that he exists—yet she perceives clearly what he is in their very first encounter, when he returns insult for insult, roar for roar, and threatens blow for blow. Neither is there anything deceptive in the terms of Petruchio's proposal of marriage:

> For I am he am born to tame you, Kate,
> And bring you from a wild Kate to a Kate
> Conformable as other household Kates.
> (Ibid. 278–80.)

In this same openness, with equal vision shared by participants and ourselves, the entire action of the shrew plot is conducted.

In sharpest contrast is the management of the minor plot, which is all composed of false supposes and unperceived realities. Multiple exploitable gaps between participant and participant and between

participants and ourselves are opened at once. In the latter half of
I. ii the familiar stair-stepped structure of awarenesses rises with
unusual abruptness—to endure through four acts as the machinery
of action and source of comic effect. Its creation results from practices perpetrated by four principal practisers—each of whom is
simultaneously the victim of others' practices; the four are Lucentio, Tranio, Hortensio, and Gremio. We are first advised of Lucentio's and Tranio's double-edged device; thus Lucentio:

> Thou shalt be master, Tranio, in my stead,
> Keep house and port and servants, as I should.
> I will some other be, some Florentine,
> Some Neapolitan, or meaner man of Pisa.
> 'Tis hatch'd and shall be so.
>
> (I. i. 207–10.)

Lucentio's practice is designed to deceive Baptista and gain admit-
tance for himself to Bianca. Hortensio's practice, to the same end,
briefly involves Petruchio also as a deceiver:

> Now shall my friend Petruchio do me grace,
> And offer me disguis'd in sober robes
> To old Baptista as a schoolmaster
> Well seen in music, to instruct Bianca;
> That so I may, by this device, at least
> Have leave and leisure to make love to her
> And unsuspected court her by herself.
>
> (I. ii. 131–7.)

The tangle of deceivers and deceived is complicated further when
Gremio employs Lucentio, disguised as 'Cambio', to woo for him:

> Hark you, sir; I'll have them very fairly bound,—
> All books of love, see that at any hand;
> And see you read no other lectures to her.
> You understand me?
>
> (Ibid. 146–9.)

Gremio here holds the lowest rung on the ladder, knowing neither
of his rival Hortensio's scheme to woo Bianca in person as her tutor
nor of his own tutor's true identity and purpose. Hortensio, holding
the edge over Gremio as proprietor of his own practice, is at the
same time deceived by both Gremio and Lucentio. Lucentio, holding the highest place as deceiver of both Gremio and Hortensio, is
himself ignorant of Hortensio's device. The entrance of Tranio,
posing as Lucentio, puts the peak to the structure, above the levels
of Gremio and Hortensio, who, ignorant that 'Cambio' is in fact
Lucentio, are ignorant also that 'Lucentio' is in fact Tranio.
 Such is the composition of the structure that the dramatist has

established in our minds by the end of Act I. The action thereafter, through all scenes of the minor plot until the denouement, has meaning and produces effect only by reference to this structure. The structure remains essentially unchanged until the last, when it is further complicated by the arrival of the 'supposed' and the 'right' Vincentios. It is the most elaborate framework for foolery that Shakespeare had yet devised.

So far as the minor plot is concerned, then, the scenes that lie between the end of the first act and the denouement are given over to exploitation of the discrepant awarenesses of six persons. It is noteworthy that, whereas often Shakespeare's exploitation of such discrepancies makes a dazzling exhibition, with bold flashes of irony struck in line after line, throughout this action the exploitation is relatively subdued. The persons go about their business: Hortensio wooing Bianca as 'Licio', Lucentio wooing her as 'Cambio', and betraying his employer Gremio the while, Baptista promising Bianca to Tranio, supposing him to be Lucentio, unaware that all the while she is being wooed by false tutors under his own auspices. Merely the image in our minds of the true situation is allowed to suffice as interpreter of the action, without special comment in the lines themselves. Most often Shakespeare exploits discrepant awarenesses by centring attention on the unaware persons, giving them speeches which—sometimes by their remoteness from the truth that we perceive, sometimes by their accidental closeness to it—illuminate the chasm between the speakers' understanding and ours. But here the unawareness of Baptista, for example, is not the subject of exploitation when he is confronted in quick succession with several impostors: Petruchio presents 'Licio' as tutor when in fact he is Hortensio and a suitor; Gremio presents 'Cambio' as tutor when in fact he is Lucentio and a suitor, deceiving Gremio, Hortensio, and Baptista; Tranio presents himself as 'Lucentio', a suitor and a gentleman, when in fact he is Tranio, a servant, and no suitor. Baptista's unawareness is exploited only in that our view of the scene is controlled by the image of the true situation which was set in our minds earlier. In contrast, in Shakespeare's mature usage, when Malvolio in *Twelfth Night*, victim of the practices of Maria and Toby, is positive that Olivia loves him, it is he, in all his richly exploitable obliviousness, who is central, and the comments of bystanders as well as his own remarks serve to exploit his condition.

But in *The Taming of the Shrew*, with Shakespeare still feeling his way, the centre of attention is more often the deceiver than the deceived—or, more precisely, since most of the principal persons are both deceivers and deceived, attention is directed to them more often as deceivers than as deceived. During the bidding for Bianca that ends Act II, for example, while Tranio poses as 'Lucentio' and, in the name of the latter's father, Vincentio, outbids Gremio, the centre of attention is Tranio, as deceiver, rather than either Baptista or Gremio, each of whom is doubly deceived. So, too, in the very heart of the minor plot—the scene of the wooing of Bianca by Lucentio as 'Cambio' and Hortensio as 'Licio' (III. i)—it is as deceivers rather than deceived that the two suitors take turns as centre of attention; thus, while Lucentio 'construes' a Latin passage for Bianca and in the process reveals his identity to her, it is his practice rather than Hortensio's unawareness that holds the attention, and while Hortensio instructs Bianca in 'gamut in a briefer sort, / More pleasant, pithy, and effectual / Than hath been taught by any of my trade', and thus reveals his identity to her, it is his practice rather than Lucentio's unawareness that is central. Moreover, though each suitor continues ignorant of the other's identity, each immediately suspects the intentions of his rival tutor; thus Lucentio, aside:

> And watch withal; for, but I be deceiv'd,
> Our fine musician groweth amorous.
> (III. i. 62–63.)

And thus Hortensio:

> But I have cause to pry into this pedant.
> Methinks he looks as though he were in love.
> (Ibid. 87–88.)

Here, however, although Hortensio's ignorance of his rival's identity is little exploited for comic effect, it is the basis for action, since it motivates Hortensio's withdrawal from the race to win Bianca; and since Tranio, acting as 'Lucentio', has already outbidden Gremio, it is made apparent at this point that Lucentio must emerge victor. Thus says Tranio, summing up the situation:

> We'll over-reach the greybeard, Gremio,
> The narrow, prying father, Minola,
> The quaint musician, amorous Licio,
> All for my master's sake, Lucentio.
> (III. ii. 147–50.)

It is not until Act IV that the exploitable unawareness of Baptista and other uninformed persons takes a central place. Tranio, needing an old man to pose as Vincentio and give 'assurances' to Baptista, deceives the newly arrived Pedant into supposing his life is in danger in Padua and prevails upon him to play the part. Baptista, from the beginning held to the bottom of the structure of awarenesses, is once more victimized, and his remarks on meeting 'supposed' Vincentio form a passage remarkably ribbed and studded—indeed, girt around—with the scraps of ignorance:

> Your plainness and your shortness please me well.
> Right true it is, your son Lucentio here
> Doth love my daughter and she loveth him,
> Or both dissemble deeply their affections;
> And therefore, if you say no more than this,
> That like a father you will deal with him
> And pass my daughter a sufficient dower,
> The match is made, and all is done.
> Your son shall have my daughter with consent.
>
> (IV. iv. 39–47.)

Here Baptista addresses a false Vincentio about a false Lucentio and a non-existent love match, while the true Lucentio, whose love match is real, looks on as 'Cambio'. So, too, in his next speech every line throws into relief some aspect of Baptista's darkness:

> Cambio, hie you home,
> And bid Bianca make her ready straight;
> And, if you will, tell what hath happened:
> Lucentio's father is arriv'd in Padua,
> And how she's like to be Lucentio's wife.
>
> (Ibid. 62–66.)

In the comedies it is always darkest just before the denouement. In the confusion at the opening of Act V, when Vincentio arrives at Lucentio's house, all except Lucentio and Tranio are deep-sunk in the condition of unawareness. Even Petruchio and Katherina are briefly affected, having encountered the true Vincentio on the road and brought him with them to Padua, knowing him to be Vincentio but supposing his son to be not the true Lucentio but the masquerading Tranio. As was earlier stated, however, the error is irrelevant to their own affairs; whether Tranio is Lucentio or Lucentio 'Cambio' interests them only as spectators. But for the others, their heads filled with half-truths or total falsities, all their illusions are relevant, exploitable, and exploited. First to bare his ignorance is Gremio, who, just after we have seen Lucentio and Bianca flee to the church to be married, arrives at Lucentio's house still expecting that his rival will fail to provide the 'assurances' demanded by Baptista and that therefore Bianca will be his by default. 'I marvel Cambio comes not all this while', he remarks from his pit of darkness, ignorant that 'Cambio' is a fiction, that Tranio is not Lucentio, that the false 'Lucentio' is even now inside the house giving 'assurances' to Baptista—these being confirmed by a Pedant as 'Vincentio' —and finally that the true Lucentio, at this instant, is marrying

Bianca. Next to have his ignorance exploited is the Pedant, who peers from the window at Vincentio's knock, ignorant that this is that very Vincentio whom he is impersonating, that the 'Lucentio' for whom he had agreed to provide assurances is really the servant Tranio, that the true Lucentio is now marrying Bianca, and, finally, that he need not have become involved in his present plight at all, there being in fact no danger to him in Padua as Tranio had made him think. Next is the 'right' Vincentio, father of the 'right' Lucentio, who has come suddenly in upon this bewildering world from outside, like Sebastian stepping into the Illyrian fog compounded by his sister in *Twelfth Night*; here Vincentio finds—he knows not what:

> *Ped.* What's he that knocks as he would beat down the gate?
> *Vin.* Is Signior Lucentio within, sir?
> *Ped.* He's within, sir, but not to be spoken withal.
> *Vin.* What if a man bring him a hundred pound or two, to make merry withal?
> *Ped.* Keep your hundred pounds to yourself; he shall need none, so long as I live.
> *Pet.* Nay, I told you your son was well beloved in Padua. Do you hear, sir? To leave frivolous circumstances, I pray you, tell Signior Lucentio that his father is come from Pisa and is here at the door to speak with him.
> *Ped.* Thou liest. His father is come from Padua and is here looking out at the window.
> *Vin.* Art thou his father?
> *Ped.* Ay, sir; so his mother says, if I may believe her.   (v. i. 17–35.)

Though ignorant of particular aspects of the situation he has come into, Vincentio sees some facts more clearly than those involved in the tangle whose eyes are bleared with counterfeit supposes. He knows, at least, that he is in fact Vincentio, that 'Lucentio' is in fact Tranio, and that whatever the Pedant is, he is not Vincentio. He stands, therefore, a rung or two above Baptista, who remains, at the end as at the beginning, mistaken in his view of everything around him. In the last wild moments of confusion, he remains ignorant that Tranio and the Pedant are impostors, that 'Cambio' Lucentio has run off with Bianca to be married, and that the new arrival, whom he would have an officer drag away summarily—'Away with the dotard! To the gaol with him!'—is in fact Vincentio. The exploitation of his errors, long compounded, continues central until the 'right' Lucentio enters and dispels the fog.

The gaps between awarenesses of participants involved in the minor plot are all closed at the end of v. i. In v. ii we share with Petruchio a final advantage over all these persons. It is an advantage which has been long in preparation—indeed, the entire action of

31

the shrew plot has moved toward this end. We have seen Katherina hailed up and down the road between Petruchio's house and Padua; at his command, we have heard her call the sun the moon, the moon the sun, indifferently, call old Vincentio a 'young budding virgin, fair and fresh and sweet', and finally, just before the last scene—for Shakespeare must always make assurance doubly sure—we have been given a clenching proof that the taming is complete:

> *Kath.* Husband, let's follow, to see the end of this ado.
> *Pet.* First kiss me, Kate, and we will.
> *Kath.* What, in the midst of the street?
> *Pet.* What, art thou asham'd of me?
> *Kath.* No, sir, God forbid; but asham'd to kiss.
> *Pet.* Why, then let's home again. Come, sirrah, let's away.
> *Kath.* Nay, I will give thee a kiss; now pray thee, love, stay.
> *Pet.* Is not this well? Come, my sweet Kate:
> Better once than never, for never too late.
>
> (v. i. 147-55.)

With Petruchio, therefore, we are well prepared to relish the exposure of all Padua's error, bluntly expressed by Tranio's remark: ''Tis thought your deer does hold you at a bay.' The exploitation of our enormous advantage is brief. It extends through only twenty-five lines and ends abruptly with Kate's cheerfully obedient entrance: 'What is your will, sir, that you send for me?'

On this proof the play closes; and with it closes also, until the first romances, Shakespeare's search for 'the way'.

CHAPTER II

All Shall Be Well: The Way Found

FROM whatever point they are viewed, *A Midsummer-Night's Dream* and *The Merchant of Venice* are evidently very different plays. But it is appropriate to consider them together, not only because they are Shakespeare's first comic masterpieces, closely related in time, but because, from the point of view of the disposition and uses of awareness, they represent, for all their dissimilarity, a common advance along the chosen road.

In the earlier plays, which exhibit some masterful individual scenes but lack the last fine touch that confers artistic wholeness, technique itself occupies a proportionately large place in the total work, and, accordingly, to describe a basic principle of technique has an obvious justification. With *A Midsummer-Night's Dream* and *The Merchant of Venice*, however, the bones of dramatic structure become deeply concealed in the live flesh of the whole creation, and, being unexposed, may seem insignificant—indeed, may seem not to exist; hence to examine the submerged mechanics of illusion when it is certainly not the mechanics but the illusion itself that counts may appear merely perverse. But in the masterpieces no less than in the exploratory comedies it is the inner structure that confers and sustains the outward shape. If, then, an approach to the great comedies through examination of the disposition and uses of awareness appears less relevant than a direct assault upon the moonlight, the lyricism, and the marvellous beings, human and other, who inhabit these extraordinary worlds, nevertheless it does afford a way of coming at these and other conspicuous manifestations of Shakespeare's imagination. And Oberon and Portia, Bottom and Shylock, the fairy world and the world where merchants most do congregate are creations of so great magnitude that any approach should be taken if it will lead to a new view of them.

1. *A Midsummer-Night's Dream*

In *The Comedy of Errors* a wide but single discrepancy in awarenesses resulted when we were given and the participants were denied one all-important fact, that two sets of identical twins are at large on the streets of the same city. The entire comic action of the play is an exploitation of this single discrepancy. In the other early comedies, multiple discrepancies both among participants and between them and us were created by deceptive practices of several sorts—wearing disguise, overhearing, overpeering, feigning ignorance, exchanging identities, secret conspiring, outright lying. In *A Midsummer-Night's Dream* the ultimate creator of the main discrepancy is again single, as in *The Comedy of Errors*; it is, of course, the magical property of a certain flower:-

> Yet mark'd I where the bolt of Cupid fell.
> It fell upon a little western flower,
> Before milk-white, now purple with love's wound,
> And maidens call it love-in-idleness.
>
> (II. i. 165–8.)

Squeezed upon the eyelids of two mortals and one fairy, the juice of this extraordinary pansy is the ultimate source—subtler than disguise, eavesdropping, or plain falsehood—of discrepancies which make possible the main action and comic effects of the play.

Though it touches the eyes of only three, the magic juice affects directly or indirectly all the principal persons. It is primarily responsible for the fact that at some time in the action each of them stands on a level of awareness below ours, and for the fact that we hold advantage over some person or persons during seven of the nine scenes. Yet although everything starts with it, the magic juice is not the only means by which the dramatist divides the awarenesses of characters. Here, as in the other major comedies, the disposition of awarenesses is elaborate, with many degrees of differentiation represented between Bottom's bottomless oblivion and Oberon's near omniscience. Though the juice is the first cause of the main gap, additional discrepancies are wrought by more ordinary means—even as ordinary as eavesdropping, and, in the case of Puck's initial error, as common as simple lack of sufficiently precise information, plus a touch of irresponsibility.

In *A Midsummer-Night's Dream*, for the first time, Shakespeare uses an 'outside force' which interferes in and controls the affairs of men. Oberon moves unseen, unheard, and unsuspected to the solution of the sole problem of the play (so far as the mortals are concerned)—that of restoring Demetrius's love to Helena. Although he differs in form and nature from Shakespeare's later notable forces of control as markedly as they differ from one another, the fairy king is like them all both in his essential dramatic function and in the attributes which enable him to perform this function—superior power and superior awareness. Like the Fate that operates throughout *Romeo and Juliet* (according to the Prologue) and the Fate of which the witches are the visible figureheads in *Macbeth*, but unlike Duke Vincentio in *Measure for Measure* and Prospero in *The Tempest*, Oberon is supernatural and immortal. Like Vincentio and Prospero, and unlike Fate in the tragedies, he is benevolent. Like Fate itself and unlike the others, he remains always invisible to the mortal participants—but, unlike Fate, he is visible to us. Like all the others except the Fate of *Romeo and Juliet*, he makes observable contact with mortals, either directly or through an intermediary. Also like all the others except the Fate of *Romeo and Juliet*, he requires special aids or 'props' in wielding his power. Unlike all the others, he is concerned quite incidentally with the affairs of mortals. And, finally, he falls a little short of the others' omniscience and omnipotence: under his direction things can temporarily get out of hand.

Although he has come on purpose to bless the bed of Theseus and Hippolyta, Oberon's interference in the dilemma of the four Athenian youths comes about by chance. The juice of the flower for which he sends Puck was meant only for Titania's eyes, to compel her to surrender her little changeling boy. It is while he awaits Puck's return that Demetrius and Helena enter, quarrelling. 'I am invisible,' says the fairy king, 'and I will overhear their conference.' The 'conference' of the angry young man and the hurt and bitter maid runs through fifty-six lines and represents the play's first use of a discrepancy between the participants' vision and ours: the couple are ignorant by what immortal eye they are being watched. When they have gone, Oberon speaks:

> Fare thee well, nymph. Ere he do leave this grove,
> Thou shalt fly him and he shall seek thy love.
> (Ibid. 245–6.)

Neither now nor ever after are Helena and Demetrius—or, indeed, any of the other human participants—to know that a force from outside their mortal circle has looked on their affairs, apprehended their dilemma, and interceded in the cause of true love. From this first point on, a gap divides the human participants' view from ours. This gap is unique in Shakespeare's comedies in that it remains open even at the end of the play. We alone know that an immortal spirit has manipulated human events and solved a mortal problem.

Immortal, yet not quite omniscient: 'Anoint his eyes,' says Oberon to Puck,

> But do it when the next thing he espies
> May be the lady. Thou shalt know the man
> By the Athenian garments he hath on.
>
> (II. i. 261–4.)

'Fear not, my lord,' replies Puck, 'your servant shall do so.' But even as Oberon gives these directions, we know, since the dramatist has taken care to advise us, that not one but two young men in Athenian garments are in the forest. Having seen only Demetrius, and being preoccupied with Titania, Oberon does not foresee the possibility of error. From this point until well into III. ii our Olympian perch is set not only above mortals but above immortals also. Dutifully seeking out a youth in Athenian weeds, and finding Lysander and Hermia sleeping far apart on the ground, as Hermia's sense of propriety has required, fallible Puck concludes that these are the estranged mortals who must be made to love each other. 'Believe me, king of shadows, I mistook', he asserts later, when he and Oberon discover what abuse their errors have wrought. Puck errs because Oberon erred in directing him, and thus, though the ultimate cause is the magical juice of the little western flower, the immediate cause of the comic action involving the lovers is a blunder made because immortal intelligence has fallen, for once, a little short of omniscience.

The principal business between the time Puck drops the juice on Lysander's eyes and the time the fault is finally rectified, however, is exploitation not of Oberon's unawareness that Puck has blundered but of the lovers' unawareness of what has happened to them. In the truly enchanted forest outside Athens as in the seemingly bewitched city of Ephesus, where Antipholus of Syracuse and his Dromio are mistaken for their brothers, the effects of error are a chain reaction of surprise, misunderstanding, mystification, and near frenzy. The beginning is Lysander's waking, ignorant of what has happened as he slept, to perceive Helena through enchanted eyes:

> *Hel.* Lysander, if you live, good sir, awake.
> *Lys.* (*Awaking.*) And run through fire I will for thy sweet sake.
> Transparent Helena! Nature shows art,
> That through thy bosom makes me see thy heart.
>
> (II. ii. 103–5.)

Not knowing the real cause of his change of affection, he attributes it to 'reason':

> The will of man is by his reason sway'd;
> And reason says you are the worthier maid.

36

Things growing are not ripe until their season,
So I, being young, till now ripe not to reason;
And touching now the point of human skill,
Reason becomes the marshal to my will
And leads me to your eyes, where I o'erlook
Love's stories written in Love's richest book.
                    (Ibid. 115–22.)

Equally innocent of the truth, Helena mistakes Lysander's protestations for mockery, thus compounding the initial error, and, startled and angry, runs off into the forest pursued by her bewitched lover. Hermia, waking, is removed even further from the truth, being ignorant not only of the cause of Lysander's change but of the fact that he *has* changed; mystified, filled with false imaginings, she, too, runs off, seeking Lysander. Thus in short order the potent magic of the little flower, misapplied by the fallible Puck, has affected three of the four youths, and exploitation of the swiftly multiplying discrepancies is under way. Briefly, moreover, the world of the mortals is in fact, in our own perspective, out of control, for Oberon is still preoccupied with Titania.

Regularly in the mature comedies, the climactic peak rises in the final scene of Act III or in the opening scene of Act IV, or in both. From *The Comedy of Errors* to *The Tempest*, too regularly to be coincidence, it is also during this portion that exploitation of discrepant awarenesses is at its peak—that is to say that at this point *the greatest number of participants are ignorant of the greatest number of facts in a situation that has attained its greatest complexity*. In *A Midsummer-Night's Dream* the climactic portion begins with Act III, ii, and runs through Act IV, i. Everyone who enters the first of these scenes, six in all, mortals and fairies, is oblivious to some aspect of the situation. Oberon, first to appear, unwittingly reminds us that his knowledge of events in the world he rules has not kept pace with ours. We have just come from seeing Titania lead Bottom to her bower; but Oberon muses thus:

I wonder if Titania be awak'd;
Then, what it was that next came in her eye,
Which she must dote on in extremity.
                    (III. ii. 1–3.)

Puck enters, and his report brings Oberon's understanding of one part of the total situation up to ours: 'Titania wak'd and straightway lov'd an ass.' But in the next lines both fairies exhibit ignorance of the havoc which, as we have just seen, their love charm has begun to work in mortal affairs:

Obe. But hast thou yet latch'd the Athenian's eyes
With the love-juice, as I did bid thee do?
Robin. I took him sleeping,—that is finish'd too,—
And the Athenian woman by his side;
That, when he wak'd, of force she must be eye'd.
(III. ii. 36–40.)

Of this matter also, however, the fairies' unawareness is short lived, for when Demetrius and Hermia enter quarrelling, Puck perceives that this is not the youth whose eyes he had anointed, and soon, overhearing Hermia's accusations against Demetrius, both spirits perceive the cause of the quarrel, and from this time on their vision matches ours. It is to be noted, finally, that although Shakespeare allowed the fairies, for a time, to be unaware of important facts known to us, he did not exploit their unawareness so as to make them laughable. On the contrary, Oberon suggests that Puck deliberately anointed Lysander's eyes instead of Demetrius's; and although Puck denies the charge—'Believe me, king of shadows, I mistook'—still he is quite ready to relish the spectacle of confusion among mortals: 'And so far am I glad it so did sort, / As this their jangling I esteem a sport.' Upon Puck, as upon the great professional fools, Shakespeare confers a special immunity, making laughter at his expense unlikely even during a moment when unawareness makes him vulnerable to laughter.

Exploitation not of the fairies' brief unawareness, then, but of the mortals' mystification and confusion is the business of the first great climactic scene. It begins with the entrance of Lysander and Helena immediately after the final act of deception has been performed, the anointing of Demetrius's eyes by Oberon. Says Puck,

Then will two at once woo one;
That must needs be sport alone.
(Ibid. 118–19.)

The next 400 lines show Shakespeare's finest achievement to this date in representing the comic effects of error. Rushing through moonlight and shadow in the enchanted forest, unknowingly observed by immortal spirits, the confused couples act the 'fond pageant' that answers Puck's hopes. The profound oblivion of the young men, neither knowing what has happened to him, each distrusting the other's motives, is the basis of the action. Each accepts unquestioningly the reversal of his affection, as a plausible and natural event—as in dreams one regards fantastic experiences as ordinary. Thus whereas Lysander had confidently attributed his conversion to the force of 'reason', Demetrius now explains his own change as a natural homecoming:

> Lysander, keep thy Hermia; I will none.
> If e'er I lov'd her, all that love is gone.
> My heart to her but as guest-wise sojourn'd,
> And now to Helen is it home return'd,
> There to remain.
>
> (Ibid. 169-73.)

Eyes open but glassy, accepting without surprise or wonder events that should astonish them, the rival lovers prefigure the greater heroes of the later comedies. But Bassanio of *The Merchant of Venice*, Claudio of *Much Ado about Nothing*, Orsino of *Twelfth Night*, and most notably of all, Orlando of *As You Like It*, need no magic anointment in order to attain that state of obliviousness which is the normal condition of romantic masculinity in Shakespearian comedy. On the other hand, Helena and Hermia less notably anticipate the heroines to follow, who are superior in awareness and mistresses of all they survey; Julia of *The Two Gentlemen of Verona* more truly prefigures these. At first incredulous and then mystified by the shift of the men's affections—for unlike the men they do not see, here or hereafter, with the dreamer's eye—the two 'lovely berries moulded on one stem' do nevertheless seek a rational explanation. Hermia, who never before had cause to doubt her power over men, seeks in vain:

> Hate me! wherefore? O me! what news, my love!
> Am not I Hermia? Are not you Lysander?
> I am as fair now as I was erewhile.
>
> (Ibid. 272-4.)

Incredulity and amazement lead to mystification—a higher if not less painful state of awareness than mere obliviousness—and in this sense the heroines are true to their kind in the world of comedy. They see farther, wider, more clearly than the males; they demand more plausible answers to questions. Yet the vision of Hermia or Helena is hardly comparable to that of Orlando's Rosalind or Bassanio's Portia: they lack the all-encompassing understanding that these have. Mystification leads them to try interpretation, and misinterpretation leads to angry quarrel which threatens violence: all this, for the women as for the men, is the effect of the same basic unawareness of the situation. The heroines of *A Midsummer-Night's Dream*, unlike those of the later comedies, hold advantage over the heroes only in realizing that the situation is unnatural, in distrusting and refusing to accept what Lysander and Demetrius view without surprise.

The quarrel scene ends with a threat of actual violence and physical injury, when Lysander and Demetrius withdraw into the forest to fight it out with their swords and Helena of the longer legs flees the sharper nails of Hermia. It is just here that the dramatist gives us reassurance—even as he did at the comparable place in *The Two Gentlemen of Verona*, showing us Valentine just before the savage Proteus threatens Silvia. Precursor of Vincentio and Prospero, Oberon has seen all. 'Stand aside', he said to Puck after anointing the eyes of Demetrius, and the pair silently watched what happens when 'two at once woo one'. At the outset, then, we have occupied a vantage-point from which to view the action not merely as a quarrel, but *as a quarrel of mortals overwatched by benevolent omnipotence*. Given a perspective that includes Oberon, knowing that he knows all and means to direct true love to a happy ending, we can maintain during the violent 'jangling' of the rivals a sense that all is really well. Our awareness provides a perfect climate for comic effect. If we forgot the presence of Oberon during the action, and thus narrowed the vision which the dramatist enabled us to use at full advantage, by so much would the force of the scene be diminished for us. But to make sure that our comfortable sense of Oberon's presence does not fail at the crucial moment, Shakespeare prods it immediately after the confused, angry, desperate mortals run off into the forest. For Oberon here reminds us that he has understood all, chides Puck for his error, and orders him to prevent the youths from hurting one another in their ignorance. And again also the dramatist reminds us that this spirit which has intervened in mortal affairs is benevolent. Seeing the day approach, Puck remarks that 'Damned spirits all' which must 'for aye consort with black-brow'd night' have already gone to their wormy beds. 'But we', says Oberon—stating a principle by which are run the worlds of the great comedies—'are spirits of another sort.' Oberon, Duke Vincentio, and Prospero are forces of benevolent control in their worlds, and similarly good though less absolute forces control the worlds of the other comedies also. These powers are our means of assurance that however large danger may loom in the view of the participants who lack our perspective, no lasting harm will be done and all will at last be well. Providing an environment in which comic effects can flourish even in dark moments, this assurance is an indispensable condition and a hall-mark of Shakespearian comedy.

In the enchanted forest of *A Midsummer-Night's Dream*, governed by a fairy king, error can be introduced into mortal affairs by the anointment of human eyes with the juice of a flower, and so also it can be removed by the simple expedient of crushing on the eyes another herb. While the couples sleep in exhaustion after their night-long chase in the forest, Puck anoints Lysander's eyes with the 'remedy' and thus corrects the error without which there would have been no misunderstanding, no quarrel, no danger —and no action. But the magic juice is left in Demetrius's eyes, to make the false lover see true, even as it had made the true one see false. So when the lovers wake, enchantment has ended, and, even as Oberon had foretold, none can recall the night's events. Our advantage over them continues, therefore, after the spell is broken, even to the end of the play, and forever. In this way *A Midsummer-Night's Dream* is unique among Shakespeare's comedies, for in others the denouement closes the gap between the participants' awareness and ours. A principle of Shakespeare's dramatic method is reflected in the fact that in his comedies, histories, and tragedies, the denouement never is needed or used to explain matters of which *we* have been ignorant, but to raise the participants' awareness up, at last, to ours. By coincidence or otherwise, it is only in *A Midsummer-Night's Dream* and *Romeo and Juliet*—plays possibly written in the same year—that the participants' level is not raised to equal ours at the end.

Theseus's party of hunters come upon the sleeping lovers even as the Prince, the rival families, and the citizens of Verona come upon the bodies of Romeo and Juliet, lying dead with Paris in the Capulet tomb. And though the lovers in the comedy wake, whereas those in the tragedy do not, yet they cannot tell their story. 'When they next wake, all this derision / Shall seem a dream and fruitless vision', Oberon had predicted; and so it is. It is Egeus who expresses the hunters' mystification:

> My lord, this is my daughter here asleep;
> And this, Lysander; this Demetrius is;
> This Helena, old Nedar's Helena.
> I wonder of their being here together.
> (IV. i. 132–5.)

For the participants this joyous conclusion is inexplicable, as is its woeful counterpart in the Capulet tomb:

> . . . here lies the County slain;
> And Juliet bleeding, warm, and newly dead,
> Who here hath lain this two days buried.
> Go, tell the Prince, run to the Capulets;
> Raise up the Montagues; some others search.
> We see the ground whereon these woes do lie;
> But the true ground of all these piteous woes
> We cannot without circumstance descry.
> (*R. & J.* v. iii. 174–81.)

It is Theseus's theory that the lovers 'rose up early to observe / The rite of May'; but this does not explain their present friendliness. Lysander tries to answer the all-important question; but the events of the night have been washed from his memory by the *vertu* of the herb, and he can barely recall even how he came to be in the forest:

> My lord, I shall reply amazedly,
> Half sleep, half waking; but as yet, I swear,
> I cannot truly say how I came here.
> But, as I think—for truly would I speak,
> And now I do bethink me, so it is,—
> I came with Hermia hither.
>
> (IV. i. 150–5.)

Demetrius tries next; but the magic juice of the little western flower abides in his eyes as it must for ever, the only permanent evidence that the events of this night were real:

> . . . I wot not by what power,—
> But by some power it is,—my love to Hermia,
> Melted as is the snow, seems to me now
> As the remembrance of an idle gaud
> Which in my childhood I did dote upon;
> And all the faith, the virtue of my heart,
> The object and the pleasure of mine eye,
> Is only Helena.
>
> (Ibid. 168–75.)

'Of this discourse we more will hear anon', says Theseus; but none of the lovers will be able to report his adventures. For in truth, on waking after the night is over, the youths have fallen still farther below our vantage-point. While the action of the night continued, they were aware of it even though they were ignorant of the cause; but now that it is over, their remembrance has failed, and they know neither the what nor the why of the night or the morrow.

So also Bottom, the state of whose awareness, in its relation to ours, remains to be probed. As Oberon is first in a line that includes Vincentio and Prospero, so Bottom is first in a line that includes such notables as Dogberry, Malvolio, and Sir Andrew Aguecheek. These are the mortals whom nature has made oblivious both of the facts of the situation which bounds them and of themselves. Their competitors for the lowest level of awareness are the romantic heroes of the comedies; but even these—in situations that do not involve business with heroines—have moments when they see themselves and their surroundings with clear eyes: Bassanio, in borrowing from Shylock, sees better than Antonio; and Orlando, seeking help for old Adam, at least manages to find his way through the woods. Other persons in Shakespeare's plays, totalling hundreds and representing many ranks and occupations—brilliant ones like Hamlet and shrewd ones like Cleopatra, even heroines of comedy, villains, and professional jesters, not to mention the vast middle group who are only ordinarily circumspect—are occasionally unaware of vital facts of their situations. But these are *made* unaware by some device, such as disguise, falsehood, eavesdropping, or other practices perpetrated by persons bent on deception. Their unawareness is rarely attributable to their own natures; usually they appear unaware to us only because the dramatist has given us specific information that is denied them and which they cannot possibly know at the time, however circumspect they are. In short, the hundreds who on occasion are ignorant of the facts of their situations are typically so because circumstances make their ignorance unavoidable. But for the select few who dwell at Bottom's depth no device of deception is needed. The dramatist creates them as beings with insulated minds, without perspective, oblivious wherever they are. They are congenitally, chronically unaware. If Rosalind carries an immunity to unawareness, Bottom carries one to awareness. For Rosalind, brightest of heroines, the dark is light enough; for bully Bottom the light is too dark, and the dark no darker.

To this Bottom alone of the mortals it is given to see the fairies—indeed, to converse with them, shake hands with them, be loved by their queen. And yet to him the fairies are no more remarkable than his hard-handed fellows who work in the shop. If Puck mistook in anointing Lysander's eyes when he should have anointed those of Demetrius, he does not err in selecting from among the homespun players—indeed, in selecting from all the world—none but this Bottom, 'the shallowest thickskin of that barren sort', to be the object of Titania's passion. Bottom's oblivion is fixed and immutable; he sees neither himself nor his situation truly at any moment in the action, either before, during, or after his sojourn with immortals. With his first words, without the dramatist's using any device except the words themselves, a chasm opens between his understanding and ours, and it remains so, neither wider nor narrower, through all the action to the end. With the artisans, casting the play:

> . . . let me play Thisby too. I'll speak in a monstrous little voice, 'Thisne! Thisne!' (1. ii. 53–55.)

—planning the rehearsal in the forest:

> We will meet; and there we may rehearse most obscenely and courageously. (Ibid. 110–11.)

—left alone, after his fellows' flight, with the ass's head on his shoulders:

I see their knavery; this is to make an ass of me, to fright me, if they could.
(III. i. 123–4.)

—first perceiving Titania, and replying to her declaration of love:

Methinks, mistress, you should have little reason for that; and yet, to say the truth, reason and love keep little company together now-a-days; the more the pity that some honest neighbours will not make them friends. (Ibid. 145–9.)

—consorting with the fairy train:

Bot. Give me your neaf, Mounsieur Mustardseed. Pray you, leave your courtesy, good mounsieur.
Mus. What's your will?
Bot. Nothing, good mounsieur, but to help Cavalery Cobweb to scratch.
(IV. i. 20–24.)

—alone in the forest when the night is over, awaking from sleep after his fellows, the fairies, the Duke's hunting party, and the lovers have all gone their ways:

I have had a most rare vision. I have had a dream, past the wit of man to say what dream it was. Man is but an ass, if he go about to expound this dream. Methought I was—there is no man can tell what. Methought I was,—and methought I had,—but man is but a patch'd fool if he will offer to say what methought I had. (Ibid. 208–15.)

—and, finally, momentarily interrupting his Pyramus role to explain to Theseus a fine point of dramatic production:

The. The wall, methinks, being sensible, should curse again.
Pyr. No, in truth, sir, he should not. 'Deceiving me' is Thisby's cue. She is to enter now, and I am to spy her through the wall. You shall see it will fall pat as I told you. Yonder she comes. (V. i. 185–9.)

—in short, from the time we first see him until his last exit (having just raised himself from the dead to remind Demetrius that the wall is now down that parted the fathers of Thisbe and Pyramus) our advantage over Bottom is constant. He is neither more nor less oblivious in the ass's head; this head is the palpable extension of his native condition: it is unawareness concretized. When the new situations rise about him, he is neither less nor more aware of them than of the old. He steers an undeviating course through the ordinary and the marvellous alike. All places, persons, and things are alike to him; his insulated mind makes no distinction between Theseus and Peter Quince, Peaseblossom and Snout. With Oberon's wife who dotes on him—'O how I love thee! how I dote on thee!'—he behaves just as he would with Snug's or Flute's wife: 'I pray you, let none of your people stir me; I have an exposition of sleep come upon me.' Not Titania's compulsive doting, but Bottom's unruffled oblivion is the exploitable substance of the first fifty lines of Act IV, which brief scene complements and completes that of the mortal lovers' quarrel and frantic chase through the forest, the two scenes standing together at the summit of the play.

From the perfect vantage-point on which Shakespeare seats us throughout *A Midsummer-Night's Dream*, we perceive more, of course, than the activities of any single group of participants. We are set where our sweep of vision takes in all actions at once—high enough to see that the worlds of fairies, lovers, and artisans, quite separate and alone so far as the participants know, are all one world. We have full view alike of the bewitched lovers overwatched by Oberon in the enchanted forest; of Theseus and Hippolyta awaiting the impending wedding for which the fairies have come to this forest; of Peter Quince and his hard-handed crew, in their relations with both mortals and immortals; and, of course, of the fairies themselves. Except briefly, Oberon and Puck sit with us and see all that we see. But the other groups of participants, whose visions are too confined to take in even what is going on in their own circles, are quite cut off from a view of the whole. The lovers, running, quarrelling, sleeping in the forest, are ignorant of the fairies' existence and of Quince's rough crew. The artisans, except for Bottom, who is transformed and bewitched at the time and can tell nothing even to himself in secret afterwards, know nothing of either the lovers or the fairies. The fact of their ignorance of the lovers' affairs, which have loomed large in our view during the central portion of the play, is subtly underscored by a remark of Snug's as the actors ready themselves to perform before Theseus: 'Masters, the Duke is coming from the temple, and there is two or three lords and ladies more married.' These 'two or three lords and ladies', anonymous shapes to Snug, are of course those very lovers whose tangled affairs have long claimed our main attention. Finally, the royal pair, though they are well acquainted with the young couples, neither know nor can learn what happened in the forest: 'No doubt they rose up early to observe / The rite of May, and, hearing our intent, / Came here in grace of our solemnity', says Theseus, finding the lovers asleep after their frantic night. Only Hippolyta senses that there is more than 'fancy's images' in the lovers' incoherent and fragmentary account of the night, and in her opinion that

> ... all the story of the night told over,
> And all their minds transfigur'd so together,
> More witnesseth than fancy's images,
> And grows to something of great constancy;
> But, howsoever, strange and admirable ...

she nears the truth as does no other mortal; accordingly, the gap between her awareness and ours comes nearest being closed. But Hippolyta is half supernatural herself, and has an appreciation of things strange and admirable, even as, in contrast, she has no patience with gross reality: 'This is the silliest stuff that ever I heard', she says of the artisans' dramatic effort. For the rest of the mortals, including the lovers who have run themselves half to death in the woods, and Bottom, whose itches have been scratched by fairy hands, their ignorance of the marvels we have witnessed from an Olympian peak is epitomized in Theseus's casual, magnificently unwitting words spoken an instant before Oberon, Titania, Puck, and all the fairy train take over the royal household: 'Lovers, to bed; 'tis almost fairy time.'

2. *The Merchant of Venice*

From our high point of observation during *A Midsummer-Night's Dream*, we perceive that Oberon presides over a world of reality, magic, and dream in which mortal and immortal affairs are mingled. Once Shakespeare has shown us Oberon and made clear what he is, we hold a steady and telling advantage over every participant who steps within our range of vision. No such high vantage-point is provided us in *The Merchant of Venice*: a partial reason is that though Portia replaces Oberon she does not replace him early or completely. During the first three acts our vision is more nearly the mere equal of the participants' than is usual in Shakespeare's comedies. We hold advantage over certain participants in only six of twenty scenes, and in two of these it is not of great dramatic use. Further, an exploitable gap separates our level from that of only six of twenty named persons: Antonio, Bassanio, Gratiano, Shylock, the Duke, and Old Gobbo. We never hold advantage over everyone at once, and in this respect also *The Merchant of Venice* differs from other major comedies, in which the climactic scenes usually exploit universal unawareness. In short, in his second comic masterpiece Shakespeare relies less on exploitation of discrepancies in awareness than in any other comedy after *Love's Labour's Lost*.

But though discrepancies are few they are thoroughly exploited. In the scenes in which we do hold advantage, both the means of our gaining it and the effect of our holding it are subtle and telling. In the court scene, for example, perhaps the most masterful scene Shakespeare had yet composed for comedy, a scene whose every stroke is dramatically potent, it is our advantage over all persons but the 'lawyer' and the 'clerk' that, like a lever, raises innate greatness to yet another degree. Moreover, though exploitation of discrepant awarenesses is notable in only six scenes, yet four of these compose the heart of the play, being central to the four main lines—the affairs of the bond, the elopement, the caskets, and the rings.

During the first and second scenes of Act I, exposition gives our view slight margin. In these scenes the situations at Venice and Belmont, exhibited separately, are bound together, first by Bassanio's glowing account of Portia and by Antonio's promise;

> That shall be rack'd, even to the uttermost,
> To furnish thee to Belmont, to fair Portia.
>
> (I. i. 181-2.)

—and next by intimate dialogue of Portia and Nerissa:

> *Ner.* Do you not remember, lady, in your father's time, a Venetian, a scholar and a soldier, that came hither in company of the Marquis of Montferrat?
> *Por.* Yes, yes, it was Bassanio,—as I think, so was he call'd.
> *Ner.* True, madam. He, of all the men that ever my foolish eyes look'd upon, was the best deserving a fair lady.
> *Por.* I remember him well, and I remember him worthy of thy praise.
>
> (I. ii. 122-33.)

When this talk occurs, it is true, we hold a passing advantage over the women, whose wishfulness is evident but who do not know that Bassanio is just now pushing Antonio's means 'even to the uttermost' for the journey to Belmont in quest of a new golden fleece.

In Scene iii, when Bassanio and Antonio agree to Shylock's terms for the loan of 3,000 ducats, we gain a more significant advantage over certain participants. Shakespeare uses subtler means to provide us with this advantage than hitherto in the comedies. Indeed, so subtle are they that here for the first time in the comedies the exact disposition of the awarenesses becomes difficult for us to fix with certainty. The sealing of the bond is an event of enormous importance in the total action, since all that follows depends upon it—the wooing and winning of Portia, the climactic court scene, the ring plot, even the elopement of Jessica and Lorenzo. The question of the disposition of the awarenesses at the moment Shylock's terms are accepted is therefore crucial: do we or do we not hold advantage over Antonio and Bassanio in our understanding of the peril to which the bond exposes the merchant? Danger is of course written large in the terms themselves—but perhaps it is written as large for them as for us:

> If you repay me not on such a day,
> In such a place, such sum or sums as are
> Express'd in the condition, let the forfeit

47

> Be nominated for an equal pound
> Of your fair flesh, to be cut off and taken
> In what part of your body pleaseth me.
> (I. iii. 147–52.)

We know, moreover, that Shylock is a villain, obsessed to wreak ages of vengeance on the merchant. As elsewhere, Shakespeare guards against the possibility of our missing this kind of point; not once in his plays does he deceive us about the intent of a villain. Though falsehood is indeed often like a goodly apple rotten at the heart in the view of participants, it never is in ours. If Shylock's direct speeches to the Christians were insufficient to suggest his true purpose, his unequivocal 'aside' makes it impossible that we should miss the truth:

> If I can catch him once upon the hip,
> I will feed fat the ancient grudge I bear him.
> (Ibid. 46–47.)

This is typically Shakespearian warning that we, however badly the participants may be deceived, must not be taken in by Shylock's later soothing assertions. We are made to know, then, that Shylock opens the bond not 'in a merry sport', but in deadly earnest, in hope that it will be forfeit. So much for our view. But does ours exceed Antonio's and Bassanio's? Are we to take it that because we, and not they, hear Shylock's vindictive 'If I can catch him once upon the hip', they are deceived by his seeming kindness?

On the contrary: from much that they say to Shylock and to each other it appears that they are as aware as we. Shylock's 'aside' is given because it is needed by us—not by them. It exists not to give us advantage, but to bring our knowledge up to theirs. The speech would add nothing to their awareness. Their eyes are open, and therefore the Jew, though a villain, is not a deceiver—though of course he would deceive if he could. Iago, Richard of Gloucester, Don John, Iachimo, Aaron, Timon's flatterers, Claudius are all deceivers, practising on the unsuspecting. Shylock does not belong with these, because he neither deceives anyone, nor deceives himself that he does. Antonio's clear-sightedness with respect to Shylock is evinced repeatedly; without hearing the 'aside', he knows to say,

> If thou wilt lend this money, lend it not
> As to thy friends; for when did friendship take
> A breed for barren metal of his friend?
> But lend it rather to thine enemy,
> Who, if he break, thou mayst with better face
> Exact the penalty.
> (Ibid. 133–8.)

Again, when Shylock—deceiving no one and aware of the fact—
has quoted Scripture, the merchant says to his face,

> Mark you this, Bassanio,
> The devil can cite Scripture for his purpose.
> An evil soul producing holy witness
> Is like a villain with a smiling cheek,
> A goodly apple rotten at the heart.
> O, what a goodly outside falsehood hath!
> (Ibid. 98–103.)

When Shylock 'in a merry sport' has named his terms, Antonio
speaks of the 'kindness' of the Jew:

> Content, i'faith, I'll seal to such a bond,
> And say there is much kindness in the Jew.
> (Ibid. 153–4.)

But this is not to suggest that he has been deceived; Shylock's offer
of the pound-of-flesh bond is 'kindness' only as measured by Antonio's opinion of the Jew's nature—which is harsh indeed if this is
'kindness'. Bassanio's awareness is no less keen. 'You shall not seal to
such a bond for me; / I'll rather dwell in my necessity', he says on
hearing the terms; and again, 'I like not fair terms and a villain's
mind.' Like Antonio, he refers to the Jew's 'kindness' with underlying irony:

> *Shy.* I would be friends with you and have your love,
> Forget the shames that you have stain'd me with,
> Supply your present wants, and take no doit
> Of usance for my moneys, and you'll not hear me.
> *Bass.* This were kindness.
> (Ibid. 139–43.)

And that is to say, 'Kindness indeed—if it were so!'

Shylock leaves the scene knowing that he has deceived no one,
and so the sides are equal: the Christians know that the Jew would
destroy the merchant if he could, and Shylock knows that they
know. Nor has Shakespeare given us advantage over the Christians
in our understanding of Shylock's purpose. But in another matter he
has given us an advantage over Antonio that is of great dramatic
importance.

Antonio's decision to accept Shylock's terms is made not because
he believes in Shylock—but *because he believes in his ships*. Twice
he voices his confidence:

> Within these two months, that's a month before
> This bond expires, I do expect return
> Of thrice three times the value of this bond.
> (Ibid. 158–60.)

And again:

> Come on; in this there can be no dismay;
> My ships come home a month before the day.
> (I. iii. 181–2.)

Antonio thus evinces perfect trust in his ships, and it is partly because he does so that anxiety about the ships begins to grow in our minds.

If their loss is to occur in the future, yet the danger exists in the present, when Antonio accepts the bond, and in our sense of this danger we hold advantage over him. But how have we gained this sense? Do we have it merely because we know we are dealing with a *play*, and our experience with plays has conditioned us to expect disaster when someone is overconfident, as Antonio is? Undoubtedly our margin owes something to dramatic sophistication; perhaps if nothing within the play itself prompted us, our experience would forewarn us. But almost always (the lone exception is *Troilus and Cressida*) Shakespeare trusted only to dramatic means in matters as indispensable to his method as is an exploitable advantage on the side of the audience. He did not leave it to experience or knowledge outside the play to supply the extra light by which a scene is to be viewed. In the present case, it is by dramatic means that he gives us a margin over Antonio and Bassanio—dramatic means more subtle than prologue, aside, or soliloquy, but no less effective. He begins early, with the conversation of Antonio, Salanio, and Salarino at the opening of the play; thus Salanio, twitting the merchant about his melancholy:

> Believe me, sir, had I such venture forth,
> The better part of my affections would
> Be with my hopes abroad. I should be still
> Plucking the grass to know where sits the wind,
> Peering in maps for ports and piers and roads;
> And every object that might make me fear
> Misfortune to my ventures, out of doubt
> Would make me sad.
> (I. i. 15–22.)

These are not casual lines to get the play going; though spoken in jest, fondly, because everyone loves and wants to cheer Antonio, they subtly turn our attention to the real dangers of ships at sea and to the insecurity of Antonio's estate. Thus Salarino takes up after Salanio:

> My wind, cooling my broth,
> Would blow me to an ague when I thought
> What harm a wind too great might do at sea.

> I should not see the sandy hour-glass run
> But I should think of shallows and of flats,
> Vailing her high-top lower than her ribs
> To kiss her burial.
>
> (Ibid. 22–29.)

Salarino speaks to rouse Antonio from his dumps; but though he speaks in jest, a sense of the hazards of ocean is alerted in our minds. It is only a little later that Bassanio asks Antonio for money, and the merchant replies, 'Thou know'st that all my fortunes are at sea'; and it is only a little farther on that we hear Shylock, calculating the risk of a loan to the merchant, say this:

... ships are but boards, sailors but men; there be land-rats and water-rats, water-thieves and land-thieves, I mean pirates, and then there is the peril of waters, winds, and rocks. (I. iii. 22–25.)

These warnings give to Antonio's repeated expressions of confidence—'Come on; in this there can be no dismay; / My ships come home a month before the day'—an ominous, ironic overtone. As scene follows scene, and we realize that, although alert to Shylock's vindictive nature, Antonio is oblivious to the dangers of waters, winds, and rocks, a disquieting advantage builds up in our minds. Though neither Salanio, Salarino, nor Shylock, whose comments make our advantage, can *know* that the ships will be lost, yet the repetition of their remarks feeds a growing anxiety, and by the time Antonio agrees to the bond our advantage over him is as strong as if the dramatist had begun with a prologue stating that the ships are doomed. Had he followed his later, typical practice, Shakespeare would have informed us secretly that the ships are already lost at the time Antonio signs the bond. But here the loss is in the future, and only the danger exists in the present. Yet if the means of advantage differ, the effects are identical: we can hardly fail to understand that in agreeing to Shylock's terms Antonio has imperilled himself.

Much action intervenes, however, between the signing of the bond and the brush with disaster that occurs in the court scene. Throughout this action our spot of anxiety for Antonio grows. As early as II. viii Salanio and Salarino come to share our sense of the merchant's peril, and their concern aggravates ours. In the main, however, such use as Shakespeare makes of discrepancies in awareness during the second and third acts is confined to incidents only indirectly connected with our principal advantage. These incidents are Launcelot's deception of his father, Shylock's loss of Jessica, and Bassanio's choice of the casket.

The Clown's practice serves no purpose but that of fun and is motivated by nothing more impressive than his declaration of intent to 'try confusions' with his father. Old Gobbo, being 'more than sand-blind, high gravel blind, knows me not', says Launcelot at the outset. Our advantage over the father is no sooner established than it is put to use. Twice the fool deceives his father, first by pretending to be someone else, next by seeming (with the back of his head turned to his father) to have grown a beard. Perhaps the scene has some significance in the fact that, desiring a comic incident to lighten the dark tenor of the main action, Shakespeare chose one whose basis is an exploitable difference in awareness. But the observation is nothing new: long before *The Merchant of Venice*—indeed, in the very first comedy—his predilection for this method of creating comic effect is evident.

More complex and more germane to the central action are the scenes culminating in Shylock's loss of Jessica, scenes in which we hold advantage over the Jew. The mixed effects of these scenes contrast with the simple comic effect that arises from Launcelot's exploitation of his advantage, and ours, over Old Gobbo. The means by which the dramatist places our vantage-point above Shylock's represent nothing new in his technique. First is the brief soliloquy spoken by Jessica after saying farewell to Launcelot:

> O Lorenzo,
> If thou keep promise, I shall end this strife,
> Become a Christian and thy loving wife.
> (II. iii. 19–20.)

This is the first information given us on the romance of Lorenzo and Jessica, and as yet we know nothing of their specific plans. But in the following scene we learn more, when Lorenzo reveals the elopement scheme:

> I must needs tell thee all. She hath directed
> How I shall take her from her father's house,
> What gold and jewels she is furnish'd with,
> What page's suit she hath in readiness.
> (II. iv. 30–33.)

These lines of Lorenzo's stand at the very end of one scene. The next opens directly upon Shylock, who inevitably stands under their light. Shylock's mood at the moment is savage: Launcelot has declared his intention to leave the Jew's service; the evening is to be noisy with the gay masques of Gentiles; and Shylock has earlier committed himself forth to sup with Christians. In his wrath the Jew is made to appear both ludicrous and odious:

> ... I'll go in hate, to feed upon
> The prodigal Christian.
> (II. v. 14–15.)

And again, venting his spleen after the retreating Launcelot:

> Drones hive not with me;
> Therefore I part with him, and part with him
> To one that I would have him help to waste
> His borrow'd purse.
>
> (Ibid. 48-51.)

Further, in the midst of this storming at Launcelot, rage at the idea of supper with Christians, and angry anticipation of masques with 'the vile squeaking of the wry-neck'd fife' is set a reminder for us of Antonio's grim plight: mention of Bassanio's 'borrow'd purse' prods the memory. Darting his wrath at multiple targets, then, Shylock cuts an evil figure which at best invites derision and at worst demands abomination. Certainly, in any event, presented in his grotesque rage and as a menace to the unwitting, good Antonio, he is a creature who repels sympathy. But Lorenzo's words, shrewdly placed immediately before the scene, complicate the effect—for they set Shylock beneath our vantage-point in the character of a father who does not know that 'Jessica, my girl' is about to desert him and his way of life.

It is Shylock's ignorance of his impending loss that Shakespeare exploits as the scene proceeds. 'There is some ill a-brewing towards my rest', says the Jew; and Launcelot, leaving the scene, sings for Jessica's ears:

> There will come a Christian by,
> Will be worth a Jewess' eye.
>
> (Ibid. 42-43.)

'Do as I bid you', says Shylock to Jessica as he departs to feast with Bassanio, 'shut doors after you; / Fast bind, fast find; / A proverb never stale in thrifty mind.' Jessica, left alone, closes the scene: 'Farewell; and if my fortune be not cross'd, / I have a father, you a daughter, lost.' Scattered throughout the scene, mixed with the angry sparks from Shylock's hate, which demand our antipathy, these sharp reminders that when the Jew returns from the feast he will find a house emptied both of 'Jessica, my girl' and of his precious stones represent a first, strong bid for sympathy: though a monster of vindictiveness, Shylock is also a father who stands unknowingly on the edge of great loss. The use of our superior awareness is inevitably the introduction of pity into what otherwise forbids pity.

Shakespeare makes no further use of a discrepancy between awarenesses until Act III, iii, in which Bassanio wins Portia. The five scenes intervening present only persons who know as much of both the general and the particular situations as we. Their action is our exposition; we learn as much as they do, and no more. Yet these scenes are indispensable, for they prepare the two significant advantages we hold over Bassanio in the casket scene.

With its music, setting, poetry—and its superb Portia—this scene would be a feast for eye and ear though we enjoyed no advantage at all. But in the climactic moments Shakespeare is rarely content to have us perceive only what is acted on the stage, hear only what is said, and there an end. Virtually without exception, the total experience of the great scenes includes not only perception of what is taking place at the moment but also apprehension of this action in the light of the context that has been established in our minds beforehand. We are reminded repeatedly to mark and measure the space between our Olympian seat and the participants' lower plain. In Bassanio's casket scene our double advantage contributes to effects which the spectacle, magnificent as it is, could not otherwise achieve.

As the scene opens, we share with Portia one obvious margin over Bassanio: she and we know which casket contains her image. We have been given this knowledge by deft, pleasant, thoroughly dramatic means. The seventh and eighth scenes of Act II, in which, respectively, the Princes of Morocco and Arragon choose the gold and the silver caskets, are admirable in themselves. Their poetry, like their setting, is gorgeous. They are wonderfully suspenseful and otherwise dramatically forceful—for they are miniature tragedies in which the natures of the protagonists drive them to reason toward personal catastrophe; moreover, they portray the world of Portia's Belmont, lodestar of Jasons in quest of the rarest golden fleece; further, preceding Bassanio's scene, they mount toward it, heightening the climactic moment of his choice. These are their general excellences as drama. But while they do all this, they also tell us surely without seeming to tell us at all, dramatically rather than expositorily, that Portia's image lies in the leaden casket.

In the Morocco and Arragon scenes, not knowing where the image lies, we see with the competitors' eyes; but in Bassanio's scene we watch with the eyes of Portia, since she, like us, knows the secret. Indeed, not only do we see with Portia's eyes, but we are invited to share her passionate interest in the outcome—and perhaps even to aid her in guiding Bassanio to the right choice. It was to win Portia, her golden hair, and her gold that he had placed his friend in peril and come to Belmont; guided by his own impulses, he would seem at least as likely as Morocco to pass up lead and silver for gold. Yet he reasons to this conclusion:

54

> Therefore, then, thou gaudy gold,
> Hard food for Midas, I will none of thee;
> Nor none of thee, thou pale and common drudge
> 'Tween man and man. . . .
>
> (III. ii. 101–4.)

'If you do love me, you will find me out', Portia had said; and again:

> Go, Hercules!
> Live thou, I live. With much, much more dismay
> I view the fight than thou that mak'st the fray.
>
> (Ibid. 60–62.)

We are invited for Portia's sake to exercise our awareness actively and to will Bassanio to the right casket. And it is by the force of Portia's will and ours—who perhaps wish the man well only for Portia's sake, and Antonio's—that he reasons in a fashion which must astonish himself—'thou gaudy gold . . . I will none of thee'— and settles on meagre lead whose plainness 'moves me more than eloquence'.

Such is the use of our first advantage over Bassanio. But even while we rejoice, with Portia, as this Jason wins his prize, our greater advantage shadows the glorious scene: *we know, better than Bassanio, why he must not fail.* The lines that Shakespeare has placed immediately to precede Bassanio's casket scene carry a dreadful import:

> *Tub.* But Antonio is certainly undone.
> *Shy.* . . . I will have the heart of him, if he forfeit. . . .
>
> (III. i. 129–32.)

From an early premonition, inspired by Salanio and Salarino's conversation, by Antonio's repeated expressions of confidence in his ships, and by Shylock's talk of waters, winds, and rocks, that the ships would be lost, we have been led through rumour and doubt to final certainty that they have in fact been lost. Thus Salarino, in the interim between the Morocco and Arragon scenes:

> I reason'd with a Frenchman yesterday,
> Who told me, in the narrow seas that part
> The French and English, there miscarried
> A vessel of our country richly fraught.
> I thought upon Antonio when he told me;
> And wish'd in silence that it were not his.
>
> (II. viii. 27–32.)

And again, in the interim between the Arragon and Bassanio casket scenes:

> *Salan.* Now, what news on the Rialto?
> *Salar.* Why, yet it lives there uncheck'd that Antonio hath a ship of rich lading wrack'd on the narrow seas; the Goodwins, I think they call the place.
>
> (III. i. 1–4.)

This is the beginning of the scene; but Shylock has heard more than Salarino, and Tubal more than Shylock: 'Antonio, as I heard in Genoa . . . / Hath an argosy cast away, coming from Tripolis.' By the end of the scene the fact is established: 'Antonio is certainly undone.' Moreover, even while the certainty of Antonio's forfeiture is being driven into our consciousness through a succession of shrewdly placed scenes, the fact of Shylock's vindictive malignity is being intensified also. His daughter has gone, leaving a trail of squandered ducats and jewels between Venice and Belmont, and his grief and rage over this loss aggravate the ancient grudge he bears Antonio, whose flesh has now become for the Jew the dearest thing in life: 'If it will feed nothing else, it will feed my revenge.' At last the two sinister themes, of the loss of ships and of the Jew's malice, which have been developed relentlessly during two full acts, converge in the last words we hear before Portia and Bassanio enter for the joyous casket scene: 'I will have the heart of him, if he forfeit.'

To all this—which Shakespeare has driven into our consciousness with an insistence rare even for him—Bassanio is of course oblivious. The potential danger of Shylock, certainly, he had feared at the first—but his fear was allayed by Antonio's confidence: 'My ships come home a month before the day.' Moreover, not only has Shakespeare made our advantage over Bassanio unforgettable, but he has given it a rare intensity by his characterization of Antonio and of the friends' mutual affection. The play is rightly named for the merchant, who is its centre; and the centre of Antonio's character is his goodness; and the centre of his goodness is that very heart which Shylock threatens. From the first lines of the opening scene, where Salanio and Salarino seek to jest away his melancholy, to the final scene, Antonio is presented as a rare spirit who has won the love of his friends by selflessness. Even the loud-mouthed, oblivious Gratiano makes his first appearance expressing concern for Antonio:

> You look not well, Signior Antonio;
> You have too much respect upon the world.
> They lose it that do buy it with much care.
> Believe me, you are marvellously chang'd.
> (I. i. 73–76.)

The merchant's unquestioning readiness to supply Bassanio's needs at the risk of his own life is a telling evidence of the man. But the sharpness of Bassanio's retort, 'Have you heard any imputation to the contrary?' when Shylock, thinking of collateral, has remarked with some hesitance that 'Antonio is a good man', is one of many subtly powerful means by which the dramatist builds our sense of

the merchant's quality and of the esteem in which he is held by his
friends. Perhaps most striking of all is the dialogue of Salanio and
Salarino after the first rumours that a ship has been lost:

> *Salan.* You were best to tell Antonio what you hear;
> Yet do not suddenly, for it may grieve him.
> *Salar.* A kinder gentleman treads not the earth.
> I saw Bassanio and Antonio part;
> Bassanio told him he would make some speed
> Of his return; he answer'd, 'Do not so;
> Slubber not business for my sake, Bassanio.
> And for the Jew's bond which he hath of me,
> Let it not enter in your mind of love.
> Be merry, and employ your chiefest thoughts
> To courtship and such fair ostents of love
> As shall conveniently become you there.'
> And even there, his eye being big with tears,
> Turning his face, he put his hand behind him,
> And with affection wondrous sensible
> He wrung Bassanio's hand; and so they parted.
>
> (II. vii. 33–48.)

In other passages, by other ways, Shakespeare renders the full image
of an extraordinary man. It is not idly that he makes Antonio as he
is. He does so for the dramatic purpose of requiring us to be deeply
concerned for the merchant's safety and welfare, even as Salanio
and Salarino are, and, above all, as Bassanio would be, during the
casket scene, if he knew in what danger his peerless friend stands.

Because Shakespeare has made us care for Antonio, then, our
advantage over Bassanio in his casket scene is supremely functional.
If we wish that he win Portia for her sake and his own, we must
wish also that he win her and her gold for Antonio's sake. 'I will
have the heart of him, if he forfeit': so emphatically has Shakespeare demanded our concern for this particular 'him' that we
cannot easily forget the merchant and his plight even during the
long scene in which Bassanio debates, makes his happy choice, wins
Portia, and turns ecstatically to claim her. Though we rejoice with
Bassanio, our advantage forbids us to forget, in this moment of
ecstasy, Antonio's peril; and our discomforting sense is not dispelled until the advantage itself is surrendered when Bassanio reads
Antonio's letter, brought by Salerio, and discovers the truth. Says
Portia, observing as he reads:

> There are some shrewd contents in yon same paper
> That steals the colour from Bassanio's cheek.
> Some dear friend dead, else nothing in the world
> Could turn so much the constitution
> Of any constant man.
>
> (III. ii. 246–50.)

57

Some part, certainly, of the total experience of a scene in which our vantage-point is higher than the participant's consists of anticipation of the moment *when the participant will learn what we know.* Always, when this moment comes, Shakespeare exploits it fully, squeezing the last drop of dramatic effect from our advantage as it expires. Portia's description of Bassanio's reaction is a part of this exploitation. And Bassanio's own words confirm the fact that if we have forgotten, during the casket scene, the goodness of Antonio, in spite of the dramatist's elaborate efforts to prevent, our realization of the potential effect has been only partial; thus Bassanio:

> The dearest friend to me, the kindest man.
> The best-condition'd and unwearied spirit
> In doing courtesies, and one in whom
> The ancient Roman honour more appears
> Than any that draws breath in Italy.   (III. ii. 295-9.)

Regularly in the comedies the middle of Act III finds exploitation of our margin over the participants approaching a climax. At that point, normally, some central secret—as, for example, that of Viola's identity in *Twelfth Night*—has gathered several satellite secrets, which are themselves exploited in individual scenes. The central secret itself is typically one of long duration, sometimes made known to us in the opening scene and withheld from most participants until the final scene. Thus the controlling power of Oberon is shown us at the beginning of Act II of *A Midsummer-Night's Dream* and never revealed to the participants, even at the end. Viola confides her intent to change identities in the second scene of *Twelfth Night*, and we keep her secret until the final scene. Duke Vincentio asks for a friar's garb in the third scene of *Measure for Measure*, and his identity is secret until Lucio plucks off his hood at the end of the play. The controlling power of Prospero in *The Tempest* is shown to us in the second scene and hidden from most participants until the end. Such secrets as these, the means of our indispensable advantage, are usually the ultimate resources for exploitation during the greater part of the play. In contrast, in *The Merchant of Venice* our principal secret, of Antonio's plight, is surrendered at the end of Bassanio's casket scene, and during the remaining three scenes of Act III—a large portion at dead centre of the play—we hold no advantage over anyone. But during this period, and even earlier, preparation is being made for the great new advantage—a double one—which we are to hold over everyone except Portia and Nerissa during Acts IV and V. Thus, at almost exactly the same time we lose the discomforting secret of Antonio's plight, we gain the comforting secret that all will be well.

The court scene is one of a very few climactic scenes in the comedies in which our vantage-point, though high, never exceeds nor equals that of some participants. We hold steady advantage over Bassanio and Gratiano, Antonio, Shylock, the Duke—all the world of Venice; but Portia sits above us during most of the action. Besides its other sources of dramatic power, the court scene owes much to a complex disposition of awarenesses among the participants, and most of all to the double advantage with which we are provided. Here as in other climactic scenes the total effect depends as much on the context in our minds as on the action represented on the stage.

We are, first, aware of the true identities of lawyer and clerk. This advantage was provided in advance by typical means:

> *Por.*   We'll see our husbands
> Before they think of us.
> *Ner.*   Shall they see us?
> *Por.* They shall, Nerissa; but in such a habit
> That they shall think we are accomplished
> With that we lack.
>   (III. iv. 58–62.)

We are thus prepared to relish a continuous comic flavour from Nerissa's entrance at line 118 to the end of the court scene. At only one point is our advantage directly exploited: in their zeal for Antonio's safety, both Bassanio and Gratiano overstep themselves:

> *Bass.* Antonio, I am married to a wife
> Which is as dear to me as life itself;
> But life itself, my wife, and all the world,
> Are not with me esteem'd above thy life.
> I would lose all, ay, sacrifice them all
> Here to this devil, to deliver you.
> *Por.* Your wife would give you little thanks for that,
> If she were by, to hear you make the offer.
> *Gra.* I have a wife, who, I protest, I love;
> I would she were in heaven, so she could
> Entreat some power to change this currish Jew.
> *Ner.* 'Tis well you offer it behind her back.
> The wish would make else an unquiet house.
>   (IV. i. 282–94.)

Except for this brief exchange, when flashes of irony light the space between the husbands' awareness and ours, the effect of our advantage is only a general lightening of the mood. Most often in the climactic scenes of the comedies one participant's ignorance of another's identity is the primary dramatic fact exploitation of which yields the main effects of the scene, but here the fact of the husbands' unawareness of the presence of their wives is of secondary importance and is exploited only incidentally. Throughout the court scene, in fact, Bassanio and Gratiano's ignorance of their wives' presence lies fairly quietly, a potentiality to be exploited later. Our more active advantage during the greater part of the scene is our knowledge that, despite all, Antonio is saved. We gain this advantage abruptly at line 118, with the entrance of Nerissa, and surrender it as suddenly after line 305, with Portia's 'Tarry a little; there is something else'. During this period Portia and Nerissa share our advantage over all Venice. But at the same time Portia holds a shrewd advantage over us.

In part, as we have seen, the advantage we held over Bassanio and Antonio at the time the terms of the bond were accepted was a result of our playgoer's sophistication; yet, not trusting to this, Shakespeare also provided dramatic basis for our expectation that Antonio's ships would be lost. So, in the present case, our awareness that all will finally be well may derive in part from a general experience with comedy. A law of Shakespeare's comedies is that no permanent harm shall befall good persons; indeed, harm is not likely to come even to villains and wretches. *Much Ado about Nothing*, for example, closes on Benedick's light-hearted promise to devise 'brave punishments' for Don John, and Shakespeare's extreme care to preserve this law is evinced in *Measure for Measure*, when, though a head is urgently needed to substitute for Claudio's, the life of the condemned and worthless Barnardine is spared and the head of a pirate already dead 'of a cruel fever' is used. Yet again, as before and after, in the court scene Shakespeare trusts nothing to our experience outside *The Merchant of Venice* itself: wishing us to hold assurance that Antonio will not be harmed, he uses his characterization of Portia as the means of giving us this assurance. Our understanding of what she is—not as Bassanio's wife but in herself—is the source of our comforting advantage.

Development of this understanding begins long before her entrance as 'Balthazar', substitute for Bellario. When first we hear of her, in Bassanio's description, she is fabulous:

> In Belmont is a lady richly left;
> And she is fair, and, fairer than that word,
> Of wondrous virtues. . . .
>
> (I. i. 161-3.)

The final description we have, which is placed immediately before the court scene opens, is Jessica's; if the first description must be discounted, being a lover's, this need not, for it is a woman's description of another woman:

Lor. How dost thou like Bassanio's wife?
Jes. Past all expressing. It is very meet
    The Lord Bassanio live an upright life;
    For having such a blessing in her lady,
    He finds the joys of heaven here in earth;
    And if on earth he do not merit them,
    In reason he should never come to heaven.
    Why, if two gods should play some heavenly match
    And on the wager lay two earthly women,
    And Portia one, there must be something else
    Pawn'd with the other, for the poor rude world
    Hath not her fellow.
(III. v. 77–88.)

Besides these are other descriptions, such as Bassanio's when he finds Portia's portrait in the leaden casket. But more persuasive than these are the lady's own words and conduct during her six scenes before she enters the court. Everywhere the dramatist's method is calculated: by representing her as not only unmatched but unmatchable, the paragon not only of women but of mortals, and not in beauty and virtue only, but in all things, he gives us a sense of Portia's infallibility. In the opening scenes of the play, our doubts grew to certainty that Antonio's ships must fail and himself be imperilled; so, in the scenes following the first description of Portia and leading up to her entrance in the court scene, our estimate of her is steadily heightened until at her arrival, heralded by Nerissa, she has taken her place as an 'outside force' of benevolent control.

Portia's intervention as the controlling force which assures us that all will be well occurs much later in the action than is usual in the comedies. In *A Midsummer-Night's Dream* Oberon's intervention in problems of Helena and Demetrius occurs in II. i. In *Measure for Measure* Vincentio reveals his intent to be a looker-on in Vienna in I. iii. In *The Tempest* we learn directly after the first scene that all things on and about the island are safe in Prospero's hand. In comparable ways we gain assurance early in *Much Ado about Nothing*, *Twelfth Night*, and *All's Well that Ends Well*. In *Twelfth Night*, as we shall note, Shakespeare goes out of his way somewhat awkwardly in order to inform us that Viola's problems are solvable. In contrast, during the first three acts of *The Merchant of Venice* our discomforting awareness of Antonio's plight grows ever more intense, and no Oberon, Vincentio, or Prospero rises to say that all is well.

Indeed, although the preparation of the comforting assurance has been under way during the full period of Portia's characterization, the opening 118 lines of Act IV introduce nothing to alleviate dark anxiety. Shakespeare's argument during this time is the utter hopelessness of Antonio's predicament. On the one side is represented Shylock's unyielding demand:

> You'll ask me why I rather choose to have
> A weight of carrion flesh than to receive
> Three thousand ducats. I'll never answer that;
> But say it is my humour.
>
> (IV. i. 40–43.)

On the other appears the impotence of law to do aught but enforce the terms of the bond; thus Antonio's statement of the fact: '. . . no lawful means can carry me / Out of his envy's reach.' And Shylock's reassertion of the same:

> If you deny me, fie upon your law!
> There is no force in the decrees of Venice.
>
> (Ibid. 101–2.)

Such situations Shakespeare always paints with heavy, black strokes. The Duke makes the ugly twin facts explicit—his own helplessness and Shylock's inhumanity:

> I am sorry for thee. Thou art come to answer
> A stony adversary, an inhuman wretch
> Uncapable of pity, void and empty
> From any dram of mercy.
>
> (Ibid. 3–6.)

Thereafter, all the passages that precede Nerissa's entrance underscore the impossibility of finding a way out for Antonio. Over and over, Shakespeare makes the point: the Duke pleads with Shylock to show such humanity as even 'stubborn Turks and Tartars' would show in the same circumstance; Bassanio offers money, attempts to reason with the Jew, alternately rages and entreats. And always the answer is the same:

> The pound of flesh, which I demand of him,
> Is dearly bought; 'tis mine and I will have it.
>
> (Ibid. 100–1.)

By the time of Nerissa's entrance, after 118 lines of heavy emphasis, Shakespeare has left no room for doubt; Antonio's doom is sealed.

If we hold any advantage over the participants during these 118 lines, it is a very uncertain one. More likely we are intended to hold none at all, since, when he intends us to have an advantage, Shakespeare customarily makes the fact unmistakable. We have been advised earlier only that the wives will see their husbands, but when, where, or in what circumstances the meeting will occur we are not told: 'I'll tell thee all my whole device / When I am in my coach', says Portia to Nerissa—and we are not invited into her coach. In denying us a higher vantage-point than the Venetians occupy, the dramatist requires us to share their anxiety, and though the denial is contrary to his usual practice, it is here a psychologically shrewd deviation. Since Antonio is so rare a mortal, it is dramatically right that we experience something of his friends' concern for him, as in Bassanio's words 'The dearest friend to me, the kindest man . . .'. Then, with Nerissa's arrival, comes sudden advantage and abrupt alleviation of our anxiety, for Nerissa heralds Portia, who will make all well. Though the single idea that Antonio is doomed has long been beaten into our minds, yet the idea is false, for Portia is infallible. When at last she steps forth, we have been made ready to observe with greater objectivity than before, as spectators now rather than participants, and to experience effects finer, richer, more complex than those of terror.

One of these effects, which grows ever stronger, is sympathy for Shylock. This sympathy is made possible only by removal of concern for Antonio. With Portia's arrival, the monster goes out of the man—not in the participants' view, of course, but in ours. He is transformed suddenly, unknowingly, into an underdog, dangerous no more, certainly incapable of mayhem. At his worst, when he whets his knife on his sole and snarls the imperious demand—'My deeds upon my head! I crave the law, / The penalty and forfeit of my bond'—Shakespeare has made it, paradoxically, possible for us to pity him as one ignorant that his cause is already lost, his plot prevented, indeed, as one who may be lucky to escape with his life. When he praises the 'judge' ecstatically, as he does on five occasions —'A Daniel come to judgment! yea, a Daniel! / O wise young judge, how do I honour thee!'—flashes of irony encircle his head, for his very ignorance strikes what, in truth, Portia is.

Shakespeare keeps Shylock unaware that the tables have turned through nearly 200 lines, from Nerissa's entrance to Portia's 'Tarry a little; there is something else'. But during this time, though he has made sympathy for the Jew possible by removing our anxiety for Antonio, he has also kept our vantage-point below Portia's, with the result that suspense is also possible for us even while we know that all will somehow be well. For although Nerissa's arrival gives notice that Antonio is saved, it does not suggest how he is to be saved. Knowing Portia, we know that she will have the answer; but we are not told the answer. The suspense made possible by the difference between Portia's awareness and ours is exploited at the same time that we are certain all will be well and that we extend our sympathy to the ruined Shylock. It is present even while we laugh at the antics of the overwrought Gratiano—who, it is worth noting, was not allowed to speak a word during all the lines preceding Nerissa's entrance, when Shakespeare was wholly concerned with building our anxiety for Antonio and intensifying hatred of the Jew, but is allowed a clown's freedom immediately after her entrance removes our anxiety. Even so, if Portia's delay in presenting her solution were explainable only as means of keeping us in suspense, the heart of the scene would be fine melodrama but inferior Shakespeare. Or if she delayed merely to play cat-and-mouse with Shylock, tormenting him by repeatedly expressing opinions that seem in his favour, whetting his expectations only to make his defeat more crushing, when she might have pronounced her inevitable verdict at the outset—then Portia would be a sadistic heroine indeed, quite unlike the paragon she seemed before. But Shakespeare is not the less Shakespeare for Portia's delay, nor is Portia the less Portia.

The answer she finally gives, which she has long denied Shylock, the other participants, and us, is evidently one that she would have preferred never to give at all. Starting high and moving by degrees downward, she extends three generous invitations to Shylock to prove his affinity with humankind—and he rejects each. First, her speech on the quality of mercy asks that he show his kinship with God by showing mercy, 'an attribute to God himself'. This plea the Jew rejects summarily: 'My deeds upon my head! I crave the law, / The penalty and forfeit of my bond.' She tries again, stepping lower, appealing to his human greed: 'Shylock, there's thrice thy money off'red thee.' Again he refuses, and she repeats the first two offers simultaneously: 'Be merciful; / Take thrice thy money; bid me tear the bond.' Again he fails, and demands an immediate judgement. A third time she offers, making a request that is at once a last invitation to prove his possession of at least the commonest human feelings, and, if he fails even in that, a trap to catch him: 'Have by some surgeon, Shylock, on your charge, / To stop his wounds, lest he do bleed to death.' When this bid for simple charity is rejected on the grounds that the provision is not named in the bond, she has no choice but to spring the trap into which Shylock's own vindictiveness, in spite of her generosity, has led him: 'This bond doth give thee here no jot of blood.' With the utterance of this answer, the major discrepancies between awarenesses are obliterated. Portia's advantage over us is gone, as is ours over the Venetians, who now perceive what we have long known, that all is well. There remains our single advantage over Bassanio and Gratiano, who remain ignorant of the identities of the doctor and the clerk.

An artistic whole in itself, the court scene is also preparation for

Act V. By means of incidental exploitation during the long action, Shakespeare has kept alive but inactive our awareness of the relationship of lawyer and clerk to Bassanio and Gratiano. As we watch Antonio's fate being decided, we are made to anticipate the full exploitation of this final gap, and the very length of the time during which exploitation is suppressed contributes to the force of the explosion when it comes. After the intensity of the court scene, any action would be likely to seem anti-climactic: it is indicative of Shakespeare's faith in the effectiveness of this dramatic method that in seeking to avoid a bad falling off of interest in the final act of *The Merchant of Venice* he placed his whole reliance on exploitation of discrepant awarenesses.

Like other heroines of the comedies, Portia and Nerissa teach their men a lesson by taking advantage of their unawareness. When Bassanio and Gratiano confront their wives in Belmont after the trial in Venice, they are enveloped by double folds of ignorance. The preparation of their exploitable condition was begun far back, when Bassanio accepted Portia's ring after the casket scene:

> ... when this ring
> Parts from this finger, then parts life from hence;
> O, then be bold to say Bassanio's dead.
> (III. ii. 185-7.)

It continued with Portia's veiled promise that the wives would visit their husbands, 'but in such a habit / That they shall think we are accomplished / With that we lack'. It yielded comic effect in a brief passing exchange between husbands and wives during the court scene, at the moment of greatest intensity just before Portia's 'Tarry a little; there is something else'. After the Duke's departure, in the same scene, exploitation of the immediate situation and preparation for the future occur simultaneously. 'Three thousand ducats, due unto the Jew, / We freely cope your courteous pains withal,' says Bassanio with a hero's magnanimity and a hero's obliviousness—holding out to 'Balthazar' one of Portia's own bags of gold. But she will have only the ring on his finger, and when he withdraws his hand she shames him—relishing her advantage in words set in an arch of irony:

> *Por.* I see, sir, you are liberal in offers.
> You taught me first to beg; and now methinks
> You teach me how a beggar should be answer'd.
> *Bass.* Good sir, this ring was given me by my wife;
> And when she put it on she made me vow
> That I should neither sell nor give nor lose it.

> *Por.* That 'scuse serves many men to save their gifts.
> An if your wife be not a mad-woman,
> And know how well I have deserv'd this ring,
> She would not hold out enemy for ever
> For giving it to me.
>
> (IV. i. 438–48.)

The preparation is continued in the brief sequel to the court scene, when Gratiano presents Bassanio's ring to Portia and his own to Nerissa. And it is completed by Portia's words to Nerissa, which carry us to the edge of the long-promised exploitation:

> We shall have old swearing
> That they did give the rings away to men;
> But we'll outface them, and outswear them too.
>
> (IV. ii. 15–17.)

One half of the lines of Act V are given directly to this exploitation, which, after the tense drama of the court scene, provides unclouded hilarity. Aided by the report that Antonio's ships have after all come home safely, it counteracts the long period of anxiety, darkness, and danger and asserts emphatically that the world of *The Merchant of Venice* is one in which goodness and mirth prevail. The ladies' practice on their husbands, though severe, is lightly executed; Bassanio and Gratiano are stretched long on the rack, but they are released before they are pulled apart. Supposing that their wives have remained in Belmont and that they alone know the story of Antonio's trial, their consciences uneasy because the rings are gone but soothed by the certainty that they were given to men and not women, they here occupy that depth of unawareness reserved for Dogberrys, Aguecheeks, Bottoms—and romantic heroes. Poor Orlando will stand there soon, as will Orsino and Bertram.

'This is the man, this is Antonio, / To whom I am so infinitely bound,' begins Bassanio grandly—presenting to Portia the merchant whose life she has just saved. 'I gave it to the judge's clerk,' says Gratiano, righteously, explaining the absence of his ring to Nerissa: 'Would he were gelt that had it.' More than 100 lines of dialogue strike up a dazzling cross-play of flashes over the gap between obliviousness and omniscience. Some are flashes to which the speaker is blind: 'I gave it to a youth, / A kind of boy, a little scrubbed boy'; some are sparks struck by the speaker for joy of the game: 'I'll die for't but some woman had the ring.' The pyrotechnics might go on indefinitely; Portia breaks them off because the good Antonio grows uncomfortable and Gratiano bawdy: 'What, are we cuckolds ere we have deserv'd it?' When the secret is out, the exploitable gap is closed. Eventually Bassanio and Gratiano, unlike the mortals of *A Midsummer-Night's Dream*, will know all that we have known, for Portia promises full detail.

Indeed, presumably they will come to know more than we do if the letter brought Antonio by Portia explains how it can be that his three argosies—which we were first assured would be lost and then informed were lost in fact—'Are richly come to harbour suddenly'. Portia is only the bearer of the good news and can of course have had no actual part in saving the ships: *yet the effect is as though she had saved them*. The sudden, surprising announcement, coming from her after we have been assured that they were lost, makes it seem almost as if she had wrought the miracle. Fabulous when we first hear of her, dazzling in the casket scene, all-knowing and seemingly all-powerful in the court scene, nowhere does she more truly prefigure the ultimate Prospero than in the effect of this closing moment. Antonio's comment on the miraculous news is alone adequate for participant and spectator: 'I am dumb.'

CHAPTER III

For the Love of Mockery: Approach
to the Summit

THE spectacular cross-play over the gap between awareness and unawareness that breaks out in the last act of *The Merchant of Venice* heralds the worlds of *Much Ado about Nothing*, *As You Like It*, and *The Merry Wives of Windsor*—plays which are all compact of practices, practisers, and practisees. In these, as in *Twelfth Night*, to which they are themselves the prelude, Shakespeare leaves no room for doubt that his preference is for dramatic effects, comic and other, that are created by exploitation of discrepancies in awareness. The primary features common to these worlds are, at the one extreme, an extraordinary alacrity of the inhabitants in initiating practices, and, at the other, an extraordinary susceptibility to the practices of their fellows. Between these two poles flash the sparks of incident and effect.

Yet the inhabitants of these worlds are not sharply divided, some serving only as practisers and others only as practisees, some always deceivers, others always deceived. A few do occupy only one camp; Rosalind is immune to deception, and Orlando is incapable of deceiving. But Beatrice and Benedick are by turns deceivers and deceived, as are Hero and Claudio, the Fords and the Pages, and indeed the great majority of residents, within whom quickness to deceive and quickness to be deceived are in remarkable balance. Among the inhabitants are also a few of the race of Bottom, who need no deception to be deceived, for whom oblivion is the normal state. Such is Dogberry. Such is Silvius. Such are Caius and Sir Hugh Evans. And, alas, almost such is Falstaff too—except as he may be saved by our memory of what he was in the days of Prince Hal.

1. *Much Ado about Nothing*

No comedy of Shakespeare's is more aptly named than *Much Ado about Nothing*, all the ado of which, from our vantage-point, is indeed about nothing. The Prince of Arragon and his party arrive to visit the Governor of Messina. If guests and hosts saw with our eyes, nothing memorable would occur during the visit. Claudio would marry Hero and remain at Messina. The other visitors, including Benedick, would go their way at month's end—unless monotony dispatched them earlier. Beatrice would die an old maid.

But because the inhabitants of the Messinian world do not see with our eyes, monotony finds no time to afflict them. All the action is impelled by a rapid succession of 'practices'—eight in all, the first of which is introduced at the end of the opening scene, the last exploited in the final moments. These practices are the means by which multiple discrepancies in awareness are created and sustained, some briefly, some over long periods. Sharing the practisers' confidence in each case, we hold advantage over some participants during fourteen of seventeen scenes, and at some time we hold advantage over every named person. Not only heroines and villains —the inveterate practisers in Shakespearian comedy—but very nearly all participants, including old fathers, uncles, and the Friar, take turns at deceiving others; and, conversely, each takes a turn at being deceived. No crowd of characters in a Shakespearian world exhibits more universal predilection for the game, such readiness to exchange and then exchange again the roles of deceiver and deceived. Nor does any play demonstrate more conclusively the dramatist's devotion to situations characterized by exploitable differences in awareness.

The first practice is devised by Don Pedro within minutes of the opening, after Claudio—having first ascertained that she is Leonato's only heir—has confessed that he loves Hero; says Don Pedro:

> I know we shall have revelling to-night.
> I will assume thy part in some disguise
> And tell fair Hero I am Claudio.
> And in her bosom I'll unclasp my heart
> And take her hearing prisoner with the force
> And strong encounter of my amorous tale;
> Then after to her father will I break;
> And the conclusion is, she shall be thine.
> (I. i. 322–9.)

The basis of this practice is hardly more than a pretext. Though young, Claudio is no shy Orlando, incapable of wooing for himself. He is a brash and ambitious would-be sophisticate, who might be thought more likely to ravish a heroine than be speechless. Don Pedro's gratuitous offer, then, is the first expression of that alacrity to perpetrate a practice which infects the people of this world.

The next scene presents the first example of the converse alacrity, that of seizing on and believing in what is false. Antonio reports to his brother Leonato:

> The Prince and Count Claudio, walking in a thick-pleached alley in mine orchard, were thus much overheard by a man of mine. The Prince discovered to Claudio that he loved my niece your daughter and meant to acknowledge it this night in a dance; and if he found her accordant, he meant to take the present time by the top and instantly break with you of it. (I. ii. 8–16.)

'Hath the fellow any wit that told you of this?' asks Leonato—but does not bother to question the servant. He hurries to tell Hero of her good fortune, and thus, abruptly, Leonato, Antonio, and Hero have dropped to a level below ours. Inevitably, they have also pushed down Don Pedro, who proceeds with his wooing, ignorant that his device has been overheard and misconstrued.

By the end of the second scene, then, from a servant's mis-overhearing and a readiness of Antonio and Leonato to mistake, a tissue of error has grown. To this point all persons involved are well intentioned, their aims honourable, and the worst result of their error should be only disappointment for Hero and Leonato when they discover that Claudio is the real suitor. But in the third scene wicked fingers insinuate themselves into the tangle. Borachio, follower of Don John, has also overheard Don Pedro and Claudio arrange their innocent deception; but, unlike Antonio's man, he has not mistaken:

> ... as I was smoking in a musty room, comes me the Prince and Claudio, hand in hand, in sad conference. I whipt me behind the arras, and there heard it agreed upon that the Prince should woo Hero for himself, and having obtain'd her, give her to Count Claudio. (I. iii. 60–66.)

'That young start-up hath all the glory of my overthrow,' says Don John. 'If I can cross him any way, I bless myself every way. . . . Shall we go prove what's to be done?' At the end of Act I, then, an innocent plot set by amateurs has become snarled with a wicked one, woven by professionals.

At the opening of Act II, we share our vantage-point only with villains, other participants being ignorant both of Don John's threats and of other aspects of the suddenly complex situation. The Prince and Claudio suppose themselves sole proprietors of their innocent plot, not knowing that it has been misunderstood by Leonato and perverted by Don John; Leonato and Hero, believing a false report, are of course ignorant of the Prince's true purpose and know nothing of Don John's malicious interest. During the opening dialogue, while the gay, sharp wit of Beatrice is featured,

Shakespeare repeatedly prods recollection of the secrets he has given us to hold. Thus, in the first line, Leonato inquires after Don John: 'Was not Count John here at supper?' These are the first words we have heard since Don John's threats closed the preceding act, and inevitably they remind of the immediate danger to this gay, unwitting group preparing for revels. Through remarks that twice interrupt Beatrice's flashing wit, we are reminded also of the widespread misunderstanding of the Prince's purpose; thus Leonato addresses Hero: 'Daughter, remember what I told you. If the Prince do solicit you in that kind, you know your answer.' And again, Antonio speaks to Hero: 'Well, niece, I trust you will be rul'd by your father.' Even Beatrice's sharp vision is blurred by the general error: 'If the Prince be too important, tell him there is measure in every thing, and so dance out the measure.' More remarkable than that Beatrice should embrace false belief, however, is that even Don John, whose henchman had told him of the Prince's true purpose, himself slips into error: 'Sure my brother is amorous on Hero and hath withdrawn her father to break with him about it.' In a minor practice, pretending to mistake him for Benedick, he accosts Claudio:

> D. John. Are not you Signior Benedick?
> Claud. You know me well; I am he.
> D. John. Signior, you are very near my brother in his love. He is enamour'd on Hero. I pray you, dissuade him from her; she is no equal for his birth. You may do the part of an honest man in it.
> Claud. How know you he loves her?
> D. John. I heard him swear his affection. (II. i. 167-75.)

No incident in the play better exposes the stuff of which *Much Ado about Nothing* is made, the mutually complementing alacrities in deceiving and being deceived: Don John had known the Prince's plan but permits the slightest evidence to the contrary to deceive him; Claudio, who had been the Prince's partner in the plan, falls instantly into the general error on the testimony of one he knows to be a villain: ''Tis certain so; the Prince wooes for himself.' When in the next moment Benedick enters to add his misapprehension to the rest—'the Prince hath got your Hero'—the 'proof' is superfluous. Claudio has already been convinced and slinks away 'to creep into sedges'.

At this point, midway through Act II, everything indicates that the main plot of *Much Ado about Nothing* will grow from the misunderstanding that has occurred. Act I and more than half of Act II have been used to bring about this situation. Every principal person has become involved in an error of which it appears that the inevitable consequence must be conflict between the two friends. Even the villain has made it his purpose to separate Don Pedro and Claudio—and ordinarily a villain's declaration of interest in an issue is proof enough that it will become central. It can scarcely be other than startling, therefore, that after another flurry of exploitation, Shakespeare suddenly destroys the error that he has taken nearly two acts to make general; thus Don Pedro:

> Here, Claudio, I have wooed in thy name, and fair Hero is won. I have broke with her father, and his good will obtained. Name the day of marriage, and God give thee joy! (II. i. 309-12.)

Even so abruptly is the affair ended—and momentarily the play, two acts nearly spent, is left without the beginning of a plot. Even the villain must start anew.

The termination of what seemed the beginning of a main action suggests that Shakespeare changed his mind while writing the opening acts; for if, at the outset, he did not intend to base his plot on the misunderstanding between Claudio and the Prince, why did he give this breach such large emphasis? Elsewhere, in comedies, histories, and tragedies alike, his way is to use Act I to lay the basis for the main action; nowhere else is there occasion for such surprise as is caused by the termination of the conflict between Claudio and the Prince. It is possible, of course, that the dramatist did change his mind. The idea of making Don John's slander of Hero the heart of the plot may not yet have occurred to him. He had already told one story of division between friends, in *The Two Gentlemen of Verona*; he may have become bored with the Claudio–Don Pedro division almost at once and sealed it quickly in order to take a fresh start.

On the other hand, the best evidence that he did not change his mind, but intended from the outset to drop the Claudio–Don Pedro conflict and to make the slander of Hero his principal matter is, first, the very excessiveness of his initial emphasis on the alacrity of persons to perpetrate practices and to be deceived by others' practices; and, second, the fact that these are precisely the human conditions out of which the slander of Hero rises and is taken for truth. Though the threatened breach is healed in Act II, yielding to different matter that becomes central, yet there is continuity in the means and the environment. The major incident of Hero's slander depends as completely on the mutually complementing factors of practice and susceptibility to practice as does the Claudio–Don Pedro division. The initial, swift-moving tangle of confusions is thus illustrative of the world in which the later, greater misunderstanding is set. Its purpose is to establish the character of this world and its inhabitants, to condition our minds for the general acceptance of Hero's slander and its consequences. And it must be said that this purpose is achieved: after the initial demonstration of the Messinian predilection for deceiving and being deceived, we can believe that any falsehood will thrive in the Messinian climate. The opening incident has demonstrated that here much ado can arise from nothing. Perhaps Shakespeare allowed the initial misunderstandings to grow too great; it is certainly bad that their abrupt breaking-off causes surprise. But the gain is greater than the loss if we have been conditioned to accept a world in which Hero's slander can be perpetrated and believed. What at first seemed a fumbling start may appear in view of the total work to be a calculated introduction.

Nor is the initial tropical growth of error the only means by which Shakespeare illustrates the character of this world: Beatrice and Benedick, lights of the first magnitude in Shakespeare's universe, may attract us so strongly that we will be sorry to find them and their affair also, like the Claudio–Prince affair, primarily a means of high-lighting this character. It is true that, whereas the initial business is snuffed out and abandoned, that of Beatrice and Benedick grows to the end; even so, it is secondary: these sparkling lovers help make the environment credible in which occurs the story of the nearly speechless Hero and the insufferable Claudio. Again, it is possibly a structural fault that Beatrice and Benedick, resembling stars but serving as planets, outshine those about whom they revolve. Yet Shakespeare's subordinate devices are often memorable in their own right: besides these, witness Falstaff and Mercutio.

The illustrative initial incident is barely closed when Don Pedro —such is the way of the world—whose practice precipitated it and threatened disaster, falls to devising anew:

> I will teach you how to humour your cousin, that she shall fall in love with Benedick; and I, with your two helps, will so practise on Benedick that, in despite of his quick wit and his queasy stomach, he shall fall in love with Beatrice. (Ibid. 395-400.)

Immediately, residents and guests alike, all incurably addicted to practising, are plunged into another indulgence. The new practice, like the first, is innocent enough. But even as Don Pedro—who has never even learned of the ado stirred up by his previous practice— prepares to unite Beatrice and Benedick by deceiving them, Don John and Borachio devise a wicked practice against Hero and Claudio. 'How canst thou cross this marriage?' the bastard asks his shadow; and Borachio outlines a plot 'to misuse the Prince, to vex

73

Claudio, to undo Hero, and kill Leonato'. Though the purposes of Don Pedro and Don John stand in direct contrast, their means are parallel. Says the Prince: 'If we can do this, Cupid is no longer an archer. His glory shall be ours, for we are the only love-gods.' And of Borachio's plot Don John speaks thus: 'Grow this to what adverse issue it can, I will put it in practice.' The repetition of the pattern of practices with which the play opened is striking: then Don Pedro devised an innocent practice to win Hero for Claudio, and Don John countered with a sinister scheme to divide and destroy Don Pedro and Claudio; now Don Pedro devises an innocent practice to unite Beatrice and Benedick, and Don John counters with a sinister plot aimed to destroy all the innocents there are.

At the beginning of II. iii, then, Shakespeare has completed preparations for claiming varied and conflicting responses of us, who are perched high above the action. The first of these effects is simply comic. Benedick speaks at length, to prove his immunity to Cupid's arrow:

> I do much wonder that one man, seeing how much another man is a fool when he dedicates his behaviours to love, will, after he hath laugh'd at such shallow follies in others, become the argument of his own scorn by falling in love.... (II. iii. 6–11.)

This, with twenty-five lines more, is uttered directly after Don Pedro's promise that Benedick, 'in despite of his quick wit and his queasy stomach, he shall fall in love with Beatrice'—and our recollection of this promise overcasts the speech. Moreover, here as elsewhere, Shakespeare ensures against our drowsily neglecting to use our advantage: when Benedick, hearing 'the Prince and Monsieur Love' coming, retires to watch unseen—as he supposes—and the practice designed to snare him is begun, our awareness is sharply prodded from both sides by comments of practisers and victim. When the Prince, Claudio, and Leonato have outdone one another in telling the degree of Beatrice's passion, the gull who thinks himself an eagle is made to speak—shrewdly, as he supposes—from the shadows:

> I should think this a gull, but that the white-bearded fellow speaks it. Knavery cannot, sure, hide himself in such reverence. (Ibid. 123–5.)

And from the other side, baldly reminding us that this is a gull indeed, Claudio's whisper encourages his fellow practisers: 'O, ay, stalk on, stalk on; the fowl sits.' The practice continues through a scene of nearly 200 lines, until Benedick 'hath ta'en th' infection'. When Beatrice comes to call him to dinner, knowing nothing of what has happened, she inevitably becomes joint victim of the gulling. He takes her sharpest lashes for expressions of love, and each remains ignorant of the other's mind.

So much for the comic, which is only part of the total effect; a shadow hangs over the action, unsuspected by either the practisers or the victims: the wicked plot hatched by Don John and Borachio. That this cloud might not escape our notice, Shakespeare has set Borachio's explanation of the plot immediately before the scene of Benedick's gulling:

> ... tell them that you know that Hero loves me; intend a kind of zeal both to the Prince and Claudio, as,—in love of your brother's honour, who hath made this match, and his friend's reputation, who is thus like to be cozen'd with the semblance of a maid,—that you have discover'd thus. They will scarcely believe this without trial. Offer them instances; which shall bear no less likelihood than to see me at her chamber-window, hear me call Margaret Hero, hear Margaret term me Claudio; and bring them to see this the very night before the intended wedding. ...   (II. ii. 34–46.)

The effect of this plot—designed to hurt the very persons who are having holiday sport with Benedick and Beatrice—is a dark overcasting of the comic effect of that scene. Shrewdly, the dramatist keeps our awareness of the menacing cloud active during the scene, not only through the presence of those who will be hurt—Claudio, most of all, and Leonato—but also by repeated naming of Hero, and, more pointedly, of Hero's chamber-window, mentioned earlier by Borachio; thus Don Pedro: 'I pray thee, get us some excellent music; for to-morrow night we would have it at the Lady Hero's chamber-window.' Our sense of the enveloping danger is further alerted by the careful paralleling of Benedick's gulling and the practice by which Don John intends to precipitate general catastrophe. It is only in their purposes that the two practices contrast.

The stair-stepped disposition of awarenesses thus makes possible here the double and conflicting effects that Shakespeare seeks in the climactic scenes of the mature comedies. The same purpose governs the opening scene of Act III, which presents the gulling of Beatrice. Unaware that Benedick has already been gulled in a way that affects herself, Beatrice is herself tricked as the scene proceeds, hence is doubly deceived at the end. Like Benedick, she thinks herself a practiser in that she hears while unseen; thus Hero: '. . . Look where Beatrice, like a lapwing, runs / Close by the ground, to hear our conference.' And, as in the parallel scene, through pointed comments, Shakespeare makes assurance doubly sure that we will savour the situation fully; thus Ursula:

> The pleasant'st angling is to see the fish
> Cut with her golden oars the silver stream,

And greedily devour the treacherous bait.
So angle we for Beatrice, who even now
Is couched in the woodbine coverture.
(III. i. 26–30.)

And again, like Benedick, Beatrice swallows completely 'the false sweet bait'; thus, at the end:

... Benedick, love on; I will requite thee,
Taming my wild heart to thy loving hand.
(Ibid. 111–12.)

The comic effect created by exploitation of her unawareness matches that created by exploitation of Benedick's. But even darker now is the overcasting of the comic effect by our enforced recollection of Don John's wicked plot. It is darker partly because the danger is nearer, but principally because of the presence in the scene of Hero herself, who is to be most injured. Elsewhere reserved and nearly silent, in this scene Hero is active and gay, taking the lead in gulling Beatrice in that same pleached orchard where, as we know, she is herself to be undone by a practice the mechanics of which are like these. So emphatic is her participation in the present business, and so strongly does the pattern of the practice parallel that threatened by Borachio, that the glow of irony smoulders steadily; only once, when she suggests a mild slandering of Beatrice to discourage Benedick's passion, does the more typical flash of irony occur:

... I will go to Benedick
And counsel him to fight against his passion;
And, truly, I'll devise some honest slanders
To stain my cousin with.
(Ibid. 82–85.)

The gulling of both wits contributes the more effectively to rendering the success of Hero's defamation plausible because these two are as they are—quick, alert, sceptical by nature. The point is persuasive: if such as these can be deceived thus, then surely the world of *Much Ado about Nothing* is one in which a Don John can propose a monstrous falsehood and have it believed. The very success of the practices by which amateurs unite Benedick and Beatrice builds anxiety for Hero, against whom, as the dramatist will not let us forget, a plot has been mounted by professionals.

In *The Merchant of Venice*, anxiety for Antonio grows during the opening portion of the court scene and is most intense just before Nerissa's arrival. During this period our awareness, though superior to that of the participants, holds nothing comforting; on the contrary, Shylock's menace is drawn in such strong colours and the helplessness of the City is so emphasized that we must think Antonio's doom inescapable. So, in *Much Ado about Nothing*, anxiety is most intense during the closing portion of III. ii, when Don John makes his first move, beginning, Iago-like, with insinuation:

> D. John. (*To Claudio.*) Means your lordship to be married to-morrow?
> D. Pedro. You know he does.
> D. John. I know not that, when he knows what I know.   (III. ii. 91–95.)

He slanders Hero; and just as the underscoring of Shylock's vindictiveness and the helplessness of Venetian law inspired fear for Antonio's safety, so now our repeated proofs of Messina's susceptibility to gulling deepen anxiety for Hero. That defamation will be taken for truth in such a world appears certain; indeed, so apt are Claudio and Don Pedro to believe false report that we might expect them to take Don John's word even without waiting for the proof he promises. The gullible Claudio needs only to hear it breathed that Hero is false; as if exhilarated, he devises a practice as inhumane as the villain's:

> If I see anything to-night why I should not marry her to-morrow, in the congregation, where I should wed, there will I shame her.   (Ibid. 126–8.)

Don Pedro quickly agrees; their recent participation in the practice on Beatrice and Benedick has taught them nothing of wariness: their alacrity in believing still balances their alacrity in deceiving. Claudio's manner carries a hint of eagerness for the morrow; possibly he would be disappointed if, Don John's 'proof' failing, he were prevented from going on with the denunciation. In short, Hero appears as good as doomed at the first breath of calumny, even from a known villain's throat.

The ominous note on which III. ii closes marks an important dividing line. Up to this point our knowledge of Don John's plot against Hero and Claudio shadowed the bright scenes of the gulling of Beatrice and Benedick very much as in *The Merchant of Venice* our knowledge of Antonio's peril in Venice shadowed the casket scenes at Belmont. Now, abruptly, the dramatist reverses the use of our superior awareness: where formerly it darkened light scenes, hereafter it lightens dark ones. It was the source whence discomfort swelled; it now brings a flood of reassurance.

In *The Merchant of Venice* Nerissa's arrival, announcing Portia's, changed the use of our awareness and enabled us to watch the trial of Antonio with confidence. In *Much Ado about Nothing* it is the arrival of Dogberry and his assistants that makes the change. Says Dogberry, instructing those assigned to the Prince's watch:

77

One word more, honest neighbours. I pray you, watch about Signior Leonato's door; for the wedding being there to-morrow, there is a great coil to-night. Adieu! Be vigitant, I beseech you.   (III. iii. 97–100.)

With this, our advantage becomes a source of reassurance; it brightens the scene for us even while the same scene, in the participants' view, grows darker. Though Hero will be slandered and denounced, yet ultimately truth will prevail. Directly after Dogberry has instructed his men, Borachio and Conrade enter and the two Watchmen stand by to observe. For us, this is the turning-point of all the action: for the first time the forces of evil are caught in the condition of unawareness, overwatched by the forces of right. Ignorant that he stands in the eye of the Law, Borachio reports the fraud he has just perpetrated:

. . . know that I have to-night woo'd Margaret, the Lady Hero's gentlewoman, by the name of Hero. She leans me out at her mistress' chamber-window, bids me a thousand times good night,—I tell this tale vilely:—I should first tell thee how the Prince, Claudio, and my master, planted and placed and possessed by my master Don John, saw afar off in the orchard this amiable encounter.

(Ibid. 153–61.)

'Call up the right master constable,' shouts the Second Watchman. 'We have here recovered the most dangerous piece of lechery that ever was known in the commonwealth.'

In its effect on our view of the action that follows, the actual apprehension of Borachio and Conrade parallels the entrance of Portia in the court scene of *The Merchant of Venice;* and, true to his way, Shakespeare has placed this incident immediately to precede the scene of Hero's preparation for her wedding. This is a gay scene, enlivened by the salacious wit of Margaret, particularly as she and Hero twit Beatrice for her change of spirit, exploiting her unawareness that she has been put upon. But we hold a double advantage over these women; indeed, over Beatrice we hold a triple advantage. Though Hero and Margaret share our knowledge that Beatrice and Benedick have been gulled, they are ignorant that they have themselves been victimized in much more serious fashion: Hero is unaware that she has been defamed, that the defamation has been taken for truth, and that even now Claudio awaits the moment of denunciation; Margaret (who has taken up the mocking role that Beatrice has let fall) is unaware that her presence at the window in conversation with Borachio supplied evidence against Hero. Our sense of these facts darkens the gaiety of the scene, since it reminds us of the anguish that must come to this Hero who is just now so brightly unsuspecting. Yet above the shadow is another light: all will yet be well, for Don John's henchmen are in custody. We hold assurance that, however sharp the pain, Hero's injury will not be permanent. As we were assured that Portia would ultimately curb the menace of Shylock, so we have been assured that Dogberry will ultimately expose Don John's plot.

Yet Dogberry is no Portia! It is one thing to share our vantage-point with an Oberon, a Portia, a Vincentio, a Prospero—and quite another to share it with a Dogberry: the use of precisely this bumbler in a position of authority, in precisely this place, where he inspires simultaneous reassurance and exasperation, is a Shake-spearian masterstroke. Because both constable and 'compartners' are inordinately blundering, suspense is added to other effects, already multiple and conflicting, created by the scenes leading to Hero's denunciation. Except for Dogberry's marvellous stupidity in the scene that just precedes the denunciation, Leonato would learn the truth that would prevent shame and hurt to Hero and himself. The scene begins auspiciously:

> *Leon.* What would you with me, honest neighbour:
> *Dog.* Marry, sir, I would have some confidence with you that decerns you nearly.
> *Leon.* What would you with me, honest neighbour?
>
> (III. v. 1–6.)

But Dogberry is tedious and irrelevant, and the facts that would spare Hero lie fallow in his mind. When he can bear no more of the constable's digressive philosophizing—'Well, God's a good man; an two men ride of a horse, one must ride behind'—Leonato ends the interview and directs Dogberry himself to examine his pair of 'aspicious persons'.

The race to spare Hero is thus lost; but though we are now denied hope that truth will out soon enough to prevent Claudio's denuncia-tion, yet nothing has shaken our confidence that it will come out in due time: Dogberry will never quite lose the scent. The last words of the scene are reassuring:

> *Dog.* We are now to examination these men.
> *Verg.* And we must do it wisely.
> *Dog.* We will spare for no wit, I warrant you. Here's that shall drive some of them to a non-come; only get the learned writer to set down our excom-munication, and meet me at the gaol. (Ibid. 64–69.)

Though the significance of what he discovers may never penetrate his own insulated mind, yet Dogberry will obey Leonato's instruc-tion: 'Take their examination yourself and bring it me.' It will all eventually be set in writing, too, for Dogberry dispatches Verges to bring one Francis Seacole, with his pen and inkhorn.

79

These comforts, strategically provided just before the entrance of Hero, Claudio, and others for the wedding, hang overhead throughout the action of the most poignant scene in Shakespearian comedy, that of Hero's denunciation at the altar. The bundle of awarenesses given us to carry during this action is heavy, yet each item of the burden contributes to the multiple and conflicting effects which the scene is calculated to produce. At the opening, with every principal person in view, we hold simultaneously comforting and discomforting advantages over all. On the bottommost level of awareness stand Hero and Leonato, ignorant that Don John's plot has blackened Hero's name, that even now Claudio is framing the words of Hero's denunciation, and, of course, that just now, also, Dogberry's 'excommunication' is drawing out the facts that will clear Hero's name. Our perception of their condition demands pity—indeed, because Hero is Hero, anguish. However she may compare with the great heroines of the comedies, Portia, Rosalind, and Viola, Hero is a gentle girl, modest and tender, composed of such fine sensibilities that Claudio's brutal condemnation must crush her utterly. The more forceful heroines of other comedies, circumspect and aggressive, would weaken the scene. A Portia or a Rosalind would never do: supposing that either could be caught in such a situation in the first place, we would have scant need of anguish on her account—being sure that she would shatter the predicament like glass, free herself, and leave Claudio's coxcomb bloody. Leonato, like Hero, is right for the situation. He is a doting father, an open-hearted and trusting friend; Borachio's boast that his plot will kill Leonato is believable. Standing on the lowest level of awareness, then, quite oblivious to the facts of their terrible situation, Hero and Leonato invite our pity—even while we know that joy lies just beyond, once Francis Seacole's pen has recorded the 'excommunication'.

On the level next above stand Claudio and Don Pedro, who know what Claudio intends but do not know either that their opinion of Hero is false or that it will shortly be corrected. Yet though they hold advantage over Hero in knowing what they mean to do at the altar, both are inferior to her in another way: their opinion of her character is false, and hers is true; once Claudio's accusation has been made, and she knows what is thought of her, it is she who holds the real advantage—albeit without satisfaction. The most insufferable of Shakespeare's heroes of comedy, combining the hero's usual oblivion with priggish egocentricity, Claudio, too, is perfectly right for his role here: one sees why Shakespeare made him thus. The eagerness which once showed in his anticipation of the moment when he would shame Hero becomes passionate as the moment nears. He therefore deserves the backlashes which, in our view, slash himself more sharply than those he intends to hurt. Shakespeare makes his 'knowing' words betray his terrible ignorance; they strike flashes of irony that engulf the speaker:

Friar. If either of you know any inward impediment why you should not be conjoined, I charge you, on your souls, to utter it.
Claud. Know you any, Hero?
Hero. None, my lord.
Friar. Know you any, count?
Leon. I dare make his answer, none.
Claud. O, what men dare do! What men may do! What men daily do, not knowing what they do! (IV. i. 12–21.)

A frequent way of Shakespeare's is to make a person speak at length in ignorance of the reality around him, erroneously denouncing the subjects of their wrath: thus Othello, coming to the murder of Desdemona; Capulet, raging at Juliet for her refusal to marry Paris; Posthumus Leonatus, condemning all womankind because Iachimo's false report has made him believe Imogen untrue; Leontes, excoriating Hermione because his own idiotic imagination has accused her. These utterances made in ignorance most often demand of us more pity than anger, for though they speak fiercely, these men have no joy in their denunciations. They are themselves deeply hurt. Even while he speaks, Othello so loves Desdemona that his emotion almost persuades Justice to break her sword. But Claudio, in his great moment, seems calculated to kindle only our anger, for his denunciation of Hero has an exuberance that borders sadism:

There, Leonato, take her back again.
Give not this rotten orange to your friend:
She's but the sign and semblance of her honour.
Behold how like a maid she blushes here!
O, what authority and show of truth
Can cunning sin cover itself withal!
Comes not that blood as modest evidence
To witness simple virtue? Would you not swear,
All you that see her, that she were a maid,
By these exterior shows? But she is none.
She knows the heat of a luxurious bed;
Her blush is guiltiness, not modesty.
(Ibid. 32–43.)

Spoken to Rosalind, these words would meet replies that would blast the speaker; spoken, with other cruel ones, to Hero, they draw only a faint, solicitous question: 'Is my lord well, that he doth speak so wide?' Though we are made to remember that Claudio speaks in ignorance, the excessiveness of his outburst destroys the mitigating effect of our awareness: ignorance cannot excuse so much zeal. When the evidence of his conduct both before and after the denunciation is added to this exhibition, the dominant impression left by Claudio is of one unworthy even of such a Hero as he thinks her to be.

Present throughout the scene, Beatrice and Benedick are hardly more than bystanders; yet their presence contributes to the complex total effect, because they steadily remind us of the way of the Messinian world. Further, their presence tempers the mood of this bitter scene: we cannot observe them without being aware, at one depth of consciousness, of their own recent gulling and of their agitated states of mind even now, while this terrible scene goes on. Seen out of a corner of the mind's eye, they add a touch of high comedy to the moment of heartbreak.

Also significantly present is Don John, the best reminder of the greatest advantage we hold during this action. Don John stands above Hero and Leonato, Beatrice and Benedick, Claudio and Don Pedro in his knowledge of the facts; indeed, his vantage-point is just under our own. He knows at the outset, as Hero and Leonato do not, what Claudio intends, and knows, as Claudio and Don Pedro do not, that they were abused by false evidence. But he does not know, as we do, that his accomplices have been caught and that even now the learned Seacole should be transcribing their 'excommunication'. This was the fact that Shakespeare fixed in our minds immediately before the church scene began, and, because it is comforting, it is the most precious fact in our possession during the action. For Hero and Leonato, momentarily stricken, the truth is better than it appears; for Don John, momentarily triumphant, most ignorant of what he is most assured, it is worse: in the comedies this is a regular formula, the pattern of which is always open to the view from our vantage-point. In the tragedies, conversely, the truth during climactic scenes usually favours villainy, and for heroes, heroines, and other innocents it is worse than they suspect. The climactic scene of *Much Ado about Nothing*, one of the most moving in the comedies, is true at last to its comic kind, for the razor's edge of anguish is blunted by our assurance that all will be well.

The climactic incident ends with Hero's swooning and the callous departure of Claudio, Don Pedro, and Don John. At once, even now, the prevailing spirit of the Messinian world reasserts itself. First Beatrice insists that her cousin has been belied; next the Friar, reading the innocence of Hero's face, risks his reputation for wis-

dom on the claim that she lies 'Under some biting error'. 'The practice of it lives in John the Bastard,' says Benedick, 'whose spirits toil
in frame of villainies.' In the world of *Much Ado* the mere word
'practice' is a cue: abruptly all who have just been gulled turn
gullers. It is the Friar—surely akin to Romeo's ghostly father, an
unhappy practiser—who now proposes the seventh major deceptive
device of the play:

> Your daughter here the princes left for dead.
> Let her awhile be secretly kept in,
> And publish it that she is dead indeed.
> Maintain a mourning ostentation
> And on your family's old monument
> Hang mournful epitaphs, and do all rites
> That appertain unto a burial.
>
> (IV. i. 204–10.)

The purpose of this practice is to 'Change slander to remorse'. Not
knowing Claudio as well as we do, the Friar anticipates that Hero's
reputed death will grieve him:

> Then shall he mourn
> If ever love had interest in his liver,
> And wish he had not so accused her,
> No, though he thought his accusation true.
>
> (Ibid. 232–5.)

The Friar, Hero, Leonato, Beatrice, and Benedick thus become
proprietors of a new practice just before the most recent old one,
that of Don John and his henchmen, is due to be exposed by Francis
Seacole's transcription. By the time the one is finished, the next will
be full-blown—and still the next preparing: such is the action of
Much Ado, propelled by Messina's addiction to practising.

The closing scene of Act IV gives final confirmation to our
assurance that all will be well, for in it Dogberry completes his
'excommunication'. It is given to Bottom alone of mortals to see and
converse with fairies; yet he finds nothing wonderful in his asso-
ciation with them, nor can he report his experience afterwards:
'Man is but an ass, if he go about to expound this dream.' It is given
to Dogberry to bring to light the dark plot of Don John. 'What
your wisdoms could not discover,' says Borachio to Don Pedro and
Claudio, 'these shallow fools have brought to light.' The significance
of his accomplishment never quite penetrates the consciousness of
Dogberry: 'Flat burglary as ever was committed' is his conclusion,
and his final wrath is spent on Conrade for calling him an ass: 'O,
that I had been writ down an ass.'

At the opening of Act V three large facts, the residue of practices, occupy our minds: that Hero was slandered; that Dogberry is on the way to Leonato's with the truth; that Hero, reported dead, is living. Two secondary facts reside with these: that Benedick and Beatrice were victimized by practices; and that Beatrice has bound Benedick, on his love for her, to kill Claudio. Leonato's ignorance of the first two facts is exploited first, in his long lament for Hero's dishonour. But the centre of attention is Claudio, whose reactions to three moments which the dramatist asks us to anticipate follow in quick succession. These are the moments in which he learns of Hero's 'death', in which he learns of her innocence, and in which he learns of her survival. The most powerful effects of Shakespeare's exploitation of discrepant awarenesses most commonly occur, first, at the time a participant, acting in ignorance, commits a wrong against another and, second, at the time he learns what he has done. In the scene of denunciation at the altar we have already tasted the first of these fruits. Claudio's successive reactions during Act V together represent the second, and the taste is sour.

The first of these moments, when Claudio learns of Hero's 'death', passes almost without notice. Leonato confronts him with the news, and this is the moment at which Claudio, by the Friar's reckoning, should begin to mourn Hero. But the Friar mistook his man: Claudio is merely self-defensive. With the entrance of Benedick only a moment after he has learned of Hero's death, he is ready with an ill-timed jest: 'We had like to have had our two noses snapp'd off by two old men without teeth.' Whatever is on his mind, it is not Hero. He speaks no word of her, but complains of boredom—'high-proof melancholy'—and challenges Benedick to a duel of wits. The fact that, in our consciousness, Hero is not really dead cannot mitigate the fault of Claudio's conduct here: she is dead to him, and he should weep for her. That he does not do so is damning. 'Well, I will meet you,' he tells Benedick, who has accused him of killing Hero and challenged him to fight, 'so I may have good cheer.' By sustained and conspicuous representation of his indifference, Shakespeare exhibits the measure of the man. That the dramatist's exposure of Claudio's insufferableness was intentional is evinced by the speech given the Friar, predicting Claudio's reaction to Hero's death, and in effect advising us how a worthy human being should act in the circumstances: 'Then shall he mourn / If ever love had interest in his liver, / And wish he had not so accused her, / No, though he thought his accusation true.' Claudio's actual reaction, quite contradicting this expectation, is damning.

In the second anticipated moment, when he learns that Hero died

84

innocent, the hero's reaction approximates 'Ah! Then she was worthy of me after all!' Thus he speaks:

> Sweet Hero! now thy image doth appear
> In the rare semblance that I lov'd it first.
> (v. i. 259-60.)

Borachio, outright villain, confessing his guilt to Don Pedro, concludes with: 'The lady is dead upon mine and my master's false accusation; and, briefly, I desire nothing but the reward of a villain.' Not to be outfaced, Claudio says to Leonato:

> Impose me to what penance your invention
> Can lay upon my sin.
> (Ibid. 283-4.)

—but he adds, defensively, 'yet sinn'd I not / But in mistaking'. On this cause, Othello kills himself; Claudio, no Othello, gladly grasps Leonato's offer of a 'niece' to replace Hero: 'I do embrace your offer; and dispose / For henceforth of poor Claudio.' Leonato, in making the offer, makes a point of saying that this child of his brother 'alone is heir to both of us'—a fact which helps Claudio to bear his penance heroically, with only the suggestion of a whimper: 'poor Claudio'.

Before the final moment arrives, when Claudio discovers Leonato's 'niece' to be Hero herself, a brief scene represents his mourning at the 'tomb' of Hero. It is noteworthy that this visit was not Claudio's idea, but Leonato's. Earlier, when Claudio asked Leonato to impose some penance, the father replied:

> ... if your love
> Can labour ought in sad invention,
> Hang her an epitaph upon her tomb
> And sing it to her bones, sing it to-night.
> (Ibid. 292-5.)

The formal rite accomplished, Claudio and Don Pedro summarily withdraw with no comment but Claudio's expression of hope that his next matrimonial venture will turn out better.

Meanwhile Leonato's household prepares to work a final practice on the visitors; says Leonato:

> Well, daughter, and you gentlewomen all,
> Withdraw into a chamber by yourselves,
> And when I send for you, come hither mask'd.
> The Prince and Claudio promis'd by this hour
> To visit me. You know your office, brother.
> You must be father to your brother's daughter,
> And give her to young Claudio.
> (v. iv. 10-16.)

Here, as usual, the dramatist has not trusted us to guess: we must be told plainly that the 'niece' earlier promised Claudio is Hero herself; the surprise is to be Claudio's, not ours. We are required, in advance of every action, to understand its true nature, and we are not allowed to disregard the advantage we hold. Clear in our facts, then, we are able to observe Claudio objectively as the great moment of his reaction to the final truth approaches. Though he has just returned from the mourning rite at Hero's tomb, his sensibilities remain undisturbed beneath the callous: 'I'll hold my mind, were she an Ethiope,' he declares valiantly—and then he jests at Benedick:

> I think he thinks upon the savage bull.
> Tush, fear not, man; we'll tip thy horns with gold
> And all Europa shall rejoice at thee,
> As once Europa did at lusty Jove,
> When he would play the noble beast in love.
>
> (v. iv. 43–47.)

His greeting of the veiled bride is of the same character: 'here comes other reck'nings'. When Hero is unveiled, the sum of his reaction is contained in 'Another Hero!' Shakespeare gives him no more words on the matter, either of love, joy, or apology; his only remaining remarks are directed at Benedick and Beatrice. Viewed from our Olympian height, Claudio's conduct during his journey through several stages of ignorance has hardly appeared heroic. Believing Hero false, he was bestial; believing her dead, he gave her no more thought; learning that she had been true, but still supposing her dead, he compromised his formal expressions of grief with protestations that he should not be blamed; and finally, learning that she is both living and innocent, he is relieved to find that the face behind the veil is not an Ethiope's.

It is the affair of Beatrice and Benedick, though suspended and almost unexploited for two acts, that best sustains the comic spirit during this period and finally lifts it for a joyful close. One or the other has been present in almost every scene, serving the business of Hero and Claudio; though there has been little comment on the condition in which their gulling has left them, their presence alone reminds us that it continues. The fact of their error makes a gay backdrop for anguished scenes. Awareness of their state brings warmth and mirth even to those moments which demand grief and anger for the main action. In preserving the climate of comedy, thus, the subordinate action indispensably serves the central one. Unlike Claudio, both Benedick and Beatrice shine as gloriously in their ignorance as in their awareness. Each was won to love the other through a humane and noble sympathy which was not dimmed but made more luminous by error. Theirs is the final mis-apprehension to be cleared away, and when they perceive how they have been gulled, the revelation makes no difference in their love: 'Peace!' cries Benedick as he kisses his bride, 'I will stop your mouth.'

2. *As You Like It*

The worlds of *Much Ado about Nothing* and *As You Like It* contrast in notable ways, even as do their inhabitants. In the world of *Much Ado* all is astir, for its people will not suffer it to stand motionless for a moment. Twelve active practisers, nine amateur, three professional, deceiving one another and being deceived in turn, keep Messina bustling. Beside it the world of *As You Like It* is still and golden, and most of its inhabitants would be content if some of its moments endured for ever: Jaques weeping with the stricken deer, 'Ganymede' being wooed by Orlando, Duke Senior hearing Amiens sing, Phebe being chided by 'Ganymede'. While Oliver sleeps, the serpent will not sting nor the lioness claw him. Although the first two acts are much given to contrasting good and evil in country and court, old times and new, and the motives of men, the ultimate criticism of life is gentle: it is the mellowest of Shakespeare's many worlds. Here a brilliant heroine, a duke's daughter, driven into the forest, finds such joy in the shepherd's life that she does not trouble to seek out her banished father: 'What talk we of fathers, when there is such a man as Orlando?' Here a stalwart hero wins the heart of a princess by cracking a professional wrestler's bones and gains a fortune by felling a 'suck'd and hungry lioness' with his bare hands. Here hardened villainy simply cannot endure, but is dissolved and absorbed by the goodness of environment. Here Melancholy grows lean, finding nothing left to nourish itself on, and at last banishes itself:

> Duke S.   Stay, Jaques, stay.
> Jaq.   To see no pastime I.
> (Ibid. 200–1.)

From the point of view of the disposition and uses of awareness the two plays stand in marked contrast also. In the first place, *As You Like It* depends far less than *Much Ado about Nothing* upon discrepant awarenesses for its movement and effects. Although we are given advantage over certain participants in eleven of twenty-two scenes, the gap between awarenesses is rarely the central dramatic fact in these scenes and is sometimes left quite unexploited; moreover, in several of these scenes our advantage functions during

87

only a portion of the action. Further, the play exhibits no very complex arrangement of awarenesses at any time; usually, in scenes in which we hold any advantage, it is a single one, which we share with one or two persons at the expense of one or two others. Near-universal ignorance is exploited only in the closing moments. In *Much Ado*, swarming with practisers, many secrets are shared by many persons and hidden from many more. *As You Like It* has only two notable practisers, Rosalind and Celia, and the only notable secret concerns their identities. All in all, then, *As You Like It* makes less use of the difference between advantage and disadvantage than any other mature comedy except *The Merchant of Venice*.

Nevertheless both the effects and the action of the climactic scenes of *As You Like It* depend on this difference quite as much as do those of the comparable scenes in *Much Ado about Nothing*. In that play the scene of Hero's denunciation could not occur but for Claudio's error in thinking Hero false; in *As You Like It* the scene of Orlando's wooing could not occur but for Orlando's error in thinking Rosalind to be Ganymede. In their degree of dependence on a gap for the central action, then, the two plays are alike even though the complexity of the patterns differs widely. No less significantly, the plays are related, as are both to *The Merry Wives of Windsor* and *Twelfth Night*, in the love of practising exhibited by certain participants. Again the difference is in complexity rather than degree: in the other plays virtually all persons are incorrigibly addicted to the art whereas in *As You Like It* only Rosalind and Celia are devoted to it. But their zeal for the game compensates for their numerical deficiency. In Rosalind the holiday spirit of the dedicated practiser has its most exuberant expression. 'I will speak to him like a saucy lackey,' she says to Celia, 'and under that habit play the knave with him.' It is with no better excuse that she begins her sport with poor Orlando.

Her practice produces no important consequence until Act III, however, and we hold no great advantage over anyone until then. Aside from the heroines, Oliver is the only practiser, and his two devices, like those that fill the opening scenes of *Much Ado*, yield no noteworthy effects, though they bear significantly on subsequent action. Our first advantage is over Charles the wrestler, deceived by Oliver's description of Orlando:

. . . thou wert best look to 't; for if thou dost him any slight disgrace, or if he do not mightily grace himself on thee, he will practise against thee by poison, entrap thee by some treacherous device, and never leave thee till he hath ta'en thy life by some indirect means or other; for, I assure thee, and almost with tears I speak it, there is not one so young and so villainous this day living.   (I. i. 153–61.)

But although we hold brief advantage over both contestants, nothing comes either of Charles's ignorance of Orlando's true nature or of Orlando's ignorance that Charles, in his error, is determined to 'give him his payment' so decisively that he will never walk again. For Orlando proves competent to hold his own in muscular terms with man or beast, and presumably if he knew of Charles's intent he would throw him no harder than he does in ignorance: 'Bear him away.' Oliver's second device, even wickeder, comes to no more than the first in terms of an exploitable situation, since Orlando learns from Adam as soon as we of his brother's intent to burn Orlando's lodging 'where you use to lie / And you within it'. For subsequent action, of course, this practice proves indispensable: it precipitates Orlando's flight to the forest, after which Oliver's own departure in pursuit is occasioned by the error of Duke Frederick in supposing that Orlando, for whose act he holds Oliver responsible, aided the flight of the princesses.

A few other moments of participants' unawareness are either represented or alluded to during the first two acts, but all are left unexploited. Thus Duke Senior appears at the opening of Act II, directly after we have learned that Celia and Rosalind are coming to the forest to seek him, and our knowledge of their decision inevitably casts special light upon him; but he is busily contrasting court and forest life, and Shakespeare gives him no mention of Rosalind or otherwise capitalizes on his ignorance that she is coming. Little more is made of Orlando's ignorance that he is in the presence of a great Duke when in the last scene of Act II he bursts upon the forest camp, sword drawn, demanding food. Some sparks of irony do indeed flash from his ignorance: 'If ever you have look'd on better days, / If ever been where bells have knoll'd to church,' he tells the Duke, 'Let gentleness my strong enforcement be; / In the which hope I blush, and hide my sword.' In return, there is a quiet flash from the Duke's reply: 'True is it that we have seen better days.' The period of Orlando's unawareness extends to a hundred lines, until the Duke ends it with an abrupt 'I am the Duke / That lov'd your father'. But except for the quick flashes of irony, the unconscious and the conscious, the fact of the hero's ignorance is not essential to the action itself or to the main dramatic effects of the scene. Finally, in the first encounter of Rosalind and Celia in their masked identities with a resident of Arden, Corin, little is made of the gap between awarenesses. The purposes of this scene (II. iv) are mainly preparatory: to introduce the rural lovers, Silvius

89

and Phebe, to show us that the heroines are in their disguises, and to get them settled in the forest. The fact that Corin does not know he is in the presence of princesses is irrelevant to these purposes, and it is uncapitalized. Besides, old Corin is a rooted element of the country-side, and revelation of their identity would presumably make no difference to him: whether for the churlish old master or for the new, and whether the new be master or mistress, of royal blood or common, he will continue to feed the sheep and shear the fleeces.

Exploitation of the great central secret of the play, then, takes its real start in Act III—the point at which the heart of the play begins to beat—and does not reach a climax until IV. i, with the wooing of 'Ganymede'. The approach to this scene is made by degrees, as Rosalind, acting her masquerade in a spirit of pure mischief, meets successively Orlando, Phebe and Silvius, and Jaques. She meets her father also during this period, but the hilarity of their interview Shakespeare leaves to the imagination, merely having Rosalind report the incident in passing to greater matters:

> I met the Duke yesterday and had much question with him. He asked me of what parentage I was. I told him, of as good as he; so he laugh'd and let me go.
>
> (III. iv. 38–41.)

No more is made of her encounter with Jaques, with which Act IV opens. Jaques's ignorance of her identity, like Corin's, is irrelevant and is therefore appropriately left unexploited. It is, then, primarily through the interview with Phebe and Silvius and the preliminary interview with Orlando himself that Shakespeare prepares the climate for the great scene.

'I'll prove a busy actor in their play,' Rosalind promises Corin, who has invited her to witness the 'pageant truly play'd' between Silvius and Phebe. The line reminds of Oberon's when he enlists himself in the service of true love for Helena's sake: 'Fare thee well, nymph. Ere he do leave this grove, / Thou shalt fly him and he shall seek thy love.' It is the first clear placement of Rosalind in the line of Oberon, Duke Vincentio, and Prospero. Later, when the denouement nears, as we shall observe, she takes upon herself increasingly the role of the omniscient, omnipotent controlling force. Further, the present interview with Silvius and Phebe anticipates the interviews of Viola with Olivia in *Twelfth Night*; but it has striking contrasts with those scenes also, for Rosalind's temperament is as far from Viola's as Phebe's from Olivia's. Rosalind's is a zestful, mischievous, even mildly wicked delight in the masquerade; with a keen relish like Prospero's, of her role and her advantage, she lashes Phebe with words meant to sting:

No, faith, proud mistress, hope not after it.
'Tis not your inky brows, your black silk hair,
Your bugle eyeballs, nor your cheek of cream
That can entame my spirits to your worship.

(III. v. 45–48.)

And, again:

Down on your knees,
And thank heaven, fasting, for a good man's love;
For I must tell you friendly in your ear,
Sell when you can; you are not for all markets.

(Ibid. 57–60.)

Phebe is the first real victim of Rosalind's mockery. She looks on to
Olivia, innocent victim of Viola's disguise, but she differs from
Olivia in deserving to be humiliated. Presumptuous, pretentious,
proud, she scorns the poor slave of a shepherd who dotes on her,
killing him over and over with darted looks—all the while insisting
that 'there is no force in eyes / That can do hurt'. When Olivia falls
in love with 'Cesario', the gentle Viola pities her and strains to avoid
hurting her; not so Rosalind, when she perceives Phebe's error:
'Why do you look on me? / I see no more in you than in the
ordinary / Of nature's sale-work.' Olivia's declaration of love invites
no derision, but only compassion: 'A cypress, not a bosom, / Hides
my heart.' In contrast, Phebe deserves the corrective medicine of
ridicule which Rosalind, of all Shakespeare's heroines, is best quali-
fied to administer.

Yet it is not Phebe who occupies the lowest vantage-point in this
scene, or in any scene in which the shepherd lovers participate.
Here, as elsewhere, that place is reserved for the hapless male.
Ignorant of 'Ganymede's' sex and rank, Silvius fails to comprehend
the more obvious and equally significant fact, that Phebe has fallen
in love. 'There be some women, Silvius, had they mark'd him / In
parcels as I did,' asserts Phebe, 'would have gone near / To fall in
love with him; but, for my part, / I love him not nor hate him not.'
Seeing nothing in this but a plain statement, Silvius gladly agrees to
bear to Ganymede Phebe's 'very taunting letter'. The display of
Silvius's masculine oblivion in the presence of Phebe is prelude to
the full-scale exhibition of the same condition in the climactic
scene, when Orlando is pitted in unequal combat with Rosalind.
Indeed, the entire scene of Rosalind's encounter with Silvius and
Phebe, presenting the first real exploitation of the gulf between
her awareness and the ignorance of the persons she meets in the
forest and overthrows one by one, serves as an approach, itself
climactic, to that summit of the comedy.

The scene is not the only preparation for the climactic period of some 200 lines that immediately follows Jaques's departure at the opening of Act IV: every preceding scene in which either Orlando or Rosalind appears is preparation in that it builds our sense of the *rightness* of these two for their roles in the climactic scene and thus increases the comic potentiality of that scene. For certainly the great scene does not exploit an ordinary discrepancy between the awarenesses of two ordinary lovers. It is in large part because these two are precisely as they are, with a wider gap between their awarenesses than between just any two lovers, that the climactic scene is so memorable. //

The width of this discrepancy is due not only to the fact of Rosalind's disguise, although of course that is essential. Nor is it attributable wholly t⌐ the fact that she possesses, besides the disguise that hides her identity, extraordinary native gifts that make her the most circumspect of heroines. Without disguise, her natural gifts would set her above everyone else in the play. 'She is too subtle for thee,' says Duke Frederick to Celia in banishing Rosalind. 'She robs thee of thy name, / And thou wilt show more bright and seem more virtuous / When she is gone.' With disguise to supplement her gifts, hers is a towering advantage, and not only Orlando but all the persons she meets in the forest are reduced to a state of oblivion when they encounter her. The cream of the cream of the jest is that such a one is confronted in the climactic scene with precisely such a one as Orlando.

Rosalind is the brightest of Shakespeare's bright heroines, and Orlando is the least conscious of his unconscious heroes. The gap between them is that between omniscience and oblivion. It is not that Orlando is a stupid man: Bardolph, Dogberry, Aguecheek are stupid men, and their quality differs from his. Moreover, in our view, Orlando is more admirable as a human being than Shakespeare's other heroes of comedy—than Proteus, the incipient rapist; Bassanio, the fleece hunter; Claudio, the sadistic prig; Bertram, the liar and ready adulterer. But though good, and not stupid, Orlando is afflicted to an extraordinary degree with that obliviousness that is common to the heroes. Perhaps Orsino of *Twelfth Night* stands nearest him in this respect—but Orsino has only to deal with gentle Viola, and Orlando is at the mercy of Rosalind.

Orlando is right for the great scene just as Bottom, equipped with an ass's head, is right for the profoundly ironic moments with Titania. Despite the deserved praise which Oliver heaps upon Orlando as reason for getting rid of him—'he's gentle, never schooled and yet learned, full of noble device, of all sorts enchantingly beloved, and indeed so much in the heart of the world, and especially of my own people, who best know him, that I am altogether misprised'—Shakespeare begins early to qualify his hero for his miserable role with brilliant Rosalind. Orlando is exposed repeatedly in situations of which the truth eludes him. Ludicrous comments, outrageously damaging to his heroic prestige, are made about him when he is absent: 'I found him under a tree, like a dropp'd acorn', says Celia—and the image stays. His abrupt disposal of Charles the wrestler; his first tongue-tied meeting with Rosalind; his sword-brandishing, valiant, but frightfully unaware entrance to demand food of Duke Senior—all these are parts of the preparation. By III. ii, when he runs about the forest, scattering bad verses and blemishing trees—'Run, run, Orlando; carve on every tree / The fair, the chaste, the unexpressive she'—he has been readied for the climactic moment. But there is even more preparation—indeed, 300 lines of it—after which, entering, Orlando can seem only a sturdy booby. First, samples of his verse, at its simultaneous best and worst, are exposed:

> Sweetest nut hath sourest rind,
> Such a nut is Rosalind.
> He that sweetest rose will find,
> Must find love's prick and Rosalind.
> (III. ii. 115–18.)

Next the verse and the man are subjected to the biting wit, in turn, of Touchstone, Rosalind, Celia, and Jaques. 'This is the very false gallop of verses,' says the fool. 'Why do you infect yourself with them?' And Rosalind to Celia: '... look here what I found on a palm tree. I was never so berhym'd since Pythagoras' time, that I was an Irish rat, which I can hardly remember.' At what exact instant in the course of this universal belittlement Rosalind learns that the maker of these verses is Orlando, it is impossible to tell. Evidently she knows by the time of Celia's comment, 'And a chain, that you once wore, about his neck. Change you colour?' Probably we are expected to understand that she guesses the truth at the outset, when she enters reading aloud: 'From the east to western Ind, / No jewel is like Rosalind.' In any event, during part of the scene she feigns ignorance of the poet's identity, and, true to her nature, uses her pretended ignorance as an excuse for adding wicked touches to the growing portrait of Orlando: 'Is he of God's making? What manner of man? Is his head worth a hat or his chin worth a beard?' It is at the height of this discussion that Celia adds the definitive stroke: 'I found him under a tree, like a dropp'd acorn.'

It is an Orlando whom the dramatist has subjected to such levity that we are next shown conversing with Jaques, while Rosalind and Celia observe unseen. And it is with the departure of Jaques, when the disguised princesses move in on their victim—'I will speak to him like a saucy lackey, and under that habit play the knave with him'—that the main action commences. The first interview of Orlando and 'Ganymede', ending with her promise to wash his liver 'as clean as a sound sheep's heart, that there shall not be one spot of love in't', is itself a prelude to the climactic scene of the wooing of 'Ganymede'. The scene of 200 lines, after Jaques leaves at the opening of Act IV, is the climactic peak, the point which the rest of the play, including Jaques and all the golden world of the Forest of Arden itself, supports. Though it lacks the fullness and complexity of corresponding moments in *The Merchant of Venice*, *Much Ado about Nothing*, *Twelfth Night*, and *Measure for Measure*, the scene deserves its crowning place. It has one distinction: it is the only cloudless climactic scene in Shakespeare's romantic comedies. The others are characterized by a complex disposition of awarenesses, and exploitation produces multiple effects, some pleasant, some painful. But here are only two levels—Rosalind's (and ours) and Orlando's —and the result of exploitation is unadulterated fun. Our equipment for the climactic scenes of other mature comedies includes a heavy burden of advantages, some over all participants, some shared with a few. Our equipment for the wooing scene is a single advantage, which we share with Rosalind alone over Orlando alone. Lacking the typical tensions and conflicting appeals of the others, the climactic scene of *As You Like It* is structurally simple. Indeed, having but one matter to exploit—the discrepancy between the lovers' awarenesses—it is unique as a climactic scene not only among the comedies but among all Shakespeare's plays. Complexity in both cause and effect being his favoured way, the climactic scene of *As You Like It* might be expected to be inferior; instead, it is a magnificent exercise in simplicity.

Inferior it might be if there were no compensation for the lack of complexity. The compensating factor is the width of the discrepancy, so carefully prepared, between the awarenesses of the lovers. Though single, this gulf is wider than that between any other lovers in the comedies—as wide as that between any other two persons in any play. Even Bottom and Titania are not so separated as these, for though Bottom's understanding approximates Orlando's, Titania's eyes, bewitched by the juice of the little western flower, lack the clarity of Rosalind's. Neither are Hero and Claudio so far apart, since Don John's practice has blinded the callow youth, and Hero is ignorant that she has been defamed. The

awarenesses of Bassanio and Portia, in the court scene, are far apart
with respect only to a minor aspect of the situation; the court scene
does not exist primarily to exploit the discrepancy resulting from
Bassanio's ignorance of Portia's identity: its main business is the
trial of Antonio, and the facts of the case are known to both. In
Act V, however, when the affair of the rings becomes central,
division of awarenesses of Portia–Bassanio and Nerissa–Gratiano
is both wide and central.

The exclusive business of the wooing scene of *As You Like It* is
exploitation of the gap between the awarenesses of Orlando and
Rosalind; but for this gap the scene could not exist. Though extended, the exploitation is not thin; it is a virtuoso piece played on
one string, as is no other major scene in Shakespeare. Neither the
relation of the participants nor the situation changes at all during
the action. At the beginning Rosalind knows everything and
Orlando nothing; at the end, the same. So wide is the space between
them that Rosalind can repeatedly insist that she is 'very very Rosalind' without risk of losing her advantage. She plays one game, and
Orlando, thinking it all one, another:

> *Orl.* But will my Rosalind do so?
> *Ros.* By my life, she will do as I do.
> *Orl.* O, but she is wise.
> *Ros.* Or else she could not have the wit to do this.
>
> (IV. i. 158–62.)

Rarely flattering to his comic heroes, Shakespeare treats Orlando
abominably! An open-hearted and open-minded innocent, incapable of suspecting that reality might differ from appearance, he
is permitted no glimpse of the truth. Even Bottom has moments of
dim wonder, finding his face hairy and his stomach wanting hay;
and Orsino, though without realizing the fact, comes to the edge of
truth in remarking that 'Cesario's' voice 'is as the maiden's organ'.
Orlando is made to play out the scene without even touching the
truth unaware. Ironical flashes are sparked by Orsino's and Bottom's
near approaches; Orlando's utterances, despite Rosalind's repeated
assertions that she is Rosalind, flare up in irony only when they
illuminate his remoteness from the truth: 'Who could be out, standing before his beloved mistress?' he inquires—standing before her.

Since Orlando has learned nothing to the purpose at the end of
the scene and since the time of a second meeting is fixed, the
same discrepancy remains the principal exploitable condition up
to the time we learn that Orlando cannot keep the two o'clock
appointment. In the interim occurs a scene in which Silvius briefly
replaces Orlando as Rosalind's victim—and Phebe's unawareness of

'Ganymede's' identity is capitalized also, through her 'very taunt-ing' letter borne to Rosalind by Silvius. 'Can a woman rail thus?' asks Rosalind, starting to read her admirer's love poem; and Silvius, sup-posing himself wise indeed, alarmed that 'Ganymede' has stolen his love, replies, 'Call you this railing?' The tangle of awarenesses that involves Rosalind, Phebe, and Silvius is more complicated than is the knot that involves Rosalind and Orlando. For Phebe, ignorant of Rosalind's sex, is in love with her; and Silvius, ignorant also of Rosalind's sex, at first does not realize that Phebe has fallen in love and therefore gladly bears the 'chiding' letter, and then, perceiving the lesser truth—that Phebe is in love—but not the greater—that 'Ganymede' is no formidable rival—is needlessly distressed. 'Alas, poor shepherd,' says Celia—not, certainly, because he has lost Phebe, but because he has been doubly deluded.

Rosalind's next victim is Oliver—who, however, is victim only of her disguise and not her mockery, for she is briefly too unhappy to play games. Indeed, for about fifty lines the dramatist gives us advantage over both Rosalind and Celia, since we and not they know that their visitor is Orlando's brother; it is an insignificant advantage, however, and is left unexploited. The main advantage remains with the disguised heroines. Orlando has described them to Oliver, and in doing so has transmitted his own error to his brother; thus Oliver:

> If that an eye may profit by a tongue,
> Then should I know you by description:
> Such garments and such years. 'The boy is fair,
> Of female favour, and bestows himself
> Like a ripe sister; the woman low,
> And browner than her brother.'
>
> (IV. iii. 84–89.)

The femininity of Rosalind is manifest in her swooning at sight of the napkin red with Orlando's blood; very briefly at this point she anticipates Viola of *Twelfth Night*, who has greater difficulty than other heroines in maintaining her masquerade. Yet Rosalind recovers quickly and resumes her role even as she reopens her eyes. Oliver is doubly deceived: not only does he, like his brother, take Rosalind to be 'Ganymede' pretending to be Rosalind, but he takes Celia for no more than the proprietor of 'the cottage and the bounds / That the old carlot once was master of', and as such woos and wins her.

It is Oliver's success in wooing and the setting of the wedding date for 'Tomorrow' that abruptly terminates Rosalind's sport, which she might otherwise continue indefinitely, and precipitates the denouement. For Orlando, seeing his brother's success, 'can live

APPROACH TO THE SUMMIT

no longer by thinking': 'Ganymede' will no longer serve. Finding it impossible to perpetuate the static situation, Rosalind takes upon herself the role of the external, controlling force. As 'Ganymede' she has enjoyed an advantage in awareness, overpeering all Arden. But even omniscience will no longer serve; so upon her practice as 'Ganymede' she grafts a second practice:

> Believe then, if you please, that I can do strange things. I have, since I was three year old, convers'd with a magician, most profound in his art and yet not damnable. If you do love Rosalind so near the heart as your gesture cries it out, when your brother marries Aliena, shall you marry her. I know into what straits of fortune she is driven; and it is not impossible to me, if it appear not inconvenient to you, to set her before your eyes to-morrow, human as she is, and without any danger. (v. ii. 64–75.)

Earlier, going with Corin to watch the 'pageant truly play'd' between Silvius and Phebe, she had promised to 'prove a busy actor in their play', identifying herself with the role played by Oberon in the affairs of the Athenian lovers. She now identifies herself more explicitly with this role. Her omnipotence—which seems magical to the participants—is, of course, only feigned, where Oberon's, and later Vincentio's and Prospero's, is real. In our view it is a patent fraud. Even so, we know also that she can do all she promises —and she promises infinitely:

> (*To Phe.*) I will marry you, if ever I marry woman, and I'll be married to-morrow. (*To Orl.*) I will satisfy you, if ever I satisfi'd man, and you shall be married to-morrow. (*To Sil.*) I will content you, if what pleases you contents you, and you shall be married to-morrow. (*To Orl.*) As you love Rosalind, meet. (*To Sil.*) As you love Phebe, meet. And as I love no woman, I'll meet. So, fare you well. I have left you commands. (Ibid. 122–31.)

Portia of *The Merchant of Venice*, coming to Antonio's trial dressed as 'a young doctor of Rome', resolves the dilemma of the court without magic or pretence of magic. Her superior awareness is leagued with merely mortal power—her own brilliance and the 'opinion' of the learned Bellario of Padua. Rosalind, in affecting to have been 'tutor'd in the rudiments / Of many desperate studies' by a 'great magician / Obscured in the circle of this forest', moves well beyond Portia toward Prospero: in effect, if not fact, her control of the world of Arden and the destinies of its inhabitants is as complete as Oberon's control of the enchanted woods outside Athens and Prospero's control of his island, its winds, waters, residents, and visitors.

To accomplish all the miracles she has promised to perform by magical acts, she need really only reveal her own identity. She surrenders her advantage spectacularly, in a burst of music and mystic song, a kind of magic in itself—and somehow, magically perhaps, she does manage to produce Hymen in person for the occasion. In this denouement, which has only one gap to close, the discrepancy in awarenesses vanishes as suddenly as a burst bubble; our own advantage over the inhabitants of the Forest is lost at the same instant Rosalind surrenders hers. In this as in other great final moments, Shakespeare sharply limits the comments of participants for whom dark has suddenly become light. 'If there be truth in sight,' says the Duke, 'you are my daughter.' 'If-there be truth in sight,' says Orlando—who has had cause to doubt—'you are my Rosalind.' Shakespeare gives the Duke four additional speeches, the hero not another word. Another kind of man, now seeing what a game was played with him—recalling the outlandish spectacle he had been tricked into making—would bide his time until fast married to this Rosalind and then would beat her until she begged for mercy. Orlando, of course, will not do so. Even from the first, he was as other heroes of the comedies are at the end—hooked and gasping for air. At last, then, Rosalind having ended her sport with him, he is properly left speechless.

3. *The Merry Wives of Windsor*

A fundamental difference between *As You Like It* and *The Merry Wives of Windsor* appears in the fact that whereas in the one the brilliant Rosalind stands at the apex of the structure of awarenesses, in the other Mistress Quickly perches there. Serving as accomplice in the wives' multiple practices on Falstaff, managing a thriving personal enterprise at the expense of sweet Anne Page's three suitors, and at last—quite unexpectedly—serving as Queen of the Fairies in command of ouphes and elves at Herne's oak, 'that foolish carrion' is *The Merry Wives of Windsor*'s nearest equivalent to Oberon, Portia, Rosalind, Viola, Vincentio, and Prospero. Between her peak and—in a startling inversion of their positions in *Henry IV*—Falstaff's nether depth range the other major participants without whose practices and counter-practices there would be neither action nor comic effects.

The play differs markedly also from *As You Like It* in its extra-ordinary multiplicity of practices, in the number of persons involved as practisers, practisees, or both, and in the great complexity of its awareness–unawareness patterns. We hold advantage over some persons during sixteen of twenty-two scenes. Only Mistress Quickly and Anne Page are spared moments of unwitting exposure

(Anne is apart from the main stream of action, being the destination of much of it). Eleven distinct practices, several of which run concurrently, inextricably bound with others yet whole in themselves, compose the material and the means of action and effect: that of Falstaff on the wives; that of Pistol and Nym on Falstaff in betraying him to Page and Ford; that of Mistress Quickly on Sir Hugh (acting for Slender, incapable of acting for himself), Caius, and Fenton in their respective suits to Anne; that of the wives on Falstaff, involving Mistress Quickly as go-between; that of the Host on Caius and Sir Hugh in appointing them different meeting places for a duel; that of Ford on Falstaff in posing as Master Brook; that of Sir Hugh and Caius on the Host in the affair of the 'Germans'; that of all Windsor on Falstaff in the affair of Herne's oak; that of Page on his wife in arranging for Anne to be taken by Slender; that of Mrs. Page on Page in arranging Anne's elopement with Caius; and, finally, that of Fenton on both husband and wife in stealing Anne for himself. This is the greatest accumulation of practices in any play of Shakespeare's except *Cymbeline*.

Peopled with practisers addicted to the game, the world of *The Merry Wives of Windsor* resembles—in this respect—that of *Much Ado about Nothing*. Both worlds bustle with activity; no moment is quiet: while one intrigue is starting, another has reached a peak of exploitation, and another is ending. Nearly all the inhabitants, taking turns at gulling and being gulled, are often gulling and gulled simultaneously. Yet the world of Windsor also contrasts significantly with the world of Messina: *it holds no dark corner where evil lurks, ready to inflict injury and grief*. The nearest to Don John here is Falstaff—in whom wickedness is only comic. The nearest to Claudio's violent passion is Ford's jealousy, and that, too, is comic, not dangerous. The nearest to Hero's anguish is Falstaff's discomfort from the odour of dirty linen, from the drubbing handed him by Ford, from the pinching and finger-end burning administered by assorted ouphes and elves. While it resembles *Much Ado about Nothing* in its multiplicity of practices, practisers, and practisees, then, *The Merry Wives of Windsor* resembles *As You Like It* in that it uses discrepancies in awarenesses only for fun. Our many advantages include no knowledge of present or impending danger or grief, hence produce no war of conflicting emotions. Accordingly, though the disposition of awarenesses is highly complex during the climactic scenes, as in *Much Ado about Nothing*, yet the absence of any sinister shadow prevents creation of such effects as those of Hero's denunciation scene.

Nearly all its discrepancies in vision, more numerous in *The*

Merry Wives of Windsor than elsewhere except *Cymbeline*, result from activities of the many practisers. The two main gaps—that between the wives and Falstaff and that between Ford and Falstaff —are exploited, with shrewd variations on each occasion, three times each, the six scenes which exploit them constituting the principal action of the play. In one scene Falstaff is deceived by three persons in succession, each time with respect to a different fact of the complex situation. In five of the sixteen scenes whose business and effects are made by exploitation of discrepancies in awareness, not one participant commands a whole view of the situation. Not even *Twelfth Night* exhibits more scenes of universal confusion. In addition to the gaps created by the activities of practisers are others that result from the participants' native lack of perspective: both Caius and Sir Hugh are so made as to be deceived when no one is deceiving them; their outstanding scenes are those which exhibit their natural follies in situations in which they are also abused by practices. Though their individual idiosyncrasies differentiate them superficially from all other persons, these two are essentially of the race of Bottom, Dogberry, and Aguecheek. Less conspicuously of this breed, but nevertheless of it also, is Shallow:

> *Slen.* They may give the dozen white luces in their coat.
> *Shal.* It is an old coat.
>
> (I. i. 16–17.)

Not a blood brother but a cousin of the race is Slender, who, unlike Bottom, has a certain pitiful awareness despite a lack of brains. The one poignant note in the play is that sounded from time to time in the minor key, asserting Slender's humble worship of sweet Anne Page. Unlike Bottom, who is not astonished to find a fairy queen doting on him, and unlike Malvolio, who nothing doubts that he deserves Olivia, Slender has a corner somewhere in head or heart that knows Anne is not for him; his is the desire of the moth for the star—if the moth could also sense futility. Mistress Quickly, though she occupies a vantage-point higher than any other's, does so not by virtue of superior intellect but because circumstances make her an accomplice in the wives' practice at the same time she is the foxy-foolish proprietor of her own triple game: she simply holds a good place. Conversely, Falstaff, in *Henry IV* the supreme comic example of wit and circumspection, is here reduced by multiple practices mounted against him to a level from which he sees no more of the total reality than Caius and Sir Hugh. Deceived by all and deceiving none, he holds the bottom despite his wit, as Mistress Quickly is hoisted to the top despite her lack of it. 'Have I laid my brain in the sun and dri'd it,' he asks at last, 'that it wants matter to prevent so gross o'erreaching as this?' Though natively of Rosalind's breed, he is here made kin to Bottom and Malvolio. Whether his nature itself has been transformed by the reversal of roles is a question to be tested in the analysis that follows.

At the end of II. i twelve persons are involved in six practices and counter-practices, most of the perpetrators of which double as deceiver and deceived. Shakespeare creates enough gaps at the outset for the whole play, and he announces the practices in rapid succession. Falstaff's is first: 'I have writ me a letter to her [Mrs. Ford]; and here another to Page's wife. . . . I will be cheaters to them both, and they shall be exchequers to me.' Next is Nym and Pistol's practice on Falstaff:

> *Nym.* I will discuss the humour of this love to Page.
> *Pist.* And I to Ford. . . .
>
> (I. iii. 104–5.)

Next is the private game run by Mistress Quickly, who in a brief scene instructs Simple to tell Sir Hugh that she will intercede with Anne Page for Slender, assures Caius that 'the maid loves you, and all shall be well', and accepts Fenton's money for her good words to Anne on his behalf: 'I'll be sworn on a book, she loves you.' Next is the wives' practice on Falstaff, and, simultaneously, on the jealousy-ridden Ford; thus Mrs. Page, 'Let's consult together against this greasy knight.' Next is the Host's practice, with Shallow and Page, on Caius and Sir Hugh; thus Shallow, 'My merry host hath had the measuring of their weapons, and, I think, hath appointed them contrary places.' And, finally, there is Ford's practice on Falstaff, and, incidentally, on Mrs. Ford; thus Ford to the Host, 'I'll give you a pottle of burnt sack to give me recourse to him and tell him my name is Brook; only for a jest.'

Act II, ii, therefore opens with an elaborate machinery of exploitation. On the bottommost level—where he remains until the end of the play despite the fact that he himself devised the practice which set all in motion—stands Falstaff, triply abused, being ignorant that Nym and Pistol have betrayed him, that Ford intends to 'sound' him in the disguise of 'Master Brook', and that the wives have consulted against him. His own practice thus has been circumscribed from the moment he divulged it to Nym and Pistol, and his ignorance of this fact is the basic exploitable matter of the play until the final moments of Act V, when, having been pinched by fairies, he rises as from a long sleep: 'I do begin to perceive that I am made an ass.' On the level just above Falstaff's stands Ford: informed by Pistol that 'Sir John affects thy wife' and disguised also, he holds double advantage over Falstaff, who of course supposes himself to hold the advantage. But Ford is blind to his wife's staunch honesty and ignorant that she has devised her own means of dealing with Falstaff. His low place on the scale is not, therefore, due wholly to his ignorance of the practices against him. If these practices alone were responsible, Page should occupy the same low level, since he has learned from Nym as Ford from Pistol that Sir John 'loves your wife'. Ford stands lower because of the fault in his nature which makes him self-deceived as well as deceived; thus,

> I do not misdoubt my wife; but I would be loath to turn them together. A man may be too confident. I would have nothing lie on my head. I cannot be thus satisfied. (II. i. 192–5.)

Page, however, not being self-deceived, is quite unaffected by the plots and counter-plots of Falstaff and Mrs. Page; thus Page:

> If he should intend this voyage towards my wife, I would turn her loose to him; and what he gets more of her than sharp words, let it lie on my head. (Ibid. 188–91.)

On the next level above stand the wives, aware of Falstaff's double-dealing, having 'consulted' about his letters, and possessed of shrewd advantage in their joint and secret practice on the knight. But their vision, too, is imperfect, since they are ignorant that Nym and Pistol have exposed Falstaff's device and that Ford, masquerading as 'Brook', has a jealous eye on the whole affair. Furthermore, perhaps because of their middle-aged vanity, they do not guess the true purpose of Falstaff's overture, but assume that he covets their persons: that their persons are in fact secondary, being his means to their husbands' purses, is Falstaff's own well-guarded secret, never discovered by husbands or wives. In this special sense, Falstaff out-tops them all even while he is the dupe of all: thus, in spite of the odds, Shakespeare preserves a shred of the old Falstaffian prestige.

Such is the disposition of awarenesses with respect to the principal action. The preparatory arrangement for the secondary action, the manœuvring for the hand of Anne Page, is less elaborate but as firmly established. Caius and Sir Hugh hold the lowest level in this structure, being abused both by Mistress Quickly and by Shallow, the Host, and Page, who appoint them contrary places for their duel. Both Slender and Fenton escape the latter kind of abuse, but they also are abused by Mistress Quickly. Falstaff has no place in this arrangement. It is not until the final scene that his affair and that of Anne Page, which have moved along parallel lines through nearly five acts, at last converge.

Only Mistress Quickly, operating between the wives and Falstaff and between the jockeying suitors and Anne Page, commands a full view of both actions. She is the only person other than the wives who knows their game with Falstaff—and perhaps she perceives more clearly than they the deeper purpose of Falstaff's suit to them. At the same time, she is sole proprietor of a lucrative practice on the suitors. Her vision, it is true, lacks the perfection of ours: she knows nothing of 'Master Brook', and presumably she is ignorant of the Host's practice on Caius and Sir Hugh. But these matters are irrelevant; ignorance of them or of any other aspect of the complicated situation never exposes her to laughter. The pre-eminence of her position overlooking both major lines of action is appropriately signified when at last, as Fairy Queen, she presides over their convergence.

However otherwise *The Merry Wives of Windsor* may be inferior to *As You Like It* and *Twelfth Night*, one fact is evident: that no comedy exhibits a technically finer development of an initial, highly complex apparatus for subsequent exploitation. Uniquely here, Shakespeare defers all exploitation until the full structure has been erected; though five scenes are required for preparation, nothing moves until all is ready. Then, once begun, exploitation proceeds swiftly on the lines laid, with little need of further exposition. In contrast particularly to *Much Ado about Nothing*, *The Merry Wives of Windsor* makes no false starts, never needs to start anew, leaves nothing uncapitalized. In the earlier play, as we have noted, the practices launched in the first scenes serve only to illustrate the way of the world; when they are abandoned, new ones must be devised for action of the last three acts. But in *The Merry Wives of Windsor* everything that looks ahead goes ahead; no initial promise is unkept; all that has been marked for exploitation is exploited; the gaps opened between awarenesses during the first five scenes are kept open until the last measure of comic effect has been squeezed from them.

Once begun, in II. ii, exploitation of these gaps is dazzling proof of Shakespeare's mastery of his favourite comic method. Brisk and efficient despite elaborateness, this exploitation moves along two main lines of action: that of the correction of Falstaff and that of the winning of Anne. It will be best to examine these in turn.

In all scenes in which Falstaff appears the primary business is exploitation of the gap between his inferior and some superior awareness. Sometimes the superior awareness is ours alone; sometimes we share it with a participant. When Falstaff is shown with other persons who know less than we, but more than he, both discrepancies are exploited—but always Falstaff's ignorance furnishes the basic comic stuff. Thus in II. ii he appears three times in the inferior position, each time with a different person and with respect to a different part of the situation. First he rants at Pistol, ignorant that Pistol has already betrayed him to Ford: 'Go. A short knife and a thong! To your manor of Pickthatch! Go. You'll not bear a letter for me, you rogue!' 'I do relent,' says Pistol—and says nothing of the betrayal, which is of course uppermost in both his mind and ours. Next Falstaff is interviewed by Mistress Quickly, as the wives' knowing emissary. Since Pistol is also present here, we are made to remember that Falstaff has already been exposed to Ford—hence his ignorance is touched from two sides at once: he knows neither that the wives are practising on him nor that Ford's eye is on him. Neither Mistress Quickly nor Pistol sees the situation in its entirety, as we do, each being ignorant of the other's secret; hence while a great gap stands between Falstaff's understanding and ours, lesser gaps stand also between the other participants' and ours.

Further, it is during this interview that Falstaff comes nearest to self-deception. 'Setting the attraction of my good parts aside I have no other charms,' he boasts; and, at the end of the meeting:

> Say'st thou so, old Jack? Go thy ways. I'll make more of the old body than I have done. Will they yet look after thee? Wilt thou, after the expense of so much money, be now a gainer? Good body, I thank thee. (II. ii. 142-7).

The Falstaff of *Henry IV*, blessed beyond all else with a true view of himself, would of course have known better; and it appears that though the new Falstaff comes dangerously close he does not even here quite sink among those who lack perspective on themselves. Bottom, Dogberry, and Malvolio require no fooling to be fooled; Malvolio imagines himself Olivia's husband even before Maria practises on him: 'Calling my officers about me, in my branch'd velvet gown, having come from a day-bed, where I have left Olivia sleeping. . . .' It is Maria's observation of his lack of perspective that determines the nature of her practice: 'the best persuaded of himself, so cramm'd, as he thinks, with excellencies, that it is his grounds of faith that all that look on him love him; and on that vice in him will my revenge find notable cause to work.' Malvolio's fantasies are spoken in soliloquy, hence cannot be meant to impress anyone but himself. But Falstaff's expectations of the wives' persons and purses áre first told to Pistol and Nym—and it was always his fashion to *boast* to his followers, and to Hal, even when he saw that no one really believed him. It is perhaps the old Falstaff who speaks here:

O, she did so course o'er my exteriors with such a greedy intention, that the
appetite of her eye did seem to scorch me up like a burning-glass!

(I. iii. 72–74.)

This, and the rest of it—'Page's wife . . . even now gave me good
eyes too, examin'd my parts with most judicious oeillades: sometimes the beam of her view gilded my foot, sometimes my portly
belly'—is conscious bragging to an audience that must especially
be impressed just now, when Falstaff, 'almost out at heels', must
dismiss his followers. Never reluctant to undertake an enterprise—
or at least to make a show of doing so—he writes letters to the
wives: 'We will thrive, lads, we will thrive.' Whatever, if any, were
his true expectations, they were evidently different from those that
are aroused when Mistress Quickly reports that the wives dote on
him and desire an immediate appointment. 'This news distracts me!'
he shouts. His surprise at the turn of events makes it plain that he
is deceived, not self-deceived.

Falstaff's third interview, with Ford in the character of 'Brook',
marks the true beginning of exploitation made possible by the
earlier elaborate preparation. Here, though his position is inferior
to Ford's, he remains deceived rather than self-deceived. Though
victim of both Ford's and the wives' practices, he is less a victim of
his own blindness than is Ford. Ford, holding advantage only in
that he knows his own identity, is victim of that sometimes-tragic
brand of self-deception, horn-madness, which blinds and nearly
destroys Leontes of *A Winter's Tale* and does destroy Othello.
With Ford, however, the consequence is only comic; nothing more
serious results than spectacular flashes, when irony, darting about
the heads of the deceived and the self-deceived, lights two gaps,
that between us and Falstaff and that between us and Ford:

Fal. Master Brook, I will first make bold with your money; next, give me
your hand; and last, as I am a gentleman, you shall, if you will, enjoy Ford's
wife.
Ford. O good sir!
Fal. I say you shall.
Ford. Want no money, Sir John; you shall want none.
Fal. Want no Mistress Ford, Master Brook, you shall want none.

(Ibid. 262–71.)

Irony, the most spectacular but not always the finest effect of
exploitation of discrepant awarenesses, is the sole effect of this interview, as, indeed, it is of most scenes in *The Merry Wives of Windsor*. The conscious irony of Ford—'Do you know Ford, sir'—
flashes from the one side; the unconscious irony of Falstaff—'Hang
him, poor cuckoldly knave! I know him not'—flashes from the

other: and arching above both is the brighter flash from our knowledge that the speakers are alike ignorant of the wives' game. Both
men's ignorance is at once knowing and unknowing. Ford knows
his own identity and knows Falstaff's ignorance of it, but is horn-
mad, his jealousy groundless. Falstaff does not know Ford, does not
know the wives' intent—but remains the witting rogue who for
love of 'face' with others will boast of compassing anything: 'I will
use her as the key of the cuckoldly rogue's coffer; and there's my
harvest-home. . . . I will predominate over the peasant, and thou
shalt lie with his wife.' In short, Falstaff's boast to 'Brook' is of the
same stripe as his boast to Pistol and Nym.

Act III, ii, makes the final preparation for the first climactic
scene, which immediately follows. Ford, horn-mad, ignorant that
his interview with Falstaff has discovered the truth only as Falstaff
knows it, gains false confirmation of his false belief when he encounters Mrs. Page with Falstaff's little page: 'Has Page any brains?
Hath he any eyes? Hath he any thinking? Sure, they sleep; he hath
no use of them.' Hurrying homeward with the expectation of surprising his wife, he invites Page, Caius, and Sir Hugh to accompany
him: 'Besides your cheer, you shall have sport; I shall show you a
monster.' We hardly needed this scene, since we knew very well
that Ford meant to surprise his wife with Falstaff. But in the interval
between 'Brook's' interview with Falstaff and the buck-basket
scene stand two scenes relating to the pursuit of Anne Page; hence,
making assurance doubly sure as usual, that we shall let no part of
our advantage lie unused, Shakespeare has given a scene to show
that Ford's homecoming is imminent. By placing this scene immediately to precede the buck-basket scene, he makes certain that one
more level of awareness is available, besides the several already
established for exploitation in the climactic scene. The wives intend
only to make Falstaff *suppose* that Ford is approaching—and to this
end, with Mrs. Page entering on cue while Falstaff hides behind the
arras, they play the roles they have rehearsed:

> *Mrs. Ford.* Why, alas, what's the matter?
> *Mrs. Page.* Your husband's coming hither, woman, with all the officers in
> Windsor, to search for a gentleman that he says is here now in the house by
> your consent, to take an ill advantage of his absence. You are undone.
> *Mrs. Ford.* 'Tis not so, I hope.
> *Mrs. Page.* Pray heaven it be not so, that you have such a man here, but 'tis
> most certain your husband's coming, with half Windsor at his heels, to search
> for such a one.   (III. iii. 112–22.)

Quickly stuffed into the buck-basket and covered with foul linen,
Falstaff lies in profound darkness: entering the house, he had been

ignorant that Mrs. Page watched from her hiding-place while he made overtures to Mrs. Ford; hiding behind the arras when Mrs. Page's arrival was announced, he was ignorant that she knew of his presence; now, gratefully hidden in the basket, he remains ignorant that all is a practice of the wives and that his immediate fate is a drenching in the Thames. On top of all, he is ignorant that Ford, now roaring just outside the basket, is that very 'Brook' to whom he had himself divulged the secret of his assignation. On the next level of awareness is Ford, ignorant that Falstaff is in the basket and that what he has interrupted is a virtuous practice designed by a virtuous wife, but aware from his interview with Falstaff that something is certainly up. On the next level above are Page, Caius, and Sir Hugh, who—in their complete ignorance that anything at all is up except Ford's jealous temper—are actually nearer the truth than either Falstaff or Ford. On the next level are the wives, aware that Falstaff is in the basket and that their own prank is virtuous. But on the topmost level, from the beginning of the scene until Ford rushes in, are we alone, Shakespeare having taken double care to inform us that Ford is *really* approaching while the wives are busily *pretending* that he is. The cream of the jest is the wives', but the cream of the cream, as usual, is ours. At Ford's arrival, it is true, the wives rise almost to our level.

Mrs. Page. Is there not a double excellency in this?
Mrs. Ford. I know not which pleases me better, that my husband is deceived, or Sir John. (Ibid. 187–90.)

—but not quite, for they remain ignorant of Ford's masquerade as 'Brook':

Ford. I cannot find him. May be the knave bragg'd of that he could not compass.
Mrs. Page. (*Aside to Mrs. Ford.*) Heard you that? (Ibid. 211–14.)

Since the main action is shown in six scenes of the repeated duping of Falstaff, a major dramatic problem of *The Merry Wives of Windsor* was evidently that of achieving variation within repetition. The three interviews of Falstaff and 'Brook' are, respectively, preliminaries to the three scenes in which Falstaff is victimized twice by the wives and finally by all Windsor. Though he keeps Falstaff always at the bottom and though the results of exploitation during these scenes are always flashes of comic irony, Shakespeare finds variation most notably by shuffling the awarenesses above Falstaff's level. In the second Falstaff–'Brook' interview (III. v) the variation is slight. Falstaff, as before, is ignorant of 'Brook's' identity and of the fact that the wives' primary intent with the buck-basket device had been to dupe him rather than Ford; and Ford, as before, is ignorant that his wife's purpose is virtuous. The scene varies from the first interview in that both men recognize and speak much more truth, though neither understands it wholly. Falstaff tells truth when—ignorant that 'Brook' was present—he describes the buck-basket incident. Having witnessed the incident, 'Brook' perceives that Falstaff is telling the truth—but during the first twenty-five lines of this interview, not knowing that Falstaff was in the basket— he supposes that Falstaff is ignorant of it. It is, of course, Ford who profits most from the interview, since Falstaff divulges secrets of both past and future: 'Her husband is this morning gone a-birding. I have received from her another embassy of meeting. 'Twixt eight and nine is the hour, Master Brook.' But though he learns truth, its actual effect on Ford is to remove him even farther from truth by seeming to confirm his false belief: 'Master Ford, awake! awake! Master Ford! there's a hole made in your best coat, Master Ford. This 'tis to be married! This 'tis to have linen and buck-baskets!'

In the second climactic scene, which parallels the first about as closely as the second interview does the first, the principal variation is in our own view. In the former scene our vision was superior even to that of the wives, who pretended that Ford was approaching while we knew him really to be coming. During the first ninety lines of the present scene we have no reason to suppose that the arrangement is other than before—that is, that we know and the wives do not that Ford is really approaching. Falstaff having hidden himself, the dialogue that follows seems to us like a practice staged to frighten him:

> *Mrs. Page.* How now, sweetheart! Who's at home besides yourself?
> *Mrs. Ford.* Why, none but mine own people.
> *Mrs. Page.* Indeed!
> *Mrs. Ford.* No, certainly. (*Aside to her.*) Speak louder. (IV. ii. 12–16.)

'How near is he, Mistress Page?' asks Mrs. Ford loudly. 'Hard by; at street end. He will be here anon.' It is nearly fifty lines later, after Falstaff has gone upstairs to put on the witch of Brainford's dress, that we learn of our own error:

> *Mrs. Page.* Heaven guide him to thy husband's cudgel, and the devil guide his cudgel afterwards!
> *Mrs. Ford.* But is my husband coming?
> *Mrs. Page.* Ay, in good sadness, is he; and talks of the basket too, howsoever he hath had intelligence. (Ibid. 90–95.)

Until this moment we have not known that Mrs. Page shares our awareness of Ford's approach. Just how she learned is unexplained. Immediately before the opening of the scene she was shown on the street with Sir Hugh and little William; possibly, then, she had seen Ford approaching with her husband 'and the rest of their company'. In any event, for nearly 100 lines the disposition of awarenesses differs from that in the earlier climactic scene: Mrs. Ford's level is equal to ours in that both she and we suppose Mrs. Page to be only play-acting when she warns of Ford's approach; our level is superior to Mrs. Ford's because we know Ford really is coming; but it is inferior to Mrs. Page's in that we do not know that she knows what we know. This intricate little snarl in the awarenesses serves one shrewd purpose: it makes possible a second use of the buck-basket, this time as a practice on Ford alone. Thus Mrs. Ford, as soon as Mrs. Page has advised her of Ford's approach:

Go, sirs, take the basket again on your shoulders. Your master is hard at door. If he bid you set it down, obey him. Quickly, dispatch. (Ibid. 110–13.)

Had Mrs. Page not known that Ford was really at the door, the empty buck-basket incident, which adds much to the business of the scene, would have been impossible. As the scene stands, Ford is twice the victim of practices, wrongly expecting Falstaff to be in the basket, and failing, in his frenzy—'Why, this is lunatics! This is mad as a mad dog!'—to suspect that he might be in the witch of Brainford's dress. Except that he is disgracefully routed and beaten, Falstaff might be thought to come off somewhat better than Ford in the action.

Before the final Falstaff–'Brook' interview, a major adjustment is made in the disposition of awarenesses. The wives' secret, hitherto shared with us alone, is opened to Page and Ford—and, indeed, to all Windsor except Falstaff. The correction of Ford's fault is now complete and, in turn, Ford opens the secret of 'Brook' to all but Falstaff and announces that the device will serve once more: 'Nay, I'll to him again in name of Brook. / He'll tell me all his purpose.' The third interview is really unnecessary to the final practice on Falstaff, since Mistress Quickly, ubiquitous and indefatigable busybody, bears 'half Windsor's' message inviting the knight to the party at Herne's oak. Nevertheless, though brief and non-essential, the interview is noteworthy for its variation of the pattern already twice used. Before, 'Brook' was as ignorant of the underlying truth —the wives' practice—as was Falstaff. Now, 'Brook' knows all and Falstaff nothing—of 'Brook's identity or of all Windsor's plot against him. In the first interview Falstaff could give 'Brook' startling information about his coming assignation with Mrs. Ford; in the second, he could divulge the means by which he had evaded Ford and could also give news of his second assignation with Mrs.

Ford. But in the final meeting Falstaff can tell 'Brook' nothing not already better known to Ford:

> That same knave Ford, her husband, hath the finest mad devil of jealousy in him, Master Brook, that ever govern'd frenzy. I will tell you. He beat me grievously in the shape of a woman. . . . I'll tell you all, Master Brook. . . . I'll tell you strange things of this knave Ford, on whom to-night I will be revenged, and I will deliver his wife into your hand. Follow. Strange things in hand, Master Brook! Follow. (v. i. 18–32.)

Though the flashes here arch across only one discrepancy, between Falstaff's oblivion and Ford's new omniscience, the effect is spectacular, for it is the widest discrepancy in the play.

For the final climax in this comedy of successive climaxes, the disposition of awarenesses is the most complex Shakespeare had yet devised, and, except for the extraordinary structure in the last acts of *Cymbeline*, the most complex he was ever to devise in any work. The play's two lines of action converge in one busy moment:

> *Here they pinch* Falstaff *and sing about him.* Doctor Caius *comes one way, and steals away a boy in green;* Slender *another way, and takes a boy in white; and* Fenton *comes, and steals* Anne Page. *A noise of hunting is made within. All the Fairies run away.* Falstaff *pulls off his buck's head, and rises up.* (v. v, between 105 and 106.)

All persons of the play participate in this scene, and all but Falstaff, Mistress Quickly, Fenton, and Anne are involved as both deceivers and deceived: Falstaff serves only as victim, the other three only as practisers. Since the dramatist has required us to give our attention equally to the affairs of Falstaff and Anne Page in the closing scene, it is now appropriate to examine his handling of awarenesses in earlier scenes that pertain to the latter affair and lead to the convergence of the two lines.

All practices in the play that do not relate to Falstaff's affair relate to Anne's. Until the final scene, however, Anne herself plays no part in any intrigue, but is rather a destination than a participant. Until their convergence, the principal link between the two main lines is of course Mistress Quickly, at once the wives' instrument against Falstaff and proprietor of her own game with Anne's suitors, each of whom supposes that she uses her influence on Anne for him alone. Out of the lovers' competition grows Caius's challenge: 'You jack'nape, give-a this letter to Sir Hugh. By gar, it is a shallenge. I will cut his troat in de park.' And out of this challenge grows the Host's practice on both Caius and Sir Hugh; thus Shallow to Page: 'Will you go with us to behold it? My merry host hath had the measuring of their weapons, and, I think, hath appointed them contrary places.' During two scenes thereafter (II. iii; III. i) the unawareness of Caius and Sir Hugh, each awaiting the other's arrival at a wrong meeting-place, is the exploitable matter. 'I pray you,' says Caius to the Host, Shallow, Slender, and Page, the Host's accomplices, 'bear witness that me have stay six or seven, two, tree hours for him, and he is no come.' And while Caius waits in a field near Windsor, his rival waits in a field near Frogmore; thus Sir Hugh: 'How melancholies I am! I will knog his urinals about his knave's costard when I have good opportunities for the ork. Pless my soul!' It is Sir Hugh who first perceives the hoax: 'Pray you, let us not be laughing-stocks to other men's humours.' Before the scene ends, the Host's victims are devising a practice for revenge. Thus even the practice against the Host, involving the 'cozen-germans' who make off with his horses and keep his rooms empty of guests for a week, stems from the affair of Anne Page, and, therefore, from Mrs. Quickly's practice.

It should be mentioned, of course, that though discrepancies in awareness are indispensable conditions of action and effect in the scenes that involve Sir Hugh and Caius, exploitation of these discrepancies is not the sole source of comic effect in these scenes. The situations in which Sir Hugh and Caius stand ignorant of what we know, and of what their pranksters know, serve primarily as frames to set off these eccentrics' natural follies—which manifest themselves most conspicuously as linguistic peculiarities. Unquestionably the special circumstances which surround the display of these peculiarities enhance their comic force; Caius and Sir Hugh are at their linguistic best when they are put upon, abused, angry: 'By gar, you are de coward, de Jack dog, John ape', for the one, and, for the other, 'Pless my soul, how full of chollors I am, and trempling of mind!' The dialectal eccentricities are themselves specific manifestations of native unawareness, like Bottom's hairy head. The two principal scenes which exhibit Caius and Sir Hugh thus exploit simultaneously their ignorance of situation and their native condition, of which their speech is the conspicuous outward sign.

So far as Falstaff's affair is concerned, there are to be only two levels of awareness in the final scene—that of Falstaff and that of 'half Windsor', which is also ours. If the action concerned merely the duping of Falstaff, it would be simpler than in either of the preceding assignation scenes, which involved four levels and, briefly, even five. Such simplicity would hardly serve for a final climactic scene, the less so since the duping of Falstaff has already been twice represented. What saves the third representation from anti-climactic repetition is the masterful fusion of the affairs of Falstaff and Anne.

That this is a superbly wrought fusion there can be no question. Shakespeare nowhere exhibits greater technical skill in composing a whole and single thing out of myriad and disparate parts. Anne's winning and Falstaff's conclusive duping meet in one design of action, over which presides a giddy Prospero, 'that foolish carrion', Mistress Quickly, as Fairy Queen. The care of the dramatist to pack our minds with preparatory information, to direct our gaze so that it will sweep every corner of the complex array of elements, and to prod our awareness so that it will not nod and miss something is noteworthy. We are first advised in detail of the final practice on Falstaff, who will be invited to meet the wives at Herne's oak at midnight, wearing horns; thus Mrs. Page:

> Nan Page (my daughter) and my little son
> And three or four more of their growth we'll dress
> Like urchins, ouphes, and fairies, green and white,
> With rounds of waxen tapers on their heads,
> And rattles in their hands. Upon a sudden,
> As Falstaff, she, and I are newly met,
> Let them from forth a sawpit rush at once
> With some diffused song. Upon their sight,
> We two in great amazedness will fly.
> Then let them all encircle him about
> And, fairy-like, to pinch the unclean knight,
> And ask him why, that hour of fairy revel,
> In their so sacred paths he dares to tread shape profane.
>   (IV. iv. 47–59.)

This time there is to be no misunderstanding among husbands, wives, and friends—at least so far as Falstaff's duping is concerned. But there is to be great misunderstanding, created by practices and counter-practices, about the winning of Anne. By means of half a dozen lines strategically placed, Shakespeare at once binds the two matters of the final scene together and enormously complicates the pattern of awarenesses:

> *Mrs. Page.* My Nan shall be the queen of all the fairies,
>   Finely attired in a robe of white.
> *Page.*   That silk will I go buy. (*Aside.*) And in that time
>   Shall Master Slender steal my Nan away
>   And marry her at Eton.
>   (Ibid. 71–75.)

We are to share with Page an advantage over Mrs. Page; but we are also to share with Mrs. Page an advantage over Page:

Mrs. Page. Go, Mistress Ford,
  Send Quickly to Sir John, to know his mind.
                      (*Exit Mrs. Ford.*)
  I'll to the doctor; he hath my good will,
  And none but he, to marry with Nan Page.
                      (Ibid. 82–85.)

The eyes of 'half Windsor' are to be fixed on Falstaff—for 'half Windsor' knows nothing of what else is afoot. *But the dramatist fixes our own eyes on Anne Page.* We have seen Falstaff gulled and abused twice before, when his gulling was central; the variation of the pattern for the final scene is thus drastic and bold. We are to note Falstaff, of course, and all the 'urchins, ouphes, and fairies, green and white', but all this spectacle—the pageantry of fairies with song and dance, and the fat knight himself, disguised as Herne, with huge horns on his head—will appear in our perspective as setting for the main event, the elopement of Anne.

For the final scene the topmost level, matching ours, is Fenton's. Page and Slender do not know that Mrs. Page and Caius plot the abduction of Anne; Mrs. Page and Caius do not know of the rival plan for Slender to steal Anne. But Fenton knows of both plots, and also of the plot against Falstaff. It is through Fenton's conversation with the Host—still gasping from the abuse of the 'cozen-germans' —that Shakespeare directs our eyes beyond 'half Windsor's', which are fixed on Falstaff; thus Fenton:

> Her father means she shall be all in white,
> And in that habit, when Slender sees his time
> To take her by the hand and bid her go,
> She shall go with him. Her mother hath intended,
> The better to denote her to the doctor,
> For they must all be mask'd and vizarded,
> That quaint in green she shall be loose enrob'd,
> With ribands pendent, flaring 'bout her head.
>   (Ibid. 35–42.)

'Which means she to deceive, father or mother?' asks the Host, and Fenton's answer puts the cap to the structure: 'Both, my good host, to go along with me.' While 'half Windsor' deceives Falstaff, some members of the group, notably Page and Slender, Mrs. Page and Caius, intend to deceive one another; and while they are doing so Fenton will deceive them all: this is the fact which has been set in the front of our awareness. While 'half Windsor' watches Falstaff, while Page and Slender seek for a figure in white, while Mrs. Page and Caius look for one in green—we are instructed to watch for Anne herself.

Fenton's conversation with the Host reviews all parts of the situation in meticulous detail and would seem adequate preparation; the scene might proceed immediately. But Shakespeare rarely cuts off preparation at the point of mere adequacy. We do not, therefore, go at once to the elaborately intertwined spectacle of Falstaff's duping and Anne's abduction, but are conducted by stages, through four quick scenes which together review yet again every aspect of the complex situation and make assurance not doubly but triply sure that nothing will escape our understanding. In v. i the third interview of Falstaff and 'Brook' reasserts that Falstaff will be on hand, ignorant of the practice mounted against him, and that the action at Herne's oak will be spectacular: 'Follow. Strange things in hand, Master Brook! Follow.' The next scene, of only sixteen lines, reasserts that Page's favourite suitor, Slender, is to 'come to her in white, and cry "mum"; she cries "budget"; and by that we know one another'. This scene reminds us also that Page is ignorant of Mrs. Page's intent to have Anne stolen by Caius; and, finally, before the sixteen lines are done, we are once more reminded that the plot against Falstaff goes forward: 'Heaven prosper our sport! No man means evil but the devil, and we shall know him by his horns.' Act V, iii, only twenty-six lines, reminds us of Mrs. Page's plot:

Mrs. Page. Master Doctor, my daughter is in green. When you see your time, take her by the hand, away with her to the deanery, and dispatch it quickly. Go before into the park; we two must go together.
Caius. I know vat I have to do. Adieu. (v. iii. 1–6.)

This scene reminds us explicitly also of Mrs. Page's ignorance of her husband's plot: 'My husband will not rejoice so much at the abuse of Falstaff as he will chafe at the doctor's marrying my daughter.' And at the same time, obviously, it reminds yet once again of the practice on Falstaff:

Mrs. Ford. We'll betray him finely.
Mrs. Page. Against such lewdsters and their lechery
Those that betray them do no treachery.
(Ibid. 22–24.)

Moreover, both this and the preceding scene exploit the gap between the Pages' ignorance and our knowledge of Fenton's plan to deceive both husband and wife. The two glimpses of the Pages exhibit the intricate pattern of their awarenesses: both hold advantage over Falstaff, each holds advantage over the other, each is at the same time at disadvantage in relation to the other, and both are at a disadvantage in relation to Fenton.

The fourth and final preparatory scene immediately precedes the

entrance of Falstaff 'with a buck's head upon him'. It is a scene of
four lines, showing the fairy crew, led by Sir Hugh, himself disguised as a fairy, nearing Windsor Park:

> Trib, trib, fairies; come; and remember your parts. Be pold, I pray you.
> Follow me into the pit, and when I give the watch-'ords, do as I pid you.
> Come, come; trib, trib.   (v. iv. 1–4.)

This is the crew whose singing, dancing, and pinching will provide
Falstaff's final lesson, and it accords with Shakespeare's usual method
that we see them in the instant before we see the knight.

Together the four scenes make Shakespeare's most elaborate set
of directions for witnessing a single scene. So familiar have we been
made in advance that the action itself may look like something
already seen. But with every movement known beforehand, our
minds are free to contemplate the complex cross-play of awarenesses for which the fantastic rout of fairies, ouphes, and elves, great
and small, with their song and dance, is the setting. First comes Falstaff, entering on the midnight tolling of Windsor bell; appearing
immediately after the four scenes that have gone over and over the
situation, he stands in an appallingly un-Falstaffian light:

> Now, the hot-blooded gods assist me! Remember, Jove, thou wast a bull for
> thy Europa; love set on thy horns. O powerful love! that, in some respects,
> makes a beast a man, in some other, a man a beast. . . . Send me a cool rut-time,
> Jove. . . .   (v. v. 2–15.)

The Falstaffian wit—'A fault done first in the form of a beast. O
Jove, a beastly fault! And then another fault in the semblance of
a fowl; think on't, Jove; a foul fault!'—here equal to that which
once delighted Prince Hal, strikes with an incongruous sound. To
be compelled to display so fine a faculty in a moment when he is as
unaware of his situation as a Bardolph, a Dogberry, or an Aguecheek: this is Falstaff's fate in *The Merry Wives of Windsor*. Magnificently self-aware, Falstaff was once Shakespeare's great example
of the mind that most contrasts with the unknowing intellect of
Bottom and his successors. And the quality of his wit never showed
better than now, as he addresses the wives: 'Divide me like a brib'd
buck, each a haunch. I will keep my sides to myself, my shoulders
for the fellow of this walk, and my horns I bequeath your husbands.'
And again, at the sound of the fairies' approach: 'I think the devil
will not have me damn'd, lest the oil that's in me should set hell on
fire; he would never else cross me thus.' These are brilliant, even for
Falstaff. But even while his wit shoots sparks and flashes as of old,
every line he speaks betrays woeful ignorance of the immediate
situation; and all the while he speaks the buck's horns atop his head

render this same ignorance palpable. The ass's head on Bottom's shoulders signifies his native condition; the addition is not incongruous, being a projection of what is within. But Falstaff's horns are a monstrous contradiction. At the lowest point of his disgrace, as he lies flat, swarmed over by ouphes and elves, his wit flashes as of old: 'Heavens defend me from that Welsh fairy, lest he transform me to a piece of cheese!' It is almost, but, alas, not quite, as if he saw through the whole trick and feigned ignorance to delight his tormentors, as he used to do with Hal. Indeed, when at last his disillusionment comes, Ford and the wives having cast their last barbs into his sides, he comes near to claiming as much: 'I was three or four times in the thought they were not fairies.' But he does not press the claim: 'See now how wit may be made a Jack-a-Lent, when 'tis upon ill employment!'

The worse employment, if legend is true, was neither Falstaff's nor Shakespeare's, but the Queen's. To be required to show Falstaff in love was to be required to make him somebody's fool. 'Who cannot be crush'd with a plot?' asks Parolles in *All's Well that Ends Well*. In *Much Ado about Nothing* Shakespeare had already put down with a plot, but not crushed, a fine pair of wits, Benedick and Beatrice. The answer to Parolles's question is that *even Falstaff can be crushed with a plot—if the Queen commands*. Indeed, had Elizabeth lived to order some special sequel to *The Tempest*, Shakespeare might have crushed Prospero himself. 'Have I laid my brain in the sun and dri'd it, that it wants matter to prevent so gross o'erreaching as this?' The crushing of Falstaff is a fault in nature. Shakespeare does his best to save him by preserving his native wit. Moreover, he has shrewdly saved the most dazzling display of this wit for those moments when the man is most deceived in his situation. But the Queen's terms—if there were such—were impossible: a wonderfully circumspect man, of great wit, who is exhibited in a moment of deep unawareness, cannot look other than foolish at last.

If the incongruous spectacle is painful to us, it must have been infinitely more so to Falstaff's creator. The fairies who pinch the great man fallen in Windsor Park are sometimes taken as a compliment to Queen Elizabeth; but it is possible to take them quite otherwise. Despite all the preparation the dramatist makes for the final scene—packing our minds with detail, conspicuously illuminating the several gaps between the participants' vision and ours, repeatedly reviewing each aspect of the situation, going over everything again and again—one monumental surprise looms up at last. It is one which could so easily have been avoided as to occasion suspicion that it may have been deliberate—and in that case it is the more conspicuous because it is one of very few surprises in all the plays. Sweet Anne Page was to have been Queen: her mother said so, her father said so, *even Fenton said so*, whose design capped those of the parents and who gave us the final word on the matter. Our minds were conditioned, our eyes trained to catch sight of this sweet girl; a rare one even among Shakespeare's heroines of comedy, 'loose enrob'd, / With ribands pendent, flaring 'bout her head', whether all in white, as her father planned, or quaint in green after her mother's wish, or in some other colour as her lover directed— but in any event presenting the Fairy Queen, exquisite compliment to a mortal one. Instead, suddenly and shockingly, leading a fairy rout that includes Sir Hugh as a Satyr, Pistol as Hobgoblin, and no telling what rabble else, appears that sly old schemer, ubiquitous busybody, double and triple dealer, Mistress Quickly. She it is who first directs the gang of ouphes to make Windsor Castle 'Worthy the owner, and the owner it'—an equivocal utterance—and then sets them at the torment of Falstaff, which but completes a humiliation that was inevitable from the moment it was commanded that he fall in love: 'About him, fairies; sing a scornful rhyme; / And, as you trip, still pinch him to your time.'

The shock of seeing Mistress Quickly instead of Sweet Anne Page might have been avoided by but one sentence spoken by Fenton before the action. The dramatist's extraordinary care to inform us in advance of the action—indeed, to describe the whole scene in detail for us beforehand—argues against an oversight. Mistress Quickly can be only a deliberate surprise. Moreover, the pains taken in preparing the scene makes this surprise the more conspicuous—like something suddenly gone dreadfully wrong in a well-rehearsed and otherwise flawless performance. It is the more startling, finally, because it contradicts Shakespeare's regular method: there is only one other clearly deliberate surprise in all the plays, the restoration of Hermione in *The Winter's Tale*. Coming as such a surprise, in such a setting, Mistress Quickly, more hag than queen, may be taken as a left-handed compliment, well deserved by her who had condemned Falstaff, of the race of Rosalind and Prospero, to play the role of Bottom.

CHAPTER IV

The Fruits of the Sport: *Twelfth Night*

Much Ado about Nothing presents a powerful climactic scene during which exploitation of the gap between the participants' and our understanding yields multiple, conflicting effects that touch both joy and pain. *As You Like It* presents an extraordinary heroine, whose native brilliance, supplemented by disguise, gives her advantage in her world and places her with the fairies, heroines, and dukes who are landmarks on the road to Prospero. *The Merry Wives of Windsor* moves swiftly and riotously on a massive but precise machinery of practices and counter-practices in which each movement exhibits the dramatist's mastery of his favoured comic method. Yet each play lacks a virtue or two of the others: the first lacks a Rosalind to command its world—for Beatrice is a bystander; the second has no complex dramatic moment in which exploitation of discrepant awarenesses precipitates a war of contradictory emotions; the third lacks both the first's rich and moving moment and the second's superb heroine. Each thus achieves only a part of the artistic wholeness of *Twelfth Night*, with its scenes that rival the greatly moving moment of *Much Ado* in that play's special virtue of conflicting effects, its heroine who surpasses Rosalind in femininity and rivals her in awareness—though hardly in control—of her world; its rich pattern of practices, cunningly interwoven, of which the multiplicity of strands and the workmanship rival those of *The Merry Wives*.

In the world of *Twelfth Night*, as in the worlds of the comedies just preceding, the spirit of the practiser prevails. Seven of the principal persons are active practisers, and they operate six devices. All action turns on these, and the effects of the play arise from exploitation of the gaps they open. During all but the first two of eighteen scenes we have the advantage of some participant; in seven—an unusually high proportion—we hold advantage over all who take part. In the course of the action, every named person takes a turn below our vantage-point, and below the vantage-point of some other person or persons: in this play neither heroine nor clown is wholly spared. Although Viola shares the great secret with us alone, Shakespeare early establishes our vantage-point above hers, and once even makes her the unwitting victim of another's practice. Although Feste is either 'in' on most practices or unaffected by them, he, with all Illyria, is ignorant of the main secret of the play, the identity of 'Cesario'. Here, then, even heroine and clown stand below us, and below them the others range down to the bottom, where sit Aguecheek and Malvolio in chronic oblivion. Though also victims of others' practices, neither needs deceiving to be deceived—Nature having practised on them once for all.

But if all are exposed at some time in ignorance of their situations, yet all but Orsino and Malvolio have compensatory moments when they overpeer others: even Aguecheek, though a fool the while, briefly enjoys advantage over Malvolio. The awarenesses in *Twelfth Night* are so structured that an overpeerer gloating in his advantage is usually himself overpeered by another participant or by us: thus Sir Toby exults in his advantage over 'Cesario', knowing that Sir Andrew is not the 'devil in a private brawl' he would have 'Cesario' believe—but at the same time 'Cesario' holds advantage over him in knowing that 'Cesario' is a fiction; and the last laugh is ours, on Sir Toby, for even he would hardly have made his jest of a duel had he known 'Cesario' truly. From much use of such arrangements, in which a participant's understanding is inferior with respect to some elements of a situation and superior with respect to others, emerge the richest effects of *Twelfth Night* and some of the finest in Shakespeare.

Of the six practices, the central one is of course the heroine's masquerade. It is the longest, and, in its relations with the play as a whole, the most important such masquerade in the comedies. Julia's practice in *The Two Gentlemen of Verona* affects only two important scenes, and the only person whose ignorance of it is exploited is Proteus. Rosalind's impersonation of 'Ganymede' in *As You Like It* lasts longer than Julia's, but it, too, is exploited in only two major scenes, and the only victims whose ignorance of it greatly matters are Orlando and Phebe. Portia's disguise in *The Merchant of Venice* is worn during only one act, and its consequences furnish the substance of another. Helena's masquerade in *All's Well that Ends Well* makes the central incident of the plot, but its only victim is Bertram. Imogen's practice in *Cymbeline*, though it yields spectacular effects in the climactic moments, is one among a multitude of intrigues in that play. But the force of Viola's masquerade in *Twelfth Night* prevails in all but the opening scenes and relates to every incident and person. Though it most affects two victims,

Viola's is truly a practice on the whole world of Illyria, as Duke Vincentio's is on the world of *Measure for Measure*, and as, in tragedy, Iago's is on his world and as Hamlet's antic disposition is on the whole world of Denmark. Viola rightly belongs in this company of most notable masqueraders in all the plays.

Viola takes up her masquerade with somewhat less urgency and altruism than moved Portia, but with somewhat more of both than moved Rosalind to perpetrate her fraud in the Forest of Arden. Washed up on the shore of Illyria, she goes to work at once. Quickly ascertaining the name of the place, the name of its ruler, and the fact that he is still a bachelor, she makes up her mind:

> I'll serve this duke.
> Thou shalt present me as an eunuch to him.
> It may be worth thy pains, for I can sing
> And speak to him in many sorts of music
> That will allow me very worth his service.
> What else may hap, to time I will commit,
> Only shape thou thy silence to my wit.
> (I. ii. 55–61.)

This speech creates at one stroke the discrepancy in awarenesses which will endure until the closing moments of the play, giving advantage to us and disadvantage to all Illyria. And as swiftly as he creates the gap, Shakespeare begins its exploitation. When next we see Viola, in man's attire, after three days at Orsino's court and already his favourite, Valentine's remarks give first expression to the general Illyrian error:

> If the Duke continue these favours towards you, Cesario, you are like to be much advanc'd. He hath known you but three days, and already you are no stranger.　　　　　　　　　　　　　　　　　　　　　　　　(I. iv. 1–4.)

But a stranger, of course, this 'Cesario' is to the Duke, and to all others. The Duke's unawareness is next exploited: 'Cesario,' he says, 'thou know'st no less but all'—and so she does, more than he dreams. When Orsino directs her to bear his lovesuit to Olivia, his remarks come near enough to strike sparks from the truth, and these flashes of irony are the first to result from the great discrepancy:

> . . . they shall yet belie thy happy years,
> That say thou art a man. Diana's lip
> Is not more smooth and rubious; thy small pipe
> Is as the maiden's organ, shrill and sound;
> And all is semblative a woman's part.
> (Ibid. 30–34.)

As the scene ends, the basic exploitable gap is opened wider; says Viola,

> I'll do my best
> To woo your lady,—(*aside*) yet, a barful strife!
> Whoe'er I woo, myself would be his wife.
>
> (Ibid. 40–42.)

As suddenly as her adoption of disguise created the first discrepancy, this confession creates a second. Henceforth her advantage, and ours, over the Duke is double: the secret of her right identity and the secret of her love.

The first major clash of the discrepant awarenesses of Viola and Illyria occurs, however, not in the Duke's court but in Olivia's house. Before meeting the recluse, Viola has encountered, in succession, Maria, Sir Toby, and Malvolio, who must be accounted first in the household to fall victims of her disguise even though the meetings are only reported; thus Malvolio: 'Not yet old enough for a man, nor young enough for a boy; as a squash is before 'tis a peascod, or a codling when 'tis almost an apple.' But the principal exploitation occurs in the interview with Olivia, whose attitude changes in the course of 100 lines from haughty scorn to flirtatious interest and finally to love. The effect of exploitation of the difference between our understanding and Olivia's is here not merely comic, although that is certainly part of the total. Though the play is not yet a full act old, the dramatist has already packed our minds with so much that simple laughter is an inadequate response. In this respect the meeting with Olivia contrasts with the comparable incident in *As You Like It*, when Phebe falls in love with 'Ganymede', and the contrast becomes even more marked in the later interviews of Viola with Olivia and with Orsino, which we are required to watch with minds packed with sympathy that forestalls laughter.

Until the end of this scene, when Olivia, moved by a passion she thinks futile to resist—not knowing how futile it is to succumb—dispatches Malvolio to run after 'that same peevish messenger' and give him a ring—'He left this ring behind him / Would I or not'—Shakespeare has established only two levels of awareness. These are Viola's, shared with us, and all Illyria's ignorance of 'Cesario's' identity. Two levels sufficed in *As You Like It*, even during the climactic scenes, when Rosalind's view is equivalent to ours and Orlando's represents that of all the Forest. But this relative simplicity is abruptly abandoned at the opening of Act II in *Twelfth Night* with the introduction of Sebastian. The instant effect of Sebastian's appearance, safe and sound on the very coast where Viola had inquired 'What country, friends, is this?' and been advised 'This is Illyria, lady' is the creation of a third level, a vantage-point above

Viola's, to be held by ourselves alone until the end of Act III—and possibly but not probably until the last moments of Act V.

The placement of the scene informing us of Sebastian's survival and immediate destination—'I am bound to the Count Orsino's court'—is a notable example of Shakespeare's way of handling the awarenesses. It is the more significant for being conspicuously early in the action, and the more conspicuous for its rather awkward interruption of the expected sequence of incident. Our notification of his rescue and arrival in Illyria might readily have been post-poned until Act IV, when, in front of Olivia's house, the Clown mistakes Sebastian for 'Cesario'. Or he might have been introduced inconspicuously between almost any two scenes in either Act II or Act III. Instead, he is thrust between Viola's departure from Olivia's house and her meeting with Malvolio on the street. Ordinarily, no scene would intervene in this space, as is demonstrable many times over in the plays. The closest parallel occurs in *The Merchant of Venice*. At the end of the court scene Bassanio sends Gratiano to overtake Portia and give her a ring; the very next scene shows Portia and Nerissa on the street, overtaken by Gratiano after Portia has spoken only four lines to mark the passage of an appropriate period of time. In contrast, the introduction of Sebastian splits the sequence with a scene of some fifty lines that entails also a shift from the vicinity of Olivia's house to the sea-coast. From the first history play onward, Shakespeare's method avoided violence to the normal order of action unless there was something special to be gained. By the time of *Twelfth Night*, certainly, the only disruptions of sequence are calculated ones. In the present case the dramatist evidently wished us to learn as early as possible that Sebastian is alive, and, more precisely, to learn it *just before Viola discovers that Olivia has fallen in love with her*.

In short, Sebastian's introduction is our assurance that all is well and will end well, an assurance which contradicts Viola's distress on recognizing what seems a hopeless entanglement:

> She loves me, sure. . . . If it be so, as 'tis,
> Poor lady, she were better love a dream.
> Disguise, I see thou art a wickedness
> Wherein the pregnant enemy does much.
> (II. ii. 23–29.)

When we saw her leave Olivia's house, her vantage-point was ours. Now, overtaken by Malvolio—who is himself wrapped in fourfold ignorance—she has slipped below, for we have seen Sebastian. She is nevermore quite the match of Rosalind, who overpeered all and was never overpeered. Yet her mind is packed with almost as much

understanding as ours: she realizes, by the ring that Olivia, ignorant
of 'Cesario's' sex, has fallen in love; she recognizes that Malvolio,
besides being a fool, is ignorant also of her sex and of his mistress's
meaning in sending the ring; and certainly she observes irony's
bright flashes about his head when, with intolerable condescension,
he announces that Olivia has commanded 'Cesario' to come no more
'unless it be to report your lord's taking of this'—thereupon tossing
Olivia's, not Orsino's, ring on the ground. But her mind is chiefly
on Orsino and his oblivion, which includes ignorance of her identity, of her love for him, and of the fact that just now his beloved
has given her heart to 'Cesario':

> My master loves her dearly;
> And I, poor monster, fond as much on him;
> And she, mistaken, seems to dote on me.
> What will become of this?
>
> (Ibid. 34–37.)

By making Viola voice dismay for the several matters that burden
her awareness, Shakespeare bids our own be alert; he comes as near
as a dramatist can to saying: 'Bear this in mind, and this, and yet
this.' He prods our remembrance also with utterances that illuminate the newly opened gap between our understanding and
Viola's:

> As I am woman,—now alas the day!—
> What thriftless sighs shall poor Olivia breathe!
>
> (Ibid. 39–40.)

And, finally:

> O time! thou must untangle this, not I.
> It is too hard a knot for me t' untie!
>
> (Ibid. 41–42.)

Viola's distress should be ours also—but we have just seen Sebastian,
in the shape of another 'Cesario', and his words still sound in our
ears: 'I am bound to the Count Orsino's court.' Olivia's sighs therefore need not be thriftless: the knot is looser than Viola thinks, and
time is, indeed, capable.

Sebastian's introduction is thus a strategic move, giving us assurance that all is and will be well. But it is also a tactical move, multiplying the possibilities of exploitation. Sebastian's unawareness—
exploitable the instant he appears on the sea-coast, weeping for a
'drowned' sister who is in fact doing quite well for herself in Illyria
—provides one such possibility. All Illyria's unawareness that Sebastian is not 'Cesario'—who, of course, is not 'Cesario' either—provides another. Add to these the possibilities already in existence,

including the main secret of Viola–'Cesario' and the subordinate ones born of Aguecheek's and Malvolio's chronic oblivions, and it is evident that by the start of Act II the exploitable potentiality is enormous.

Although Sebastian's appearance gives us advantage over Viola, her demotion is hardly damaging to her prestige as heroine and prime practiser. Her ignorance that her brother is at hand does not expose her to ridicule or pity, for the truth that she cannot see is better than the appearance. Though the heroines of comedy always look about them with a wider sweep of the eye than others enjoy, Shakespeare occasionally cuts off their view of a segment of the full circle; only Rosalind and Portia escape such limitation of their vision. Other heroines, though momentarily blind to some specific aspect of a situation, usually retain a commanding view of all else and in any event are spared exposure to laughter. Beatrice is an exception; but she is a secondary heroine, and besides, like Benedick's, her nature invites corrective effect. Later heroines, Isabella, Imogen, and Perdita, are blind to significant facts of their situations, but their ignorance does not make them vulnerable to laughter. Viola stands between these and Beatrice; she is caught in a condition of laughable unawareness during two incidents in Act III.

During Act II, however, except that she does not know about Sebastian, Viola escapes unawareness and enjoys an advantage over Orsino that matches Rosalind's over poor Orlando and Portia's over Bassanio. Indeed, her advantage grows during this period. When she left for her first interview with Olivia, Orsino was ignorant only of her identity. When she returns, he is still ignorant of that, of the fact that she loves him, that she is loved by Olivia, and that therefore his suit to Olivia is truly hopeless. His fourfold ignorance is the exploitable substance of the second Viola–Orsino interview. Shakespeare capitalizes the opportunity fully but tenderly, and the result is an artistic triumph. Lacking the complexity of some later scenes, in which stair-stepped levels of awareness provide the structure for dazzling cross-play, the scene nevertheless makes a powerful demand for simultaneous conflicting responses. Luxuriating in melancholy, loving love, affecting the agony of the disdained lover, feasting on music and song that aggravate his craving, Orsino stands naked to laughter—a foolish plight for a hero, like that into which Shakespeare previously thrust Orlando, rehearsing with 'Ganymede' his love for Rosalind.

Like Orlando's, then, a brutally ludicrous representation of romantic masculinity, Orsino's exposure should inspire roaring laughter. Yet as the scene moves on laughter becomes inappropriate and is perhaps finally made impossible by the force of a contradictory impulse. The latter force is enhanced by the music, song, and poetry of the scene—but its original stimulation is the presence of Viola, whose quality is as right for this moment as are the qualities of Rosalind and Orlando for their wooing scene. Whereas Orsino sees nothing, Viola sees too much; her mind is burdened with understanding. 'Thus far I will boldly publish her', said Sebastian; 'she bore a mind that envy could not but call fair.' If she could know that Sebastian lives, that the solution to her dilemma is even now on the road to Orsino's court, her distress would be lightened and the pain of the scene would be eased. Everything that she does know, beyond Orsino's knowledge, hurts her; and what she does not know—that the dramatist has taken care to have *us* know—hurts her also. Deliberately, with a psychologically shrewd manœuvre, Shakespeare has balanced our own awarenesses between laughter and pain.

These contradictory impulses, equal in power, stimulated by complex awarenesses, do not cancel each other out, leaving indifference; they battle for supremacy, and the intensity of their struggle determines the degree of our involvement. Shakespeare's way in the great scenes is to involve us deeply, by packing our minds with private awarenesses that confer a sense of personal responsibility toward the action.

> *Duke.* My life upon't, young though thou art, thine eye
> Hath stay'd upon some favour that it loves.
> Hath it not, boy?
> *Vio.* A little, by your favour.
> *Duke.* What kind of woman is't?
> *Vio.* Of your complexion.
> *Duke.* She is not worth thee, then. What years, i' faith?
> *Vio.* About your years, my lord.
>
> (II. iv. 24–29.)

Here the Duke's oblivion, illuminated by each line he speaks, is laughable—but opposing it is Viola's too-feminine awareness, reaching to every corner of the situation, shining brightly in her every utterance, demanding our concern. Toward the end of the scene, when the same sort of exchange is repeated, with the same tension of opposed awarenesses sustained, the dialogue is laden with pathos:

> *Duke.* What dost thou know?
> *Vio.* Too well what love women to men may owe.
> In faith, they are as true of heart as we.
> My father had a daughter lov'd a man,
> As it might be, perhaps, were I a woman,
> I should your lordship.

Duke.   And what's her history?
Vio.   A blank, my lord. She never told her love,
        But let concealment, like a worm i' th' bud,
        Feed on her damask cheek. She pin'd in thought,
        And with a green and yellow melancholy
        She sat, like Patience on a monument,
        Smiling at grief. Was not this love indeed?
        We men may say more, swear more; but indeed
        Our shows are more than will, for still we prove
        Much in our vows, but little in our love.
Duke. But died thy sister of her love, my boy?
Vio.   I am all the daughters of my father's house,
        And all the brothers too;—and yet I know not.
                              (II. iv. 107–24.)

Although the exchange glitters with irony, to describe the total effect as that of irony is to leave its rarer metals unassayed. The effect is compounded of many simples; elements of the comic and elements of the pathetic are exquisitely blended, with the final unity conferred by the alchemy of poetry. Innately rich, vibrant, the lyric voices gather resonance from the sounding-board of awareness which the dramatist, with calculated art, constructed and fixed in our minds before the start of the duet. Perhaps Shakespeare never achieved a richer tone—though he rises to this once more in *Twelfth Night*—than with these voices reverberating over the chasm between the speakers' awarenesses.

In the interim between this scene and Viola's second interview with Olivia occur the beginnings, along with much else, of Maria's practice on Malvolio. But it is best to postpone discussion of the antics of the clowns, wits, and dolts who make up Olivia's household, both in order that these may all be examined together and in order that we may follow the progress of the heroine and come at once to a scene which is closely knit to that just reviewed.

In the second Viola–Olivia interview, Shakespeare deals gently with Olivia's unawareness. Here, if he chose, he might cause a lady to look as ridiculous as Orlando rehearsing for 'Ganymede'. It is not so: we are required to pity Olivia, for she has caught the plague. With Phebe, suddenly smitten by passion for 'Ganymede', the dramatist dealt otherwise, making her ignorance of Rosalind's sex a means of mockery. But though Phebe stands to 'Ganymede' as Olivia to 'Cesario', Phebe and Olivia are contrasting spirits. Phebe's contemptuous treatment of the shepherd who follows her with dog-like devotion demands that she be exposed to laughter; she deserves Rosalind's sharpest barbs: 'Sell when you can; you are not for all markets.' Olivia, though she has rejected Orsino, has not treated him contemptuously, and her 'cruelty' is only a figment of Orsino's

music-fed imagination; nor, certainly, has she rejected him suddenly, at first sight of a seemingly better match, as Phebe did
Silvius. Derisive exploitation of Olivia's disadvantage would be dis-
cordant here, and there is none. Moreover as Phebe differs from
Olivia, Viola differs from Rosalind. To Rosalind the masquerade in
the name of Jove's page is mocking, malicious, high-holiday sport.
She relishes her advantage, exploits it with a conscienceless zest for
the game that makes boobies of her victims. As the action continues, her exhilaration mounts; appropriating a magician's reputation, promising to make all things even at last, she enjoys astonishing
all Arden. No practiser has a more glorious time of it. Devastating
in her thrusts at Phebe, perhaps she would claw even Olivia, though
not deeply, if that unfortunate were at her mercy. It is otherwise
with Viola, who would deal tenderly even with Phebe.

Viola did not take up the masquerade for the love of mockery.
Hers is not a mocking nature. The thing she starts threatens to get
out of hand almost at once. Hopelessly wooing Olivia for Orsino,
hopelessly loving Orsino, hopelessly loved by Olivia, ignorant that
Sebastian is alive to make all right at last, she is caught in what is to
her a frightening dilemma such as Rosalind would never be caught
in—for Rosalind is superior to dilemmas. It is in accord with her
nature that Viola bears her advantage mercifully in the second
interview, and the gap between the pair is exploited tenderly: 'A
cypress, not a bosom, / Hides my heart', Olivia begins, and Viola
replies, 'I pity you'. These are not Rosalind and Phebe, the one
exuberantly mocking, the other brazen-bold; these are Viola and
Olivia, the one bearing her advantage as if it had suddenly become
a cross, the other so deeply stricken that laughter at her condition
would be gross. Exploitation is concentrated in one principal exchange that finds what is hilarious girt round with pathos:

> *Oli.* Stay!
>   I prithee, tell me what thou think'st of me.
> *Vio.* That you do think you are not what you are.
> *Oli.* If I think so, I think the same of you.
> *Vio.* Then think you right. I am not what I am.
> *Oli.* I would you were as I would have you be!
>   (III. i. 149–54.)

Olivia's confession of love is a compulsive outburst of such frank-
ness as only rudeness could laugh at:

> Cesario, by the roses of the spring,
> By maidhood, honour, truth, and everything,
> I love thee so, that, maugre all thy pride,
> Nor wit nor reason can my passion hide.
>   (Ibid. 161–4.)

Yet the frame of the situation is comic, even grotesque: the reversal of roles, the woman wooing the man, an incongruity in society if not in nature, is a perennial subject of jest; and the fact that this 'man' is not even a man adds a joke to what is already a joke. But within this laughable frame the presentation of human qualities stifles laughter. Olivia's nature conflicts with her plight; her genuineness disarms laughter. And the 'man' is not only a woman, but a woman of rare sensitivity, who carries her masquerade with uncertainty, in a sprightly manner but with rising alarm and forced bravado. Earlier heroines—Julia, Portia, Rosalind—had no such difficulty with this role. Besides the fact that their capabilities were greater, they had female companions to confide in: before donning men's clothes Julia jests with Lucetta, Portia with Nerissa, Rosalind with Celia. They carry their roles with a certain elation. But in her disguise Viola is as much alone in the great world as when she floundered in the sea. Acutely feminine, she finds the role hard, is distressed by it, comes soon to wish she had not undertaken it: 'Disguise, I see thou art a wickedness / Wherein the pregnant enemy does much.'

The emotional conflict which rises from this unlaughable treatment of a laughable situation, complex already, is further complicated by the force of the crowning fact in our superior awareness: our knowledge that Sebastian lives and must now be close at hand. If Olivia can love 'Cesario', she can love Sebastian. The 'thriftless sighs' that arouse Viola's pity and prevent us from laughing need not be thriftless; the hand that can free Olivia will also sever the knot that is too hard for Viola to untie. Thus while the laughter implicit in the situation is drowned in the sympathy demanded by the gentleness of both women, the struggle is also flooded with comforting assurance; all is well and will end well.

And there is more: the total effect of this scene is lightened by the character of the action which surrounds it. The scene which immediately precedes it has ended on a high note of promised hilarity as Maria speaks of Malvolio to her accomplices:

If you will then see the fruits of the sport, mark his first approach before my lady. He will come to her in yellow stockings, and 'tis a colour she abhors, and cross-garter'd, a fashion she detests; and he will smile upon her, which will now be so unsuitable to her disposition, being addicted to a melancholy as she is, that it cannot but turn him into a notable contempt. If you will see it, follow me. (II. v. 217–25.)

This invitation is followed by the entrance of Viola, who matches wits with Feste, then proceeds to the interview with Olivia. *Maria's promise of the ludicrous spectacle that is to be the highest point of hilarity in all the action thus hangs over the tender scene.* Though both women are ignorant that a practice on Malvolio is under way and its exploitation imminent, Olivia is integral to it, for the practice on Malvolio is necessarily a practice on her also; hence her mere presence in the interview helps keep awareness of the promised hilarity alive, and this awareness lightens the effect of the interview.

Shakespeare's preparation of our minds for the climactic scene of the yellow stockings and cross-gartering has been long and elaborate. It has included introduction to the back stairs of that household in which Olivia—exhibited in a predicament as deliciously ironical as any in Shakespeare—has vainly vowed to walk for seven years in mourning veil 'And water once a day her chamber round / With eye-offending brine: all this to season / A brother's dead love'. It is not only Orsino's suit that threatens her solemn purpose; the stamp of futility is set on her vow by the lunatic character of her household: vain dream, to pass seven years in weeping under the same roof with Malvolio, Maria, Belch, and Aguecheek! Before it is visited by Viola, practising as 'Cesario', and before Maria devises her practice on Malvolio, Olivia's house harbours another practice: Sir Toby is revelling at Sir Andrew's cost, the bait being Olivia. This practice was begun before the action of the play commences, and it continues until the final scene when, after Sebastian has half killed both the guller and the gull, Sir Toby breaks it off abruptly:

> *Sir And.* I'll help you, Sir Toby, because we'll be dress'd together.
> *Sir To.* Will you help?—an ass-head and a coxcomb and a knave, a thin-fac'd knave, a gull! (v. i. 210–13.)

Though inconspicuous, this long-standing practice is central to much action, for it precipitates both Maria's practice on Malvolio and Toby's practice on Sir Andrew and Viola–'Cesario' which brings them near to duelling and very nearly ends Viola's masquerade; indeed, it underlies the entire secondary action, which itself provides the comic environment for the main 'Cesario'–Orsino–Olivia–Sebastian plot.

This initial practice is introduced to us before we are shown Sir Andrew himself; in our first sight of Olivia's household, Sir Toby alludes to it:

> *Mar.* I heard my lady talk of it yesterday, and of a foolish knight that you brought in one night here to be her wooer.
> *Sir T.* Who? Sir Andrew Aguecheek?
> *Mar.* Ay, he.
> *Sir T.* He's as tall a man as any's in Illyria.
> *Mar.* What's that to the purpose?
> *Sir T.* Why, he has three thousand ducats a year. (I. iii. 15–23.)

Nightly, Sir Toby and Sir Andrew drink healths to Olivia: 'I'll drink to her', says Toby, 'as long as there is a passage in my throat and drink in Illyria.' Toby's is a lucrative practice; much later, he estimates the gross:

> *Fab.* This is a dear manikin to you, Sir Toby.
> *Sir To.* I have been dear to him, lad, some two thousand strong, or so.
> (III. ii. 57–59.)

Before we see him, then, we hold advantage over Sir Andrew in knowing that he is being gulled. At first sight, in I. iii, we gain another: we perceive at once that his ignorance of Toby's practice is only an acute manifestation of a native condition. Of the race of Bottom, Sir Andrew would be at a disadvantage if he were not being gulled; being gulled, he is doubly 'out'.

The practice on Sir Andrew goes forward in back-room cater-wauling; and it is this caterwauling that precipitates the practice on Malvolio, whose high-handed manner of relaying Olivia's command that the bacchanal cease provokes the wrath of the revellers and inspires Maria's genius: 'If I do not gull him into a nayword, and make him a common recreation, do not think I have wit enough to lie straight in my bed.' Her device is adapted precisely to that singular lack of self-perspective which is Malvolio's whole vice and whole virtue:

> ... it is his grounds of faith that all that look on him love him; and on that vice in him will my revenge find notable cause to work.   (II. iii. 163–6.)

Besides other attributes, Maria has a gift for forgery: 'I can write very like my lady your niece.' Says Toby,

> He shall think, by the letters that thou wilt drop, that they come from my niece, and that she's in love with him.   (Ibid. 178–80.)

Such is the practice which places Maria and her accomplices, with ourselves, on a level above Malvolio and Olivia. Our advantage over Malvolio, however, like that over Sir Andrew, is double. Possibly Malvolio's pit is the darker, since Sir Andrew has moments when he apprehends the possibility that he lacks wit: 'I am a great eater of beef and I believe that does harm to my wit.' Though foolish enough to dream of Olivia's hand, he is scarcely hopeful. He adores Olivia, with an adoration that is hardly bolder than Slender's remote and silent worship of sweet Anne Page. If Toby did not egg him on—'Send for money, knight. If thou hast her not i' the end, call me cut'—he would lose all hope and go home; if Toby had not first prompted him he would never have aspired. Sir Andrew, then, is deceived, and foolish, but not self-deceived.

Malvolio, on the other hand, is self-deceived before he is deceived. Sir Hugh Evans and Justice Shallow together cannot arouse real hope in Slender's breast; Sir Toby's assurances do not allay Sir Andrew's grave doubts. But Malvolio's fire is the product of spontaneous combustion, and his sense of worthiness is unalloyed by misgivings. Shakespeare makes this fact clear by exhibiting the man's vainglory just before he finds the forged letter: 'To be Count Malvolio!' and, again:

> Having been three months married to her, sitting in my state.... Calling my officers about me, in my branch'd velvet gown, having come from a day-bed, where I have left Olivia sleeping.... (II. v. 49–55.)

This exhibition of self-deception continues until Malvolio picks up the letter, when deception is welded to self-deception by a gaudy flash of irony: 'What employment have we here?' The 100 lines that follow, during which Malvolio manages to find his own name in the letters M, O, A, I, and arrives at confirmation—'I do not now fool myself, to let imagination jade me; for every reason excites to this, that my lady loves me'—make simultaneous exploitation of deception and self-deception:

> M, O, A, I; this simulation is not as the former. And yet, to crush this a little, it would bow to me, for every one of these letters are in my name. (Ibid. 151–4.)

Exhibiting the seduction of a mind eager to be seduced, the scene surpasses everything resembling it in Shakespeare. In comedy the nearest to it is the scene in which Falstaff hears the wives' propositions recounted by Mistress Quickly; yet Falstaff hears with astonishment and believes in spite of himself, so that deception prevails over self-deception. And in tragedy, the nearest is the witches' initial winning of Macbeth—which leaves him, however, not yet wholly committed.

'Observe him, for the love of mockery', said Maria to her accomplices. Hidden in the box-tree, they hold a triple advantage over Malvolio, in that they watch him when he does not suspect, recognize his self-kindled folly, and, of course, know that the letter which sets him ablaze is forged. Yet the master practiser here is Shakespeare, whose way it is to set participants where they over-peer others while they are also overpeered. The practice on Malvolio is contained by frames which the practisers do not suspect, as we are privately reminded when Maria describes Olivia as 'addicted to a melancholy', a disposition which will render Malvolio's smiles intolerable to her. The fact is that Olivia is not now addicted to a melancholy, but is in love with 'Cesario'—and her world has changed. Hence even Maria, knowing nothing of the change, drops below our level. As for Sir Andrew, Shakespeare does not let us forget that the man is a fool all the while he joyously overpeers Malvolio—and that, besides, he is practice-ridden. Maria has just described her scheme to gull Malvolio when we are reminded that Andrew's own gulling continues:

> *Sir To.* Let's to bed, knight. Thou hadst need send for more money.
> *Sir And.* If I cannot recover your niece, I am a foul way out.
> *Sir To.* Send for money, knight. If thou hast her not i' the end, call me cut.
> (II. iii. 198–203.)

And while he is most enjoying his advantage over Malvolio, Sir Andrew is made to expose the depth of his congenital unawareness:

> *Mal.* 'Besides, you waste the treasure of your time with a foolish knight,'—
> *Sir A.* That's me, I warrant you.
> *Mal.* 'One Sir Andrew,'—
> *Sir A.* I knew 'twas I; for many do call me fool. (II. v. 85–90.)

Maria's invitation to see 'the fruits of the sport', which is the final word of preparation for the climactic scene of the yellow stockings, thus carries even higher promise than she intends, since the gullers as well as their gull will, in our perspective, contribute to the fun.

The climactic scene does not follow immediately: Maria's promise, suspended, conditions the environment of three scenes before it is fulfilled. The first of these, the pathetic interview of 'Cesario' with Olivia, totally encircled by past, continuing, and promised hilarity, has already been examined. Sentimentally conceived, permeated with emotion, Olivia's declaration of love demands sympathy: yet, placed where it is, it gathers an echo from Malvolio's affair: Olivia's passion for 'Cesario' is as preposterous as Malvolio's for Olivia. The second scene (III. ii) is affected also, but differently: Sir Toby, assisted by Fabian, puffs up Sir Andrew's collapsing hopes of winning Olivia, and Sir Andrew, foolish and practice-ridden, fails to see in Malvolio's delusion the very portrait of his own. At the same time that it exploits the old practice on the brainless knight, this scene also prepares a new one; says Toby,

> Challenge me the Count's youth to fight with him; hurt him in eleven places; my niece shall take note of it; and assure thyself, there is no love-broker in the world can more prevail in man's commendation with woman than report of valour. (III. ii. 36–41.)

The new practice is in fact born of ignorance, not only Andrew's but the practisers', for Toby and Fabian do not guess that the 'favours' which Andrew reports he saw Olivia do 'the Count's serving-man' in the orchard were expressions of true love—or that they were misspent, this youth being no man at all. 'For Andrew', says Toby, 'if he were open'd and you find so much blood in his liver as will clog the foot of a flea, I'll eat the rest of the anatomy.' Fabian's reply flares up in irony that marks a hit of error upon truth: 'And his opposite, the youth, bears in his visage no great presage of cruelty.'

The third scene set between Maria's promise and its fulfilment shows Sebastian on a street in Illyria and confirms our long-held, comforting assumption that the solution to Viola's 'insoluble' problem is at hand. Placed between the announcement of Sir Toby's practice (the challenge) which will surely terrify 'Cesario', and the exploitation of multiple practices in the climactic scene, Sebastian's declaration that he will walk abroad to view the town is our reassurance that all is well. It comes just as the climactic scene of the yellow stockings begins and is the dramatist's last bid to make certain that all useful information is in our minds.

And it is truly an enormous bundle of awarenesses that we must carry into this scene, during the action of which all nine of the persons present are blind to some part of the situation. Though not the first of Shakespeare's scenes in which everyone stands below our vantage-point, it is the most complex of such scenes until the climactic portion of *Cymbeline*. Four principal situations comprise the scene: first, that in which Malvolio's delusion is central; second, that in which Olivia's unawareness of 'Cesario's' identity is central; third, that in which Viola and Sir Andrew's unawareness of Toby's practice is central; fourth, that in which Antonio's mistaking of 'Cesario' for Sebastian is central. Yet these are only the basic situations. The total context which has been established in our minds and from which the action draws its full meaning is beyond explicit description; yet it is in the totality that the cream of the jest—or of four jests—lies.

First up for exploitation is Malvolio's unawareness—but Shakespeare delays Malvolio yet again, until we have been reminded of the state of Olivia's mind. Her remarks stand like the topic sentence for what follows:

(*Aside.*) I have sent after him; he says he'll come. How shall I feast him? What bestow of him? For youth is bought more oft than begg'd or borrow'd.
(III. iv. 1–3.)

Not Malvolio, as he thinks, or her dead brother, as Maria and her accomplices suppose, but 'Cesario' fills her mind: *we are not to be allowed to forget, even at the very edge of it, that Malvolio's outrageous performance before his lady is set within the frame of*

133

Viola's masquerade. Remembrance of Olivia's vain love thus is made to hang darkly over the hilarious spectacle very much as, earlier, Maria's promise of this hilarity hung brightly above the tender and embarrassed interview of Viola and Olivia. The second fold of Olivia's ignorance is next exposed:

> Where is Malvolio? He is sad and civil,
> And suits well for a servant with my fortunes.
> Where is Malvolio?
>
> (III. iv. 5–7.)

Malvolio's gulling is also Olivia's; says Maria:

> Your ladyship were best to have some guard about you, if he come; for, sure, the man is tainted in's wits. (Ibid. 12–14.)

Unaware of Maria's forgery, both servant and lady are victims of the practice. But Olivia stands on the higher level: mystification is up the scale from oblivion. Maniacally smiling, cross-gartered, yellow-stockinged, a veritable bodying-forth of ignorance, Malvolio is the central figure amid circles of error. His smile, his garters, his stockings are unawareness rendered visible; his words, unawareness rendered audible. Orlando's unawareness of 'Ganymede' and Orsino's of 'Cesario' are exploited mainly by words whose flares illuminate the space between their depths and our height. But Malvolio's is ignorance not so much of another person as of himself, hence is aptly exhibited not only by words but by physical signs—like Bottom's superadded head and Falstaff's horns. 'His very genius', says Sir Toby, when the incident is past, 'hath taken the infection of the device.' The smile, the garters, the stockings—the immediate effects of Maria's practice on him—are ultimately the signs of Malvolio's practice on himself.

Here and in Feste's later practice (IV. ii) Malvolio's exposure to derision is well deserved. Not only is his aspiration self-kindled, lacking the excuse that it was set going by an external practice, but it is contemptible in its nature. Sir Andrew, with Toby's prompting, aspires to Olivia's hand because, in his booby fashion, he loves her. But Malvolio sees Olivia as means to Great Place. Shakespeare exhibits four such deceived, futile aspirants: Sir Andrew and Malvolio of *Twelfth Night*, Slender of *The Merry Wives of Windsor*, and, in the tragic case, Roderigo of *Othello*. Sir Andrew's aspiration is nearest Slender's in its innocence; Malvolio's, tainted with self-love and social ambition, nearest Roderigo's, which is lust.

Though a climax in itself, Malvolio's scene is framed by the main situation: it opens with Olivia awaiting the arrival of 'Cesario' to dine with her; 'Cesario', not Malvolio, is foremost in her mind then and thereafter—and Malvolio's performance, in her perspective, is only an odd episode which occurs while she is waiting. Moreover, the comic effect of Malvolio's scene arises partly from his ignorance of 'Cesario's' identity and of Olivia's misspent passion; indeed, in this ignorance Malvolio stands on the same level as his tormentors, for even Maria believes Olivia still to be grieving for her brother. And Toby incites Andrew to challenge 'Cesario', not because he thinks there are grounds for his gull's jealousy but merely for the love of the game. Amid preparations for Toby's newest practice, Shakespeare sets the third interview of 'Cesario' and Olivia, which reminds us—should the several interludes have obscured the fact—that Olivia's passion is real enough. Though brief, the interview is indispensable: it looks before and after, and its twenty lines bind together the four episodes of this very long climactic scene.

The third of these episodes, which primarily exploits Sir Andrew's ignorance, is at once the result of Sir Toby's old practice on him and of 'Cesario's' practice on all Illyria. The episode parallels that of the yellow stockings: his aspiration fed by Maria's practice, Malvolio makes a spectacle of himself before Olivia; his aspiration fed by Sir Toby's practice, Sir Andrew makes a spectacle of himself by challenging 'Cesario'. 'Marry', says Toby, when the opponents are brought front to front, 'I'll ride your horse as well as I ride you.' Even Malvolio is not so practice-ridden as is Sir Andrew at this moment. Victim, first of all, of nature's practice, he has next been deceived by Sir Toby into supposing that Toby's dry gullet is the way to Olivia's heart; next, he is deceived by Viola's practice into supposing that 'the Count's serving-man' is a serious rival; next, egged on to challenge 'Cesario', he is abused when his foolish letter is replaced by Toby's description of his ferocity: 'this letter, being so excellently ignorant, will breed no terror in the youth; he will find it comes from a clodpole'; and, finally, he is abused by Toby's exaggerated report of his adversary: 'Why, man, he's a very devil; I have not seen such a firago. . . . They say he has been fencer to the Sophy.' The densest concentration of the Illyrian fog which rolled in from the sea with Viola here settles about the head of Sir Andrew. Of the total, infinitely complex situation which the dramatist has spread out plainly to our view, he sees nothing in its right shape, colour, or dimension. 'So soon as ever thou seest him, draw', Sir Toby has directed him; 'and, as thou draw'st, swear horrible.' When the time comes, Sir Andrew's resolution is shattered by the terrifying images looming through his wall of fog: 'Let him let the matter slip, and I'll give him my horse, grey Capilet.'

If it concerned him alone, the effect of the episode would be purely comic. But Sir Toby's device makes sport of 'Cesario' also: 'This will so fright them both that they will kill one another by the look, like cockatrices.' For the very first time, yoked with a booby as the butt of a joke, Viola is in danger of looking ridiculous. Hitherto our only advantage over her has been our knowledge of Sebastian's survival—an advantage that has provided comforting assurance but given no cause for laughter. Yet again, as in the case of Olivia stricken with passion for 'Cesario', though the plight is laughable the victim is not. It bears repeating that Viola is one of the most feminine of Shakespeare's heroines. No other heroine is less suited to brave it in man's role—unless it were Hero, who would not dare. To Viola, a duel with a warrior such as Sir Toby describes is unthinkable:

> He is knight, dubb'd with unhatch'd rapier and on carpet consideration; but he is a devil in private brawl. Souls and bodies hath he divorc'd three; and his incensement at this moment is so implacable, that satisfaction can be none but by pangs of death and sepulchre. Hob, nob, is his word; give't or take't.
>
> (III. iv. 257–63.)

Rosalind could manage this Aguecheek; but even if Viola knew the truth about him, duelling would not be for her. 'I am one that had rather go with sir priest than sir knight', she tells Fabian; 'I care not who knows so much of my mettle.' Shakespeare has balanced the scales delicately between laughter and tears, and Viola's exquisite femininity keeps them so; capable Rosalind would destroy the tension. From the outset the trials in which Viola's disguise involves her have been hard; this one frightens her nearly to surrendering her secret: 'A little thing would make me tell them how much I lack of a man.'

The line prods our awareness at a crucial moment: the grotesque basis of the duel, the blubbering terror of Sir Andrew, and the swaggering, gross humour of Sir Toby would assuredly tip the scales to the side of hilarity if we should momentarily forget what 'Cesario' is. Further, this particular line of Viola's, being set just after Sir Toby's loudest exhortation to the reluctant duellists, subtly reminds us that Sir Andrew and Viola are not the only butts of this joke: they are the butts in Sir Toby's perspective, but Sir Toby is the butt in ours. If Sir Andrew is ignorant that 'Cesario' is not 'a very devil . . . a firago', and if 'Cesario' is ignorant that Sir Andrew is all hare and no lion, yet Toby is ignorant that 'Cesario' is Viola. This is the cream of the cream: that the boisterous manipulator, perpetrator of multiple practices on Sir Andrew, overpeerer also of 'Cesario' by virtue of his better acquaintance with the silly knight's valour, absolute master, in his own perspective, of all

elements in the situation, as self-assured as Malvolio in his utterances
—should be all the while ignorant of the most important fact in the
entire action. 'Marry', he tells us confidentially of Aguecheek, 'I'll
ride your horse as well as I ride you.' But Shakespeare has enabled
us to ride Sir Toby.

Perhaps, then, Viola gets off free here, when her unawareness
invites laughter at her expense. But in the final episode of the scene,
though she escapes laughter, she is exposed under an unflattering
light. The fault, of course, is not hers, but Antonio's, in mistaking
her for Sebastian. In a sense, Antonio's level is lower than Illyria's,
for Orsino, Olivia, and others have only supposed Viola to be
'Cesario', while Antonio, ignorant alike of 'Cesario' and Viola, takes
her to be Sebastian. Yet in another sense Illyria's error is deeper, for
'Cesario' is a fiction, whereas Sebastian is a fact.

For this episode the dramatist has so arranged the awarenesses
that they set contradictory responses fighting for supremacy. Here
again, also, the initial preparation lies far back, in the scene which
first shows us Sebastian. Antonio has saved him from the sea, weeps
with him for his drowned sister, is solicitous for his welfare, begs to
serve him, and, finally, braving old enemies in Orsino's court, insists
on accompanying him: 'I do adore thee so / That danger shall seem
sport, and I will go.' When next we see the pair, the expression of
Antonio's regard for his young friend is emphatic to the point of
being conspicuous; what is more, it is backed up by action: 'Hold,
sir, here's my purse.'

Perhaps Shakespeare remembered another Antonio, who risked
his flesh for his friend Bassanio: had the sense of that Antonio's
goodness not been established in our minds, our anxiety for him
while danger increased would hardly have been stirred, and the
tensions that make the court scene great would have been flabby.
Sebastian's magnanimous Antonio is like Bassanio's; hence, when he
mistakes 'Cesario' for Sebastian, is arrested, asks return of his purse
—'It grieves me / Much more for what I cannot do for you / Than
what befalls me'—is stared at and refused, our knowledge of his
kindness compels sympathy for him—and resentment towards the
cause of this sudden shock given to his nature:

> Will you deny me now?
> Is't possible that my deserts to you
> Can lack persuasion?
> (Ibid. 381–3.)

It is a moment shrewdly wrought, which brings into conflict
two urgent awarenesses—of Antonio's selflessness and of Viola's

femininity and perfect innocence. Though we know Antonio to be in error and Viola blameless, yet in the eyes of this kind man she is terribly guilty. Shakespeare's devotion to such moments of extreme tension sometimes leads him to the edge of psychological calamity; perhaps here he goes too near, and his heroine, despite our awareness that she is innocent and despite her eagerness to do what she can for Antonio—'My having is not much. / I'll make division of my present with you'—is singed by an involuntary flash of our resentment.

The incident closes the scene. Presenting four interlocked episodes all the relationships of which are constantly exposed to our Olympian view; parading forth nearly all the persons of the play in their relative states of ignorance, none understanding all, and some —Malvolio, Aguecheek, Olivia, Antonio—understanding nothing that is going on; moving from the hilarious exhibition of Malvolio's delusion to the painful representation of Antonio's sudden disillusionment with humankind, it is, from the point of view of the creation, maintenance, and exploitation of multiple discrepant awarenesses, the most remarkable achievement in Shakespearian comedy before *Cymbeline*.

The brief scene which follows is the very cap atop the action of the play, the tip of the summit. In short space are exploited the gaps between the several levels—all inferior to ours—of the six persons who enter. In Shakespeare's comedies, almost infallibly, two contrasting moments make the great peaks: first, the moment in which, errors having been compounded and various lines of action brought to a central point, confusion is nearest universal, visibility nearest zero; second, that in which confusion is dispelled. In the present scene, the first moment is marked by Feste's doubly ironical expostulation with Sebastian:

No, I do not know you; nor I am not sent to you by my lady, to bid you come speak with her; nor your name is not Master Cesario; nor this is not my nose neither. Nothing that is so is so.   (IV. i. 5-9.)

So speaks the Clown, wise enough to *play* the fool, yet lost like the others in the Illyrian fog. He is the first of five who in quick succession mistake Sebastian for 'Cesario'. The formula is the same on which the entire action of *The Comedy of Errors* is based, but it is here used with a difference. In the early play, when Adriana mistakes Antipholus of Syracuse for her husband, she is only once removed from the truth apparent to us—for there is indeed an Antiphilus of Ephesus. But the 'Cesario' for whom Sebastian is mistaken is himself a fiction. All five persons, thus, being twice removed from truth, hold a level even lower than Sebastian's. For Sebastian, though he has come from outside into a situation of which he is totally ignorant—knowing neither that Viola lives nor that she poses as 'Cesario', that Olivia loves this 'Cesario', or that Sir Andrew is jealous of him—is nevertheless well enough aware that he is himself Sebastian and no other; not seeing the illusion that blinds the others, he is nearer reality than they. Oblivion is a lower level than mystification; they are oblivious, and he is mystified:

> What relish is in this? How runs the stream?
> Or I am mad, or else this is a dream.
> (Ibid. 64–65.)

His mystification continues through his next scene, when it contrasts with Olivia's blissful error as she draws him home in the company of a priest. In all Shakespeare's comedies, only the twin brothers of *The Comedy of Errors*, masters and servants, remain longer in this precise degree of awareness; indeed, among the enormous number of persons in the comedies shown ignorant of their situations, only a few are truly mystified. For a moment or two in *Love's Labour's Lost*, upon their return to the ladies after posing as Russians, the King and his companions stand in this condition. Briefly also, Bassanio and Gratiano, in *The Merchant of Venice*, are mystified when Portia and Nerissa suddenly show the rings earlier presented to the 'doctor' and the 'clerk'. In *Much Ado about Nothing* Hero is briefly mystified by Claudio's harsh indictment of her honour. In *The Merry Wives of Windsor* Ford is twice mystified by his failure to find Falstaff in his wife's company. In the later comedies, as we shall note, moments in which a participant's mystification is exploited are similarly rare and brief. In both intensity and duration, Sebastian's mystification comes nearest that of Antipholus of Syracuse; thus, after his first meeting with Olivia:

> This is the air, that is the glorious sun,
> This pearl she gave me, I do feel't and see't;
> And though 'tis wonder that enwraps me thus,
> Yet 'tis not madness.
> (IV. iii. 1–4.)

His relation to the illusion-ridden city of Illyria differs in one particular from that of Antipholus of Syracuse to Ephesus. Until Antipholus and his Dromio arrived, no illusion existed in Ephesus; what follows is all of their own making. But when Sebastian came out of the sea to Illyria, Viola had preceded him, bringing in the fog that now engulfs everyone. 'Madman, thou errest', the Clown tells Malvolio in the continuing practice on this most extreme case of the

Illyrian affliction. 'I say, there is no darkness but ignorance, in which thou art more puzzl'd than the Egyptians in their fog.' Malvolio best represents also the Illyrians' inability to perceive their illusion: 'I tell thee, I am as well in my wits as any man in Illyria.' In contrast, coming from outside into all this, Sebastian knows enough to be mystified; though he cannot see through the fog, he can see that it is there: 'There's something in't / That is deceivable.'

At the opening of Act V the burden of the context which preceding acts have established in our minds is staggering. *During Acts II, III, and IV no fully aware person except Viola has appeared before us*—and during part of this time she too has lacked full vision. At precisely what moment she rejoins us in our omniscience is the final question to be considered; indeed, the question of the state of Viola's awareness during the last two acts is the great question of the play.

At the close of Act IV we saw Olivia and Sebastian go to be married. We therefore hold advantage over Viola and Orsino upon their entrance in Act V. Over Orsino, of course, we hold other advantages also—the same that we have held for three acts. But are we to suppose that we hold any additional advantage over Viola? She is ignorant that her brother—in a state like that of shock—is now repeating the marriage oath before Olivia's priest. But is she still ignorant that he escaped drowning and has arrived in Illyria?

At the end of Act III, when Antonio interrupted her match with Sir Andrew, the cause of his error was as open to her as to us. That she then perceived the truth there can be little doubt:

> Methinks his words do from such passion fly
> That he believes himself; so do not I.
> Prove true, imagination, O, prove true,
> That I, dear brother, be now ta'en for you!
> (III. iv. 407–10.)

And again:

> He nam'd Sebastian. I my brother know
> Yet living in my glass; even such and so
> In favour was my brother, and he went
> Still in this fashion, colour, ornament,
> For him I imitate.
> (Ibid. 414–18.)

But now, at the opening of Act V, with Orsino, again meeting Antonio, she speaks with wide-eyed amazement:

> He did me kindness, sir, drew on my side,
> But in conclusion put strange speech upon me.
> I know not what 'twas but distraction.
> (v. i. 69–71.)

'That most ingrateful boy there by your side, / From the rude sea's enrag'd and foamy mouth / Did I redeem', asserts Antonio. The sea captain who had saved Viola had told her:

> I saw your brother,
> Most provident in peril, bind himself,
> Courage and hope both teaching him the practice,
> To a strong mast that liv'd upon the sea;
> Where, like Arion on the dolphin's back,
> I saw him hold acquaintance with the waves
> So long as I could see.
>
> (I. ii. 11–17.)

And she had replied:

> Mine own escape unfoldeth to my hope,
> Whereto thy speech serves for authority,
> The like of him.
>
> (Ibid. 19–21.)

From the first she had entertained hope; then Antonio had mistaken her and named Sebastian, whom she imitated in her masquerade; and, finally, Antonio describes a sea-rescue that accords with other evidence of Sebastian's survival. When Antonio has finished his account of the rescue and his three-months' life with Sebastian, Viola could, with few words, disabuse the tormented fellow, whose experience with ingratitude is maddening him. Instead, wide-eyed as before, she inquires, 'How can this be?'

That is to say, she holds to her masquerade in spite of all at this crucial moment—and even, in feigning ignorance, grafts a new practice on the old. Why does she do so? A damning answer is that Shakespeare is willing to sacrifice plausibility in order to preserve to the last moment the richly exploitable gap between Illyria's oblivion and Viola's awareness, so that when all lines have converged upon that moment, he can achieve a spectacular denouement, with Illyria's awareness shooting up like a rocket when Sebastian and 'Cesario' come face to face. That Shakespeare always set a high rate on exploitable gaps and that he here forces the situation to yield its utmost effect before he explodes it is unquestionable. But that he sacrifices plausibility in doing so is not so sure.

At the opening of Act V Viola is yet ignorant of one fact: that Olivia and Sebastian are married. *If she knew that*, she would know that time, on which she early set her hope—'O time! thou must untangle this, not I'—has already solved her problem. Not knowing it, and being Viola, feminine as no other, she maintains her old fiction and compounds a new one of silence and innocence. Like Portia and Rosalind, Vincentio and Prospero in that she plays the role of chief practiser and controlling force, she is unlike these in her attitude toward it. She has found no joy in the role; she has been tempted to abandon it: 'A little thing would make me tell them how much I lack of a man.' More significantly, whereas the other controlling forces manipulate persons and contrive practices to bring their ends about, she has contrived nothing beyond her initial disguise. Though her goal—implied in 'He was a bachelor then' at her arrival in Illyria and shortly thereafter confirmed in 'Whoe'er I woo, myself would be his wife'—has always been to catch this Duke, she has played fair with both him and Olivia, serving faithfully, twisting nothing to her own purpose, striving only to stay out of trouble—and waiting on time. When trouble came, in the form of Olivia's passion and Sir Toby's practice, she rode it out despite embarrassment, pity, and even terror. When at last Antonio's error advised her of her brother's survival, her hope took ecstatic new life: the end was in sight. Being Viola, she could not then break faith with time, even to save the good Antonio from misanthropy. Feminine in her patient waiting, she is no less so in her persistence: it is not enough that the end is in sight; it must actually be reached. When the Duke berates her, even threatening death, she opposes her patience to his fury:

> And I, most jocund, apt, and willingly,
> To do you rest, a thousand deaths would die.
> (v. i. 135-6.)

The final silent moments of her masquerade are the hardest.

So great is her subtlety at the last that it is difficult to identify the instant at which she perceives that time has performed its final chore in her behalf. But she must be fully aware by the time of Olivia's exclamation: 'Cesario, husband, stay!' Nevertheless, to the Duke's enraged 'Her husband, sirrah!' she replies with a wide-eyed denial that we should perhaps take instead as a victory whoop: 'No, my lord, not I.' The priest confirms Olivia's word that 'Cesario' is her husband. Sir Andrew and Sir Toby berate 'Cesario' for hurting them. Still Viola keeps silent, except to deny the charges. Then follow fifty lines of dialogue in the course of which Sebastian enters and astonishes all Illyria except herself. And still she speaks never a word. The arrival of Sebastian cannot be a surprise to her; his tender greeting of Olivia can be none. The long, superb silence, more wonderful than the Illyrians' ejaculations of amazement, is almost but not quite the extremest demonstration of her femininity. That demonstration comes only after Sebastian has subjected her to direct questioning, when she replies with wide-eyed and incredible incredulity:

Such a Sebastian was my brother too;
So went he suited to his watery tomb.
If spirits can assume both form and suit,
You come to fright us.

(Ibid. 241–3.)

In this last instant before giving over her long masquerade, she thus
devises a final fiction: neither husband, brother, nor sister-in-law
will ever learn from her lips anything other than that she had been
ignorant, *until this instant*, of her brother's survival, his arrival in
Illyria, and his marriage. This shred of a great secret she will never
give up, that she had ridden her masquerade to the very end, biding
time—'O time! thou must untangle this, not I'—until it took Olivia
off her hands and gave her Orsino.

143

CHAPTER V

When Degree is Shak'd: *All's Well* and *Troilus and Cressida*

OBSERVED from the point of view of the uses of discrepant aware-nesses, *Much Ado about Nothing*, *As You Like It*, and *The Merry Wives of Windsor* make an approach to the summit of *Twelfth Night*. Observed from the same point, *All's Well that Ends Well* marks the downward turn from this summit toward the depth of *Troilus and Cressida*. From any point of view, these two 'dark comedies' must appear puzzling creations to follow after the bright-ness of *Twelfth Night*; perhaps from none do they look more strange than from that of the management of awarenesses. So seen, they look at times even un-Shakespearian.

They stand together, isolated, at the centre of a period in which the dramatist's other works, histories and tragedies as well as comedies, exhibit elaborately structured dispositions of the aware-nesses, with our vantage-point regularly at the top, and shrewdly calculated exploitation of multiple discrepancies in awareness. The five years preceding produced *The Merchant of Venice*, *Much Ado*, *As You Like It*, *The Merry Wives*, and *Twelfth Night*, the comedies; the great histories of *Henry IV* and *V*; *Julius Caesar* and *Hamlet*, the tragedies. The five years after produced *Measure for Measure*, *Othello*, *King Lear*, and *Macbeth*. In all these, the propor-tion of scenes in which we hold advantage is very high; and not only is the proportion high, but our advantage—with the noteworthy exception of some crucial moments in *Hamlet*—is invariably made unmistakable: *the dramatist's method requires us to know and to remember where we stand, and to mark the gap between our vantage-point and that of the participants*. In the comedies of this ten-year period we are provided with an early and fast assurance that, however ill all looks to the participants, all is in fact well because all is under control. Thus the balmy climate of comedy is made to prevail even in moments of acute distress.

But *All's Well* and *Troilus and Cressida*—the one partially, the other wholly—stand as contradictions of what would otherwise seem to be Shakespeare's habitual method during these years. In both, the proportion of scenes in which we hold significant advantage is low: indeed, in the latter it is lower than in any other play except *Henry VI*, when Shakespeare was still seeking his way and stumbling from the way. Moreover, in these two plays we are not only not compelled to know where we stand, but often, especially in *All's Well*, prevented from knowing; and in *Troilus and Cressida* we escape from 'this ignorant present' that engulfs the participants only because we live later and know their story. Elsewhere Shakespeare makes assurance doubly sure that we shall use the advantage given us, so that no effect of exploitation may be wasted; but in *All's Well* and *Troilus and Cressida*, perhaps deliberately in the first, but inexplicably in the second, he is ambiguous. Ambiguity in the management of awarenesses is the most conspicuously un-Shakespearian characteristic of both these plays. Finally, whereas in earlier comedies we have been assured at once, by dramatic means, that all will at last be well, in *All's Well*—despite the title itself—assurance is denied until late; and in *Troilus and Cressida* it never comes, and all is never well.

1. *All's Well that Ends Well*

The dramatic effects of only five of the twenty-three scenes in *All's Well that Ends Well* arise primarily from exploitation of discrepant awarenesses. Though at some time we hold advantage over each named person—except, perhaps, the heroine—the ignorance of only two, Bertram and Parolles, serves as the exploitable condition for whole scenes. Until the last scene, while the long and tortuous denouement is under way, the play erects no structure of awarenesses so elaborate as the arrangements exploited in earlier comedies and attaining greatest complexity in *Twelfth Night*. Moreover, whereas in previous comedies Shakespeare regularly gave us early advantage to hold until the denouement, in *All's Well* we are not explicitly invited to share a large secret until the last scene of Act III—late indeed; and though thereafter we share Helena's deep secret, our general awareness is sustained falteringly, often by belated injections of information; hence we sometimes find suddenly, after action has passed, that our vantage-point was not as high as we had supposed. Our awareness is not similarly treated in any earlier play except the *Henry VI* trilogy when the apprentice dramatist, striving to keep our understanding merely equal to the participants', introduced messenger upon messenger, each with news of happenings elsewhere.

In *All's Well that Ends Well*, until II. iv, such advantages as we gain are minor. At the end of I. ii the sick King says:

> How long is't, Count,
> Since the physician at your father's died?
> He was much fam'd.
>
> (I. ii. 69–71.)

'Some six months since, my lord', replies Bertram;-and the King: 'If he were living, I would try him yet.' It accords with Shakespeare's usual method that at the end of the scene just preceding we have heard Helena:

> The King's disease—my project may deceive me,
> But my intents are fix'd and will not leave me.
>
> (I. i. 243–4.)

Though she is here, as hereafter, darkly inexplicit about her intentions, Helena says enough to cast special light on the conversation of Bertram and the King, who are ignorant that the famed physician's daughter is up to something that will affect them both. Again, in I. iii, we hold brief advantage over Helena herself; this deserves notice because it is probably the only time we do so—though later we are allowed to *suppose* that we hold a great one. Says the Steward, having overheard Helena: 'Her matter was, she lov'd your son.' Helena enters, and Shakespeare lets her remain ignorant, for about fifty lines, that the Countess knows her secret. Finally, in II. iii, after Helena has cured the King, we share her advantage over Bertram, Lafeu, the King, and the four Lords as she feigns to make a choice of husband. For the participants there is suspense as she passes before them, seeming to consider, moving ever nearer to Bertram; for us, prepared beforehand, there is none.

Though minor, these gaps and their exploitation are in any event handled in Shakespeare's usual way. The major ones which follow are not all handled so. The first scenes in which, by the dramatist's typical usage, we should hold significant advantage, are the last two of Act II, when we, but not Helena, have been advised that Bertram intends to desert his new bride for the wars. Perhaps we hold an advantage here—and perhaps we do not: our insecurity is the result of a peculiar ambiguity in the management of awarenesses which obscures the true nature of the action until the end of Act III. We know for sure that Helena is aware of Bertram's disdain; his scorn has been made as obvious to her as to us from the outset. On leaving Rousillon in I. i he spoke to her as to a servant: 'Be comfortable to

my mother, your mistress, and make much of her.' In her soliloquy
ending that scene, Helena spoke thus: ''Twere all one / That I
should love a bright particular star / And think to wed it, he is so
above me.' When she had saved the King's life and claimed her husband, this 'unseasoned courtier' showed contempt in her presence
as if she had been insensible:

> But follows it, my lord, to bring me down
> Must answer for your raising? I know her well;
> She had her breeding at my father's charge.
> A poor physician's daughter my wife! Disdain
> Rather corrupt me ever.
>   (II. iii. 119–23.)

'I cannot love her, nor will strive to do't', he said to her face, and
it is evident to her that only the King's threat to destroy all his
hopes in life caused Bertram to acquiesce: 'I take her hand.' She sees
as clearly as we that marriage has merely changed indifference to
active dislike.

When, therefore, Parolles—lying for his master after the wedding—explains to her that 'a very serious business calls on him'
and that

> The great prerogative and rite of love,
> Which, as your due, time claims, he does acknowledge,
> But puts it off to a compell'd restraint;
> Whose want, and whose delay, is strew'd with sweets,
> Which they distil now in the curbed time,
> To make the coming hour o'erflow with joy
> And pleasure drown the brim.
>   (II. iv. 42–48.)

—when Parolles tells her this, Helena should have no doubt of her
husband's disdain. Yet her reply is that of an obedient and trusting
wife; she *seems*—so Shakespeare represents her action to us—to
accept Parolles's explanation, with its implication that Bertram will
shortly join her at Rousillon: 'In everything I wait upon his will.'
With this, she goes to seek the King's permission to leave the court.
So also, parting from Bertram, she seems not to suspect his true
purpose:

Ber.   This to my mother:
                                    (*Giving a letter.*)
      'Twill be two days ere I shall see you, so
      I leave you to your wisdom.
Hel.   Sir, I can nothing say,
      But that I am your most obedient servant,—
Ber. Come, come, no more of that.

Hel.   And ever shall
        With true observance seek to eke out that
        Wherein toward me my homely stars have fail'd
        To equal my great fortune.
Ber.   Let that go.
        My haste is very great. Farewell; hie home.
                                                (II. v. 74–86.)

Says Bertram, to us alone: 'Go thou toward home, where I will never come / Whilst I can shake my sword or hear the drum.' We hardly need the closing couplet: we knew already that Bertram means this cold parting to be final, and we can guess the content of the letter he hands his wife for the Countess. With respect to Bertram's intention, then, Shakespeare's handling of the scene is characteristic. Moreover, the evidence of his method in earlier comedies should leave no question about the relation of our awareness to Helena's: we should take the scene as an exploitation of her pathetic unawareness of Bertram's true purpose. *At the time the scene is acted*, that is to say, we have no cause to suspect that Helena is other than an object for pity, abandoned and still unaware of the fact.

If we do hold advantage over her here, we lose it in III. ii. At Rousillon the Countess first reads her letter from Bertram, the tenor of which we could predict: 'If there be breadth enough in the world, I will hold a long distance.' In the next moment Helena, having read her similar letter from Bertram, enters in apparent amazement: 'Madam, my lord is gone, for ever gone.' Her conduct here suggests that she had truly been deceived by her husband's earlier promise to rejoin her within two days. Bertram not having taken us wholly into his confidence before, we learn for the first time, with Helena, of the mocking 'terms' by which he must be re-won:

'When thou canst get the ring upon my finger which never shall come off, and show me a child begotten of thy body that I am father to, then call me husband; but in such a "then" I write a "never".'   (III. ii. 59–63.)

The remainder of the scene creates no new advantage for us over a participant. Helena, in a seemingly uncertain, quite un-heroinely soliloquy, discloses her intent to leave Rousillon so that Bertram will have no need to stay from home. The soliloquy gives no hint that she means other than she says. Nor does the curious sonnet-letter which she somehow finds time and spirit to phrase before leaving. 'I am Saint Jaques' pilgrim, thither gone': if at this point she has another purpose in mind, Shakespeare does not invite us to share her secret. She is to be a pilgrim to a distant shrine—indeed, a pilgrim seeking Death, 'Whom I myself embrace, to set him free'. Taken literally—as their unequivocal presentation suggests they must be—both the soliloquy which ends III. ii and the sonnet-letter read by the Steward to the Countess in III. iv picture a forlorn, abused wife, deserted by a contemptuous husband in the hour of her wedding, denied the fruits of her hard-won preliminary victory, fleeing from home to a foreign shrine to embrace Death. So she tells us herself, categorically, and, having said so much, suits action to the word, donning pilgrim's habit and stealing, 'poor thief', from Rousillon.

Thus the action of the play, in the very middle of its course, appears diverted if not devoid of direction. The heroine's announced purpose seems woeful but dramatically irrelevant. We are left blind to what will follow; the dramatist himself seems uncertain. In short—unnatural condition for Shakespearian comedy—the world of *All's Well that Ends Well* seems out of control.

Then, suddenly, we see Helena in Florence—the very city which Bertram came to serve in the wars!

It therefore becomes necessary, in the light of this unexpected conjunction, to do what has not been necessary in examining any earlier play: to look again at action just passed, which has already been examined *by the best light the dramatist provided at the time*. And it becomes especially necessary to probe the nature of this heroine.

She is fifth and last in the succession of heroines who—all practisers, overpeerers, proprietors of central secrets about which large actions revolve, and in varying degrees controllers of their worlds —stand in the line of Prospero. Helena is the great pivot in Shakespearian comedy: after her, heroines do not control the suddenly and terribly worsened world which has come into being with *All's Well* and which endures without improvement to the last moments of *The Tempest*. After Helena the role passes to men—benevolent, omniscient, and omnipotent ones, Vincentio of *Measure for Measure* and Prospero himself, who control their worlds easily and absolutely despite the worst that evil tries; to elemental and divine forces in *Pericles*, *Cymbeline*, and *The Winter's Tale*; or, as in *Troilus and Cressida*, world altogether without management, the role does not exist at all except as it is neglectfully infested, by a bystander, Thersites.

Helena, then, is a turning-point heroine for a turning-point world. Portia and Rosalind, brilliant and disguised, could manage their healthy worlds readily: all Belmont was golden, and all Venice was sound except for Shylock—no match for Portia and the general goodness; the world of *As You Like It* contained nothing worse than the usurping Duke and Oliver—besides a green and gilded snake and a sucked and hungry lioness, easily managed by Orlando, who is managed by Rosalind; Illyria, though inhabited wholly by persons suffering some degree of frustration, held no darker menace than Aguecheek, so that Viola could safely trust time alone to resolve her difficulties. Helena's world, following Viola's, is the last that is controllable by a heroine; after it, the words of the comedies and romances are either uncontrolled or mastered by forces of extraordinary magnitude.

Viola can trust all to time: in her world Helena trusts nothing to time, for time would solve nothing. Viola's gentle femininity is sufficient in a world of sentimental cast, characterized by the melting softness of Orsino and Olivia, the selflessness of Antonio, the mellow buffoonery of Belch, the innocence of Aguecheek. The world in which Helena operates requires a heroine of sterner stuff: she must be shrewder than Portia, more self-sufficient than Rosalind; her nails must be sharper than Beatrice's.

For there is a fistula to be cured in her world, which corrupts not only the King's flesh but the time itself. Shakespeare himself has grown older: *All's Well that Ends Well* is the first comedy whose point of view is not youth's, but that of the older generation looking at youth's world and finding it not good. The old, great days are gone: in the land, as in the King's body, 'Nature and sickness / Debate it at their leisure'.

Though Helena's is youth's world still, and not age's, as are Marina's, Imogen's, Perdita's, and Miranda's, yet it is youth's world as seen through age's eyes. It is the world of Parolles, seen as Lafeu sees Parolles:

> The devil it is that's thy master. Why dost thou garter up thy arms o' this fashion? Dost make hose of thy sleeves? Do other servants so? Thou wert best set thy lower part where thy nose stands. By mine honour, if I were but two hours younger, I'd beat thee. Methinks thou art a general offence, and every man should beat thee. I think thou wast created for men to breathe themselves upon thee. (II. iii. 264–72.)

Yet the world of this action is exactly at the turning-point: youth's story is set within a frame of jaundiced age's conception. To master such a world is quite too much for a gentle heroine: control requires a force nearer Vincentio's than Viola's. The dazzling Rosalind, who easily rules her world and makes all perfect by inventing a fiction of magical powers, would not suffice here. Helena, however, suffices: single-minded, secretive, cunningly aggressive, she is all that a heroine must be to thrive in such company, in such a world.

A trace of the emerging Helena shows in the deep and subtle silence in which Viola hides from the time of her first meeting with Antonio in Act III of *Twelfth Night* through the last moments, when, confronted and questioned by Sebastian, she still keeps her wide-eyed mask: 'If spirits can assume both form and suit / You come to fright us.' It is Helena's silence, from the end of I. i until near the end of III. vii, on the matters that most concern her, that leaves us to 'square our guess by shows'—and to accept too readily her self-portrait drawn in the soliloquy of III. ii and the sonnet-letter of III. iv as an obedient and crushed wife, forlorn, abandoned, selflessly anguished that her presence keeps Bertram from home and imperils him in foreign wars. In not taking us into her confidence on vital matters during this crucial period, she represents a drastic departure from Shakespeare's customary way of handling our awareness of a heroine's mind and purposes.

That Helena does in fact have in her mind a secret thing-to-do, all the while from the time Bertram sends her from the court to the time she describes her scheme to the Florentine widow, there is reason to believe from the very beginning. The soliloquy which ends I. i, re-examined in the light of Helena's unexpected appearance in Florence, is very revealing: it is the most explicit statement of her philosophy in the entire play. Set where it is, it gains significance as conforming to Shakespeare's regular method. Such statements, as common in the histories and tragedies as in the comedies, serve as topic sentences for subsequent action. This looks less like a heroine's reasoning than like Edmund's in *King Lear*; more emphatically, as an announcement of purpose, it harks back to Richard of Gloucester's promise to slay more gazers than the basilisk and like a Sinon take another Troy. It is no utterance for a Viola—'O time! thou must untangle this, not I. / It is too hard a knot for me t' untie!'—but neither is this a world for a Viola. 'But my intents are fix'd and will not leave me': this is our guide to interpretation of Helena's action until Bertram is prostrate at her feet. Presumably we should understand that this declaration claims precedence over any contradictory speech, even a soliloquy, made afterwards. It provides our advantage during those scenes in which Helena must otherwise appear to have left her intents and to have become an object of pity.

Even so, Helena's characteristic way—uncharacteristic of Shakespeare—of neglecting to be specific in telling us what is in her mind rules the key soliloquy itself, where she does not make even her incidental purpose explicit—the cure of the King—let alone the deeper purpose to be served by that cure:

The King's disease—my project may deceive me,
But my intents are fix'd and will not leave me.
(I. i. 243–4.)

Both purposes are left to be divined from the tenor of the soliloquy
and to be perceived fully only in the subsequent action, which is
their implementation. Though this method is contrary to Shakespeare's normal way, it is appropriate to Helena's character, which
in turn is appropriate to the world against which she must hold her
own. Though it is never made unmistakable, in Shakespeare's usual
way of making indispensable facts unmistakable, that the opportunity to save the King's life is, to her, but a lucky chance in her
campaign for Bertram, yet it is implied both by the key soliloquy
and by her later admission to the Countess:

Hel.   There is a remedy approv'd set down
          To cure the desperate languishings whereof
          The King is render'd lost.
Count.   This was your motive
          For Paris, was it? Speak.
Hel.   My lord your son made me to think of this,
          Else Paris and the medicine and the King
          Had from the conversation of my thoughts
          Haply been absent then.
(I. iii. 234–41.)

If his fistula did not offer a means to catch Bertram, the King could
die of it; it would be all one to Helena—like the recent death of her
own father:

Laf. Farewell, pretty lady. You must hold the credit of your father.
Hel. O, were that all! I think not on my father,
        And these great tears grace his remembrance more
        Than those I shed for him. What was he like?
        I have forgot him.
(I. i. 88–93.)

Re-viewed thus nakedly, Helena's philosophy and its implementation take on an unheroinely cast. Had Shakespeare followed, in
this play, his customary method of making explicit statement in
advance of action, her conduct might well have appeared even
worse. To thrive in this world, she must be as she is; yet if what she
is were boldly represented at the outset, she would appear brazen.
Perhaps, then, the ambiguities which Shakespeare permits in the
management of awarenesses in *All's Well* are calculated: Helena's
motives and means are such that it is expedient to leave them obscure
until the goal is won; in retrospect they will not look so bad.

In any event, it is better to leave them obscure until some moment comes when they can be shown to serve a pious purpose—such as preventing an act that has no relish of salvation in it: Bertram's flirtation with the sin of adultery, his attempt to seduce the virgin Diana, is such an act. It is when Helena catches him at this that, for the first time in the play, Shakespeare allows her to be explicit about her devices:

> *Hel.*   Let her, in fine, consent
> As we'll direct her how 'tis best to bear it.
> Now his important blood will nought deny
> That she'll demand. A ring the County wears,
> That downward hath succeeded in his house
> From son to son, some four or five descents
> Since the first father wore it. This ring he holds
> In most rich choice; yet in his idle fire,
> To buy his will, it would not seem too dear,
> Howe'er repented after.
> *Wid.*   Now I see
> The bottom of your purpose.
> *Hel.* You see it lawful, then. It is no more
> But that your daughter, ere she seems as won,
> Desires this ring; appoints him an encounter;
> In fine, delivers me to fill the time,
> Herself most chastely absent.
>
>   (III. vii. 17–34.)

Though the indispensable soliloquy which ends I. i gave us a deep look into Helena's philosophy, it exposed nothing of immediate means and ends. It permitted us to surmise, but not to know with that certainty with which we are usually equipped in the comedies. With the help of other passages it gave us enough light to see that the King's cure is a means rather than an end. Moreover, it gave cause to pry into Helena's seemingly unsuspecting acceptance of Bertram's instructions after the wedding. Lacking the soliloquy (II. v. 75–78), we should have to see Helena here as naïvely trusting and deceived. Having it, though left unsure whether we hold advantage over her or over Bertram in his assumption that he is deceiving his wife, we at least know enough to view the scene with some suspicion. The same kind of ambiguity veils the truth of the scenes (III. ii and iv) of Helena's soliloquy and sonnet-letter on leaving Rousillon. Lacking the key soliloquy of I. i, we should have to take her at her word and pity her as an abused innocent, selflessly fleeing home as a pilgrim to St. Jaques and Death. Having that early statement, we have cause to question whether she leaves Rousillon to pursue Death, or to pursue Bertram. On the one hand, being spoken with only us to hear, and carrying the ring of truth, Helena's departing plaint seems intended for truth:

> I will be gone.
> My being here it is that holds thee hence.
>   (III. ii. 125–6.)

Against this impression, the words of the first soliloquy are persistent:

> The fated sky
> Gives us free scope, only doth backward pull
> Our slow designs when we ourselves are dull.
>   (I. i. 232–4.)

And more:

> —my projects may deceive me,
> But my intents are fix'd and will not leave me.
>   (Ibid. 243–4.)

This is paltering with us in a double sense. With two key soliloquies in conflict, we cannot be positive, when she leaves Rousillon,
that Helena means what she says. The dramatist veils the truth,
though recollection of the first soliloquy must inevitably breed a
kind of question in the second, which would otherwise stand for
truth itself.

Then, in pilgrim's habit, as we noted, Helena arrives in Florence,
where Bertram is. Her destination, she tells the Widow, is 'Saint
Jaques le Grand'. Since the Widow, familiar with the destinations
of pilgrims, evinces no surprise or offers correction, we must understand that Helena's proper route to this shrine does in fact lie
through Florence; indeed, 'There's four or five, to great Saint
Jaques bound' already stopping at the Widow's house. Therefore
Helena has not gone out of her way: *or so, for the moment, we are
required to understand.* But was it coincidence that she chose a
saint the road to whose shrine ran through Bertram's present loca-
tion? Had she, at first, a real intention of going beyond Florence?
Or was the pilgrimage a mask for the true purpose—like her visit
to Paris to cure the King's fistula? Added to the statement of her
philosophy made in the first soliloquy and to her use of the King's
cure as the means of marrying Bertram, her arrival in Florence is
cause for suspicion that the pilgrimage to Saint Jaques was a masquerade from the outset. But the dramatist allows it to do no more
than arouse suspicion at this time.

Shakespeare continues to hold up the veil of ambiguity during
Helena's first conversation with the Widow and Diana. He does,
however, give us our first unequivocal advantage here, in that the
Widow and Diana are ignorant of Helena's identity and of her

relation to Bertram. Moreover, the gap between their awareness and ours is the first in the play that is exploited with his old relish. The exploitation of the situation is extended and elaborate—as though Shakespeare particularly enjoyed this one major indulgence of the sport which had been a speciality since *The Comedy of Errors*. The peculiar relation of Helena to Bertram, known to us and not to the Florentines, is touched directly or obliquely many times; the Count's reported rejection and abandonment of his bride, Parolles's reported vilification of the deserted wife, Bertram's improper overtures to Diana—everything in the conversation strikes close to Helena; finally, the sustained display is brightly climaxed when Bertram, ignorant of her presence, marches along the street, past her and the Florentine ladies, ignorant of her relation to him. In all but one respect the exploitation is conducted as Shakespeare had conducted exploitation of comparable situations from the first. The closest parallel is the scene in *The Two Gentlemen of Verona* (iv. ii) when Julia, just arrived in Milan, in boy's clothes and unobserved by Proteus, converses with the Host while her lover serenades Silvia. But the contrast is as striking as the resemblance. We know precisely why Julia has come to Milan, because she told us before she left Verona. We do not know with certainty why Helena is in Florence. We share completely in Julia's advantage over Proteus, whose passes are overwatched by one who means to thwart them. Bertram's passes are also overwatched—but we cannot be sure whether Helena has come deliberately to overwatch them and claim her husband or is in Florence merely because it lies on the road to Saint Jaques's shrine. Because our vision is imperfect, the effects of the scene are uniquely ambiguous. Knowing Helena's relation to Bertram while the Widow and Diana's ignorance of it is exploited, we cannot fail to mark the flashes of irony. But, being unsure of Helena's intentions since she left the King's court and, more recently, since she left Rousillon with the assertion that she was going to Saint Jaques, we cannot tell how to respond to the scene. If we knew that she has truly abandoned the pursuit and is honestly, as she represents herself, a homeless pilgrim seeking Saint Jaques and Death, our knowledge would flood the spectacle with pathos. Or if we knew beyond doubt that she has come to Florence as a relentless hunter who has never lost the scent, and that even now as she eyes the quarry her mind is shrewdly sifting the Widow's facts for materials of a device to bring him down, our knowledge would provoke either simple joy that the victory is in sight—or, perhaps, sympathy for the quarry, marching jauntily by, oblivious of the keen, hard eye that has him in the sights. The confused effects which result from our deficient knowledge are the heaviest penalty Shakespeare pays in the play for ambiguity in the management of awarenesses: it seems a monumental missed opportunity at the dead centre of the play. For such a crucial scene he would usually have begun preparation far back, so that when it came we could have no doubt how to take it.

At the end of III. v Helena continues to hold the veil between herself and us; thus she speaks to the Widow:

> I humbly thank you.
> Please it this matron and this gentle maid
> To eat with us to-night, the charge and thanking
> Shall be for me; and, to requite you further,
> I will bestow some precepts of this virgin
> Worthy the note.
>
> (III. v. 99–104.)

'I will bestow some precepts of this virgin / Worthy the note': this pious sentiment seems proper for a holy pilgrim; yet the promise of bestowing precepts may be like the journey to Paris to cure the King's fistula—means to another end. That Helena does have a scheme in mind at the very moment she makes this promise is proved when we next see her. She has then sounded the Widow about co-operating, and the preliminaries are already out of the way when they arrive at the Widow's house:

> *Hel.* If you misdoubt me that I am not she,
>   I know not how I shall assure you further
>   But I shall lose the grounds I work upon.
> *Wid.* Though my estate be fallen, I was well born,
>   Nothing acquainted with these businesses,
>   And would not put my reputation now
>   In any staining act.
>
> (III. vii. 1–7.)

In leading up to her description of the device which she must have perfected since arriving in Florence and meeting the Widow and Diana in the street, Helena shows noteworthy insight into the nature of that passion which, she has perceived, has Bertram in its power. Earlier, Helena had gone to Paris ostensibly to cure the King —and by curing him had won her husband: now she will save the honour of two young people whose emotions are not as well controlled as her own—and by doing so will claim her husband for good and all. Says the Widow, 'Now I see / The bottom of your purpose': it is also our own first view of the bottom of Helena's purpose. We gain, at the end of Act III, the degree of awareness which we gained in *Twelfth Night* in I. ii, and in *As You Like It* in

i. iii, when Viola and Rosalind openly announced the beginnings of their masquerades.

But now that we have reached this pinnacle, belatedly, it becomes necessary to make a third examination of earlier scenes which, in a reversal of long habit, the dramatist did not equip us to see in their true colours when they were acted. Once more resurveyed, the facts of earlier action appear startlingly different: since the end of i. i Helena has never faltered in the intents which she then said were fixed and would not leave her. She has not made even us partners in her enterprise; she has deceived us as she has deceived those of her own world. She has long been a masquerader without our knowing it; it is as though Rosalind had vanished into the character of 'Ganymede' without notifying us. Her eyes saw quite through Bertram and Parolles when, after the forced marriage, they sought to make her believe—and themselves were deceived in thinking that they succeeded—that Bertram would rejoin her at Rousillon within two days. The soliloquy of III. ii and the sonnet-letter of III. iv, key statements both, unequivocally announcing her purpose to seek the shrine of Saint Jaques and Death, were practices upon our own credulity: her pilgrimage was never meant for Jaques, but for Priapus. She left Rousillon for Florence, not intending to go farther, with no purpose but to get the ring from Bertram's finger and a child of his fathering. Trusting nothing at all to Time, being no Viola, she arrived with head up, hard-eyed beneath her pilgrim's hood, alert for means to implement her ends. Circumspect and opportunistic from the outset—when she saw the King's fistula as a way to a husband—she sniffs out Bertram's unholy suit to Diana and converts it to her purposes. Indeed, observant of Bertram of the arched brow, hawking eye, and curls, and familiar also with the reputation of Florence—having conversed frankly with such a man as Parolles—she may, even before leaving Rousillon, have imagined the outline of such a situation as this which, by subtle prying, she now discovers:

> *Wid.* Ay, right! Good creature, whereso'er she is,
> Her heart weighs sadly. This young maid might do her
> A shrewd turn, if she pleas'd.
> *Hel.*   How do you mean?
> May be the amorous Count solicits her
> In the unlawful purpose.
> *Wid.*   He does indeed;
> And brokes with all that can in such a suit
> Corrupt the tender honour of a maid.
>   (III. v. 68–75.)

Such has been the past action, and such are the motives and methods of Helena. *Or such—it is necessary to qualify even now—they appear on the third examination, from the highest vantage-point we have so far been provided.*

Not only are the means at hand, but the circumstances are such that now, for the first time, without risk, Helena can tell us all that she has in mind. For in reclaiming her husband on his own terms she will both prevent him from sinning and save Diana's honour: this is a virtuous purpose, about which she can be forthright. That Bertram would ultimately have triumphed over Diana is evident, for this virgin, less strong than her namesake, is half lost already. 'They say the French count has done most honourable service', she is saying when we first meet her, and she keeps returning, fascinated, to the subject: 'He, that with the plume; 'tis a most gallant fellow.' Again, 'Is't not a handsome gentleman?' It would be only a matter of time: the warnings spoken by the Widow and Mariana are those of worried elders addressed to one tottering on the brink. In these circumstances, Helena can be outright with us without risking her heroinely prestige: reclaiming her husband by saving the honour of two innocents is obviously as noble an act as first winning him by curing a king's fistula.

Helena's acute practice on Bertram in which Diana assists is less a new practice than an implementation of the old one, which began stealthily with the soliloquy that ends I. i. Mainly, the management of the device parallels that in earlier comedies in which masquerading heroines deceive heroes. However, unfortunately for the structure of *All's Well* as a whole, there is one notable difference: because of its delicate nature the climactic moment of exploitation cannot be actually represented. In *As You Like It* we witness the two scenes, at the heart of the play, when Orlando makes love to Rosalind, thinking her 'Ganymede' pretending to be Rosalind. In *Twelfth Night* we witness the interviews of 'Cesario' with Orsino and Olivia, climactic scenes which bring the heroine face to face with the persons whose ignorance of her masquerade is most exploitable. The exploitation of these moments, in the earlier plays, is the fruition of long preparation. In *All's Well*, obviously, we cannot witness Helena's crucial meeting with Bertram, and the play therefore lacks exploitation of its climactic moment. We are advised immediately before the meeting that it will occur, and afterwards we are told that it has occurred. But, except for pointed allusions, the nearest the dramatist comes to showing the event itself is the action of IV. ii, when Bertram solicits Diana 'in the unlawful purpose'. Since our advantage over Bertram is perfect here—Helena having for once included us in her planning—and since Diana is Helena's proxy, exploitation of the discrepancy in the awarenesses of Bertram and Diana approximates that of the climactic scenes of earlier comedies. Yet it is not quite the same: Rosalind as 'Ganymede' and Viola as 'Cesario', in their scenes with Orlando and Orsino, are Rosalind and Viola still in our eyes; they carry out their practices in person. Helena is present only as an image in the mind's eye. Moreover, the Bertram–Diana scene itself is only a prelude to the main event, which is unpresentable.

A second attempt to compensate for the absent climactic scene consists of not one but three closely related scenes, totalling 600 lines and surrounding the point which in the typical structure of the comedies is the climactic peak. Gaining enormous emphasis from both this position and their length, these scenes, unfortunately for the total structure, have only an indirect relation to the main action of the play. They are the scenes which develop and exploit the practice on Parolles.

Unlike Helena's practice, which impels the main action, the practice on Parolles is managed quite in Shakespeare's usual fashion: well established beforehand, our advantage over the victim is perfect; the exploitation strikes the usual flashes of irony; the disposition of awarenesses grows ever more complex as exploitation nears a climax. Considered alone, from the point of view of dramatic conception and execution of details, the three scenes are among the finest in the play. But though superbly managed within itself, the fact is that the affair of Parolles is given space disproportionate to its significance for the main action. Parolles appears in thirteen of twenty-three scenes and figures in the dialogue of others. The principal scene of his unmasking, taking 376 lines, is the longest in the play and is set at the normal peak of the comedy—where the consummation of Helena's practice on Bertram should have stood. That Shakespeare permitted Parolles's affair so large emphasis without binding it securely to the main plot—as, for example, the affairs of Malvolio and Aguecheek–Belch are bound to the main plot of *Twelfth Night*—suggests that the inexplicably un-Shakespearian slippage of focus which so damages *Troilus and Cressida* had its beginning in *All's Well*.

Himself a practiser by reputation, Parolles no longer deceives anyone except, allegedly, Bertram. Reportedly 'first smok'd by the old lord Lafeu', his corruption is actually revealed to us first by Helena, whose sharp eyes have pierced him through and through. Already a 'notorious liar' in the opening scene, he is a practiser whose best days are past when the action commences. He is next 'smok'd' by Lafeu:

I have now found thee. When I lose thee again, I care not; yet art thou good for nothing but taking up, and that thou'rt scarce worth.   (II. iii. 217-20.)

'Methinks thou art a general offence, and every man should beat thee', he adds; and, later, he warns Bertram of the company he keeps. Learning that Bertram has deserted his new bride, the Countess instantly blames Parolles:

> A very tainted fellow, and full of wickedness.
> My son corrupts a well-derived nature
> With his inducement.
>
> (III. ii. 89-91.)

Diana, addressing 'Saint Jaques' pilgrim', similarly blames Parolles for Bertram's deviation:

> Yond's that same knave
> That leads him to these places. Were I his lady,
> I would poison that vile rascal.
>
> (III. v. 85-87.)

Inexplicit about Helena's subtle manipulations, Shakespeare is emphatic in advising us that Bertram is the unwitting victim of Parolles's long-standing, corruptive practice. From many remarks we are evidently expected to understand that we hold an advantage over the hero from the first scene of the play until IV. iii, when Parolles's character is exposed.

But if Parolles is in fact Bertram's Falstaff, the play leaves the fact undemonstrated; there are only testimonials of bystanders. Despite Lafeu's too-obvious warnings and despite the Countess's alacrity in assigning blame, there is no evidence that Parolles influences Bertram's relations with Helena. It is true that after the marriage Parolles seconds the hero's resolution to depart for the wars; but Bertram has made his decision before Parolles speaks: 'Although before the solemn priest I have sworn, / I will not bed her.' To this Parolles replies merely, 'What, what, sweetheart?' before Bertram continues, 'I'll to the Tuscan wars, and never bed her.' Parolles's 'influence' is only an echo: 'To the wars.'

The great emphasis given the three scenes which end in Parolles's unmasking is therefore a structural fault. If these built up to the exposure of one whose practices had directed the hero's relations with Helena—and if it were these very practices that they exposed—the emphasis they gain because of their length and position would be justified and their effect dramatically satisfying. If Bertram, on having his eyes opened to Parolles, rushed home to Rousillon, seeking Helena to make amends for wrongs done her, then they would certainly deserve their place. But these scenes teach

Bertram only that Parolles is a generally worthless creature, and nothing about his own conduct: indeed, after the unmasking of Parolles he grows worse rather than better. The relations of Bertram and Helena remain exactly as before: it is still Helena's solitary task to bring her wayward husband into line.

That fact, perhaps, explains why Shakespeare could not use the unmasking of Parolles as the means of correcting Bertram, for to have done so would have been to diminish the magnitude of the heroine's task—if, indeed, not to eliminate it altogether. Yet not to have the Parolles scenes accomplish this purpose is to have them irrelevant to the main action. In solving the dilemma Shakespeare chose the lesser of two evils, allowing the unmasking to serve little purpose rather than using it to solve the heroine's problem for her. At the same time, with some discredit to his dramatic integrity, he sought to patch up the inevitable flaw by packing the play with bystanders' testimonials to the wicked influence of Parolles on Bertram, through the weight of repetition making us suppose it a fact, but shrewdly avoiding any demonstration of the fact. Indeed, the net of the practice perpetrated on us by the dramatist is greater still: the failure of Parolles's unmasking to open Bertram's eyes to himself makes Helena's already seemingly impossible task appear even more difficult—for if the hero has learned nothing from the gross example of Parolles, he must be hard indeed to teach. Thus the main plot is apparently strengthened by some shrewdly crooked devising, and the heroine's prestige is enhanced; out of the unfortunate fact that the unmasking of Parolles and the single-handed reclamation of Bertram by Helena are incompatible elements, Shakespeare has managed to make a good thing.

Within themselves, it should now be repeated, the three scenes of Parolles's affair are superb. As examples of the creation and exploitation of discrepant awarenesses, they show Shakespeare at his best. We hold an unbroken advantage over Parolles from the time the several lords prevail on Bertram to let them 'put him to 't' (III. vi) until he is 'unblinded' to see about him the faces of those to whom he has unwittingly exposed his inner corruption: 'Who cannot be crush'd with a plot?' Moreover, the final scene (IV. iii) of the practice gains extra force from our awareness, during the first portion, up to the entrance of Bertram, *that this period covers the very time of the midnight assignation.* The ninety lines of dialogue of the two French lords are in effect a mock climax—the presentable substitute for the real one which is just then occurring at Diana's house. That we shall not fail to make the connexion, Shakespeare has taken precautions, first by setting immediately before this scene that in which

Diana accepts Bertram's proposal and fixes the hour of the meeting, and second by concerning portions of the lords' conversation with matter that marks the time:

> *2. Lord.* We shall not then have his company to-night?
> *1. Lord.* Not till after midnight; for he is dieted to his hour.
> *2. Lord.* That approaches apace.　　　　　　　　　(IV. iii. 32–36.)

The portion of the scene that follows Bertram's joining these two lords gains extra force from our awareness that the hero has just come from his assignation, where he has unknowingly undone himself. 'I have to-night', he boasts,

> . . . dispatch'd sixteen businesses, a month's length a-piece, by an abstract of success. I have congied with the Duke, done my adieu with his nearest; buried a wife, mourn'd for her; writ to my lady mother I am returning; entertain'd my convoy; and between these main parcels of dispatch effected many nicer needs. The last was the greatest, but that I have not ended yet.
> 　　　　　　　　　　　　　　　　　　　　　　(Ibid. 98–107.)

In this scene, moreover, Shakespeare uses a more complex arrangement of awareness than elsewhere in the play. Three distinct levels are involved: Parolles, overpeered by all, holds the lowest, being blindfolded, ignorant of his whereabouts and of the identity of his interrogators; Bertram is next, overpeering Parolles and witnessing his unmasking, but ignorant that he himself has just been the victim of a deeper plot; we, with the absent, triumphant Helena, stand highest, overpeering Bertram. 'Who cannot be crush'd with a plot?' Parolles's summary line, carrying a double significance for us, points up the parallel: Bertram has been laid as bare by a practice as has Parolles by that in which Bertram takes part. At the point of Parolles's unmasking, the two exchange places on the structure of awarenesses: Parolles, looking at the faces around him, sees the truth; Bertram, seeing clearly enough what a thing is Parolles, recognizes nothing of himself in the spectacle.

Shakespeare's un-Shakespearian manner of treating our awarenesses, expressed in the heroine's unheroinely manner of neglecting to explain her campaign before she conducts it, is nowhere more noticeable than in the scenes just after the climax. In IV. iii, in the midst of the substitute climax, we hear from the Second Lord:

> Sir, his wife some two months since fled from his house. Her pretence is a pilgrimage to Saint Jaques le Grand; which holy undertaking with most austere sanctimony she accomplish'd; and, there residing, the tenderness of her nature became as a prey to her grief; in fine, made a groan of her last breath, and now she sings in heaven.　　　　　　　(Ibid. 56–62.)

'How is this justified?' asks the First Lord—who, if his showing of

astonishment were magnified, might be speaking for us; the Second
Lord replies:

> The stronger part of it by her own letters, which makes her story true, even
> to the point of her death. Her death itself, which could not be her office to say
> is come, was faithfully confirm'd by the rector of the place.   (Ibid. 65–69.)

Our advantage over the two French lords is here as firm as ever: we
know well enough that Helena is not dead, but warm and breath-
ing, her pilgrim's masquerade laid by and her masquerade as Diana
taken up. Bertram also, according to the second Lord, has already
been informed of his wife's death, 'point from point, to the full
arming of the verity'. What is more, when the scene returns to
Rousillon at the end of Act IV, we learn that the Countess, Lafeu,
and the Clown are all familiar with the report; and the King, already
apprised of Helena's death, has consented to Bertram's marriage
with Lafeu's daughter. But this report, widespread among participants, catches us quite unprepared: though we know that the report
is false, we have been given no prior hint of its existence.

*At this point, therefore, it becomes necessary yet again to re-
survey the operations of Helena.*

The manipulations of all earlier comic heroines are conducted in
the open, so far as we are concerned. Helena's are conducted behind
the scenes; her conjurer's fingers are hidden even from us. Previous
reviews of her actions have made this fact evident; but with the disclosure that verified reports of her death have been spread over Italy
and France, it becomes apparent that earlier judgements based on
as much as the dramatist allowed to be seen up to the time they were
made under-estimate her.

When did she lay the detailed proofs of her 'death'? From the
time of her arrival in Florence and her encounter with the Widow
and Diana to her midnight assignation with Bertram is only part of
a day and half a night. Yet at the hour of the assignation the report
of her death has been widely circulated, presumably by letters first
to the Countess in Rousillon and thereafter from the Countess to
Bertram in Florence. Evidently, then, Helena's proofs were arranged
before she arrived in Florence. Her first conversation with the
Widow makes it appear that she has come directly from Rousillon
and is bound for Saint Jaques. Yet in IV. iii, at midnight, shortly
after her arrival, the Second Lord states that Bertram's wife 'some
two months since fled from his house'. Moreover, this same lord
remarks that her death 'was faithfully confirm'd by the rector' of
Saint Jaques's shrine. Where, then, has Helena spent the two months
since she left Rousillon and during which time she has established

and disseminated 'proofs' of her death? On first meeting her, the Widow inquires whither she is bound. 'To Saint Jaques le Grand', she replies. This is the first we have seen or known of her since the soliloquy and sonnet-letter on the occasion of her leaving Rousillon: 'I am Saint Jaques' pilgrim, thither gone.' We have, then, when she meets the Widow, no hint that her words are false, yet false they must be. She cannot be just going to Saint Jaques, but coming *from* Saint Jaques, where, during the past two months, she has resided, written letters advertising her illness, and finally arranged with the rector of that place—by what subtle machination, who can say?—to confirm her death even 'to the full arming of the verity'.

It is not impossible, of course, that what appears to be Helena's juggling of the facts of time, place, and purpose is merely Shakespeare's carelessness. On the other hand, the belated, surprising evidence of the heroine's activities during the two months between Rousillon and Florence is consistent with the dramatist's handling of our awareness throughout the play, consistent also with our growing sense of Helena's way of operating from the beginning. Excepting the moment of openness when she needed Diana to help her trap Bertram, this heroine has not spoken straight to anyone. She has not taken us into her confidence, but has kept silent, hinted loosely, or put us off the track with falsehood. Unlike our sense of earlier heroines, our awareness of what she is grows and changes. Our understanding of her past conduct is repeatedly revised by our view of her present conduct. Her emerging character becomes gradually more consistent with the philosophy of that first soliloquy:

> Our remedies oft in ourselves do lie,
> Which we ascribe to heaven. The fated sky
> Gives us free scope, only doth backward pull
> Our slow designs when we ourselves are dull.
> (I. i. 231–4.)

All things considered, Helena appears quite capable of telling us and the Widow that she is bound for Saint Jaques when in fact she has already been there. The shock given our awareness by the news that her 'death' has been well documented and widely reported is less likely an accident of Shakespeare's carelessness than an effect of his intention.

Finally, the manner in which she capitalizes her multiple advantages in the last scene of the play justifies the most extravagant estimate of her capabilities. She contrives and executes the last practice of her campaign—the sixth and greatest—with that same secrecy, thoroughness, and determination by which she had earlier won a husband by curing the King's fistula and conquered him by managing a triple, simultaneous masquerade in the cloaks of pilgrim, Diana, and Death.

In this long final scene Shakespeare exploits with a vengeance, as though to make up for opportunities omitted in the preceding acts, the many discrepancies that have accumulated and are piled up at the end. Our vantage-point for this last action is nearly but not quite Olympian—for Helena has even now withheld all the details of her scheme. As hitherto, she has done her work behind the scenes. Although her subtle hand appears in each twist of the tortuous denouement, she is herself absent during the greater part of the last scene, present during only the final thirty-five lines. A triumphant general who has mapped the strategy from the rear, she steps forward just in time to accept unconditional surrender:

> *Hel.*   No, my good lord;
> 'Tis but the shadow of a wife you see,
> The name and not the thing.
> *Ber.*   Both, both. O, pardon!
>   (v. iii. 307–9.)

She could as well have appeared at the start of the scene, with Diana and the Widow. Her plain statement then, proved by her companions, would have settled everything at once and forestalled Bertram's pain on the rack. Indeed, she could have provided evidence enough without bringing the Florentines to Rousillon, for the King's ring is on Bertram's finger, where she had placed it in her midnight role. This ring is her greatest new surprise for us: 'And on your finger in the night I'll put / Another ring, that what in time proceeds / May token to the future our past deeds', said Diana in making her appointment with Bertram. We did not know, at that time, what ring it was: Helena, true to her nature, had told us nothing. The King's words in the final scene are therefore a revelation:

> This ring was mine; and, when I gave it Helen,
> I bade her, if her fortunes ever stood
> Necessitied to help, that by this token
> I would relieve her.
>   (Ibid. 83–86.)

Besides her extraordinary personal resources, of which we became aware slowly, Helena has possessed this token of supreme authority ever since she cured the King's fistula and has kept the fact from us. During the long while that we supposed her an abused, abandoned, defeated wife, she was in fact equipped not only with secret personal capabilities but also with a symbol of the King's power. With the discovery that she has kept this ring in reserve throughout the action, our estimate of Helena must be revised a final time: as a controlling force she has stood nearer to Vincentio and Prospero than we could know.

Though she might easily have spared Bertram his hour upon the rack, then, she does not. Portia, dealing with a villain in the court scene of *The Merchant of Venice*, mercifully extends him chance after chance to save himself by showing a sign of humanity. Helena, dealing with a hero, puts him to the torture. Yet it is not torture without purpose; Helena does nothing without purpose. This hero is so inwardly corrupt that even just before the end he cannot recognize the portraiture of his own case in that of Parolles: 'He's quoted for a most perfidious slave, / With all the spots o' th' world tax'd and debauch'd, / Whose nature sickens but to speak a truth.' So he describes Parolles—in the midst of his own desperate lies. Helena's subtly designed torture inexorably compels him to indulge in an orgy, a last wild spree of falsehood, so violent that it must purge his system of vileness for ever. When this spree is over, he lapses into a silence broken only by his cry at sight of his personal nemesis and saviour: 'O, pardon!'

So darkly designed and so efficiently executed—all the while with herself in the rear of it—is Helena's final practice that it borders on witchery, as—looked at once more—did her first device of the campaign, when with a weird chant she charmed the King into letting her treat his fistula. 'Sweet practiser, thy physic I will try', said the King, naïvely, himself being drawn into the incantation, at the end of which it would seem quite in order if Helena should cry 'Peace! the charm's wound up'. 'There's something in't / More than my father's skill', she had said darkly of her medicine, seeking the Countess's leave to go to Paris.

By application of this 'something more', first at Paris, afterwards at Saint Jaques's shrine, at Florence, and finally at Rousillon, she has prevailed at last. Like Proteus and Bassanio, who were reduced to stunned Orlandos, Bertram will require no further correction. Shakespeare's 'loveliest creation', Coleridge called Helena: 'O, pardon!' cries the prostrate Bertram, who has been scratched deep by the longest and stealthiest nails in Shakespeare. Yet the scratches are benign, for against the great odds of a corrupt world they have cured his corruption.

2. *Troilus and Cressida*

Conspicuous as it is, the falling-off of the world between *Twelfth Night* and *All's Well* is a slight dip as compared to that which occurs between *All's Well* and *Troilus and Cressida*. The King, Lafeu, and the Countess deplore the slippage from their generation to that of Parolles and Bertram; but at least the old ones still live, to lament the passing of a better world and to reflect its glory—and Helena has inherited power to cure the local manifestations of corruption in her world.

Whereas the world of *All's Well* has slipped a degree or two, that of *Troilus and Cressida* has fallen the whole way down, past hope, past cure, and physicianless. Shakespeare took up the heroic tale of Troy after it had gone a progress through the guts of a beggar and at a time when he was evidently not of a mind to restore its former glory. Never—or at least never since the days of Talbot in *Henry VI* —quite able to stomach heroics, which he saw to be excess, laughable or contemptible or both, he perhaps found the debatable argument of Troilus, Cressida, and Pandarus, already besmeared, suited to his immediate mood: 'All the argument is a cuckold and a whore; a good quarrel to draw emulous factions and bleed to death upon. Now, the dry serpigo on the subject, and war and lechery confound all!'

So says Thersites, our ubiquitous adviser, on whom has descended what, for the moment, remains of the great role of chief practiser and controller, formerly tenanted with distinction by Oberon and a succession of brilliant heroines.

The corruptive disease of the world of *Troilus and Cressida* is a contagious one, catching even to the bones of dramatic structure, leaving them too infirm to support the action. This structure is defective also in important ways not immediately relevant; but in no way is the dramatic malformation more conspicuous than in the management of the awarenesses. We hold advantage of some significance in only four of twenty-seven scenes, and the discrepancy between the participants' awareness and ours is the essential fact in only one of these. In no case is a dramatically created discrepancy the subject of exploitation of an entire scene. Of the twenty-five named persons, we hold advantage at some time over only seven— Hector, Troilus, Pandarus, Achilles, Ajax, Diomedes, and Cressida. What is more, our advantage over Hector is brief and negligible; exploitation of our advantage over Achilles is both brief and badly managed; and our advantage over Troilus, Cressida, and Pandarus, though it is the most notable in the action, *is not given us by drama-*

tic means but depends upon our extra-dramatic knowledge of out-comes. The stair-stepped structure of awarenesses, a fixture in the comedies since *The Comedy of Errors*, rises shakily in but one scene. In short, the play strangely neglects the means by which Shakespeare has hitherto maintained perspective, moved action, and created effect. Central to a period during which he made telling use of elaborate arrangements of the awarenesses, in both comedy and tragedy, *Troilus and Cressida* exhibits uncertainty in the hand-ling even of simple arrangements and a botching of more complex ones.

Always Shakespeare's practice has been to build by dramatic means, trusting no other, a context in our minds and to require us to measure and interpret by it the significance of action set before our eyes; it is one of his supreme virtues as a dramatist that he does so. *All's Well*, in which we are repeatedly required to re-examine pre-ceding scenes in the light of later ones, shows a change from his habitual method of making assurance doubly sure that our minds hold facts needed to catch the significance of a scene *at the time it is acted.* Yet the reversal in *All's Well* appears to have been cal-culated, the new method serving to obscure Helena's motives and methods, which appear less unsightly when perceived afterwards than if recognized beforehand. Moreover, though atypical, the method is followed consistently; it is a principle of the manage-ment of the awarenesses in that play. But no principle in the manage-ment of awarenesses is discoverable in *Troilus and Cressida*, where all is chaos which matches—by coincidence rather than design? —the condition of its world: 'What's past and what's to come is strew'd with husks / And formless ruin of oblivion', says Agamem-non; and so, except for our extra-dramatic knowledge, the action would inevitably appear to us also. For Shakespeare here trusts all, or nearly all, to this extra-dramatic knowledge of the major out-comes: that Cressida will prove false; that Achilles will kill Hector; that ultimately Troy will fall. The damaging effects of the substi-tution of an historical, ready-made awareness for a dramatically created one are all too evident.

Aside from our ready-made advantage, then, we hold almost none. Until II. iii our vantage-point is never higher than that of the participants. Most uncharacteristically, during this half of the play Shakespeare twice neglects opportunities to create and exploit dis-crepancies of a kind that in other plays after the series of *Henry VI* he often went out of his way to capitalize; here, though they lie directly in his path, he misses them. The first such opportunity arises in what should be the key scene of Pandarus's initial interview

with Cressida. Heretofore such a scene would be cast in a double
or triple light; here we do not know until *after* the interview what
has been in Cressida's mind throughout:

> Words, vows, gifts, tears, and love's full sacrifice,
> He offers in another's enterprise;
> But more in Troilus thousandfold I see
> Than in the glass of Pandar's praise may be;
> Yet hold I off.   (I. ii. 308–12.)

By the usual method, the sense of this soliloquy would have been
exposed to us not at the end of what, as it stands, is an interminable
scene which appears to get nowhere, but at the outset. The apparently stalemated interview is immediately preceded by a conversation of Cressida with her servant, and even as early as the *Henry VI*
group Shakespeare used such introductory passages to create a light
by which the main action to follow should be seen. Thereafter, the
device became a mark of his craftsmanship in comedy, history, and
tragedy; its use has been illustrated in every comedy before *Troilus
and Cressida*—even in *All's Well*, where, though avoided in Helena's
scenes, it is used in Parolles's. The conversation of Cressida and her
servant gave easy opportunity for the dramatist to suggest her true
attitude; we would then have shared an advantage with Cressida
over Pandarus and, by implication, over the absent Troilus. But,
inexplicably, the opportunity is let slip; the introductory talk between servant and mistress has not the slightest bearing on the key
interview which follows. It makes no mention of Troilus, of Cressida's interest in him, or of Pandarus, but irrelevantly concerns
Hecuba and Helen, Hector's anger, Andromache, and the character
of Ajax. The result of the omission is that we stand on the same footing as Pandarus during the nearly 300 lines of the interview, ignorant
of what is in Cressida's mind. When her soliloquy finally advises us,
it is too late: though it presents a spectacular pageant of Trojan
heroes returning from battle, passing singly across the stage while
Pandarus and Cressida comment, the scene fails as drama. Managed
in the usual way, it should have had great relevance and yielded
multiple effects; lacking an exploitable discrepancy it is only spectacle.

The second, more surprising failure to capitalize a situation in the
usual way occurs in the handling of Ulysses' practice on Achilles.
Conducted in three stages, with the continuing purpose of moving
the reluctant warrior to battle, this practice is one of three principal
lines of action in the play. The initial step is devised as usual, the
scheme being clearly explained for our advantage prior to the scene
of its exploitation. 'I have a young conception in my brain', says

Ulysses to Nestor: 'Be you my time to bring it to some shape.' And
he continues:

> No, make a lottery;
> And, by device, let blockish Ajax draw
> The sort to fight with Hector; among ourselves
> Give him allowance as the worthier man;
> For that will physic the great Myrmidon
> Who broils in loud applause, and make him fall
> His crest that prouder than blue Iris bends.
>
> (I. iii. 374–80.)

Announced thus early in the action by Ulysses himself and concerning a purpose so central as that of moving Achilles, this is a practice
that Shakespeare would normally develop and exploit fully, as one
that impels a main action. At its start Ulysses' device appears to have
a dramatic significance comparable to the donning of disguise at the
start of the heroine's masquerade in the romantic comedies. But then,
having reared it, Shakespeare lets the practice fall unexploited and
become lost in a mass of irrelevant matter. In the scene which follows the devising of the practice, when we should expect exploitation of the discrepancy between Achilles' awareness and ours,
shared with Ulysses, the first sixty lines are consumed with insults
exchanged by Thersites and Ajax, and the next seventy with more
of the same in which Achilles and Patroclus join. Only at the end of
the scene is there mention of the lottery devised by Ulysses as a
practice on Achilles. It is not the fault of Shakespeare's art, of course,
that Ulysses' practice fails to move Achilles! But it is unlike Shakespeare to leave unexploited a highly exploitable discrepancy which
he has taken pains to create.

In both cases of omitted opportunities, the primary matter on
which our attention would usually be concentrated is buried by
secondary or seemingly random matters. The main matter is again
obscured in the treatment of the second stage of the practice, represented in II. iii before Achilles' tent. Here again a gap is created and
then left unexploited, when the practice on Achilles becomes lost
during this scene of nearly 300 lines. The opening seventy lines are
again consumed with the unfocused raillery of Thersites; and thereafter, for 100 lines, Agamemnon makes two futile attempts to bring
Achilles from his tent, sending first Patroclus and then Ulysses for
him. It is when a third trial is intended, with Ajax as envoy, that
Ulysses invents a second device:

> O Agamemnon, let it not be so!
>
> . . . . .
> No, this thrice worthy and right valiant lord [*Ajax*]

170

Must not so stale his palm, nobly acquir'd;
Nor, by my will, assubjugate his merit,
As amply titled as Achilles is,
By going to Achilles.
That were to enlard his fat-already pride
And add more coals to Cancer when he burns
With entertaining great Hyperion.
This lord go to him! Jupiter forbid,
And say in thunder, 'Achilles go to him.'
                                        (II. iii. 192–209.)

Though the ultimate purpose of this device is to move Achilles by flattering Ajax, it is exploited not as a practice on Achilles, but merely as a practice on blockish Ajax, ignorant of the true purpose of the praise showered on him. We are given no hint that Achilles hears any of it; he has withdrawn into his tent before Ulysses and others begin to sing the praises of Ajax—and Shakespeare gives him no voice either during or immediately after this portion of the scene. This is an unexpected waste of a practice which has begun as auspiciously as that, for example, by which Benedick and Beatrice in *Much Ado about Nothing* are tricked into supposing that each is loved by the other. There we are given repeated assurances that the overhearers overhear, and all dialogue exploits the gap between practisers and victims. Here not only does Achilles give no sign of overhearing, but the practisers carry on their baiting of Ajax as though that were the end, though there is nothing to be gained by swelling up Ajax unless Achilles is thereby moved. It is an excessive practice if it serves merely to dissuade Ajax from entering the tent to invite Achilles out. It is true that Ajax is to be the Greeks' champion in the coming combat with Hector—but that fact was earlier made known to both Ajax and Achilles; Ajax then demonstrated that he required no fattening of pride to accept the challenge, and Achilles was untouched by the insult to himself when Ajax was chosen by lottery: 'I know not what; 'tis trash.' All circumstances considered, therefore, the seventy-five lines exploiting the gap between our awareness and Ajax's fail in the same way other scenes and portions of scenes in *Troilus and Cressida* fail—by including elements that obscure the primary purpose, which is allowed to go under without notice.

The third stage of Ulysses' campaign to move Achilles is unfortunately separated from the second by the long scene in which Troilus and Cressida are brought together. The very separation impairs the dramatic force of the practice. But more disastrous to it is the intrusion of the affair of Calchas—the arrangement for the exchange of Antenor and Cressida. This business—of profound

significance in the affair of Troilus and Cressida—has none at all in
the affair of Achilles; yet, amazingly, it stands as the introduction to
the scene which represents the culmination of Ulysses' practice. It
is the second gross violation of Shakespeare's virtually universal
method of using the opening of a scene to light the remainder. Once
begun, exploitation of Ulysses' final device is well managed. Says
Ulysses at the beginning,

> Achilles stands i' th' entrance of his tent.
> Please it our general to pass strangely by him,
> As if he were forgot; and, princes all,
> Lay negligent and loose regard upon him.
> I will come last. 'Tis like he'll question me
> Why such unplausive eyes are bent, why turn'd on him.
> If so, I have derision med'cinable
> To use between your strangeness and his pride,
> Which his own will shall have desire to drink.
>
> (III. iii. 38–46.)

In succession Agamemnon, Nestor, Menelaus, and Ajax pass Achilles
with indifferent greetings; and this time, whereas the first two
devices of the campaign—the choice of Ajax by lottery and the
fattening of his pride by flattery—failed to affect Achilles, the
device succeeds. The actual exploitation of the gap between our
awareness, shared with the four practisers, and that of Achilles
takes up only fifteen lines; but, along with the Diomedes–Cressida
scene of Act V, it best accords with Shakespeare's normal method.
Ulysses' interview with Achilles, which directly follows this initial
exploitation and includes the great speech on the transitory nature
of fame ('Time hath, my lord, a wallet at his back') is itself a continuation of the practice—indeed, the speech is itself a practice. For
although Ulysses aptly characterizes the way of the world in general
—'For Time is like a fashionable host / That slightly shakes his
parting guest by th' hand, / And with his arms outstretch'd as he
would fly / Grasps in the comer'—yet the fact is that the particular
application is false: Time and the Greeks have not forgotten Achilles
and begun 'to worship Ajax', but need him direly, as none knows
better than Ulysses, the speaker. No moment in the play is more
shrewdly managed than this in which Ulysses, with a speech superb
in itself and enhanced by the practice that frames it, exhorts Achilles
to guard his honours. Our knowledge of the true purpose of the
speech acts as a lever to lift a high utterance even higher.

When Ulysses turns away at last—'Farewell, my lord; I as your
lover speak'—the third and final stage of the long practice ends. The
management of the entire practice shows faults such as Shakespeare
does not commit except in this play. Three have been identified: the

failure to exploit the situation in the first stage, when the selection
of Ajax by lottery is buried under other matter; the shifting of the
focus from Achilles to Ajax as victim in the second stage; and
the awkward intrusion of the affair of Calchas as introduction to the
scene in the final stage. Two additional, more fundamental faults
mar the practice also. First is the use of Thersites, present almost
constantly during each stage of the practice. An effect of his blight-
ing utterances is that it becomes increasingly difficult to care
whether Achilles is or is not ever incited to action. The effect of the
presence of Thersites on the play as a whole will be assessed hereafter.

The second fault is yet graver and more baffling. Ulysses' long
practice on Achilles, taking large space and building toward the
climactic speech on the nature of fame, is based on the assumption
that the hero keeps to his tent because he is swollen by pride and
that if he can be made to think his fame waning he will return to the
field. Yet after making his final, powerful argument to this effect,
Ulysses abruptly introduces matter which suggests that the entire
practice has been falsely based:

> 'Tis known, Achilles, that you are in love
> With one of Priam's daughters.
> *(Ibid. 193-4.)*

Belated proof that this is the true reason for his idleness comes in
Act V from Achilles himself:

> My sweet Patroclus, I am thwarted quite
> From my great purpose in to-morrow's battle.
> Here is a letter from Queen Hecuba.
> A token from her daughter, my fair love,
> Both taxing me and gaging me to keep
> An oath that I have sworn.
> *(v. i. 42-47.)*

In the end, thus, all Ulysses' practice not only comes to nothing, but
is rendered irrelevant. In Homer, of course, the slaying of Patroclus
is necessary to dislodge Achilles from his tent, where he has remained
in wrath for wrong done him by Agamemnon; so, too, in Shakespeare it is finally the slaying of Patroclus that rouses him. But what,
in Shakespeare, is the cause of his long idleness? If it is his swollen
pride, then why are both Ulysses and Achilles made to speak so
absolutely of Polyxena? And if it is Polyxena, then why does wise
Ulysses—who evidently knows of Achilles' love from the outset—
invent an elaborate practice to deflate the hero's pride as a means of
moving him?

Even this is not the end of the confusion. Directly after Ulysses has made his last argument, Patroclus suggests an additional, or a substitute, reason for Achilles' inaction:

> They think my little stomach to the war
> And your great love to me restrains you thus.
> (III. iii. 220-1.)

This is a persistent theme also, of course, of Thersites' harping. Perhaps the force that restrains Achilles is pride, perhaps love for Polyxena, perhaps doting on Patroclus, perhaps the combination of all. In any event the dramatist has played fast and loose with our awareness in making us suppose, throughout Ulysses' long practice, that the cause is pride alone. And by mismanaging our awareness he has mismanaged the practice itself—the greatest of three lines of action in the play. It is a final irony that, as deviser of the brilliant but unsuccessful and misdirected practice, Shakespeare should have used Ulysses—potentially the shrewdest master practiser available in all his materials of romance, legend, and history.

Despite Ulysses' great botch in erecting an elaborate practice on a false basis, the affair of Achilles is better handled than the affair of Troilus and Cressida; or, perhaps, it merely seems superior because it occasions the surpassing speeches of Ulysses—among others that on degree (I. iii) and that on fame (III. iii)—which, if little else in the play did, clearly engaged Shakespeare's whole mind. The affair of Troilus and Cressida boasts no such redeeming features; besides, from the point of view of the management of the awarenesses, it is damaged by even worse faults.

The preliminary scene of this affair, when Pandarus speaks to Cressida for Troilus, has already been reviewed as an example of opportunity missed. At the end of the scene Cressida advises us that she was won—though 'Nothing of that shall from mine eyes appear' —even before Pandarus spoke. Since she advises us in soliloquy, Pandarus should know nothing of her state of mind. From Cressida's conversation, it must appear to him that Troilus's suit is either unwelcome or, at best, not yet successful:

> *Cres.* Adieu, Uncle.
> *Pan.* I'll be with you, niece, by and by.
> *Cres.* To bring, uncle?
> *Pan.* Ay, a token from Troilus.
> *Cres.* By the same token, you are a bawd.
> (I. ii. 303-7.)

These are the most receptive words spoken by Cressida in the interview. At best they may suggest indecision to Pandarus; at worst, the same flat rejection which Cressida has repeated throughout the interview. To this point we have been given no more insight than Pandarus. Further, the soliloquy which follows, and which does give us insight, proves that Cressida herself believes that she has told Pandarus nothing interpretable as encouragement to Troilus: 'Then though my heart's content firm love doth bear, / Nothing of that shall from mine eyes appear.' If Pandarus is shrewder than Cressida thinks him, he is also shrewder than Shakespeare has given us cause to think him—and shrewder than ourselves, since we discovered nothing until the soliloquy.

In view of the ending of the interview, it must appear startling that when we next meet Pandarus—after a thoroughly bad interruption of four scenes totalling some 1,022 lines and including two-thirds of the representation of Ulysses' practice on Achilles—he is asking Paris to make Troilus's excuse to Priam 'if the King call for him at supper'. It is one great violation of Shakespeare's typical method that the long interruption puts the affair of Troilus and Cressida out of our minds; it is another that while we were watching Ulysses' efforts to move Achilles, heeding the finest speeches of the play, Pandarus—behind our backs—has moved Cressida and made arrangements for her to meet Troilus. When, therefore, in III. ii we find Troilus waiting in Pandarus's orchard and Pandarus, approaching, greeting him with 'Have you seen my cousin?' it becomes startlingly apparent that our vantage-point, instead of being above that of the participants, as we have grown accustomed to have it, is not even up to theirs. Even in *Henry VI*, when situations changed so fast that the apprentice dramatist could never quite keep us abreast of the news, there is no such omission of an indispensable link.

The cause is the same that damages the affair of Troilus and Cressida throughout: Shakespeare's trust in our 'outside' knowledge of events. Even though the earlier Pandarus–Cressida scene ended at best inconclusively, we are presumably expected to ignore the fact and to understand—because we know that was the way the old story went!—that Pandarus's next efforts proved successful. We are thus brought abruptly to the meeting of Troilus and Cressida— a climactic situation of such stature that Shakespeare would normally have begun stocking our minds in preparation as early as the opening scene of the play. But here our only 'preparation' is prior acquaintance with the story and its outcome. We do in any event hold enormous advantage over the participants in this scene, and at the end the difference between their perspective and ours is exploited with uncommon obviousness. The gaudiest effects of irony since *Richard III* are struck:

Tro. True swains in love shall in the world to come
Approve their truths by Troilus. When their rhymes,
Full of protest, of oath and big compare,
Want similes, truth tir'd with iteration,
As true as steel, as plantage to the moon,
As sun to day, as turtle to her mate,
As iron to adamant, as earth to th' centre,
Yet, after all comparisons of truth,
As truth's authentic author to be cited,
'As true as Troilus' shall crown up the verse,
And sanctify the numbers.
Cres.   Prophet may you be!
If I be false, or swerve a hair from truth,
When time is old and hath forgot itself,
When waterdrops have worn the stones of Troy
And blind oblivion swallow'd cities up,
And mighty states characterless are grated
To dusty nothing, yet let memory,
From false to false, among false maids in love,
Upbraid my falsehood! When they've said as false
As aid, as water, as wind, as sandy earth,
As fox to lamb, as wolf to heifer's calf,
Pard to the hind, or stepdame to her son,
Yea, let them say, to stick the heart of falsehood,
'As false as Cressida.'

                                        (III. ii. 180–204.)

Though far the most spectacular exploitation of a discrepancy to be found in the play, this also most contradicts Shakespeare's usual method. For our advantage—without which exploitation would be impossible and the scene undramatic—derives entirely from our extra-dramatic knowledge of what the names of Troilus, Pandar, and Cressida came in fact to mean 'in the world to come'. To this point no evidence that Cressida is either 'slyding of corage' or plain wanton has been presented by dramatic means. Though she has told us her passion for Troilus and has consented to meet him, nothing in her characterization thus far makes her later career predictable. *Except for our outside knowledge*, that is to say, we would have no cause to find her protestation of faith ironical; and if we lacked a sense of irony here the scene would create *no* dramatic effect.

Through prior characterization of Cressida, then, Shakespeare might have prepared us to perceive the ironical flashes. But he could as easily have prepared us by means of his favoured device of scene placement. It has previously been stated that the Calchas matter introduced at the start of the final stage of Ulysses' practice on Achilles (III. iii) damages the scene by irrelevant intrusion. Its obvious relation is to the Troilus–Cressida scene, which immediately precedes the Ulysses–Achilles scene. Placed as it is, it does throw light back upon the action just presented—especially on the solemn exchange of vows made as Pandarus ushers the eager couple into Cressida's chamber; thus Calchas:

> You have a Troyan prisoner, call'd Antenor,
> Yesterday took; Troy holds him very dear.
> Oft have you—often have you thanks therefore—
> Desir'd my Cressid in right great exchange,
> Whom Troy hath still deni'd; but this Antenor,
> I know, is such a wrest in their affairs
> That their negotiations all must slack,
> Wanting his manage; and they will almost
> Give us a prince of blood, a son of Priam,
> In change of him.
>
> (III. iii. 18–27.)

'Let Diomedes bear him / And bring Cressid hither', replies Agamemnon—and thereupon the conversation turns to the affair of Achilles: 'Achilles stands i' th' entrance of his tent. / Please it our general to pass strangely by him, / As if he were forgot.' Shakespeare would more typically have given the Calchas transaction a scene alone, set between Pandarus's interview with Paris and Helen (III. i) and his meeting with Troilus stalking about Cressida's door 'Like a strange soul upon the Stygian banks / Staying for vantage'. Then its light would have flooded the subsequent action on which it has immediate bearing. Thus in *Much Ado about Nothing* we are shown the capture of Don John's villains immediately before the scene in which the abused Claudio denounces his betrothed in church, so that during that scene we know that Hero will be saved at last. And in *Twelfth Night* we are shown Sebastian, the solution to Viola's problem, immediately before we hear the heroine lamenting that there is no solution. In both of these, as is usual in the comedies, the extra light provided beforehand assures us that the truth is better than it appears to the participants. In the tragedies, where the device is used with comparable regularity, the effect is typically to warn us that the truth is worse than the participants suspect. Thus in the second balcony scene of *Romeo and Juliet* we watch the scene of the lovers' parting; though anguished, they do hold some hope that all will be well:

> *Jul.* O, think'st thou we shall ever meet again?
> *Rom.* I doubt it not; and all these woes shall serve
>   For sweet discourses in our times to come.
>
> (III. v. 51–53.)

We are, however, made to watch the scene in the light of that just preceding, when Capulet promised Juliet to Paris: 'O' Thursday let it be.' Thus though the lovers know cause for grief, theirs is only a fraction of the cause we know. The situation of the lovers' meeting in *Troilus and Cressida* is comparable: simply by placing Calchas's fatal transaction ahead of the meeting Shakespeare could have enriched the effect as he most often does elsewhere. Instead he places the Calchas scene after the meeting and trusts to our extra-dramatic knowledge for the light that gives the scene meaning.

In two of the last three scenes that treat the affair of Troilus and Cressida, Shakespeare does manage discrepancies in awareness largely in his usual fashion—and the benefit to these scenes is conspicuous. At the opening of Act IV Diomedes enters Troy. Though the scene wanders badly from its principal business—a fault which, inexplicably, afflicts nearly every scene in the play—by taking up the rivalry of Diomedes and Aeneas, irrelevant at the moment, when all should be concentrated on the separation of the lovers, and by presenting Diomedes' general views on the war and on the relative merits of Paris's and Menelaus's claims to Helen, yet the main purpose at least escapes burial; says Paris to Aeneas:

> His purpose meets you; 'twas to bring this Greek
> To Calchas' house, and there to render him,
> For the enfreed Antenor, the fair Cressid.
> (IV. i. 36–38.)

Because of the placement and the relevant part (a few lines out of many) of this scene, we hold telling advantage over Troilus and Cressida when they enter in the next. Our advantage over both carries through the opening lines, until Aeneas tells Troilus that 'We must give up to Diomedes' hand / The Lady Cressida', and over Cressida it lasts longer, until Pandarus breaks the news that she must go. The exploitation of the lovers' initial unawareness is accomplished with great force by the knocking of Aeneas at the gate—the significance of which is known to us. It is noteworthy that here Shakespeare did not trust to our extra-dramatic knowledge, or even to our recollection of Calchas's transaction which opens III. iii two scenes back. Rather, he showed us Diomedes entering Troy and reasserted the purpose of his coming immediately before opening the scene on the blissfully unaware lovers. Hence the meaning of the knocking at the gate is instantly apparent.

Yet even here the care used to prepare our awareness is not Shakespeare's usual care, for though it forewarns us that the lovers must part, it does not forewarn us that Cressida will be false. Perhaps this is the greatest single fault of many great faults in the play. Cressida's conduct on learning that she must leave carries no sign that she will be or is capable of being false. Indeed, it suggests that she will be true. 'I will not go', she tells Pandarus,

> I will not, uncle. I have forgot my father;
> I know no touch of consanguinity;
> No kin, no love, no blood, no soul so near me
> As the sweet Troilus.
>
> (IV. ii. 102–5.)

As she speaks we know that she will be false—but we know it only because we know the story. Here again as hitherto, then, effect depends upon our familiarity with the outcome. That being set aside, we should have to take this as a parting of lovers who will die true. Perhaps the lovers' preoccupation with the ideas of truth and falsity carries ominous significance; but then there is no more cause to think that Cressida will be false than that Troilus will, for Cressida is as insistent that he be true as he is that she be so.

By adding together all that is told of Cressida from the time we first meet her until she leaves with Diomedes, and by weighting certain suggestions—such as Pandarus's remark that 'she fetches her breath so short as a new-ta'en sparrow' while she waits for Troilus to come in from the orchard—we can detect a possibility that in favourable circumstances she might be won by another even as she was won by Troilus. But the evidence implies that she is no more likely than Troilus to prove false. The first three and a half acts have done nothing to prepare us for Ulysses' instant assessment when she enters the Greek camp:

> *Nest.* A woman of quick sense.
> *Ulyss.*   Fie, fie upon her!
> There's language in her eye, her cheek, her lip,
> Nay, her foot speaks; her wanton spirits look out
> At every joint and motive of her body.
>
> (IV. v. 54–57.)

With this speech, set at the end of Act IV, we gain such information as in earlier plays we gained at the outset. Cressida has been a masquerader during her portions of four acts, even as her predecessors. But Julia, Portia, Rosalind, Viola took us with them from the start, and even Helena's methods and motives began to show when she appeared in Florence; moreover, when Helena's early conduct is reviewed in the light of our later understanding, all proves to be of a piece. But Cressida's mask was on before we met her: her portrait as drawn prior to Ulysses' description is irreconcilable with that description. In omitting dramatic exposition and trusting wholly to our historical knowledge of the heroine's future, Shakespeare is false to his own dramatic manner and to us.

The belated advantage given us by Ulysses' speech is ready for use at once, when Troilus comes to the Greek camp for Hector's match with Ajax. Again incredibly, however, exploitation of Troilus's unawareness is spoiled by the business of the match—indeed, iᵗ is delayed until the match is over. Arriving with the other Trojans, Troilus is speechless but for one shout to his brother—'Hector, thou sleep'st; / Awake thee!'—until the tag end of the scene, when we are reminded of his unawareness and of Ulysses' awareness of Cressida:

> Ulyss. As gentle tell me, of what honour was
> This Cressida in Troy? Had she no lover there
> That wails her absence?
> Tro. O, sir, to such as boasting show their scars
> A mock is due. Will you walk on, my lord?
> She was belov'd, she lov'd; she is, and doth:
> But still sweet love is food for Fortune's tooth.
>   (IV. v. 287–93.)

Here we hold advantage over both Ulysses and Troilus, the one not knowing that Cressida is Troilus's love, the other ignorant what Cressida is. The opportunity is a rare one—but the exploitation comes too late to be effective. *Earlier, the Calchas transaction for the exchange of prisoners intruded in and marred the climactic scene of Ulysses' practice on Achilles. Here, the mountainous matter of the Hector–Ajax combat and the first Hector–Achilles meeting rears up to split the affair of Troilus and Cressida*, which falls into a little space at each end of the scene. So placed, exploitation of a crucial instant in the affair is made to seem irrelevant matter intruding on that of Hector–Achilles.

The final scene which makes much use of a discrepancy in awarenesses is v. ii, when Diomedes and Cressida meet before Calchas's tent and are overheard by Troilus, Ulysses, and Thersites. From every point of view this is the finest *whole* scene in the play—and it can hardly be coincidence that it is also the only scene in which the management of awarenesses is flawless. The structuring is familiar: it shows the Shakespeare of old. Our vantage-point is perfect: for the first time, without relying on historical assistance, we recognize that Cressida is false, for we have heard Ulysses' description, and, immediately before the scene opens, we have heard Thersites' confirming judgement: 'That same Diomed's a false-hearted rogue, a most unjust knave. . . . They say he keeps a Troyan drab, and uses the traitor Calchas his tent.' Below our point are ranged the participants, with Ulysses and Thersites aware that Cressida is false, but ignorant, at the first, of her relation to Troilus; with Troilus aware of this relation but ignorant at the start that his love is faithless; and

with Cressida and Diomedes always ignorant that they are observed.
The main exploitable substance is the unawareness of Cressida, who
does not guess that she is playing her game with Diomedes under
the eyes of her former lover. The high point of exploitation occurs
when, with calculated art—as our new understanding of her enables
us to realize—she seems to lament over the sleeve given her by Troilus and now demanded by Diomedes:

> O, all you gods! O pretty, pretty pledge!
> Thy master now lies thinking in his bed
> Of thee and me, and sighs, and takes my glove,
> And gives memorial dainty kisses to it,
> As I kiss thee.
>
> (v. ii. 77–81.)

At the same time that it exploits her unawareness, the scene exploits
Troilus's coming-to-awareness. Beginning in a romantic hero's
typical state of oblivion, which had earlier been ruffled not by distrust of Cressida but by the boldness of Diomedes, Troilus rises
swiftly through stages of doubt and disbelief to final perception and
acceptance of the truth:

> O Cressid! O false Cressid! false, false, false!
> Let all untruths stand by thy stained name,
> And they'll seem glorious.
>
> (Ibid. 177–9.)

Most commonly, when one of Shakespeare's heroes speaks thus of
a woman, or of women in general, we know that he is in error: thus
Claudio of Hero, after Don John's trick has deceived him; Posthumus Leonatus of Imogen, after the 'proofs' laid before him by
Iachimo have deceived him; and, in tragedy, Othello of Desdemona,
after Iago's poison has affected his senses. In these typical cases
the truth which we see is better than the appearance seen by the
speakers. Troilus, however, speaks from our own vantage-point,
and the ugly truth he sees when his eyes have been disabused is the
only one to be seen. At the end of the scene Troilus is the only hero
in Shakespearian comedy who ever overpeers a heroine. But his
advantage brings him no joy.

More mismanaged than either the affair of Troilus and Cressida
or that of Ulysses' practice on Achilles is the affair of Hector and
Achilles, which looms every larger as the play nears the end. Our
advantage in knowing the outcome of this action, like our advantage in Troilus's affair, owes entirely to extra-dramatic knowledge
until nearly all is over. In the last scene of Act IV Achilles muses as
he surveys Hector: 'Tell me, you heavens, in which part of his
body / Shall I destroy him, whether there, or there, or there?'

Replies Hector, 'I'll not kill thee there, nor there, nor there; / But, by the forge that stithied Mars his helm, / I'll kill thee everywhere, yea, o'er and o'er.' Hector's confidence here carries irony only because *we have learned the outcome elsewhere*; otherwise we have no more reason to suppose Achilles' boast will be fulfilled than his. It is not until v. iii that Shakespeare attempts to do what in other plays he did no later than the beginning of Act II—advise us dramatically what the end must be. Andromache, Cassandra, and finally Priam seek to prevent Hector from going to battle, each foretelling his death; says Priam, summarizing the warnings:

> Come, Hector, come, go back.
> Thy wife hath dream'd; thy mother hath had visions;
> Cassandra doth foresee; and I myself
> Am like a prophet suddenly enrapt
> To tell thee that this day is ominous:
> Therefore, come back.   (v. iii. 62–67.)

Coming when the play is almost done, these warnings seem curiously superfluous—like empty formalities observed. In the same scene, through Troilus, Shakespeare uses another device also to give us advantage over Hector:

> *Tro.* Brother, you have a vice of mercy in you,
>   Which better fits a lion than a man.
> *Hect.* What vice is that, good Troilus? Chide me for it.
> *Tro.* When many times the captive Grecian falls,
>   Even in the fan and wind of your fair sword,
>   You bid them rise, and live.
> *Hect.* O, 'tis fair play.
> *Tro.*   Fool's play, by heaven, Hector.
>   (Ibid. 37–43.)

Here is perhaps the most curious stroke of all—the sudden imputation of a 'tragic flaw' to Hector in the middle of Act V, as though the dramatist sought thus to elevate him to the place of tragic protagonist and to weld the disparate actions of the play into the unified action of tragedy.

Hector's fault does in fact destroy him—though in highly ambiguous circumstances:

> *Achil.* Now do I see thee. Have at thee, Hector!
> *Hect.* Pause, if thou wilt.
> *Achil.* I do disdain thy courtesy, proud Troyan.
>   Be happy that my arms are out of use;
>   My rest and negligence befriends thee now,
>   But thou anon shalt hear of me again;
>   Till when, go seek thy fortune.
>   (v. vi. 13–19.)

182

Exactly what happens here is not determinable from the dialogue. Presumably some accident momentarily puts Achilles' arms 'out of use'—perhaps, even, Hector shows himself the better man by disarming Achilles. In any event Hector exposes that very mercy which Troilus, just before, had called 'fool's play'. The warning, followed by the demonstration, amply if somewhat crudely prepares us to see Hector slain when, in similar circumstance, Achilles will deny him mercy. The quick repetition of many warnings gives us advantage over Hector in soliloquy as he rests with helmet off and shield aside:

> Most putrefied core, so fair without,
> Thy goodly armour thus hath cost thy life.
> Now is my day's work done; I'll take good breath.
> Rest, sword; thou hast thy fill of blood and death.
> (v. viii. 1–4.)

Entering, as we knew they must, Achilles and the Myrmidons slay him without mercy.

It is thus Hector's affair which rears up abruptly to claim undivided attention during the final seven scenes. It is the death of Hector that inspires Troilus's fury in his last speech:

> Hector is gone.
> Who shall tell Priam so, or Hecuba?
> Let him that will a screech-owl aye be call'd
> Go in to Troy and say there, 'Hector's dead!'
> There is a word will Priam turn to stone,
> Make wells and Niobes of the maids and wives,
> Cold statues of the youth, and, in a word,
> Scare Troy out of itself.
> (v. x. 14–21.)

From the emphasis of these final scenes, crowned with Troilus's powerful speech, the play should be tragedy, Hector its protagonist, and Troilus a Horatio, left behind. Yet in fact Hector's affair is only one of four in the total action: besides the practice of Ulysses on Achilles and the affair of Troilus and Cressida, there is the underlying cause of the whole unpleasantness, the affair of Helen and Paris. What moves the fury of Troilus is represented at last to be only the death of Hector, as though his own disillusionment had no bearing—even as though it had never been: thus the affair of Troilus and Cressida—which had title to the foreground, with all else background—is itself finally reduced to the place of irrelevance.

'The specialty of rule hath been neglected', said Ulysses, accounting for the disorganization of the campaign against Troy. His full speech is an apt description both of the world represented in the play and of the play's representation of that world. Whereas in other plays Shakespeare conducts multiple, sometimes fantastically complex actions in such a way that strength and significance accrue to each from each, and all bear on the centre, in *Troilus and Cressida* 'Each thing meets / In mere oppugnancy'. The affair of Ulysses' practice on Achilles, mismanaged, confused, and ambiguous within itself, intrudes upon and damages the representation of the affair of Troilus and Cressida. That affair, in turn intrudes upon and damages it. The affair of Hector and Achilles, which should emerge as result of Ulysses' practice on Achilles, rises instead from the slaying of Patroclus, so that Ulysses' practice becomes a lengthy and complicated irrelevance; and, finally, the conclusion of the Hector–Achilles affair usurps the place of all else, claims all of Troilus's fury for itself, and thereby makes the affair of Troilus and Cressida irrelevant. Meanwhile the affair of Helen and Paris, treated scurrilously in the dialogue not only by Thersites but also by Ulysses, Troilus, Hector, and Diomedes, is represented in the action by a single scene (III. i)—upon which the affair of Troilus and Cressida intrudes and in which the face that launched a thousand ships is shrunk to merely that of 'my Nell'.

In the handling of these affairs the mismanagement of awarenesses is at once the most conspicuous fault and the source of the others. Elsewhere Shakespeare takes even excessive pains to supply us with information needed to perceive action in its true light and especially to mark the effects of exploitation of discrepant awarenesses. Here, for a dramatically established context, he substitutes ready-made knowledge of outcomes. Elsewhere he lifts us to Olympus with devices of his own contriving, and so packs our minds with sympathetic understanding that we recognize a personal stake in the matter: our advantage commits us to care greatly about the participants and their affairs. Here he wrings no sympathy, but sets Thersites to lead us about on the participants' plain and to coat persons and events with slime that repels. Individually, in the course of action, Thersites besmears Agamemnon, Nestor, Ulysses, Ajax, Achilles, Patroclus, Helen, Paris, Menelaus, Troilus, Cressida, and the four affairs in which these are involved. In the Troy scenes we have Pandarus with us, who serves for Thersites at the beginning of the affair of Troilus and Cressida and thus degrades it from the outset; for all other scenes and events we have Thersites himself. On the barest excuse, or none, Shakespeare even has him accompany Ulysses and Troilus to watch the interview of Diomedes and Cressida; but though there is no proper reason he should go, his use to the scene is obvious: 'How the devil Luxury, with his fat rump and potato-finger, tickles these together! Fry, lechery, fry!' To the same effect he is put beside us in the final battle scenes, where he speaks thus of Troilus and Diomedes: 'Hold thy whore, Grecian! —now for thy whore, Troyan!' and thus of Paris and Menelaus: 'The cuckold and the cuckold-maker are at it. Now bull! now, dog!'

As adviser of our awareness, Thersites is the strongest force of unity in the play; perhaps the sole unifying force. But unlike the heroines who precede him in this role, and unlike King Oberon and Dukes Vincentio and Prospero, he exercises no control of events in his world. 'And therefore', said Ulysses, 'Is the glorious planet Sol / In noble eminence enthron'd and spher'd / Amidst the other; whose med'cinable eye / Corrects the ill aspect of planets evil, / And posts, like the commandment of a king, / Sans check, to good and bad.' Thersites is the only Sol in the universe of *Troilus and Cressida*, and, since he controls nothing, but only observes, the several affairs which should keep their right orbits and contribute to a whole action run wild: the matter of Ulysses and Achilles intrudes on that of Troilus and Cressida and the matter of Troilus and Cressida upon that of Ulysses and Achilles; and at last the matter of Hector crowds out both. Said Ulysses:

> Take but degree away, untune that string,
> And, hark, what discord follows! Each thing meets
> In mere oppugnancy. The bounded waters
> Should lift their bosoms higher than the shores
> And make a sop of all this solid globe.
>
> (I. iii. 109–13.)

'When degree is shak'd, then enterprise is sick': the chief deviate from his normal practice, *Troilus and Cressida* is best proof of Shakespeare's need for a force to control both the world represented by the play and the play's representation of the world; of his need to exploit dramatically created discrepancies in terms of present situations rather than ready-made ones in terms of ultimate outcomes. Here the affair of Troilus and Cressida falls like the repetition of a dirty story for an audience already familiar with the ending. Perhaps because the story was so familiar Shakespeare considered his usual dramatic method of maintaining our advantage inappropriate. But his dissatisfaction with the deviation is plainly evinced by his emphatic return to the normal way in *Measure for Measure*.

CHAPTER VI

Like Power Divine: *Measure for Measure*

CENTRAL, in point of time, among the worlds of *All's Well that Ends Well*, *Troilus and Cressida*, *Hamlet*, *Othello*, *King Lear*, and *Macbeth*, the world of *Measure for Measure* would inevitably appear as wicked, dark, and dangerous as the unhealthiest of these but that our view of it is profoundly affected by our certainty that all is well and will end well. In *All's Well that Ends Well* nothing appears more than dubiously well until late, after we have recognized Helena's formidable capabilities; in *Troilus and Cressida* nothing ever appears well and is never well; and in the tragedies, of course, the dramatist's art is calculated from the beginning onward to persuade us that, character and circumstance being as they are, all is ill and must end ill. The action of *Measure for Measure* would be tragic also except that the bad world in which it occurs is controlled by an omniscient, omnipotent, and benevolent force; and it would in any event *appear* potentially tragic to us except that we know of this force.

Only *The Comedy of Errors*, which has nothing to offer besides, relies more exclusively than *Measure for Measure* on discrepancies in awareness for both action and effect. We hold advantage over all named persons except the Duke and his accomplice friars during thirteen of seventeen scenes—that is, from I. iii to the end except for IV. v, when only the Duke and Friar Peter are present. Throughout this period the gap between our awareness and the participants', like the several secondary differences in the awarenesses of participants, is not only wide but defined with unfailing clarity. Once established our main advantage remains fixed until the abrupt, spectacular denouement. In all, the management of the awarenesses represents a reversal of the methods of *All's Well* and *Troilus and Cressida* and an emphatic reassertion of the way of *Twelfth Night* and its predecessors. Here no ambiguity is allowed to exist in our understanding of the relation of our vision to that of a participant; we have no moments of uncertainty about where we stand or where participants stand. Here it is unnecessary to review and reinterpret earlier action in the light of later action and belated information, as is repeatedly necessary in *All's Well*. Before a scene begins we are provided with the light by which it is to be seen in a true perspective.

The main cleavage of awarenesses comes with a single stroke in I. iii, when the Duke tells us that he will stay in Vienna. It is therefore only in the first two scenes that our vision, like the participants', is imperfect. We are deceived by the Duke's remarks in deputizing Angelo:

> Hold therefore, Angelo:
> In our remove be thou at full ourself.
> Mortality and mercy in Vienna
> Live in thy tongue and heart.　　　(I. i. 43–46.)

Though he never actually states that he intends to leave Vienna, the Duke speaks of 'our absence', 'our remove', 'Our haste from hence', and promises to communicate by letters 'How it goes with us, and do look to know / What doth befall you here'. From such remarks we must assume, with Angelo and Escalus, that he intends to travel at some distance from Vienna and to depend upon these two for information. We remain under this misapprehension throughout the second scene, along with Lucio, Pompey, Mrs. Overdone, and Claudio—the first representatives of the general world of Vienna whom we meet after Vincentio's supposed departure. We learn from them that the new deputy is tyrannizing the city, and the specific case of Claudio is so presented as to appear as desperate to us as to them; says Claudio:

> ... the new deputy now for the Duke—
> Whether it be the fault and glimpse of newness,
> Or whether that the body public be
> A horse whereon the governor doth ride,
> Who, newly in the seat, that it may know
> He can command, lets it straight feel the spur;
> Whether the tyranny be in his place,
> Or in his eminence that fills it up....
> 　　　　　(I. ii. 161–8.)

'Send after the Duke,' cries Lucio, 'and appeal to him.' 'I have done so,' Claudio replies, 'but he's not to be found.' Claudio's hope that his sister will be able to move Angelo is made to appear vain by the earlier characterization of the deputy. At this point, then, the situation seems hopeless: Angelo is incapable of mercy, and the only higher power is beyond the reach of appeal.

In emphasizing Vienna's peril before reassuring us, Shakespeare follows his usual way in the comedies. Old Aegeon is left standing in mortal danger at the end of the first scene of *The Comedy of Errors,* condemned for lack of a thousand marks. In the next scene we are given a passing hint that all may be well when Antipholus of Syracuse hands his Dromio a purse containing a thousand marks; however, in this first comedy the pattern is atypical in that we are denied real assurance that all will be well until the end, when we meet Aemilia. The lovers' plight in *A Midsummer-Night's Dream* seems at first desperate also—and then, very quickly, we are shown Oberon. In *The Merchant of Venice* the first part of the court scene makes Antonio's doom seem certain—and then Portia enters. In *Twelfth Night,* less direly, Viola's affairs become badly tangled before we are shown Sebastian. In *All's Well* we are made to think that Helena has abandoned the chase and gone a pilgrimage to Death—when suddenly we catch sight of such formidable qualities in her that it may seem we should fear less for her than for her quarry. And finally, to take a long jump, the shipwreck scene which opens *The Tempest* is represented as real enough in its terror of sight and sound, just before we hear Prospero: 'There's no harm done.'

Claudio's imprisonment at the order of such a one as we know Angelo to be, with benevolent power gone beyond appeal, holds more frightful potentiality than anything previously represented in the comedies. Even Shylock's claim on Antonio in *The Merchant of Venice* is not utterly unjust, and his very rage seems less fearsome than the cold inhumanity already shown in Angelo's nature. 'Mortality and mercy in Vienna,' said the Duke, 'Live in thy tongue and heart.' And more, 'Your scope is as mine own, / So to enforce or qualify the laws / As to your soul seems good.' The words 'mercy' and 'qualify' are notable in the mandate as suggesting the Duke's assumption that Angelo will bear his sway humanely. But Claudio's arrest is an act of icy inhumanity, purely evil in its coldness, and it signifies that the deputy's rule will be a triumph of evil over good, which must stand abuse without redress.

'Tell your piteous heart / There's no harm done': as in *The Tempest,* so here. It is just after we have been shown the peril of the city in general and Claudio in particular that Shakespeare floods our awareness with reassurance; says the mighty Duke:

> . . . to behold his sway,
> I will, as 'twere a brother of your order,
> Visit both prince and people; therefore, I prithee,
> Supply me with the habit and instruct me
> How I may formally in person bear me
> Like a true friar.   (I. iii. 43–48.)

188

This disclosure gives us a new perspective in which the situation appears suddenly and drastically changed. It establishes a climate for comedy by assuring us that a supreme power of good yet watches over this world; that evil has a line drawn around it and will be contained; that though villainy may threaten, it can do no permanent harm. Omniscience and omnipotence are on the side of good: Vincentio, unseen and unknown, will see all and know all. Ill can no more befall good people in the benignly guarded, wicked world of Vienna than in the brutal world of *The Tempest*, snug in the palm of Prospero. These are the indispensable facts that we are not to forget for an instant during the subsequent action, for their light profoundly alters the appearance of every scene. It is noteworthy that in *The Comedy of Errors*, during the entire middle action that is the lightest, most farcical in the comedies, we are asked to remember the tragic plight of Aegeon; and that in *Measure for Measure*, during the whole course of the dark and dangerous action that takes place in one of Shakespeare's worst worlds, we are required to remember that a godlike power has everything in control. Lightness is darkened, and darkness lightened: not only in climactic scenes, but often during whole actions, Shakespeare so manages the awarenesses as to make simple, single responses impossible, and to demand complex, conflicting ones.

In assuming the role of chief practiser who maintains his own and provides our advantage by means of disguise, Duke Vincentio replaces the heroines of preceding comedies. But he masquerades for a purpose very different from theirs. Rosalind practised for the love of the game; Julia, Viola, and Helena, to catch and hold husbands; Portia, to save a life—and to teach her husband a lesson. Excepting Helena's, the worlds of these heroines were relatively free of evil, and some were golden. Such difficulties as arose in them could be overcome by the heroine's advantages of disguise and personal brilliance; Viola could simply trust everything to time and subtle silence. In short, these were such worlds as merely mortal—indeed, feminine—force could control. Only Helena's had grown so rank that the heroine needed to adopt secret, even unheroinely tactics and to borrow a 'something more', presumably from magical arts, to cure its corruption. Heroine at a crucial point, she is the last of her sex to command the worsening world. After her the self-sufficiency of heroines follows a dropping course—Isabella, Marina, Imogen, Perdita, down finally to Miranda of the marvellous innocence and utter incompetence to look out for herself.

The mighty Duke Vincentio, then, takes over the world of Shakespearian comedy at the point where it has become unsafe for heroines—at the point where godlike power alone can keep the balance of good against evil. Though he resembles the heroines in that he uses disguise and has superior awareness, his advantage over others does not depend only on the fact that his identity is secret or on the fact that he sees and knows all. The significant difference is that this particular unknown identity, seeing all and knowing all, is also omnipotent: a disguised absolute power is more than a disguised Rosalind, Viola, Portia—or even a Helena possessed of a king's ring. Hence, even in his much more wicked world he provides greater certainty than these do that all is well and will be well—greater even than does Oberon, the fallible immortal of *A Midsummer-Night's Dream*. To go further, he is the converse of the Fate which, announced in the Prologue, operates unseen during the action of *Romeo and Juliet*, and of the Fate which shows glimpses of itself in its figureheads, the witches of *Macbeth*. For these are absolute forces which contribute to our certainty that catastrophe is inevitable. Duke Vincentio as a controlling force is the nearest Shakespeare had come to Prospero: both are mortal, and both are omniscient, omnipotent, and benevolent. Though he is not quite Prospero (he must resort to eavesdropping) his relation to the world of Vienna is nearest Prospero's relation to his isle and the surrounding waters.

The chasm opened between Vienna's awareness and ours by the Duke's announcement of his masquerade is the principal dramatic fact during all subsequent action. It conditions our view of every scene after I. iii. Structurally, because of an unusually strict concentration upon one centre, *Measure for Measure* is most unlike its immediate non-tragic predecessor, *Troilus and Cressida*, in which, lacking a centre, parts have no proper orbits, but meet 'in mere oppugnancy'. Here concentration of our awareness upon the secret shared with Vincentio controls and shapes the play's representation of the world, even as the Duke's centrality controls the world represented in the play. This concentration produces effects in the next scene after the Duke's announcement. When Lucio greets Isabella at the nunnery and describes her brother's plight, the truth just opened to our view is far better than he knows. 'The Duke is very strangely gone from hence', he begins, and, after characterizing the situation as he perceives it, concludes:

> All hope is gone,
> Unless you have the grace by your fair prayer
> To soften Angelo.
>
> (I. iv. 68–70.)

The speech stands directly under the light of the Duke's words

spoken at the end of the preceding scene: '. . . to behold his sway, /
I will, as 'twere a brother of your order, / Visit both prince and
people.' Contradicting Lucio's impression, assuring us that all is well
while we observe persons who fear that all is ill, our advantage frees
us from their anxiety, so that we can contemplate action with com-
parative objectivity. This privilege becomes increasingly valuable
during the more anguished scenes that follow.

Besides reassuring us, despite participants' fears, the early scenes
serve to impress two ideas upon our consciousness: first, that Angelo's
condemnation of Claudio is truly an abuse of authority which a just
power would not tolerate; second, that his tyranny cannot be
checked unless by the action of a just and superior power. In i. i the
Duke himself has advised us of Escalus's wisdom and righteousness;
when, therefore, we hear Escalus plead for Claudio, and plead in
vain, the two ideas are impressed simultaneously. Says Escalus, alone
after Angelo's order for Claudio's execution:

> Well, Heaven forgive him! and forgive us all!
> Some rise by sin, and some by virtue fall.
> Some run from brakes of vice and answer none;
> And some condemned for a fault alone.
> (II. i. 37-40.)

Though Angelo's power exceeds his, Escalus stands for the Duke's
point of view on justice here; hence, with Escalus, we must regard
Angelo's condemnation of Claudio as an unjust act. Again, the next
scene, with Pompey, Froth, and Elbow, besides making the first
comic exploitation of the gap between Vienna's ignorance and our
awareness, reaffirms from another point of view the idea that
Angelo's conduct of office is improper. 'Does your worship mean
to geld and splay all the youth of the city?' asks Pompey. 'No,
Pompey,' replies Escalus. 'Truly, sir, in my poor opinion, they will
to't then,' Pompey warns. The widely separated intellects of
Pompey and Escalus coincide at the crucial point: Angelo's edict is
fantastic. Finally, the idea is reasserted with telling force in the next
scene, when the 'enskied and sainted' Isabella—speaking, for the
moment, with a godlike perspective that is not always hers—pleads
vainly for her brother. Vainly, not knowing Angelo as well as we
know him, Lucio and the Provost take hope that Isabella will win
mercy: 'O, to him, to him, wench!' cries Lucio, 'he will relent.' She
continues:

> Go to your bosom,
> Knock there, and ask your heart what it doth know
> That's like my brother's fault. If it confess
> A natural guiltiness such as his,

Let it not sound a thought upon your tongue
Against my brother's life.

(II. ii. 136–41.)

When Angelo invites her, 'Well, come to me to-morrow', both she and Lucio imagine that victory is in sight: 'Heaven keep your honour safe!' she exclaims. But our own sense of the situation has been alerted by Angelo's 'aside', following Isabella's plea that he consult his own bosom:

She speaks, and 'tis
Such sense, that my sense breeds with it.

(Ibid. 141–2.)

Next we are flatly told by Angelo's soliloquy that the 'mercy' she may win must be claimed at a price which, enskied and sainted, she will find it quite inconvenient to pay:

Having waste ground enough,
Shall we desire to raze the sanctuary
And pitch our evils there? O, fie, fie, fie!
What dost thou, or what art thou, Angelo?
Dost thou desire her foully for those things
That make her good?

(Ibid. 170–5.)

At scene's end, thus, we hold a curious double advantage over Isabella, knowing that, on the one hand, her hope of winning mercy is vain—and that, nevertheless, all is well because a supreme power stands by to call Angelo to account. Hence the truth is at once far worse and far better than she knows.

Together, the three scenes ending in the rebellion of Angelo's flesh overwhelm our minds with a sense that justice with mercy can triumph in Vienna only if a force greater than Angelo's exists, knows all that we know, and is disposed to intervene. So far we have been advised only that the Duke has not left Vienna; he has not learned of the situation that is shaping. Now, in II. iv—with some evidence of haste in the order of events—Shakespeare brings him in to learn all that we know. Moreover, by having him learn of Claudio's affair from Juliet, the dramatist assures us that the Duke's sympathies are engaged; it is noteworthy, however,. that he does not have Vincentio expressly commit himself to Claudio's cause. The Duke makes no such declaration as Oberon's: 'Ere he do leave this grove, / Thou shalt fly him and he shall seek thy love.' It is left to be assumed that, being benevolent, Vincentio sides with us and Claudio once he perceives what preceding scenes have made evident to us. Perhaps a declaration such as Oberon's would be both super-fluous and demeaning in a force which Shakespeare begins early to elevate to the godlike. So Vincentio, first hearing of Claudio's plight from the Provost, gets the details from Juliet, and is satisfied that her repentance is not 'hollowly put on':

Duke. Love you the man that wrong'd you?
Jul. Yes, as I love the woman that wrong'd him.
Duke. So then it seems your most offenceful act
    Was mutually committed?
Jul.   Mutually.
Duke. Then was your sin of heavier kind than his.
Jul. I do confess it, and repent it, father.
Duke. 'Tis meet so, daughter; but lest you do repent
    As that the sin hath brought you to this shame,—
    Which sorrow is always towards ourselves, not heaven,
    Showing we would not spare heaven as we love it,
    But as we stand in fear,—
Jul. I do repent me, as it is an evil,
    And take the shame with joy.
Duke.   There rest.
                      (II. iii. 24–36.)

This is a crucial interview: if there is a precise point at which the Duke commits himself to the cause, it is here, when he finds Juliet's penitence honest, and, being so, to merit forgiveness. This is also the first of the great moments in the play during which the predominant effect is exhilaration in the knowledge that a supreme power of good exists and is ready.

At the end of II. iii, then, we know that Vincentio is aware of Claudio's plight, and sympathetic. In the next scene our knowledge briefly outstrips his when we see Angelo yield to the devil in his flesh and confront Isabella with the choice of her chastity or her brother's life. Since we have been advised a moment earlier of what Angelo intends, we hold advantage over Isabella through about a hundred lines of the interview. Entering respectfully, hopeful of the mercy that Angelo's earlier invitation had seemed to promise, she quite mistakes the riddle, open to us, with which she is greeted:

Ang.   Your brother cannot live.
Isab. Even so, Heaven keep your honour!
Ang. Yet may he live a while; and, it may be,
    As long as you or I. Yet he must die.
                  (II. iv. 33–36.)

Next her lofty mind apprehends the first statement of Angelo's proposition as only an academic hypothesis:

Ang. Admit no other way to save his life,—
    As I subscribe not that, nor any other,
    But in the loose of question,—that you, his sister,
    Finding yourself desir'd of such a person

> Whose credit with the judge, or own great place,
> Could fetch your brother from the manacles
> Of the all-binding law; and that there were
> No earthly mean to save him, but that either
> You must lay down the treasures of your body
> To this supposed, or else to let him suffer;
> What would you do?

Isab. As much for my poor brother as myself:
> That is, were I under the terms of death,
> The impression of keen whips I'd wear as rubies,
> And strip myself to death, as to a bed
> That, longing, have been sick for, ere I'd yield
> My body up to shame.

Ang.   Then must your brother die.

(II. iv. 88–104.)

We are presumably to understand that she remains oblivious to the true meaning until Angelo has declared himself openly—indeed, he must repeat himself, for at first Isabella still mistakes:

Ang. Plainly conceive, I love you.
Isab. My brother did love Juliet,
> And you tell me that he shall die for it.
Ang. He shall not, Isabel, if you give me love.
Isab. I know your virtue hath a license in 't,
> Which seems a little fouler than it is,
> To pluck on others.
Ang.   Believe me, on mine honour,
> My words express my purpose.
Isab. Ha! little honour to be much believed,
> And most pernicious purpose! Seeming, seeming!
> I will proclaim thee, Angelo.

(Ibid. 134–51.)

At this point Shakespeare twice underscores the central truth of the play, that in such a world mercy and goodness must go under unless an outside force, omniscient, omnipotent, and benevolent, rescues them. Says Angelo, on Isabella's threat to proclaim him:

> Who will believe, thee, Isabel?
> My unsoil'd name, th' austereness of my life,
> My vouch against you, and my place i' th' state,
> Will so your accusation overweigh,
> That you shall stifle in your own report
> And smell of calumny.

(Ibid. 154–9.)

'To whom should I complain?' cries Isabella in the soliloquy that ends the scene. 'Did I tell this, / Who would believe me?' In the tragedies, hearing such pleas, we can only recognize their futility. Juliet, for example, appeals in vain to some benevolent force greater

194

than the malevolence that abuses her: 'Is there no pity sitting in the clouds—?' Angelo's confidence is based on his certainty that no power within hearing can challenge his; Isabella's despair comes of the same certainty. But her very cry of despair, prodding our awareness that help is at hand, stirs warming comfort.

At the opening of Act III, with a double practice—eavesdropping and disguise—the Duke again catches up with us, never to fall behind again. His argument urging Claudio to be 'absolute for death', with which this scene begins, even though it lacked a context, must stand with the greatest passages in Shakespeare; its innate force, however, is enormously enhanced by the special frame of our awareness. Vincentio clearly does not intend to let Claudio die. Though he does not yet know of Angelo's improper proposal to Isabella, his interview with the penitent Juliet showed him the right and the wrong of the case. Hence the speech urging Claudio to be absolute for death is a simultaneous double practice: neither the speaker nor the argument is truly what it seems. Simply as the speech of a humble friar, the argument has power to persuade Claudio—at least for the present; but our knowledge that the speaker who argues so brilliantly for death has both authority and intent to save the life of the person addressed works a sea-change on the whole utterance. The effect of this combination of message, speaker, and situation is not exactly paralleled elsewhere in Shakespeare; the nearest analogy is the combination in *The Tempest*, when Prospero feigns to condemn the sudden love of Ferdinand and Miranda while he is inwardly overjoyed: 'At the first sight / They have chang'd eyes.'

The anguished scene between brother and sister which follows this introduction is similarly elevated and transformed by our advantage. For the participants it is a time of conflicting emotions, all painful. Claudio, honourable but passionately human, is appalled by thought of death and the grave:

> Ay, but to die, and go we know not where;
> To lie in cold obstruction and to rot;
> This sensible warm motion to become
> A kneaded clod, and the delighted spirit
> To bathe in fiery floods, or to reside
> In thrilling region of thick-ribbed ice;
> To be imprison'd in the viewless winds,
> And blown with restless violence round about
> The pendent world; or to be—worse than worst—
> Of those that lawless and incertain thought
> Imagine howling,—'tis too horrible!
>
> (III. i. 118–28.)

195

All too human, he remains absolute for death only so long as he can conceive it in terms of life: 'If I must die, / I will encounter darkness as a bride, / And hug it in mine arms.' But his martyr's resolution is overwhelmed by that same flow of warm blood that had first swept him under Angelo's edict. In striking contrast to Claudio's human warmth is his sister's inhuman coldness. Still 'enskied and sainted', confessing to no stirring of blood within, but even yet as frozen in nature as when she spoke her first lines in our hearing, at the entrance of the nunnery—'I speak not as desiring more, / But rather wishing a more strict restraint / Upon the sisterhood, the votaries of Saint Clare'—Isabella meets her brother's plea for life with a denial that is shocking in its ferocity:

> O you beast!
> O faithless coward! O dishonest wretch!
> Wilt thou be made a man out of my vice?
> Is't not a kind of incest, to take life
> From thine own sister's shame? What should I think?
> Heaven shield my mother play'd my father fair!
> For such a warped slip of wilderness
> Ne'er issued from his blood. Take my defiance!
> Die, perish! Might but my bending down
> Reprieve thee from thy fate, it should proceed.
> I'll pray a thousand prayers for thy death,
> No word to save thee.
>
> (III. i. 136–47.)

This is perhaps the warmest feeling she has ever experienced—but it expresses itself in a shriek of fury.

Like Angelo's, Isabella's veins are filled with snow-broth at first. Angelo's ice gives way in the heat of lust, Isabella's in the heat of anger. The cases run parallel, and perhaps there is no real choice between them. In each an excess of virtue amounting to a form of inhumanity yields to its opposite excess, which is a vice of humanity. Wicked as are lust and rage, they do evince a human potentiality more promising than the 'saintliness' which formerly denied this pair's affinity with humankind. The involuntary surrender of this 'saintliness' to a frailty of humanity is thus, in a sense, a step forward for both Angelo and Isabella.

Yet the precipitation of each from one excess to another evinces also a terrible need for correction—and it is a fact not to be forgotten during subsequent action *that the Duke has seen and heard exactly what we have seen and heard of Isabella's interview with her brother*: 'Bring me to hear them speak, where I may be conceal'd', he told the Provost. If the hundred lines of dialogue between brother and sister were presented in another circumstance—the

Duke not overhearing, or we ignorant that he overhears—the effect of the scene would be quite different. We would then stand on the participants' level, subject to the emotions that tear them. Our knowledge that the Duke, like power divine, hears both the account of Angelo's moral fall and the furious shriek of Isabella's outraged inhumanity enables us to watch the scene objectively, free of the participants' frenzy. The problem of the scene is intellectual rather than emotional, and the Duke's reassuring presence enables us to view it so. With the Duke hovering at its edge, the scene is a dark and bitter parallel of that in *A Midsummer-Night's Dream* when Oberon overhears the lovers' quarrel and enlists himself in their cause. But though dark and bitter, with the participants more agonized, the scene of Claudio and Isabella should cause us no more genuine anxiety than that of Demetrius and Helena. In each case an 'outside force' equal to the occasion hears all.

During the interview Claudio and Isabella are ignorant both that they are overheard and that the eavesdropper is the one force stronger than Angelo. A fold of their ignorance is stripped off when the Duke interrupts their talk: 'Son,' he says, 'I have overheard what hath pass'd between you and your sister.' That a mere friar has overheard the report of Angelo's fall and witnessed his own confession of human frailty and his sister's exhibition of inhumanity, however, signifies little to Claudio. The greater secret, which would signify much, the Duke withholds, even at the expense of a series of plain lies:

> Angelo had never the purpose to corrupt your sister; only he hath made an assay of her virtue to practise his judgment with the disposition of natures. She, having the truth of honour in her, hath made him that gracious denial which he is most glad to receive. I am confessor to Angelo, and I know this to be true; therefore prepare yourself to death.　　　(Ibid. 162-9.)

The seven lines contain three falsehoods apparent to us: Angelo did indeed mean to corrupt Isabella; the Duke is not Angelo's confessor; and, finally, now aware of all the facts, he cannot truly intend to let Claudio die. These lies appear notably ungodlike, and here the Duke's conduct first raises a question: recognizing the perfidiousness and danger of his deputy, why does he keep up his masquerade, when the removal of his friar's hood would set matters right—or at least as right as before he gave power to Angelo? Continuation of the masquerade is essential, obviously, to the maintenance of the gap between the participants' awareness and ours—and Shakespeare's addiction to the use of an exploitable discrepancy makes him willing, sometimes, to strain probability in order to preserve the discrepancy. Most of the Duke's masquerading predecessors could also have exposed their true identities earlier than they do: Portia, after saving Antonio in the court scene—but then she would have given up the sport which teaches her husband a deserved lesson; Rosalind, at any time after she has reached the safety of the forest and found Orlando truly in love with her; Viola, at her first encounter with Antonio, when she learns of Sebastian's survival; Helena, in the climactic moment of her midnight appointment with Bertram. In all these cases the continuation of the masquerade is necessary to the continuation of the exploitable discrepancy—which is itself necessary to the continuation of the action. But also, in these cases, justification of the heroines' delay in abandoning the masquerade is to be found in their own natures. Being disposed to try a practice in the first place, they are true to themselves in riding it out until the pattern they began to weave is finished. Not one of them would be quite herself if she dropped the masquerade short of the end.

So much may be said also, first of all, for Vincentio, whom Shakespeare has made one who enjoys the practiser's role. Most like Prospero, and like his predecessors (with the possible exception of Viola in her distressed moments) he relishes his advantage, even as we do ours in sharing his. Excepting Prospero (and Iago in tragedy) no other practiser of Shakespeare's is so active in plying his art. Contriving, manipulating, overhearing, overpeering, soliciting conversations, picking the minds of the innocent, the foolish, and the wicked alike, he might be expected, from pure delight, to protract the masquerade indefinitely. And truly, as we shall note, he never does give it over voluntarily.

But there are further reasons for him to continue. He had set out to be a looker-on in Vienna, visiting 'both prince and people'. In his perspective the specific case of Claudio and Isabella is part of a whole; to abandon the practice so as to rescue the first persons he finds in trouble under Angelo would be to forfeit the larger purpose. His test of Angelo, announced to Friar Thomas at the outset, designed to discover 'what our seemers be' under the temptation of absolute power, is not yet complete; he must give the deputy rein awhile to find the limit of his propensity.

Finally, the Duke must be considered to have taken a close interest in Isabella as a result of observing her in the interview with Claudio. From what proceeds, to the very end, it is evident that he sees her to be in as great need of rescue as, in another sense, Claudio is. His first sight of her comes in the interview, when her cold inhumanity is thawed by rage and her outburst exhibits a spirit devoid of such humane virtues as understanding, tolerance, compassion,

love. After the outburst she turns her back on her brother's cries—
'O hear me, Isabella!'—and would instantly return to the nunnery,
leaving Claudio to die. Even to us her exhibition must appear startling—yet we have been partly prepared for it by an earlier glimpse
of her at the nunnery door, when she wished that the rules might
be even more confining; by the dissolute Lucio's awed description:
'a thing enskied and sainted'; by the very fact that the frozen
Angelo, seeing her, melted in desire 'to raze the sanctuary' though
he had never been so moved before; and by her last words to us
before the interview with Claudio, when she denied Angelo with
a proclamation the flat enunciation of which seems holy but inhumane: 'More than our brother is our chastity.'

The Duke has had no such preliminary acquaintance: the outburst is his introduction, and if it startles us it must appal him.
Although he never states that the regeneration—or the generation
—of Isabella's humanity here becomes part of his purpose, he does
interrupt the interview abruptly, at its crisis—as though to prevent
her from damaging her soul further by utterances even more excessive. His first remarks, moreover, carry a double-cutting edge of
sarcasm, evident to us, dark to her:

> *Duke.* Vouchsafe a word, young sister, but one word.
> *Isab.* What is your will?
> *Duke.* Might you dispense with your leisure, I would by and by have some
> speech with you. The satisfaction I would require is likewise your own
> benefit. (III. i. 152–7.)

In view of the circumstance of her brother's peril, the duke's
request for 'but one word' appears overly modest, and sharper still
is the assurance, added hastily, that the moment's conversation
requested will be of benefit to herself. Isabella's reply does her
humanity hardly more credit than did her earlier outburst; she
would prefer to spend no more time for Claudio's sake unless it
were purely superfluous time, and she consents grudgingly: 'I have
no superfluous leisure; my stay must be stolen out of other affairs,
but I will attend you a while.' What other affairs has she, that take
priority over this which involves her brother's life? Returning to
Isabella, after a brief talk with Claudio—in which he says no word
of truth—the Duke speaks with great restraint, his measured words
falling exactly between compliment and censure:

> The hand that hath made you fair hath made you good; the goodness that
> is cheap in beauty makes beauty brief in goodness; but grace, being the soul of
> your complexion, shall keep the body of it ever fair. (Ibid. 184–8.)

His own mild and tolerant pronouncement on Angelo's fall, beside

Isabella's violent outburst, implies criticism of her dearth of human understanding: '. . . but that frailty hath examples for his falling, I should wonder at Angelo.'

A benevolent power, becoming ever more godlike, the Duke is concerned for Isabella and Angelo as for the rest of Vienna. Were he to give up the masquerade, neither would be saved. Isabella would withdraw to the nunnery, where an enduring rage at Angelo and Claudio would remain her only human indulgence. As for Angelo, arrested in his course, his blood would again congeal. The Duke's task is grander than merely the saving of Claudio's life: it is the salvation of Angelo and Isabella, and that, in these cases, amounts to the humanization of two 'saints'.

To carry out the purpose he must continue the masquerade. His use of the abandoned Mariana would be an absurdly inefficient method which would hardly occur to him if his purpose were only to free Claudio. The direct way to accomplish that end would be to take off his hood and speak to the Provost. *But Mariana provides a way for the salvation of everyone in need of salvation.* Much is in the Duke's mind when he tells Isabella of Mariana's plight. From his suggestion that she will at least be able to do 'uprighteously' what she is asked to do, he advances gingerly in the education of Isabella's humanity, first seeking to move compassion for Mariana's wretched condition:

> Left her in tears, and dried not one of them with his comfort; swallowed his vows whole, pretending in her discoveries of dishonour; in few, bestow'd her on her own lamentation, which she yet wears for his sake; and he, a marble to her tears, is washed with them, but relents not. (III. i. 234–9.)

His words are heavily laden with the pity of it—and Isabella is sufficiently touched to remark that 'this poor maid' would be better off dead. On this evidence of promise in his pupil, the Duke entails the practice by which multiple ends can be accomplished: '. . . your brother saved, your honour untainted, the poor Mariana advantaged, and the corrupt deputy scaled.' These are the only appropriate ends of which he can speak to Isabella. On the deep-lying benefits he intends for her and Angelo he is silent.

In the interim between the announcement of the Duke's acute practice on Angelo, with Mariana and Isabella as his accomplices, and the event itself, Shakespeare exploits the gap which separates the Duke's awareness from all Vienna's ignorance. Our advantage over Elbow, Pompey, Lucio, and Escalus, who represent the unknowing world, is double, since they are ignorant of both the 'friar's' true identity and Angelo's moral lapse. The mere exhibition of Elbow's essential stupidity, Pompey's trade-warped view of the world, and Lucio's swaggering dissoluteness would make interesting spectacle without any special frame; taking place in the presence of the all-powerful 'looker-on'—for whom all that is seen and heard has meanings unsuspected by these persons—the scene achieves dazzling effects. The most obvious are comic, as when the conversation of Lucio and the 'friar' strikes the familiar flashes of irony, long Shakespeare's staple commodity:

> *Duke.* I never heard the absent Duke much detected for women. He was not inclin'd that way.
> *Lucio.* O, sir, you are deceived!
> *Duke.* 'Tis not possible.   (III. ii. 129–32.)

These exchanges, in which comic effect is the most conspicuous result of exploitation of the discrepancy, takes up much of the scene. But even from the first Shakespeare was rarely content to exploit differences in awareness for any single effect, comic or other. *The Merry Wives of Windsor* is nearest a whole exception; *As You Like It*, with Rosalind playing her game with Orlando for the love of mockery, is next. But even *The Comedy of Errors* has Aegeon's plight shadowing scenes in which exploitation would otherwise produce pure fun. In general, as the line of comedies runs up to *Measure for Measure* the use of our advantage for mere comic effect decreases; not only are there fewer scenes in which comic effect predominates, but even in these that effect is not exclusive. So in the present scene, the nearest to pure-comic in the play: woven throughout are reminders that Elbow, Pompey, Lucio, and Escalus, for all Vienna, continue ignorant that Angelo, whose severity has caused these woes, is himself guilty, in thought and intent, of what he has condemned; indeed, guiltier, for he would 'raze a sanctuary' of which even dissolute Lucio stood in awe. Thus Elbow, speaking of Pompey: 'He must before the deputy, sir; he has given him warning. The deputy cannot abide a whore-master. If he be a whore-monger, and comes before him, he were as good go a mile on his errand.' And Lucio: 'They say this Angelo was not made by man and woman after this downright way of creation. . . . Some report a sea-maid spawn'd him; some, that he was begot between two stock-fishes. But it is certain that when he makes water his urine is congeal'd ice; that I know to be true: and he is a motion generative; that's infallible.' If the greatest secret of the play is that of the 'friar's' identity, the second is that of Angelo's duplicity, known only to us, the Duke, Angelo himself, Isabella, and Claudio. All Vienna remains unaware until the denouement; and then, as we shall note, all would continue ignorant, or unbelieving, despite Isabella's denunciation, but that this 'friar' is the Duke.

Thus the dark strain of the mistaking of Angelo runs through the scene, intertwined with the light one, represented mainly by Lucio's hazardous maligning of the Duke's character to the 'friar'. At the end these strains are finally knotted in Escalus's virtuous but unknowing comment and the deeply ironic reply of the Duke:

> *Escal.* You have paid the heavens your function, and the prisoner the very debt of your calling. I have labour'd for the poor gentleman to the extremest shore of my modesty; but my brother justice have I found so severe, that he hath forc'd me to tell him he is indeed Justice.
>
> *Duke.* If his own life answer the straitness of his proceeding, it shall become him well; wherein if he chance to fail, he hath sentenc'd himself..
>
> (III. ii. 263–72.)

Elbow, lowest rung of both law and intellect; Lucio, the licentiate; and Escalus, sagest of mere men—'The nature of our people, / Our city's institutions, and the terms / For common justice, you're as pregnant in / As art and practice hath enriched any / That we remember'—are equally deceived by Angelo, in whom evil masquerades as virtue and in this mask would surely defeat justice. But all are similarly deceived by the 'friar', who is benign omnipotence masquerading as mere powerless goodness. Thus both Angelo and the Duke are 'seemers', and our assurance of safety for those ignorant of the evil that hides behind Angelo's mask of virtue—and for those who have already caught a glimpse of it—comes of our knowledge that this evil is circumscribed by the omnipotence hidden behind the mask of the 'friar'. Pointedly here Vincentio's own sense of his godlike relation to the situation, catastrophic but for him, is expressed in soliloquy; the description is applicable both to himself and to what Angelo seems to be and is not:

> He who the sword of heaven will bear
> Should be as holy as severe;
> Pattern in himself to know,
> Grace to stand, and virtue go. . . .
> (Ibid. 275–8.)

As is usual in the comedies, the most complex disposition of awarenesses is attained in *Measure for Measure* at the beginning of Act IV and sustained until the denouement shows the participants what we have long known. At the lowermost level stand the representatives of the unknowing world, most significantly Escalus and the Provost, but also Lucio, Elbow, Pompey, and all who become involved with either the seeming angel or the seeming friar. All these are quite ignorant of the situation beyond the fact that

Claudio has been condemned. Just above them is Angelo, who has himself discovered with surprise that he is not what he had seemed to be, but who is ignorant of the 'friar's' identity and of the trap now set for him. Above Angelo are Isabella and Mariana, knowing accomplices of the 'friar' in the practice on Angelo—but unsuspecting accomplices of the Duke in his enveloping practice on Vienna. Finally, standing with us, overpeering all levels, omnipotent, omniscient, and benevolent, is Vincentio. This structure of awarenesses stands during the entire central portion of the play, from the Duke's announcement of his acute practice on Angelo at the end of III. i until the denouement. Though less elaborate than the comparable portions of *Twelfth Night* and *The Merry Wives*, in which a great many secrets create many discrepancies, the structure, resting on ignorance of the 'friar's' identity and the deputy's duplicity, is remarkable for its centrality and its duration; it has literally become the play.

At the end of III. i, her sleeping humanity shaken partially awake by the 'friar's' plea, Isabella has consented to take part in the deception of Angelo. In IV. i the three practisers fix the details of their device. The next scene would normally present the climax—the meeting of Angelo with Mariana, masquerading as Isabella. Since this cannot well be exhibited, the time of its occurrence is marked, somewhat as the dark meeting of Bertram and Helena, masquerading as Diana, is marked by the conversation of the two French lords at the corresponding point in *All's Well*. But this is Shakespeare's second use of a substitute climax: his hand is surer now, and the result is a piece of artistry as fine as the finest in the plays.

''Tis now dead midnight,' says the Provost to Claudio, 'and by eight to-morrow / Thou must be made immortal.' Isabella had been precise about the time and circumstances of her assignation with Angelo: 'There have I made my promise / Upon the heavy middle of the night / To call upon him.' Hence, while Abhorson instructs Pompey in his new mystery, *we know that the dark practice designed to accomplish multiple purposes is in its preliminaries*: Mariana should by now have opened the 'planched gate' of Angelo's vineyard, crossed that, and, with a little key, have unlocked the door to the garden 'circummur'd with brick'. With infinite shrewdness the dramatist made Isabella describe the details of the route so vividly that now the mind's eye can trace the course while the outer eye observes the substitute action. Like a ticking clock, but more pointedly, the conversation of the Provost, Abhorson, Pompey, and Claudio fills up the time, their proxy action veiling the true one of which they are themselves quite ignorant. The very vocabulary of the participants, being compact of the terms of Pompey's former trade—'notorious bawd', 'unlawful bawd', 'bawd . . . bawd . . . bawd', 'your whores, sir, being members of my occupation, using painting, do prove my occupation a mystery', 'if you have occasion to use me for your own turn, you shall find me yare'—forms a gross parallel to the climactic event going on at Angelo's. Claudio's very presence on the stage serves also to remind of the hidden action—by which his life is being saved. The Provost's words at the sound of knocking within—'I hope it is some pardon or reprieve / For the most gentle Claudio'—serve the same purpose.

The climax of the proxy scene is the arrival of the Duke, his mind heavy with consciousness of the hour, the event, and the multiple purposes just now being served. As the Duke speaks, the action at Angelo's should be finished; the sudden 'knocking within', which commences at the end of his deeply ironic speech, signifies the completion:

> *Prov.*   It is a bitter deputy.
> *Duke.* Not so, not so; his life is parallel'd
>   Even with the stroke and line of his great justice.
>   He doth with holy abstinence subdue
>   That in himself which he spurs on his power
>   To qualify in others. Were he meal'd with that
>   Which he corrects, then were he tyrannous;
>   But this being so, he's just.   (*Knocking within.*)
>   (IV. ii. 81–88.)

'Now are they come', says the Duke.

And so they are. But both we and the Duke are deceived, for the messenger bears no countermand, but a reaffirmation of the order for Claudio's execution. 'Were he meal'd with that / Which he corrects, then were he tyrannous': when the Duke spoke these lines, a moment earlier, they were consciously ironic, subtly mixing truth and falsehood. They were false in suggesting that Angelo is not 'meal'd' with lust, but seemingly true in that Angelo will not correct in another the fault he is himself just now guilty of—for his agreement was to release Claudio. The quality of the irony in these lines —and, indeed, in the entire speech, which is composed of three distinct statements of a single idea—is violently altered when both we and the Duke learn that Angelo does intend to execute Claudio. 'Were he meal'd with that / Which he corrects, then were he tyrannous': the condition is now removed, and a new irony not intended by the Duke or perceived by ourselves at the time now engulfs the former.

The arrival of the messenger abruptly ends the parallel of the masking action and the true one. Confronted with the great disadvantage of being unable to represent the actual climactic scene, Shakespeare devised a substitute which makes advantage of disadvantage, turning an interim of waiting in the dreary hours of night in the dim prison into an artistic triumph.

With the arrival of a reaffirmation instead of a countermand arises a second occasion on which the Duke might be expected to end his masquerade and deal with the situation directly. If his purpose were but to save Claudio, he would surely do so. Or if it were but to discover 'what our seemers be', he should seek no further evidence, having now had clear sight of the seamy side of the angel. He continues the masquerade against such difficulties that neither these purposes nor the mere love of practising would be reasonable motives. First, in order to continue the old practice he must devise a new one—actually his third major practice—using the Provost this time as accomplice as he had used Isabella and Mariana in that just completed. In persuading the honest Provost to deceive Angelo by sending Barnardine's head instead of Claudio's, he encounters the hardest test so far in his masquerade, for the Provost is not so quick to agree as were Isabella and Mariana. Indeed, so firm is he that the Duke has to lower his mask a little; the 'friar', that is to say, is obliged to borrow of the Duke:

> I will go further than I meant, to pluck all fears out of you. Look you, sir, here is the hand and seal of the Duke. You know the character, I doubt not; and the signet is not strange to you.   (Ibid. 206–9.)

'I will go further than I meant': an ultimate purpose of the masquerade as is now implied is to test whether the 'friar', being only a friar, with the aid only of good but powerless mortals like Isabella, Mariana, and the Provost, could ever triumph—to prove, that is to say, what would be the fate of good in the bad world of Vienna if no force 'like power divine' existed. This moment with the Provost is therefore a critical one: with reluctance the 'friar' compromises the purity of the test a little by displaying tokens of the Duke's authority. If he did not do so—if no such power existed, or if he were truly only a friar—his efforts would fail at this point, and Claudio would die in spite of all that mere goodness could do. From this point to the end it becomes increasingly evident that mere mortal goodness, though coupled with superior awareness, is insufficient: the happy ending of *Measure for Measure* requires direct intervention of a force that is not only aware and good, as the 'friar' is, but omnipotent, as the Duke is. 'All difficulties are but easy when they are known', the 'friar' tells the Provost; but his need to use symbols of the Duke's authority argues that mere 'knowing' is not enough in Vienna, as it used to be in the worlds of Arden and Illyria.

Barnardine's refusal to be hanged is the second obstacle that confronts the Duke in his effort to discover whether the 'friar' can win the battle for justice unaided. The incident carries, besides, a special significance for all Shakespearian comedy: it underscores the fact that, whatever its iniquities and however imminent the apparent danger, this world of comedy is one in which no permanent harm shall befall anyone. Not Claudio, Isabella, Mariana—not even a Barnardine 'unfit to live or die' shall be harmed in this world; indeed, villainy itself cannot do injury to itself—for Angelo is saved, despite himself, if Claudio lives. It is noteworthy, as marking the immutability of Shakespeare's law of comedy, that even in the world of *Measure for Measure*, with all its blackness, *the head finally used to deceive Angelo is not only not the good Claudio's, not only not Barnardine's, 'unfit to live or die'—not even that of any man of any kind who must be put to death to provide a head, but that of a man already dead; and even so, not that of any casual mortal who has died, but that of a pirate, a notorious pirate—killed by a fever that is described as 'cruel'*: 'O, 'tis an accident that Heaven provides.' The incident is an extreme illustration of the way of the world in the comedies.

The sending of Ragozine's head for Claudio's is the Duke's third major practice, his second within the all-encompassing device of the masquerade itself. The lie told Isabella, which follows at once, is his fourth:

> *Isab.* Hath yet the deputy sent my brother's pardon?
> *Duke.* He hath releas'd him, Isabel, from the world.
> His head is off, and sent to Angelo.
> (IV. iii. 118–20.)

The Duke's stated reason for this practice seems abrupt and unconvincing—

> . . . I will keep her ignorant of her good,
> To make her heavenly comforts of despair,
> When it is least expected.
> (Ibid. 113–15.)

—and not conspicuously godlike. By keeping the fact of Claudio's survival hidden from Isabella, Shakespeare of course adds to the accumulation of practices, secrets, and discrepancies that can be exploited as the denouement approaches. Devoted early to an elaborate machinery of exploitation, he appears to love it ever more intensely, even greedily, as he nears the last plays. Possibly his own addiction, then—together with his Vincentio's consciousness of working in mysterious ways—is the true reason for this startling lie to Isabella. Yet the action both before and after this moment suggests a deeper reason, left unsaid. The Duke has not yet ended his work with Angelo and Isabella. Angelo must of course be kept ignorant of Claudio's survival, or Claudio's head will yet be off, and the Provost's too. And Isabella, knowing that her brother lives, would presumably retire to the nunnery. Yet she is needed by the Duke, with Mariana, to expose Angelo, and she must then play her role earnestly. Her frozen humanity has only begun to thaw. In helping the wronged Mariana against Angelo, she gave promise of coming to understand that the world holds worthy commodities besides her chastity. Further hopeful signs of her awakening humanity are manifest in her reaction to the Duke's report of Claudio's death:

> Unhappy Claudio! Wretched Isabel!
> Injurious world! Most damned Angelo!
> (Ibid. 126-7.)

This is surely the widest range of human concern that she has ever experienced; she has evidently come far from the Isabella who wished stricter restraint upon the sisterhood of Saint Clare. In our perspective, of course, she is here mistaken in each of the four exclamations, and the passage is a brief masterpiece of flashes which illuminate the gaps between truth and her understanding: for Claudio is not 'Unhappy Claudio!' but happy Claudio, being saved and soon to be reunited with Juliet; Isabel is not 'Wretched Isabel!' except in her ignorance that Claudio lives and that the Duke's eye is on Angelo; it is not an 'Injurious world!' but one so guarded against injury that the head of a dead pirate is called into service to spare that of the most worthless living man; and it is not 'Most damned Angelo!' for the benign grasp of the Duke has made it impossible even for villainy to damn itself. But though she is wrong in her facts, Isabella's impulses are more humane now than before. As the denouement proceeds it becomes apparent that her belief that Claudio is dead by Angelo's command is indispensable to the Duke's purpose of completing her humane education.

Dependent upon discrepancies in awareness for its very existence, the denouement of *Measure for Measure*, in both its workmanship and its effects achieved by workmanship, has few peers and no superiors in Shakespearian comedy. Neither so fantastically complex as that of *Cymbeline* nor so grandly spectacular as that of *The Tempest*, it exceeds both in its clarity and sharpness of detail, in its structure and movement, and in its concentration of power. As in the other comedies except *The Comedy of Errors*, where we learn belatedly of Aemilia, and *The Winter's Tale*, where we discover at last that Shakespeare lied about Hermione's death, this denouement is none for us, we having nothing new to learn, but only for the participants. For us the final scene is a spectacle of promises kept, bringing to completion two principal matters: it concludes the demonstration of the ugly truth that in this Vienna good would perish but for the intervention of a godlike force; and it finishes and tests Isabella's re-education.

Four levels make up its structure of awarenesses. At the bottom are Escalus, Lucio, and all the officers and citizens gathered at the city gate to greet the Duke. These are the yet-unknowing world, alike ignorant of truth and abused by false report. The one fact known to them is that Claudio was arrested and condemned under Angelo's strict application of the law. Of all else that has happened and that we have watched and heard, they know nothing. They believe that the Duke has been far from Vienna and is only now returning; that Angelo's veins are still as full of snow-broth as when he took office; that in the absence of the Duke the deputy has ruled with a severity consonant with his nature; and that Claudio has been executed. The absoluteness of their ignorance is a matter of great importance: *for this same ignorance would have been the Duke's also if he were in fact now returning from afar.* And it is the mask of this ignorance that the Duke does, in a new practice, put on when he resumes his place.

The next level above the unknowing world's is Angelo's alone. His only advantage over Vienna is the knowledge of his improper proposal to Isabella, which proved that blood, and not the snow-broth imagined by Vienna, flows in his veins. He is quite in error in his opinion of the sequel to that proposal, believing that Isabella visited him secretly and that Claudio is now dead. The state of his awareness is exhibited immediately before he goes to greet the Duke:

> A deflow'red maid!
> And by an eminent body that enforc'd
> The law against it! But that her tender shame
> Will not proclaim against her maiden loss,
> How might she tongue me! Yet reason dares her no....
>
> (IV. iv. 24–28.)

Like Isabella in her 'Unhappy Claudio! Wretched Isabel! / Injurious world! Most damned Angelo!' Angelo is shown in error about all he thinks true: 'A deflow'red maid!'—but she is not deflowered; 'But that her tender shame / Will not proclaim against her maiden loss, / How might she tongue me!'—but she will proclaim him and will be mightily supported; 'For my authority bears a credent bulk / That no particular scandal once can touch / But it confounds the breather'—but the Duke himself knows the truth; 'He should have liv'd'—but Claudio does live. Excepting the naïve and pitiful wretches who conspire against Prospero in *The Tempest*, no other of Shakespeare's wrongdoers, or potential wrongdoers, is so tightly pinioned and so ignorant of his helplessness as is Angelo. Paradoxically, the truth which he does not know is both better and worse than he supposes; what he thinks bad is good, and what he thinks good is bad. He believes himself guilty of the deflowering of Isabella and of abuse of authority in executing Claudio for a similar fault; but so tight has been Vincentio's rein that though he thinks he has destroyed two innocents he has not really been dangerous to either. His bad intents have been thwarted; he is saved and ignorant that he has been saved. Thus the truth is better than he supposes. But it is also worse. Though he believes that he has committed unforgivable acts whereas he has really committed none, yet he thinks these acts known only to himself and the crushed and silent victims; but in reality all of his intents have been known to the Duke from the beginning, and the truth of his acts is better known to the Duke than to the deputy. Greeting the Duke at the opening of Act V, then, Angelo stands under an extraordinary light, a figure at once odious, comic, and pathetic: supposing himself guilty of heinous crimes of which remembrance tortures him, but which he is convinced he can keep hidden, he is truly guilty of no criminal acts, but all his intents are known to the authority who can call him to account.

On the level just above Angelo's stand Isabella and, less significantly, Mariana. Isabella shares with us, the Duke, and Angelo himself an awareness of the seemer's other side. Further, with the 'friar' and Mariana, having perpetrated a midnight fraud on Angelo, she holds advantage over him in knowing the truth of that crucial incident. On the other hand, she remains ignorant of Claudio's survival and, of course, with all Vienna, of the 'friar's' identity.

On the highest level, from which every aspect of the situation is open to his vision, ready to proceed with Angelo 'By cold gradation and well-balanc'd form', stands the Duke. Friar Peter shares all his secrets, and the Provost some of them: 'The Provost knows our purpose and our plot.' Earlier, in order to win his aid in saving Claudio, the 'friar' had displayed 'the hand and seal of the Duke' to the Provost, who is now aware, of course, that Claudio is alive and possibly aware even of much more, short of the deepest secret, the 'friar's' identity.

Our own awareness of the immediate situation matches the Duke's, and we know the general outline but not the precise details of what is to follow. Vincentio has been more generous with us in drafting the design of the final action than was Helena in *All's Well*, whose shrewd machinations were conducted behind the scene. The Duke instructs Isabella and Mariana, sends letters to Angelo, lays plans with Friar Peter—all in our view. But we are denied the exact details of his design and its outcome. For us, therefore, as for Isabella in particular—'To speak so indirectly I am loath. / I would say the truth; but to accuse him so, / That is your part. Yet I am advis'd to do it; / He says, to veil full purpose'—some inscrutability remains in the Duke's purposes. It is one of the shrewdest dramatic strokes in this play, of which the workmanship is everywhere characterized by great shrewdness, that a sense of mystery and suspense is preserved amid absolute assurance that all is and must end well. Our recognition that the Duke's mind grasps the totality of action and holds purposes beyond our certain knowledge heightens his stature during this climactic period, when full effect requires that he loom 'like power divine'. Realization that he intends to proceed 'By cold gradation and well-balanc'd form', joined with uncertainty of precise means and ends, binds us to watch the proceedings with an attentive eye.

Unlike Helena of *All's Well*, the Duke is himself on hand to direct the movements of his intricate plot—indeed, he is on hand in a triple role, as proprietor of two distinct practices and as himself. As the 'friar' he continues the masquerade begun in Act I. As the Duke who feigns to have returned from some remote country he wears a mask of ignorance. Both roles are essential in the final test of the question, whether truths can be exposed, wrongs redressed, and all set right in Vienna without the intervention of an 'outside' force. Hitherto the Duke has refused to reveal his true identity in spite of all; but once, in order to have the Provost spare Claudio's life, he had to compromise the test by displaying the Duke's hand and seal. Now, as the final action proceeds, he continues his effort to right wrong without having to call upon the supreme power which exists, in effect, apart from both 'friar' and 'newly returned' Duke. As 'friar' he is omniscient, but not omnipotent. As 'newly returned' Duke he is omnipotent, but not omniscient: indeed, his is the same ignorance as all Vienna's. Omniscience and omnipotence are combined only in the Duke in the true identity that we alone perceive, apart from either masquerader.

The Duke conducts the first phase of the final test in the 'newly returned' mask. From the start, when Isabella—a conscious participant in the 'friar's' practice and an unwitting one in the Duke's—makes her first plea, the odds against the triumph of good unaided appear too great:

> Justice, O royal Duke! Vail your regard
> Upon a wrong'd—I would fain have said a maid!
> O worthy Prince, dishonour not your eye
> By throwing it on any other object
> Till you have heard me in my true complaint
> And given me justice, justice, justice, justice!
>
> (v. i. 20–25.)

To this plea Vincentio, playing with imaginative honesty the role of oblivious omnipotence, replies quite as he would have replied had he truly just returned to Vienna, ignorant of Angelo's duplicity:

> Relate your wrongs. In what? whom? Be brief.
> Here is Lord Angelo shall give you justice:
> Reveal yourself to him.
>
> (Ibid. 26–28.)

Here, and on until the moment that the friar's hood is snatched from the Duke's head, the most spectacular products of exploitation of the multiple discrepancies in awareness are bursts of irony which flare up in a succession that provides virtually steady illumination. The complex situation has been so devised that the Duke cannot address Angelo, Isabella, or Lucio without striking a shower of sparks: thus even his simple, formal greeting of Angelo at the gate —'My very worthy cousin, fairly met!'—and his first words of praise—'O, your desert speaks loud; and I should wrong it / To lock it in the wards of covert bosom / When it deserves, with characters of brass, / A forted residence 'gainst the tooth of time / And razure of oblivion'—brightly arch the gulf between our awareness and the unknowing world's oblivion. So also when he replies to Isabella's first plea: 'Here is Lord Angelo shall give you justice'; and again, when Isabella has berated Angelo as murderer, adulterous thief, hypocrite, and virgin-violator, concluding 'Is it not strange and strange?' Vincentio replies, 'Nay, it is ten times strange.' Even these are hardly simple strokes of irony; there is a double, often triple excellence in them, since every flash comes of *just such an utterance as the Duke would have made without ironical intent if he had truly just returned to Vienna.* The same remarks which now flash as conscious irony would then have struck flashes invisible to the Duke and visible only to us, Angelo, and Isabella. As the scene stands, these flashes seem unintentional to Angelo and Isabella, who know that Angelo deserves no such praise and who are ignorant that the Duke is deliberately acting the role of unwitting ruler. And while we know the flashes struck by the Duke's remarks to be intentional and Angelo and Isabella think them unintentional, all Vienna gathered at the gates, knowing nothing of Angelo's fall, can see no flashes at all.

Spectacular as they are, the ironical flashes that light the scene are rather accompanying effects than ends in themselves. And in this respect the uses of discrepancies in awareness differ significantly from those in the early comedies and in the primarily comic scenes of the mature comedies, where situations were regularly created *in order* to produce these effects alone. In *Measure for Measure* too, of course, portions of scenes exploit discrepancies mainly for their ironical flashes. The earlier interviews of the 'friar' with Lucio are such, as we have seen, and the effects of these are repeated in the present action, with the former 'friar' as 'newly returned' Duke:

> *Duke.* You were not bid to speak.
> *Lucio.*   No, my good lord;
> Nor wish'd to hold my peace.
> *Duke.*   I wish you now, then.
> Pray you, take note of it; and when you have
> A business for yourself, pray Heaven you then
> Be perfect.
> *Lucio.*   I warrant your honour.
> *Duke.* The warrant's for yourself; take heed to't.
> > (v. i. 78–83.)

The flashes that accompany the Duke's remarks to Angelo and Isabella, however, are only incidental to the demonstration of the main point—that if the Duke did not already know the truth it would go unregarded. It would not go unheard, but it would be rejected, even as it seems rejected now by the consciously ironical remarks of the Duke, which Angelo and Isabella take as unconsciously ironical. Repeatedly, with rising passion that suggests growth of her human capabilities, Isabella pleads for redress:

> He would not, but by gift of my chaste body
> To his concupiscible intemperate lust,
> Release my brother; and, after much debatement,
> My sisterly remorse confutes mine honour,
> And I did yield to him; but the next morn betimes,
> His purpose surfeiting, he sends a warrant
> For my poor brother's head.
> > (Ibid. 97–103.)

To Vienna, wholly ignorant of these events, all is incredible. To Angelo, who keeps silence, all seems true. To Isabella herself, part is

truth, part practice: 'My sisterly remorse confutes mine honour, /
And I did yield to him.' The 'newly returned' Duke replies to every
plea with the appearance of bland disbelief; so far as Isabella can
see her plight is utterly hopeless:

> Then, O you blessed ministers above,
> Keep me in patience, and with rip'ned time
> Unfold the evil which is here wrapt up
> In countenance! Heaven shield your Grace from woe,
> As I, thus wrong'd, hence unbelieved go!
>
> (Ibid. 115–19.)

This is a familiar cry of tragic heroines caught in hopeless situations.
Juliet, married to banished Romeo, commanded to marry Paris or
die in the streets, calls out for supernatural sympathy: 'Is there no
pity sitting in the clouds / That sees into the bottom of my grief?'
We hold no comforting advantage over Juliet; her skies are black
and silent to us as to her. For Isabella the dismal affair seems to have
ended in that utter defeat which Angelo foretold. But Shakespeare
has equipped us with an advantage which enables us to watch objectively: even when the Duke, in his role of ignorant omnipotence,
orders Isabella carried off we know that all is well. Such is the use
of awareness; even this darkest moment of the play is bathed in
comforting assurance that makes the effects of comedy possible.

The second phase of the final test is represented by Mariana's
efforts to win the 'newly returned' Duke's belief. Her failure is as
conclusive as was Isabella's, and it comes more abruptly, even
though she tells perfect truth whereas Isabella mixed truth with
practice:

> . . . this is the body
> That took away the match from Isabel,
> And did supply thee at thy garden-house
> In her imagin'd person.
>
> (Ibid. 210–13.)

Her truth is startling news, of course, to Angelo; but, though he
unquestionably believes it, he gives no sign: 'This is a strange abuse.'
And then, ignorant—pitifully so, in our perspective—that he is
lying in the very face of heaven, he goes on boldly:

> I do perceive
> These poor informal women are no more
> But instruments of some more mightier member
> That sets them on. Let me have way, my lord,
> To find this practice out.
>
> (Ibid. 235–9.)

'And punish them unto your height of pleasure', the 'newly

returned' Duke answers, putting the case of the women into Angelo's hands—even as he might have done if he were truly as unknowing as the deputy supposes.

In the last phase of the test the 'friar' replaces Isabella and Mariana in striving to win justice without aid from outside. Now masked as impotent omniscience rather than ignorant omnipotence, making a determined final effort, the Duke touches the highest point in his career as masquerader and perpetrator of multiple practices. His first plea hurled back at him, the 'friar' laments for the helpless victims of Angelo's tyranny:

> O, poor souls,
> Come you to seek the lamb here of the fox?
> Good night to your redress! Is the Duke gone?
> Then is your cause gone too.
>
> (v. i. 299–302.)

Angelo, of course, could not be expected to heed the appeal of the 'friar' and his fellow petitioners, but Escalus might yet be induced to heed it; hence Shakespeare puts everything on the exchanges between 'friar' and Escalus rather than on 'friar' and Angelo. Moreover, the prior characterization of Escalus gives great significance to his conduct in these last crucial moments. Escalus is the wisest mere mortal in Vienna, and is completely dedicated to the idea of justice. If, therefore, the truths told by Isabella, Mariana, and the 'friar' have failed to reach him, then the final proof is conclusive: *truth and justice cannot prevail in this world without help from without.* Guilt-ridden, Angelo would of course deny the appeal; Escalus, however, has no purpose except to find the truth—and he is one who could find it if it were discoverable by mere mortal wisdom. But like Isabella in her 'Unhappy Claudio! Wretched Isabel!' lamentation, and like Angelo in his soliloquy—'A deflow'red maid!' —that just precedes the final act, he is quite mistaken about the situation in which and of which he speaks, and his verdict is therefore appalling:

> Take him hence; to the rack with him! We'll touse you
> Joint by joint, but we will know his purpose.
>
> (Ibid. 313–14.)

In the frightfully worsened world of *Measure for Measure*, neither awareness without power nor power without awareness is enough to save truth: both 'friar' and 'newly returned' Duke fail. The wisest man of law shouts down the very principle of justice that is dearest to him—and by the blind excess of Escalus's zeal to punish, Shakespeare drives home the ugly fact:

Away with him to prison! Where is the Provost? Away with him to prison!
Lay bolts enough upon him! Let him speak no more. Away with those giglots
too, and with the other confederate companion!   (Ibid. 349-53.)

Such would be the fate of truth in a world lacking the control of an
external, benevolent, omnipotent, and omniscient force. It is noteworthy that the 'friar' does not end the masquerade voluntarily, but
might have allowed himself to be taken to prison, there to continue
his efforts to have truth prevail. It is Lucio who, by tearing off the
'friar's' hood, ends the Duke's masquerade. 'Thou art the first knave
that e'er mad'st a duke', says Vincentio—and all is well. But,
obviously, if snatching off the hood had disclosed merely the face
of a friar, evil would have prevailed; the happy ending depends
entirely on there being a duke's face beneath the hood.

The main discrepancy in awarenesses which has provided the
exploitable condition for almost five acts is thus closed with sen-
sational abruptness. Lucio, suddenly lifted to our vantage-point,
tries to sneak away. The wise and just Escalus, who in ignorance
has just been shouting loudly in the cause of injustice, is stunned,
and the Duke speaks a consoling word. But the coming-to-awareness
of these persons is relatively unimportant; in this climactic instant
the main attention is on the one to whom the sudden revelation
means most. Says Angelo:

> O my dread lord,
> I should be guiltier than my guiltiness,
> To think I can be undiscernible,
> When I perceive your Grace, like power divine,
> Hath look'd upon my passes.
>   (Ibid. 371-5.)

Angelo's conversion is effected by shock; his lesson is finished, and
the Duke has really nothing more to do with this pupil. But he has
not yet finished with Isabella.

After the 'friar' is unhooded, one secret remains, the existence of
which leaves a gap still to be closed between Vienna's ignorance
and the Duke's and our awareness; it is the secret of Claudio's survival. 'O, give me pardon,' cries Isabella, distressed at her breach of
propriety, 'That I, your vassal, have employ'd and pain'd / Your
unknown sovereignty!' The handsomest answer which the Duke
could make to this plea is that she has both pardon and her brother's
life. Pardon he gives instantly; but instead of reporting Claudio's
survival, he reasserts his former lie and adds an elaborately false
excuse:

> Your brother's death, I know, sits at your heart;
> And you may marvel why I obscur'd myself,
> Labouring to save his life, and would not rather

LIKE POWER DIVINE

> Make rash remonstrance of my hidden power
> Than let him so be lost. O most kind maid,
> It was the swift celerity of his death,
> Which I did think with slower foot came on,
> That brain'd my purpose. But, peace be with him!
> (v. i. 394–401.)

Shakespeare, as has been shown, does not give up an exploitable discrepancy while anything exploitable remains in it. Moreover, especially from *Twelfth Night* onward—'One face, one voice, one habit, and two persons'—he does not like to give it up until the ripest moment is at hand, when the space between our knowledge and the participants' ignorance can be closed with greatest effect. The master practiser Vincentio, like his master Shakespeare, evidently likes the showmanship which his advantage makes possible, and it accords with his relish for working in mysterious ways that he holds on to an exploitable situation until more effect can be gained by releasing it than by holding it longer. The snatching off of the friar's hood occurred at precisely the right moment. But the revelation of Claudio's survival, if it immediately followed that of the 'friar's' identity, would be anti-climactic—indeed, would be wasted; and it is not imaginable that either Shakespeare or Vincentio would waste an effect which had been saved for the last at some earlier cost to probability: 'I will keep her ignorant of her good, / To make her heavenly comforts of despair, / When it is least expected.' All these are obvious reasons why the Duke might now compound his lie to Isabella about Claudio; but their basis is mere dramatic expediency, and if there were no better basis Shakespeare would be the less Shakespeare—and Vincentio would hardly deserve Angelo's awe: '. . . your Grace, like power divine.'

The better reason has been suggested earlier. The Duke's introduction to Isabella came when, eavesdropping on her talk with the doomed Claudio, he heard the inhumane outburst that was her response to her brother's all too human plea for life. By careful invitation he induced her to help in the deception of Angelo—she consenting perhaps partly from rage at Angelo but partly also in pity of Mariana. Her capability of larger sympathies thereafter shows also in her reaction to the report that Claudio has been executed in spite of Angelo's promise; and finally it shows in her plea in the early part of the closing scene—a plea prompted partly by her wish for vengeance on Angelo but also, at the entreaty of the 'friar', by her wish to help Mariana. Isabella has evidently come a good way from the 'enskied and sainted' thing who wished the nunnery's rules more rigorous; from the icy prude whose pronounce-

ment in soliloquy, gratuitous, flat, and absolute—'More than our
brother is our chastity'—carried overtones of the deadly sin of
pride; and from the 'angry ape' the exhibition of whose inhumanity
—'Die, perish! Might but my bending down / Reprieve thee from
thy fate, it should proceed'—was witnessed by the Duke.

She has come a good way from this—or, more precisely, *she has
been led by the 'friar'*. But her humane education is not complete—
nor will the Duke let it stop short of completion. Hence he reasserts
his lie about Claudio's death, and then proceeds, with the same 'cold
gradation and well-balanc'd form' with which he had proceeded
with Angelo, to give his pupil a final lesson—and a test. Newly
married, Angelo and Mariana return to the scene, and the Duke
sentences Angelo to death, making plain—and speaking pointedly
to Isabella in doing so—that no malpractice of the deputy *except his
execution of Claudio* is responsible for the penalty:

> The very mercy of the law cries out
> Most audible, even from his proper tongue,
> 'An Angelo for Claudio, death for death!'
> (Ibid. 412–14.)

Knowing that Claudio lives, the Duke cannot really intend to take
Angelo's life for Claudio's. His condemnation of Angelo is, therefore, a practice. But on whom and to what end? It is not on Angelo,
already a changed man, ready to accept death, clearly in need of no
further lessons. Nor, obviously, is it a practice on Mariana, who has
never needed a lesson in humanity. It is a practice on Isabella, the
shrewdest and most drastic devised by Vincentio in the entire
action. When, speaking directly to her, he says that Angelo must
die for Claudio's death, Isabella stands silent. Mariana pleads
movingly for her husband's life. The Duke's answer is a harsh 'no'.
Isabella stands silent. Again Mariana pleads and again the Duke's
reply is cold as stone: 'Never crave him; we are definitive.' Isabella
stands silent. Once more Mariana pleads, and this time drops on her
knees before the Duke. Vincentio could hardly maintain his practice of seeming to intend the death of Angelo merely to prolong
the sport of it—or to make Mariana 'heavenly comforts of despair'
a little later; but again his reply is startling in its harshness: 'You do
but lose your labour. / Away with him to death!' Isabella stands
silent. Then Mariana—who might almost perceive the purpose of
the Duke's practice, and as if induced to act by his prompting—
turns to beg Isabella's help:

> Sweet Isabel, take my part!
> Lend me your knees, and all my life to come
> I'll lend you all my life to do you service. (Ibid. 435–7.)

Isabel stands silent. Says the Duke, pointedly,

> Against all sense you do importune her.
> Should she kneel down in mercy of this fact,
> Her brother's ghost his paved bed would break,
> And take her hence in horror.
>
> (v. i. 438–40.)

'Should she kneel down in mercy of this fact': it is the prompting of a hesitant pupil. And yet Isabel stands silent. Mariana again picks up her plea—this time rather a plea for Isabella's salvation than for Angelo's:

> Sweet Isabel, do yet but kneel by me.
> Hold up your hands, say nothing; I'll speak all.
>
> .   .   .   .   .
> O Isabel, will you not lend a knee?
>
> (Ibid. 442–7.)

Though with Mariana's help he has led Isabella to the critical point, the Duke does not ease his demand at the last instant: 'He dies for Claudio's death.' The proof must be conclusive: if Isabella asks mercy for Angelo, she must do so even with the realization at the forefront of her consciousness that Angelo killed her brother; nothing less will serve. And it is with the words 'Claudio's death' in her ears that, at long last, she goes to her knees:

> Most bounteous sir,
> Look, if it please you, on this man condemn'd
> As if my brother liv'd.
>
> (Ibid. 449–50.)

It has taken much time, shrewd deception, and sharp nudging at the last moment, but the proof is won on the Duke's uncompromising terms. Working in mysterious ways, he has transformed an erstwhile 'saint' into a creature of human sympathies and forced her to demonstrate them against odds. She who had once shrieked refusal—'Might but my bending down'—to save her brother's life has at last humbly knelt to beg mercy for one who, she believes, has done her terrible wrong. Once she has been brought to her knees, no reason remains for the Duke to keep the secret of Claudio's survival—nor does he keep it. Before Isabella can rise he has turned to the Provost—whom he had evidently prepared for this outcome—and ordered Claudio led in. In a last flash of showmanship he then yields the final secret of a trying but fruitful masquerade: 'What muffl'd fellow's that?'

During the remaining eighty lines after her plea for Angelo's life

Isabella is notably silent. Even when her brother is unmuffled and the Duke claims her as his bride she says nothing. One of two 'saints' humanized in the course of the action, she is presumably speechless at the sensation of blood flowing in her veins.

CHAPTER VII

A Lasting Storm: The Planetary Romances

Of four heroines of the romances, three, Marina, Imogen, and Miranda, narrowly miss being raped—not by clean young noblemen, momentarily beserk, like Proteus, but by brutes: Boult, Cloten, Caliban; and the other, Perdita, narrowly escapes being eaten by a bear. Despite what has been said of the romances as reflecting serenity after the storm of tragedy, the fact is that the worlds of the first three are the worst of Shakespeare's non-tragic worlds and at best no better than the tragic ones; and as for the world of the fourth, *The Tempest*, a proof that it is potentially the worst of all is the indispensability of its Prospero.

The worlds upon which Marina, Imogen, and Perdita are cast are such as might occur to the imagination of a father fearful for his own daughters after he is gone. They are worlds too large for their puny inhabitants, who become displaced and lost. They are worlds in which good people—quite safe from harm in the comedies—stumble about in a blind life and avoid disaster only by the skin of their teeth in action which might turn one way or another. They are worlds which everywhere betray the fact of their creation on the dark side of the tragedies. They are populated with creatures out of tragedy: Antiochus, Cleon and Dionyza, Leonine; Cymbeline's queen, Iachimo, Cloten; Leontes, Hermione. In them such innocuous boobies of the comedies as Slender and Aguecheek, vain aspirants to the hands of shining, remote heroines, have rotted down to Cloten, on the way to Caliban: boobies still, but now beast-boobies. These are worlds in which death may come not only, as in tragedy, from strokes that are invited by personal character and decision, but from the glancing blows of accident, from life's mere irrelevancies: 'Exit, pursued by a bear.'

Idyllic moments—the princess Marina, with her fellow maids, singing like one immortal; the princess Imogen feasting in a cave with her princely brothers; the princess Perdita among shepherds

and shepherdesses, dancing with her princely 'Doricles'—are here
set precariously in a universe which appears at best senseless and at
worst hostile; or perhaps it is the other way around, at best hostile
and at worst senseless.

*What is more, the world appears thus not only to the participants,
but to us*: from the point of view of the management of awarenesses, what most distinguishes the first three romances from the
comedies is that here, while action continues, we are denied that to
which we have grown accustomed—the comforting assurance that,
in spite of seeming danger, all is well.

1. *Pericles*

So it is especially in the first one. Imperilled at Antioch, Pericles
flees to Tyre with an assassin in pursuit. Prompted by misgivings
he flees Tyre just in time to escape the assassin's stroke, and reaches
Tarsus. Warned to flee Tarsus he sails again, is tempest-tossed, shipwrecked, cast upon the shores of Pentapolis. Later, bringing his
pregnant bride home to Tyre, he is assailed by a second tempest, at
the height of which his Marina is born and his wife, dead, is cast
into the sea. Says the buffeted Prince, with only spirit enough left
to beg the elements to leave him alone for awhile that he may die:

> Alas, the seas hath cast me on the rocks,
> Wash'd me from shore to shore, and left me breath
> Nothing to think on but ensuing death.
>> (II. i. 5–7.)

'What a drunken knave was the sea to cast thee in our way', says a
fisherman; and Pericles describes his sense of place in the universe:

> A man whom both the waters and the wind,
> In that vast tennis-court, hath made the ball
> For them to play upon. . . .
>> (III. i. 61–65.)

When news is brought him of his wife's death:

> O you gods!
> Why do you make us love your goodly gifts
> And snatch them straight away?
>> (Ibid. 22–24.)

There is no answer from the empty heavens, nor, so far as action
has permitted either Pericles or ourselves to see, can any be expected. During these violent tossings we have known of no Vincentio, no Prospero, omniscient, omnipotent, benevolent, with his eye

and his hand on hostile forces, ready to crush them to save good people. We have not been provided, that is to say, with that assurance which warms the climate of comedy. To us, as to Pericles, the universe appears only a senseless whirlwind where chance alone will decide for better or worse.

The underlying difference, then, between the handling of the awarenesses in *Pericles*, especially during the first three acts, and in the comedies through *Measure for Measure* (excepting *Troilus and Cressida*) is that here we are denied our usual unequivocal assurance that all is well. Hence the widest and most pleasantly exploitable gap which has regularly divided the participants' view from ours is lacking here. Otherwise, in the details of incidents and scenes, the management of awarenesses is sometimes typically Shakespearian and sometimes quite un-Shakespearian. Surprisingly, considering the instability of the play's general structure—its false starts, its wandering movements, its patchwork assemblage of narrative and dramatic portions—we do hold advantage over participants during fourteen of twenty-two scenes. It is a fact that the comedies which approach perfection in their dramatic construction regularly exhibit a high proportion of scenes in which we hold advantage, and that those which are most deficient exhibit a low proportion of such scenes—thus, at the one extreme, *Twelfth Night*, and, at the other, *Troilus and Cressida*.

Accordingly, in view of the awkward construction of *Pericles*—in which even the question whether the narrative or the dramatic is to dominate is not resolved until Act IV—the proportion of scenes in which we hold advantage might be expected to be negligible. That the play may have bare continuity, let alone artistic wholeness, Gower must come forward eight times to speak 300 lines of extra-dramatic exposition: 'I do beseech you / To learn of me, who stand i' the gaps to teach you, / The stages of our story.' Though a very few scenes are superbly devised within themselves, the whole is imperfect, not so much from particular faults as from the fact that the materials are incompletely converted to dramatic form. What is more, in *Pericles* Shakespeare relies infrequently upon those devices which are elsewhere his favoured and most efficient means of creating discrepancies in awareness. In most plays which show high proportion of scenes in which we hold advantage he uses either a professional practiser or a nest of amateurs whose activities create exploitable discrepancies; in *Pericles* he lacks a master practiser—though Antiochus, Simonides, Cleon and Dionyza, and Pericles himself take brief turns at deceiving. A second device often used elsewhere to create discrepancies, the strategic placement of scenes or portions of scenes to light subsequent action, is also inexplicably neglected here; until Act III there is no such placement.

In the absence of the usual dramatic devices, what accounts for the high proportion of scenes which give us advantage is, first, the extensive use of the extra-dramatic device—Gower, standing 'i' the gaps' to teach us the stages of the story; and, second, the fact of physical separation of the main persons—which is simply an accident of story rather than a dramatic device. Our main advantage during the latter half of the play derives from our knowledge that Pericles, Thaisa, and Marina have survived and are living seas apart, ignorant of one another. This is a ready-made advantage, which owes nothing to the dramatic shrewdness by which exploitable discrepancies are created in the comedies. *Troilus and Cressida* is the best evidence that Shakespeare's total construction falters when he trusts too much to the ready-made; *Pericles* offers the second-best evidence.

It is the ubiquitous presence of Gower that gives our initial and main advantage in the first half of the play. During the first seventy lines of the opening scene, until Pericles has finished reading Antiochus's riddle, we hold a valuable advantage over the Prince because we have heard Gower:

> This king unto him took a fere,
> Who died and left a female heir,
> So buxon, blithe, and full of face
> As heaven had lent her all his grace;
> With whom the father liking took,
> And her to incest did provoke.
>
> (I. 21–24.)

When the dramatized episode begins, we have been prepared to mark the flashes of irony from Pericles' awestruck comments on the purity and beauty of this daughter:

> See where she comes, apparell'd like the spring,
> Graces her subjects, and her thoughts the king
> Of every virtue gives renown to men!
>
> (I. i. 12–14.)

The use of Gower is a too-easy way of establishing exploitable discrepancies, is uncharacteristic and unworthy of Shakespeare. Yet with some exceptions it is the way of the play. Briefly, after Pericles has caught the meaning of the riddle—a feat which should require no particular acumen—there exists a relatively complex situation in which the awarenesses of Pericles and Antiochus are involved in a tension like that which occurs during interviews of

Hamlet and Claudius, when each senses what is in the other's mind and also senses that the other perceives the fact: thus Pericles catches the meaning of the king's riddle and Antiochus perceives that he does so, yet 'glozes' with him, pretending to suppose that Pericles has failed to interpret the riddle, and Pericles recognizes that the king 'glozes', but gives no sign that he does. In the brief moment of tension Shakespeare's hand shows in both the management of the situation and the cast of the language; thus Pericles:

> The breath is gone, and the sore eyes see clear
> To stop the air would hurt them. The blind mole casts
> Copp'd hills towards heaven, to tell the earth is throng'd
> By man's oppression; and the poor worm doth die for't.
>
> (I. i. 99–102.)

It is the only unmistakably Shakespearian moment before Act III.

When Pericles flees Antioch for Tyre, he bears the deadly secret of Antiochus's sin; the assassin Thaliard pursues him, and it is fear of pursuit that causes him to flee, successively, Tyre and Tarsus. But thereafter the murderer pursues no longer, and indeed, as we learn in II. iv, Antiochus himself has been destroyed for his sin. Hence the entire Antioch episode is irrelevant except as it motivated Pericles' flight. The episode of his visit to and beneficence at Tarsus is similarly irrelevant except that, later, it is to the rulers of Tarsus that he entrusts the care of Marina and from whom Marina escapes to a new life. Both Pericles and Marina thus move on, leaving behind them episodes that lack relation to their subsequent adventures. The whole action of Act I serves merely to carry Pericles ultimately to Pentapolis, where begins the history of his adventures as husband of Thaisa and father of Marina, which is the principal matter of the play. *Pericles* is the only play of Shakespeare's from which the entire first act could be removed without damage to the rest.

Act I, at all events, contributes not at all to the establishment of a context in our minds. Hence Act II opens without our holding advantage—without even any particular expectation of action to follow. Between them Gower and a dumb show have carried us and Pericles across seas, through storm and shipwreck, from Tarsus to Pentapolis. What lies behind Pericles is random adventure.

Nevertheless, during Act II we do share one secret with Pericles, that of his royalty. But why he keeps this secret is itself a question. He hides his identity, first, from the fishermen who befriend him after the sea has tossed him on their shore; second, from King Simonides and his knights; and, finally, even from Thaisa both before and for a time after their marriage. Why he does so—except that thereby we hold a secret and the dramatist maintains an exploitable discrepancy—is inexplicable. It cannot be that he does so from fear of pursuit from Antioch, for even on fleeing Tyre with a boatload of corn for Tarsus he had not gone incognito even though he then knew that an assassin was after him. Neither does he hide his identity during his long stay at Tarsus, and when he leaves Tarsus he sets off like the prince he is. It is not until he is shipwrecked and cast on Pentapolis that—with no such explanation for us as heroines always gave in taking up their disguises—he feigns to be humble. By allowing his royalty to vanish into the sea that has taken his ship, Pericles merely increases his difficulty in, first, claiming from the fishermen the rusty armour—his own, the gift of his father—hauled up conveniently in a net; and, second, winning a princess as wife.

If, however, the Prince's motive in posing as a 'mean knight' and an obscure 'gentleman of Tyre' is inexplicable, Shakespeare's purpose in having him do so is not: the discrepancy created by the Prince's pose is the exploitable condition without which Act II, like Act I, would be essentially undramatic, and might better have been narrated by Gower than dramatically represented. In any event, all dramatic effects produced in the incidents of the tournament, the banquet, and the winning of Thaisa result from exploitation of the gap between our awareness and Pentapolis's ignorance that Pericles is a prince. Thus, before the tournament, Pericles is scorned by the lords and afterwards, at Simonides' banquet, the 'mean knight' who has won the tournament sits 'too melancholy', neglected, his rusty armour and unknown origin setting him apart from the other knights. *Yet some marvellous quality shines through his apparent poverty* and attracts both Simonides and Thaisa; thus the King:

> Yon knight doth sit too melancholy,
> As if the entertainment in our court
> Had not a show might countervail his worth.
> (II. iii. 54–56.)

And Thaisa:

> (*Aside.*) To me he seems like diamond to glass.

The hidden royalty, known to us, shines through the patched apparel of 'the mean knight' and recommends itself mysteriously to those ignorant of its source. Though Shakespeare had twice before, with the King in *Henry V* and the Duke in *Measure for Measure*, exhibited royalty masquerading meanly, he had not exploited the gap between awarenesses in this way, or to this purpose—to provide the thrill, sentimental in character, that is peculiar to romance. Bates, Court, and Williams, with whom Henry V converses, mistake him for a fellow soldier and have no suspicion that he is anything more; the King's royalty does not subtly communicate itself to them through his borrowed coat. So also, in *Measure for Measure*, various persons of unknowing Vienna talk with Vincentio in his friar's hood and sense nothing extraordinary about him. Indeed, before *Pericles* Shakespeare had presented the romantic notion that royalty will shine through disguise only as the point of a colossal jest:

> *Poins.* Come, let's hear, Jack; what trick hast thou now?
> *Fal.* By the Lord, I knew ye as well as he that made ye. Why, hear you, my masters. Was it for me to kill the heir-apparent? Should I turn upon the true prince? Why, thou knowest I am as valiant as Hercules; but beware instinct; the lion will not touch the true prince. (*1 H. IV*, II. iv. 293–9.)

After *Pericles* the idea that inner greatness cannot be perfectly obscured by exterior covering or circumstance of life has its finest expression in the representation of the mountaineer princes of *Cymbeline*, whose royalty brightens their cave and captivates a princess—whose own hidden royalty in turn captivates them.

That Pericles' royalty is unknown but nevertheless recommends itself subtly to strangers: this, then, is the exploitable substance of Act II. Says Simonides, vainly trying to smother his inexplicable affection for the 'gentleman of Tyre' who sits alone and disconsolate at the banquet:

> He's but a country gentleman,
> Has done no more than other knights have done,
> Has broken a staff or so; so let it pass.
> (II. iii. 33–35.)

Shortly, the King finds himself proposing a toast to Pericles—and next orders that he be given lodgings nearest his own.

At this point the scene shifts to Tyre, and we learn that Antiochus has been destroyed by a fire sent from heaven. The significance of this news for us is that Pericles could now return safely to Tyre. A discrepancy is thus created between Pericles' awareness and ours. Superficially the placement of the scene at Tyre resembles that in *Twelfth Night* when we learn of Sebastian's survival; the purpose is also similar: to provide us with assurance, at a crucial moment, that the truth is better than it appears to the central participant—in that case Viola and in this Pericles. This placement approximates the shrewdness with which Shakespeare elsewhere regularly gives us special light just in time to add dimension to a crucial scene. But this time, though the device itself is good, its effect is negligible; for as the next scene proceeds, in which Simonides gives his blessing to the marriage of Thaisa and Pericles, it really matters little that we know and Pericles does not that he is now free to return to Tyre: he has, unaided, won a bride, a kingdom, and happiness in Pentapolis.

Though unexploited, our advantage over Pericles does add a tier to the fairly elaborate structure of awarenesses for the action of II. v, the climactic scene at Pentapolis. Beneath our level is Pericles, who sits above Thaisa and Simonides in knowing his true identity. And, on the lowermost step, are the King and his daughter, who have sensed their guest's quality but are ignorant of its basis. This structure stands as the principal dramatic situation of the scene; but what moves the action and creates the effects is Simonides' practice on Thaisa and Pericles in seeming to oppose their love when in fact he is impatient for a match. This is a curiously unmotivated practice, introduced with no more reason than Simonides' exclamation at Pericles' approach: 'Soft! here he comes. I must dissemble it.' In confronting Pericles with Thaisa's letter declaring her intention to wed 'the stranger knight', shouting 'Traitor!' at him, and threatening both lovers with terrible punishment—yet all the while assuring us in asides that he is delighted—Simonides presents a foolish picture. Thus the ending of this odd scene, the King speaking:

> Yea, mistress, are you so peremptory:
> (*Aside.*) I am glad on't with all my heart.—
> I'll tame you; I'll bring you in subjection.
> Will you, not having my consent,
> Bestow your love and your affections
> Upon a stranger? (*Aside.*) who, for aught I know,
> Nor can I think the contrary,
> As great in blood as I myself.—
> Therefore hear you, mistress: either frame
> Your will to mind,—and you, sir, hear you,
> Either be rul'd by me,—or I will make you—
> Man and wife.
> Nay, come, your hands and lips must seal it too;
> And being join'd, I'll thus your hopes destroy;
> And for a further grief,—God give you joy!
>   (II. v. 73–87.)

In the fond fatherly delight he takes in first seeming to forbid and then in abruptly giving his blessings to the marriage, Simonides anticipates Prospero, as the whole scene anticipates that in *The Tempest* (I. ii) in which Prospero masks his delight at the sudden love of Ferdinand and Miranda. But Simonides is an unmotivated, unstable, even childish Prospero, and the scene which his practice dominates fails even as he does. Though it is the most attractive scene. of the first two acts, with the characters threatening for the first time to become more than bloodless elements in a tale that is more narrative than dramatic, yet even here the management of the awarenesses, the initiation and exploitation of Simonides' practice, the actions and reactions of the three participants all suggest either that Shakespeare was only going through the motions of doing what he had done many times in earnest, with consummate skill and rich effect —or that the scene was devised by an inexperienced and indeed amateur dramatist attempting for the first time what had long since become Shakespeare's special manner of devising practices, creating and exploiting discrepancies in awareness. Whatever the facts of its genesis and intention, the scene seems to burlesque that manner.

Pericles' royal secret and our advantage over him are both lost just before the opening of Act III, and, though neither was productive of much effect, the loss is catastrophic: it destroys the dramatic connexion between the first two acts and the last three. Moreover, the two secrets are surrendered in a manner quite unlike Shakespeare's usual way. In the comedies the period in which main secrets are opened is always climactic, and it bustles with last-minute exploitation. What would normally have been celebrated in a busy scene with dialogue and action equal to the occasion is here passed over between the formal acts—in a combination of Gower's narrative octosyllabics and dumb show. It is a combination which, for all its brevity, manages to be repetitious.

The sum of the first two acts, then—as we learn from Gower standing 'i th' gap' between Act II and Act III—is the wedding of Pericles to Thaisa and the conception of a child. So much is, of course, indispensable to what follows. But the episodes of Antiochus and Tarsus —which were the whole matter of Act I—and the particular *way* in which Pericles wooed and won Thaisa—which was the whole matter of Act II—are alike irrelevant to the drama that begins with Act III. Hence during III. i, when Marina is born in a tempest, Thaisa dies, and Pericles prepares to cast the body overboard, we stand as we commonly do during I. i—merely learning, not yet sufficiently advised to hold an advantage.

Notably lacking in our preparation is any evidence that the universe is either kindlier or more hostile than it seems to Pericles. Like him we can see it only as a spiteful or a careless world. 'Th' unfriendly elements / Forgot thee utterly', laments the buffeted Prince for his dead wife, and his pleas vanish into the void:

228

Thou god of this great vast, rebuke these surges,
Which wash both heaven and hell; and thou that hast
Upon the winds command, bind them in brass,
Having call'd them from the deep!

(III. i. 1–4.)

'Blow, and split thyself', says the First Sailor, who expects no
favours from the wind. The prevailing attitude of participants
accepts the existence of some malevolent intelligence in the universe. The First Sailor identifies it with the elements themselves,
with which one must manage to stay on good terms: 'The sea works
high, the wind is loud, and will not lie till the ship be clear'd of the
dead.' Pericles, here as before and after, identifies it with the gods,
who have singled him out for torment. This second tempest, in
which he loses his wife—like the first, when he lost ship, goods, and
crew—seems to him to have been raised for his particular persecution.

Our own view, though conditioned by Pericles' expression of his,
is not necessarily identical to it. From Gower's remarks we gain the
impression that no force is bent particularly on the Prince's destruction, but that mere whimsical fortune, manifesting itself in the mere
chance of weather at sea, causes his continuing misfortunes. Thus
Gower at the opening of Act II, when the first tempest blew on
Pericles:

All perishen of man, of pelf,
Ne aught escapen but himself;
Till Fortune, tir'd with doing bad,
Threw him ashore, to give him glad.

(Loc. cit.)

What Gower presents as whim, Pericles takes for a malevolently
aimed stroke:

Alas, the seas hath cast me on the rocks,
Wash'd me from shore to shore, and left me breath
Nothing to think on but ensuing death.
Let it suffice the greatness of your powers
To have bereft a prince of all his fortunes;
And having thrown him from your watery grave,
Here to have death in peace is all he'll crave.

(II. i. 5–11.)

Again Gower takes the opposing view, when the second tempest
blows on Pericles:

But fortune's mood
Varies again. The grisled north
Disgorges such a tempest forth,
That, as a duck for life that dives,
So up and down the poor ship drives.

(III. 46–50.)

The conflict between Gower's view of the universe as something whimsically operated without regard to particular individuals, whom it abuses or blesses indifferently, and Pericles' view of it—and submission to it—as a mortal enemy bent on his personal torment, runs through the first three acts and is still strong at the opening of Act V. The consequence for us is ambiguity: from Gower we learn that the successive misfortunes of Pericles 'driven before the winds' are a meaningless and disconnected series; from Pericles, that he has been singled out for hounding by a malign intelligence. Until the second scene of Act III, then, our sense of the world of this action must waver between the alternatives, each uninviting, each denying comfort.

In fact, we gain no positive assurance until the end that all is well. We know of no benevolent power overwatching all. But in III. ii we are first given a hint that the true view of the world may be neither Gower's nor the Prince's, and thereafter the new impression grows. *What is more, it is exactly at the point of this first hint that the drama itself takes life and begins to look like Shakespeare's.*

In the course of III. ii we gain two all-important advantages over Pericles; but one is the result of an accident of story rather than of dramaturgy, and the other is left too obscure to be effectively exploitable—hence strange to Shakespeare's methodical way of making unmistakable what needs at least to be clear. We gain the first by witnessing Thaisa's restoration; says Cerimon, moving with authority like Prospero's:

> —The fire and cloths.
> The rough and woeful music that we have,
> Cause it to sound, beseech you.
> The vial once more. How thou stirr'st, thou block!
> The music there! I pray you, give her air.
> Gentlemen,
> This queen will live.
>
> (III. ii. 87–93.)

Thaisa returns to life before our eyes, and we know at scene's end that with Cerimon's care she will recover fully. From this moment until the denouement the knowledge that she lives is one of our three great secrets, kept from Pericles. What Thaisa's survival signifies is that Pericles' misfortunes, though grievous, are not, as he supposes, beyond remedy: there has been no death. To the extent that one candle brightens an enormity, the world appears less dark to our view.

But of greater significance even than the fact of Thaisa's survival is the manner of it. Evidently dead, locked in a 'caulk'd and bitumed' chest, cast into a raging sea by sailors to appease the elements, the Queen would not seem to have much chance. Either in Gower's uncontrolled world, whirling on whimsically, or in Pericles', controlled by a malign intelligence bent on his personal persecution, hope must be non-existent. Yet she is saved. Perhaps, then, this is neither Pericles' world nor Gower's, but a better one than either. It is in our sense of this possibility—not fixed in our minds with Shakespeare's usual firmness, to be sure, but nevertheless hinted—that we gain a second advantage over Pericles, and over Marina a little later—and, indeed, over our ubiquitous informer, Gower himself.

Cast overboard within sight of Tarsus, the chest with Thaisa's body is not washed ashore there, *but is swept to Ephesus and deposited almost at the feet of one who has thus introduced himself to us*:

> 'Tis known I ever
> Have studied physic, through which secret art,
> By turning o'er authorities, I have,
> Together with my practice, made familiar
> To me and to my aid the blest infusions
> That dwells in vegetives, in metals, stones;
> And I can speak of the disturbances
> That Nature works, and of her cures; which doth give me
> A more content in course of true delight
> Than to be thirsty after tottering honour,
> Or tie my pleasure up in silken bags,
> To please the fool and Death.
>
> (Ibid. 31–42.)

Calling for 'all my boxes in my closet', employing fire, cloths, a mysterious vial—all to the accompaniment of 'rough and woeful music'—this Prospero–Cerimon restores Thaisa: 'The heavens,' says the First Gentleman, 'Through you increase our wonder.' Though he asks Aesculapius for guidance Cerimon is a magical healer, with 'secret art', deeply read in 'authorities', familiarly calling to his aid 'the blest infusions / That dwells in vegetives, in metals, stones'. Though he cannot, like Prospero, control the elements themselves, make and allay storms, yet he 'can speak of the disturbances / That Nature works, and of her cures'. Though not omniscient and omnipotent in his world, like Vincentio of *Measure for Measure*, Cerimon, in his proprietorship of mantle, staff, and book, is nearer to Prospero than Vincentio is. As the scene is offered, its implication is that of all men in the world only he could have revived Thaisa: for us his existence is a sign that the world is better than Pericles has had cause to perceive—and better than Gower would allow us to suppose.

But there is more to the sign: what force brought Thaisa to the feet of this healer? 'How close 'tis caulk'd and bitum'd!' cries Cerimon, first seeing the chest. 'Did the sea cast it up?' And the First Servant utters a momentous line:

> I never saw so huge a billow, sir,
> As toss'd it upon shore.
> (III. ii. 58–59.)

Is this extraordinary billow the work of either mere chance or malign direction? At its coming, the seas of *Pericles*, hitherto seemingly either uncontrolled or wickedly purposive, appear to manifest the force of a benevolence at work in mysterious ways.

It is noteworthy that these quick signs, contradicting all appearances of the world up to their occurrence, are given in the middle of Act III—when everywhere, for the first time, other marks of Shakespeare's workmanship show also. Until Act III *Pericles* has been truly a mouldy tale of piteous misadventures, strung out narratively rather than woven dramatically, moving straight on, forming no apparent design. The extraordinary billow which brings Thaisa's body to Cerimon is the first evidence of Shakespeare's attempt to find meaning in, or to put meaning into, what otherwise is a series of mere happenings in the life of Pericles. Though the billow, standing for the seas and for whatever hidden force directs them, represents in its form a drastic deviation from the heroines and dukes who control their worlds, it is like them in function: it marks Shakespeare's effort to give dramatic pattern and meaning to episodic events by introducing into his world a means of order and control.

The widening of a gap between Pericles' and our awarenesses is the immediate result of our learning that Thaisa survives and that the world may be kindlier than the battered Prince thinks. Having taken over the management almost too late, Shakespeare wastes no more time, but exploits the discrepancy forthwith. Our two advantages gained in III. ii are put to work in III. iii, when Pericles, after a year in Tarsus, takes leave of Cleon and Dionyza:

> *Dion.*   O your sweet queen!
> That the strict fates had pleas'd you had brought her hither
> To have bless'd mine eyes with her!
> *Per.*   We cannot but obey
> The powers above us. Could I rage and roar
> As doth the sea she lies in, yet the end
> Must be as 'tis.
> (III. iii. 8–12.)

In the comedies through *Measure for Measure*, it is typically in the closing scenes of Act III that the most participants are ignorant of the most facts of a situation that has reached maximum complexity. The climax of the play is thus the exploitation of compounded confusion. Beside such scenes the closing scenes of Act III in *Pericles* are simple, undeveloped, and obvious, for they are the first in the play in which the narrative string has looped enough to make the beginning of dramatic design. In the comedies the climactic portion follows long preparation begun in the very first scenes. But in *Pericles* the preparation for the closing scenes of Act III has begun only with the sea-storm of III. i, the preceding acts having contributed nothing.

The end of Act III passes an exploitable situation on to the opening of Act IV; it is the first time that one act or scene has bequeathed a dramatic condition to the next. The inheritance of Act IV is chiefly the fact of separation: divided by seas that seem indifferent or hostile, Pericles at Tyre is ignorant that Thaisa lives; Thaisa at Ephesus is ignorant of the fate of her husband and even of the birth of Marina: '. . . Whether there / Delivered, by the holy gods / I cannot rightly say'; and Marina at Tarsus, ignorant of her mother's survival, is lost in an immense and careless universe. Moreover, having finally created an enveloping situation, Shakespeare, now behaving as usual, immediately establishes another within it. He does so by calling again on Gower, who recounts the growth and education of Marina at Cleon's court, describes the perfection of her virtues, and finally provides us with an advantage for the subsequent scene:

> Marina gets
> All praises, which are paid as debts,
> And not as given. This so darks
> In Philoten all graceful marks
> That Cleon's wife, with envy rare,
> A present murderer does prepare
> For good Marina, that her daughter
> Might stand peerless by this slaughter.
> (IV. 33–40.)

Yet another sign that Shakespeare has taken the play in hand is the use at the opening of IV. i, directly after Gower's speech, of dialogue to throw special light on the action that succeeds it, the plot against Marina's life. Though the device is for Shakespeare as old as *Henry VI*, its use here is noteworthy for two reasons: first, because until now it has been neglected in *Pericles*; second, because *it repeats the information just given by Gower*, hence suggests Shakespeare's dissatisfaction with the extra-dramatic device and marks a return to his method of equipping us by dramatic means.

It is at this point that we have our first real view of Marina—seen earlier only as a blanketed bundle in Lychorida's arms on shipboard at her birth and at Tarsus when she was left to the care of Cleon and Dionyza. At her first entrance she stands in a light unlike any in which a previous non-tragic heroine of Shakespeare's has stood. As has been shown, in the comedies a heroine is rarely permitted to occupy a level below ours. Hero's plight in *Much Ado about Nothing*, before she is denounced at the altar, is pitiful; she is a joyous bride-to-be, ignorant of the blow ready to fall. Viola of *Twelfth Night* is distressed, perceiving universal frustration when Olivia loves her, who loves Orsino, who dotes on Olivia; and later, when Sir Toby frightens her with a false image of Sir Andrew, she stands briefly in a laughable predicament. These are among the most precarious conditions of unawareness into which Shakespeare has allowed non-tragic heroines to fall. They are in truth not desperate at all, for in Hero's case we know that though Claudio will denounce her, Dogberry will clear her name, and in the case of Viola our glimpse of Sebastian, provided just before she laments, has told us that all is well. In fact, not only do heroines of the comedies not stand in such danger as Marina's, but no other persons of the comedies do, either. Antonio of *The Merchant of Venice* and Claudio of *Measure for Measure* face what they believe to be imminent, inevitable death. But at the arrival of Nerissa, heralding Portia, we know that Antonio is safe; and as for Claudio, we have barely been told of his arrest when we learn that the Duke will remain in Vienna, and thus we know that Claudio is safe. The situations of these two men are the darkest in Shakespearian comedy; yet even they are not really dark at all for us, because of the special light by which we see them. But Marina, at our first sight of her, stands unknowingly in the very mouth of death. Her assassin has been given his orders and is ready with his sword.

A basic difference between the comic world and that of *Pericles* is suggested by the fact that whereas our advantage over Antonio and Claudio tells us they are safe, our advantage over Marina tells us that she will be murdered: we have no cause to think that the blow will be averted. As we watch her in conversation with Dionyza and Leonine, our reserve of knowledge breeds anxiety, not comfort. In *Measure for Measure* our confidence in the Duke is such that we do not expect even a Barnardine, 'unfit to live or die', to be harmed. But in *Pericles* we cannot be sure that even a heroine will live to the end of her very first scene.

The fact alone is enough to differentiate the predominant effect of Marina's scene with Dionyza and Leonine from that of any

scene in the comedies. But more, the manner in which her awareness of danger is exploited contrasts notably with that in any earlier
scenes of comparable situation. Since the comedies have no truly
dire situations, it is necessary to look elsewhere for parallels. The
scene is reminiscent of the Clarence–Gloucester scene (I. i) of
Richard III, of the Princes–Gloucester scene (III. i) in the same play,
and of the Hubert–Arthur scene (IV. i) in *King John*. In all these
the dramatist exploits the discrepant awarenesses of assassin and
victim for as many flashes of irony as can be struck from them—and
apparently the more glaring the flashes, the better: 'Well, your
imprisonment shall not be long; / I will deliver you, or else lie for
you' (*R. III*, I. ii. 114–15); and, again:

> *York.* I pray you, uncle, give me this dagger.
> *Glou.* My dagger, little cousin? With all my heart.
> (Ibid. III. i. 110–11.)

In contrast, throughout Marina's scene with her assassins, dialogue
that would strike gaudy flashes is avoided. Even when Dionyza's
words directly touch our awareness of the imminent murder they
seem calculated to demand pity for Marina rather than to attract
attention to flares of irony:

> *Dion.*   Go, I pray you,
> Walk, and be cheerful once again; reserve
> That excellent complexion, which did steal
> The eyes of young and old. Care not for me;
> I can go home alone.
> *Mar.*   Well, I will go;
> But yet I have no desire to it.
> (IV. i. 39–45.)

Though these lines waken our sense of the impending murder, hence
inevitably exploit the gap between Marina's awareness and ours,
they do not seem to do so merely for the sake of striking up those
flashes that in the Gloucester-victim scenes of *Richard III* are the
whole purpose of the exploitation: 'My dagger, little cousin? With
all my heart.' Though the gap between the awarenesses of Leonine
and Marina is identical to that between Gloucester and little York,
and though both gaps are exploited, thus, the effects of exploitation
contrast.

But there is yet another dimension to be considered. Though the
difference between our awareness and Marina's ignorance is the
immediately exploitable condition, there is a larger frame which
encompasses this condition and affects the character of the scene.
When Marina enters, meeting those who—as Shakespeare has told
us twice beforehand—intend to kill her, it is her ignorance of

danger, obviously, that is foremost in our minds. But her first words do not exploit her immediate situation, but turn our minds away from this to the enveloping situation. Marina is grieving for Lychorida, whose death has just broken the link with her lost father and mother. In her grief, like her father in his, she sees only hostility in the universe:

> Ay me! poor maid,
> Born in a tempest when my mother died,
> This world to me is like a lasting storm,
> Whirring me from my friends.
> (IV. i. 18–21.)

It was suggested earlier that in the huge billow which carried Thaisa's body to Cerimon we glimpsed a benevolent universe. Now, Marina's words, spoken in a moment of peril, and being, moreover, the first that are given her to speak, gain a heavy emphasis. By Shakespeare's usual method Marina would here speak words that exploit her ignorance of the danger that is urgent in our own minds. Instead, what she speaks turns our attention away. All her speeches up to Leonine's abrupt, 'Come, say your prayers' concern only winds and seas—the conspicuous symbols of the universe throughout *Pericles*:

> *Mar.* Is this wind westerly that blows?
> *Leon.*   South-west.
> *Mar.* When I was born, the wind was north.
> *Leon.*   Was't so?
> *Mar.* My father, as nurse says, did never fear,
>   But cried 'Good seamen!' to the sailors, galling
>   His kingly hands haling ropes;
>   And, clasping to the mast, endured a sea
>   That almost burst the deck,—
> *Leon.* When was this?
> *Mar.* When I was born;
>   Never was waves nor wind more violent. . . .
> (Ibid. 51–62.)

'Come,' says Leonine, 'say your prayers.'

The effect of Marina's preoccupation with wind and wave, storm and sea is to force the mind away from the question of her present peril and back upon the abiding question: is the universe of *Pericles* that of either Gower or Pericles? or is it that of the kindly billow? This question bears strongly upon the total effect of the scene. If, having been advised by that extraordinary billow, we now believe that the world is benignly controlled—then even while her assassin fondles his sword we have comfort; references to wind and wave, storm and sea then remind us of, and exploit, the difference between her vision of the universe and ours: we know and she does not know that her mother in fact survived the crucial tempest that now occupies her mind.

Whether it is intended that we understand the scene so is difficult to tell. In the past, for a critical scene, Shakespeare has both provided unmistakable advantage and prompted us to use it at the right time. Perhaps here we are meant to experience only a sense of Marina's imminent peril; but, if so, it is inexplicable that the dramatist makes her whole conversation present her view of the world as 'a lasting storm / Whirring me from my friends', when this emphasis reminds us of the difference between her view of the world and ours. If he did not intend, just here, to remind us of this difference, why did he not simply exploit, as in the scenes of *Richard III* and *King John*, the obvious gap between Marina's ignorance and our awareness of her danger from Leonine?

The question of the nature of the universe is thus vital in this particular scene, since the answer determines whether we should take Marina's peril as real. If we have taken the extraordinary billow as a positive sign of benevolence, then we will perceive that Marina stands in no real danger from Leonine. Since Shakespeare has not yet clearly resolved the conflict between Pericles' sense of a maliced universe and the giant wave's sign of a benevolent one, we cannot know the answer, and while the action continues the effect remains ambiguous.

But then, just at the end, the conflict is abruptly resolved: *for off the same violent sea from which came the giant wave to save Thaisa come pirates who snatch Marina from under the sword and carry her to sea again. The seas have now acted twice to protect the family of Pericles.*

It seems less by virtue of an external agency, however, than by assertion of her own will that Marina survives her next ordeal. We hold no advantage over her during her imprisonment in the brothel, except as we may now have seen that a benign force is working toward some happy ending. In the brothel episodes the discrepant views of the universe are left unexploited; indeed, in these scenes the universal forces of winds and seas, which to this point, half-way through Act IV, have profoundly affected the affairs of participants, are seemingly inactive. To this point Marina, like her father, has been swept along like a chip; now she opposes her character to the enemies around her. It is a noteworthy change in the action of *Pericles*, for until now no person has tried to master his fate. Pericles —Shakespeare's only entirely will-less hero—has fled Antioch to Tyre, Tyre to Tarsus, Tarsus to Pentapolis; has been frightened by

King Antiochus, tossed by wind and sea, intimidated by King Simonides, tossed again by wind and sea—and to everything has opposed nothing, expressed no more defiance than a bitter question at the time of Thaisa's loss: 'Why do you make us love your goodly gifts / And snatch them straight away?' Thaisa, though she stood up to her whimsical father when he seemed to oppose her love for Pericles, succumbs in childbirth, is sealed in a chest, swept away without will or even life, carried ashore by a kindly wave, and restored by Cerimon. Having asserted no personal force toward preservation, she then yields unquestioningly to the certainty that 'My wedded lord I ne'er shall see again', and resigns herself to a vestal livery in which she will 'never more have joy'. Said Gower, describing the scene at Marina's birth:

> The grisled north
> Disgorges such a tempest forth,
> That, as a duck for life that dives,
> So up and down the poor ship drives.
> (III. 47–50.)

Until the brothel scenes, the family of Pericles have been passive, all tossed like Gower's ship, and must surely have perished but that the sea preserved them.

But in triumphing over Bawd, Boult, Pandar, and Lysimachus, besides sundry nameless prospective customers who came as cavaliers and departed as converts—'Shall's go hear the vestals sing?'—Marina throws off the passive role and shows the capability that distinguished the heroines of comedy. Hence, though thrust into a situation of frightful potentiality, she is no longer a pathetic case. Also, like her predecessor heroines, she is, with a difference, a masquerader: though her keepers know that she is a virgin, they are ignorant that she is a princess. But her secret, though it gives her advantage in awareness, gives her none in control. The earlier heroines chose their masquerades, mainly enjoyed their advantage in disguise, and could always escape real danger simply by dropping the mask. Marina could not extricate herself by making her royalty known. It is hard enough that her keepers know of her virginity, for the fact enables them to advertise very effectively: 'There was a Spaniard's mouth so wat'red!' If they knew of her royalty as well, presumably the rush of clients would make her position untenable. Her secret therefore gives her no advantage.

Though the royal secret is kept alive in our minds during the brothel scenes, Shakespeare does not directly exploit this difference between our awareness and that of the keepers and clients. What the proprietors see to value in Marina, besides her virginity, is summed by Boult: 'She has a good face, speaks well, and has excellent good clothes.' They come no nearer to striking the truth. So, in the interview of Marina with Lysimachus, what is exploited is the governor's unawareness not of her royalty, but of her virtue:

Lys. Now, pretty one, how long have you been at this trade?
Mar. What trade, sir?
Lys. Why, I cannot name 't but I shall offend.
Mar. I cannot be offended with my trade. Please you to name it.
Lys. How long have you been of this profession?
Mar. E'er since I can remember.
Lys. Did you go to 't so young? Were you a gamester at five or at seven?
Mar. Earlier too, sir, if now I be one.   (IV. vi. 73–82.)

Neither is it the fact of her royalty that wins her release at last from the brothel. Though she certainly owes some of her accomplishments to her upbringing at Cleon's court the degree of her talent is innate. She far outshone the daughter of Cleon and Dionyza, who had the same training, and it was then her personal perfection that nearly cost her life. She is 'absolute Marina': the power of persuasion that turns prospective clients 'out of the road of rutting for ever', alters the mind of Lysimachus from 'Come, bring me to some private place' to '. . . to me / The very doors and windows savour vilely', and finally triumphs over Boult and wins her release—this power is her own extraordinary gift.

During the brothel scenes, then, our immediate assurance that all will be well derives not from knowledge of Marina's royalty, but from perceiving that, like the capable heroines of the comedies, she possesses great personal resources including a powerful will. Her own qualities rescue her from the brothel and bring her fame in Mytilene. Partly, but certainly not solely, these qualities are responsible also for her reconciliation with her father and therefore also for his reconciliation with Thaisa. To some degree, then, the happy ending is wrought by human will.

Between the brothel scenes (IV. ii and vi) are set two at Tarsus, in the first of which Cleon and Dionyza, deceived by Leonine's report, quarrel about Marina's murder. Here the persons, the situation, and the language itself are obviously imitative of *Macbeth*: 'I do shame / To think of what a noble strain you are, / And of how coward a spirit.' But though these ingredients make a cauldron as ugly as any in *Macbeth*, the effect of the scene contrasts with the savagery of the elements. For while Cleon and his depraved queen rage at each other, discuss the assassination of Marina and the poisoning of Leonine, and plot to deceive Pericles, we know that they are themselves deceived: Marina lives. Our advantage thus provides an environment of comedy for a scene whose ingredients are uncommonly brutal and shocking. The effect of exhibiting a scene of human depravity within a reassuring frame is, to say the least, mixed; perhaps it is impossible to react at once to both the ingredients and the setting. The nearest Shakespeare had come to such a mixture previously was the Claudio–Isabella quarrel scene (III. i) of *Measure for Measure*, with Vincentio overhearing Claudio's human pleas and Isabella's inhumane denials; or, in tragedy, the wedding-morn scene (IV. v) of *Romeo and Juliet*, when Juliet's 'death' is grotesquely lamented by the Nurse and the family; or the Gloucester–Edgar 'Dover Cliff' incident (IV. vi) of *King Lear*. But none of these is perfectly analogous to the Cleon–Dionyza scene in either its components or its effects. The bringing together of a spectacle and a frame so mutually contradictory that it is impossible for response to accommodate the demands of both is a device peculiar to the romances. The ultimate in this same grotesque incongruity is reached in *Cymbeline*, when Imogen sobs over the brute Cloten's headless body, thinking it her husband's.

A less extreme example occurs in the second Tarsus scene, when Pericles arrives to reclaim Marina. Our advantage over deceivers and deceived alike is perfect: Dionyza and Cleon suppose Marina murdered by Leonine, and in their error deceive Pericles by announcing her death from another cause. But though the matter is enormously important and the situation offers greater opportunity for exploitation than exists at any previous moment, what might have been the finest moment of the play is passed over in a Dumb Show set amid fifty lines of Gower's narrative:

> *Enter Pericles, at one door, with all his train: Cleon and Dionyza, at the other. Cleon shows Pericles the Tomb; whereat Pericles makes lamentation, puts on sackcloth, and in a mighty passion departs. Then exeunt Cleon and Dionyza.* (IV. iv.)

'See how belief may suffer by foul show!' comments Gower on this speechless exhibition. Three incidents in the life of Pericles, preceding his final reconciliation with Thaisa and Marina, are momentous occasions: the winning of Thaisa, the loss of Thaisa, and the discovery of Marina's 'death'. The drama of the first is defective because the conduct of Simonides, on which exploitation is based, is unmotivated; the second is effectively managed but lacks what Shakespeare favoured in climactic scenes, an exploitable gap between the awarenesses; and now the third, with the greatest potential, and with discrepancies that would normally have been highly attractive to the dramatist—Cleon and Dionyza thinking they have murdered Marina, Pericles thinking that they mourn with him for her untimely death, we alone knowing that all are in error—is not even dramatized.

'Let Pericles believe his daughter dead,' Gower continues, 'And bear his courses to be ordered by Lady Fortune.' Spent with passion, dressed in sackcloth, Pericles puts to sea:

> He bears
> A tempest, which his mortal vessel tears,
> And yet he rides it out.
> (Ibid. 29–31.)

This is the third tempest. The first had wrecked his ship when he fled Tarsus: 'And he, good prince, having all lost, / By waves from coast to coast is tost.' The second had blown as he was carrying his bride home to Tyre, and it had precipitated premature and fatal childbirth: 'The lady shrieks, and well-a-near / Does fall in travail with her fear.' Now the third tempest bursts when he leaves Marina's tomb. Though on each occasion Gower advises us that these storms are the work of whimsical Fortune, or lays them to the eternal, uncontrolled restlessness of the seas—'Where when men been, there's seldom ease'—Pericles takes them for personal enemies sent to harass and destroy him. So they appeared when he was washed ashore on Pentapolis: 'Let it suffice the greatness of your powers / To have bereft a prince of all his fortunes'; and so they appeared when they robbed him of his bride: 'Why do you make us love your goodly gifts / And snatch them straight away?' The incident of the third tempest is not dramatized, so that we do not hear his opinion of it; but we have Gower's word that he bears his courses 'to be ordered / By Lady Fortune'. Utterly defeated, Pericles has given in to his old 'enemy'.

But at the opening of Act V we learn, again from Gower, the result of the final tempest:

> . . . we left him, on the sea. We there him lost;
> Whence, driven before the winds, he is arriv'd
> Here where his daughter dwells.
> (v. 13–15.)

It has carried him—as will-less as was Thaisa in her casket—to Marina. Once more, then, action suggests that we should have a sense of the universe that is different from that of either Pericles or Gower, our principal informants. In the seas of *Pericles* we are to recognize a controlling benevolence. At first the seas destroyed Pericles' ship and left him destitute on the shores of Pentapolis; but at once they gave up his own precious armour which had gone down with the ship, and with this armour he won a king's daughter. Next the seas so frightened Thaisa that she fell to labour too soon and succumbed; but an extraordinary billow carried her lifeless body straight to the hands of a healer—'The gods can have no mortal officer / More like a god than you'—who restored its life. Then from the same wild seas came pirates who seized Marina and sold her to brothel-keepers; but they snatched her from the stroke of the assassin. And now, finally, the unresisting Pericles is 'driven before the winds' of these seas into the harbour of Mytilene, where absolute Marina 'sings like one immortal'.

Pericles' ship is blown into Mytilene harbour, says Gower, even while 'The city striv'd / God Neptune's annual feast to keep', and Lysimachus, having come out to the ship, tells Helicanus that he had observed its arrival 'Being on shore, honouring of Neptune's triumphs'. By these remarks the centrality of the seas' place in the action is formally attested, as though to confirm the rightness of our view against the testimony of Gower and Pericles: the seas which have seemed to them respectively careless and hostile have in reality been benignly purposeful. Though they have divided, they have also preserved the family of Pericles. The emphasis would seem to provide the clinching proof for the idea that was first planted in our minds by the extraordinary billow of III. ii.

But the confirmation comes very late: it is the opening of Act V. During most of the action we have lacked our usual firm assurance. We have had instead, during Acts I and II, inconclusive evidence that in this world events either follow one another meaninglessly, or fit the design of a malevolent intelligence bent on torment and destruction. And during Acts III and IV, while the same ambiguity continued, we have been provided with growing, but still sporadic, signs of benign purpose. When this evidence at last prevails at the opening of Act V, it can hardly compensate for the preceding four acts of uncertainty.

Not only is the question of how we are to regard the universe of *Pericles* late in being resolved; it is also resolved without Shakespeare's characteristic finality. 'Ere he do leave this grove,' said Oberon in *A Midsummer-Night's Dream*, 'Thou shalt fly him, and he shall seek thy love.' And in *Measure for Measure* the Duke, in our hearing, promised to 'Visit both prince and people'. These outright statements may stand for both the certainty of the assurance with which we are usually provided and the direct means by which it is forced upon our minds. In *Pericles* it is necessary for us to spell out, from scanty signs and dubious manifestations, the existence and character of an invisible and benevolent controlling force.

Though imperfect and though gained barely in time for the denouement, the assurance which we have at the opening of Act V is at least comforting, and it provides a frame which enhances the effect of the final action. For this scene the discrepancies in awareness are numerous and richly exploitable. At the lowest level stands Lysimachus, who, though he brings Marina and Pericles together, is ignorant of the one fact that matters—their relationship. His act in bringing them together, though indispensable to the happy outcome, seems accidental. The fact is that it is not Lysimachus himself who conceives the idea of bringing Marina to Pericles; the idea is suggested by one of his Lords: 'Sir, / We have a maid in Mytilene, I durst wager, / Would win some words of him.' It is on so insecure a hinge that the final action turns. On the level above Lysimachus are Pericles and Helicanus, whose advantage consists only in knowledge of the history of grief that has reduced the King to his present condition: ''Twould be too tedious to repeat,' Helicanus tells Lysimachus, 'But the main grief springs from the loss / Of a beloved daughter and a wife.' Paradoxically, then, the very knowledge that sets Pericles and Helicanus above Lysimachus is false. Marina's awareness approximates her father's: whereas Pericles supposes both Thaisa and Marina dead, Marina also supposes her mother to be dead but presumably supposes her father still to be at Tyre. Thus, though details differ, the participants in the scene stand almost on a common footing of ignorance: each knows something unknown to the others, yet each is ignorant of those facts most pertinent to himself. On the other hand, the difference between our vantage-point and the participants' level is very wide. We know, first, that the universe is benevolent rather than malign; next, that Pericles has lost neither wife nor daughter; and, of course, that the two who now meet as strangers are father and daughter.

Of the three aspects of the total difference exploited in the course of the scene, it is of course the third, Pericles' and Marina's ignorance of each other, on which the action is itself based. In a significant way the situation was a new one for Shakespeare. In typical earlier situations that are at all comparable, one of the persons—usually the heroine—knew the identity of the other: thus Portia knew Bassanio, in the court scene of *The Merchant of Venice*, but was unknown by him; so also Rosalind and Orlando, Viola and Orsino, Helena and Bertram, and, in a reversal of the usual order, Vincentio and Isabella in *Measure for Measure*. In these cases what is exploited is the gap between the unaware participant's level and ours, which we share with the other participant. The dialogue strikes a cross-play over the gap, the one participant consciously and the other unconsciously contributing to the display. But in the present variation neither person knows the other; they occupy a common level, and the exploitable gap is that between their mutual ignorance and our understanding. Moreover, whereas in the earlier scenes the object was to exploit an unchanging gap between the awarenesses of the participants, here it is to exploit each step of their progress toward the moment of recognition. The movement is deliberate, with each stroke calculated to play its part in the massive total impact.

'I am great with woe,' says Pericles, 'and shall deliver weeping.' For him the coming-to-awareness is necessarily long and tortuous, since he must not only recognize a daughter he has thought dead, but also completely change his conception of the universe. Early in the interview he strikes out at Marina, and the blow expresses both his ignorance of her identity and his misunderstanding of the universe—which has in fact worked in mysterious ways to accomplish this very meeting. His conviction that the universe is his enemy prevents his immediate acceptance of Marina after she has told her story and her name; the revelation seems to him yet one more cruel stroke of his old tormentors:

> O, I am mock'd,
> And thou by some incensed god sent hither
> To make the world to laugh at me.
> (v. i. 143–5.)

'Thou little know'st how thou dost startle me / To call thyself Marina.' Marina little knows, indeed. For Pericles the widening of vision takes place slowly, during most of the long scene, as he is compelled in spite of himself from disbelief and distrust through degrees of doubt and uncertainty. All this while Marina remains oblivious. When at last Pericles accepts her and identifies himself she is lifted abruptly from ignorance to full awareness, without verbal exploitation of the rise. The focus of the scene is thus on Pericles' coming-to-awareness. His recovery of Marina and his reversal of attitude toward the universe leave us still with one advantage over Pericles: our knowledge of Thaisa's survival.

In the universe of his new conception, the thunder no longer threatens, the seas no longer rage as if either not controlled at all or controlled by malice. There is a different sound in this new universe.

It was the winds of the sea that wrecked his ship and stranded him at Pentapolis—where, in armour yielded by the sea, he won Thaisa; it was a sea storm that separated husband, wife, and child—and a wave of the sea that bore Thaisa straight to salvation; it was pirates from off the sea who snatched Marina from Leonine—and bore her over the sea to Mytilene; and, finally, it was the winds of the sea that drove Pericles' rudderless ship into this very harbour—where 'God Neptune's annual feast' is just being celebrated—for reunion with Marina. It is now the moon's Diana, in league with the ocean's Neptune, that accomplishes the reunion of Pericles and Thaisa. Commanded by Diana in a vision to visit her temple at Ephesus and to tell his story there, Pericles sets sail and arrives safely—for the seas are now overtly benevolent: 'In feather'd briefness sails are fill'd, / And wishes fall out as they're will'd.'

The final reunion itself is anti-climactic: it merely completes the proof of Neptune and the moon's benevolence. There is only a moment more of exploitation, for as soon as Pericles tells his story, Thaisa, as high priestess, faints, and Cerimon divulges the final secret: 'If you have told Diana's altar true, / This is your wife.' Proof quickly follows, and the final gap is closed. Pericles is overwhelmed by this sense of the generosity of forces that had long seemed perverse: 'No more, you gods! Your present kindness / Makes my past miseries sports.' The final argument that watchful goodness rules the universe is presented by the moralizing Gower —who has perhaps learned as much as Pericles; for whereas he formerly insisted that universal force was mere whim, he now sums the meanings of Pericles' trials thus:

> Virtue preserv'd from fell destruction's blast,
> Led on by heaven, and crown'd with joy at last.
> (v. iii. 89–90.)

2. *Cymbeline*

Pericles never comes to be wholly Shakespeare's. On the first two acts the dramatist puts no personal stamp. With Act III he begins attempting to give a total meaning to what seems only an aimless series of misfortunes, and to create exploitable discrepancies for dramatic purposes. But he takes command with difficulty. A quarrel is evident between Gower and himself, the one insisting on a design-less universe, in which establishment of dramatically exploitable situations is impossible; the other requiring—in the world as in the art that represents it—order and purpose, design, and design within design. As not before or after, Shakespeare is here inexplicably respectful to an untoward source—which can be no other than the original of that same narrative poem that Gower, as Chorus, recites piecemeal.[1] By Shakespeare's usual expository method, this poem would have been either stricken entirely or sharply subordinated to the drama. Instead, it is allowed to contain the drama. Until Act III it rules all, and then a conflict arises between narrative and dramatic parts, both in point of view and in the insistence of each on swallowing the .other. The struggle is never fully resolved. Though in Acts IV and V the dramatist lays bold hands upon the narrative parts—abandoning the tetrameter lines, modernizing the vocabularly, and doubtless also reducing the length of the poem and partially subordinating it to the drama—yet momentarily as late as the middle of Act IV Gower rises up, overthrows the drama, and steals entirely for himself—with Dumb Show and narration—the place of a climactic scene of enormous potential.

The root of the difficulty is that Gower's world is quite incompatible with Shakespeare's. Hitherto Shakespeare's world was dominated by man's will: in the comedies, not chance but human will wrought happiness; in the tragedies, not chance but human will wrought catastrophe. In *Pericles* Shakespeare was confronted by another kind of world in which man no longer determines his fate, but is swept along like a chip in a lasting storm: Gower's image of a boat bobbing like a duck is the dominant image of this concept of man's relation to the universe. Whether the ending is to be happy or catastrophic depends not on man, but on external forces. If a benevolent intelligence directs them, it will bring a happy ending; if a malign intelligence, it will bring catastrophe. But if there is no intelligence, but only senselessness, then whatever comes will come by chance.

Artistically if not philosophically dissatisfied with the senseless world imposed by Gower's narrative upon the first two acts of *Pericles*, Shakespeare began in Act III to imply, through scattered signs, the existence of benign direction in the universe. By doing so he also created an exploitable discrepancy between our awareness and that of the principal persons—in particular Pericles, who imagines a malign intelligence. Moreover, briefly, he attempted to restore the human will to the place it had occupied in earlier plays: her own spirit saves Marina in the brothel. But the final reunion is brought about by the gracious intervention of Neptune and Diana. The appearance of a chance ending is thus avoided, and the artistically unacceptable condition initially established by Gower is partly corrected. But unsightly evidence of the conflict between

[1] See my essay, 'The Poem of *Pericles*', in *The Image of the Work*, by B. H. Lehman and others. University of California Press, Berkeley and Los Angeles, 1955.

irreconcilable views of the universe and man's relation to it remains at every hand, and as a whole work of art *Pericles* is badly damaged by it.

Though winds and waves, tempests and seas are absent from it, the world of *Cymbeline*, too, presents a lasting storm; what is more, it offers even less assurance than was ours during *Pericles* that the storm will ever blow to a happy ending. Whereas in *Pericles*, through such signs as the billow that saves Thaisa, we sensed a force, blurred but benign, protecting the royal family, and knew during the latter half of the action that Thaisa and Marina were merely lost, not dead—in *Cymbeline* we must scrutinize the face of the universe intently in order to discern the slightest sign of comfort. In the wisdom of the physician Cornelius and the loyalty of the servant Pisanio we have signs that goodness and truth at least have allies; but these are mainly bystanders to the torrent that sweeps Posthumus and Imogen along, and though they mean well we cannot suppose that their utmost will prevail against the great odds. Moreover, even at late as IV. iii, when Pisanio hopefully ventures that 'Fortune brings in some boats that are not steer'd', we lack evidence that any 'outside' intelligence, for good or ill, watches over man; and Pisanio's comment, besides coming later in the action, is not even so reassuring as the giant billow of *Pericles*. We do not learn until Posthumus's vision in v. iv, when Jupiter claims the credit for the conduct and control of everything—

> Be not with mortal accidents opprest;
> No care of yours it is; you know 'tis ours.
> Whom best I love I cross; to make my gift,
> The more delay'd, delighted.   (Loc. cit. 99–102.)

—that any hand holds the rudder of man's ship. In this respect, then, *Cymbeline* resembles *Pericles* but goes much farther in the same direction—away from the old, insistent reassurance, toward fear that all can never be well.

But though the worlds represented are thus alike, the workmanship of representation differs as ineptness from virtuosity. On the evidence of *Pericles* and *Troilus and Cressida* alone, it would be necessary to conclude that when Shakespeare attempted to depict a world lacking design and purpose, uncontrolled by either man's will or external force, his own art caught the disorder of the world represented. *Cymbeline* is the contradiction of this evidence: as an exhibition of technical skill in the management of the dramatic devices he had favoured from the first, it has no equal. *The Merry Wives of Windsor*, which put on an earlier dazzling display, is only a finger exercise beside *Cymbeline*.

To master the representation of his new world, Shakespeare called on all the old devices—but especially on those most useful in creating and exploiting discrepant awarenesses. Whereas in *Pericles* the high proportion of scenes in which we hold advantage resulted mainly from use of extra-dramatic features, in *Cymbeline* it results entirely from dramatic devising. In managing the discrepant awarenesses of this one play, Shakespeare calls upon all the means he had found useful from *The Comedy of Errors* through *Measure for Measure*. As a result we hold advantage over some or all participants in twenty-three of twenty-seven scenes; advantage at some time over every named person; and simultaneous, multiple advantages over all persons in many scenes.

These facts would not alone make *Cymbeline* exceptional: even in *The Comedy of Errors* we held advantage in all scenes except the first and over all persons except Aemilia, and in all of the mature romantic comedies multiplicity of discrepancies created by multiple dramatic devices, and multiplicity of effects resulting from exploitation of these discrepancies are the rule rather than the exception. What does make *Cymbeline* extraordinary is at once the fantastic complexity of its uses of discrepant awarenesses and the consummate skill with which its intricacies are managed: with greater finality than does any other play, it evinces Shakespeare's mastery of infinitely complex art. From the first his methods made heavy demands on our minds in requiring them to accept, hold, and actively use the advantages provided; but the tasks imposed by our advantages in *Cymbeline* are unprecedented. Here the uses of awareness are fairly gymnastic; our awareness is compelled through a harder course of exercises than ever. From the point of view of the creation, maintenance, and exploitation of discrepant awarenesses —considered both quantitatively and artistically—*Cymbeline* is Shakespeare's greatest achievement.

The dramatist's business of opening gaps starts subtly and quickly. Before the end of i. i we hold advantages of lasting significance over both Cymbeline and the Queen. Cymbeline, at the outset, stands like another Lear, a man who has ever but slenderly known himself —and who is just now, besides, blinded by a practice. He has blundered in opposing Imogen's marriage to Posthumus; his sense of the groom's merit has been abused. We are ourselves advised of Posthumus's quality before the action is a minute old. Says the First Gentleman:

> —a creature such
> As, to seek through the regions of the earth,
> For one his like, there would be something failing

In him that should compare. I do not think
So fair an outward and such stuff within
Endows a man but he.

(I. i. 19–24.)

The estimate is not eccentric; it is shared by all the courtiers, who
are secretly pleased with the marriage. There follows one of Shakespeare's brightest encomiums, the purpose of which is to recom-
mend this Posthumus to us as a paragon. When, a moment later, the
King berates him—

Thou basest thing, avoid! Hence, from my sight!
If after this command thou fraught the court
With thy unworthiness, thou diest. Away!
Thou'rt poison to my blood.

(Ibid. 125–8.)

—the words exploit the gap newly opened between Cymbeline's
understanding and ours. Further, even before we witness the King's
misjudgement we have learned its source. He is afflicted by two
kinds of blindness, toward both his Queen and Posthumus, and the
first has caused the second. During five acts, until the final scene,
Cymbeline's ignorance of what we learn in the first scene—that the
Queen is a vicious practiser, exercising her cunning for herself and
Cloten against Cymbeline, Imogen, and Posthumus—remains a
primary dramatic fact. In *Cymbeline* practices are spawned by
practices more profusely than in any other play, and it is the
Queen's practice that begins the multiplication and precipitates the
entire action. If she had not blinded the King to Posthumus's virtues, there would have been no occasion for the banishment; none
for the wager of Posthumus and Iachimo; none for Iachimo's
wicked practice on Imogen and Posthumus—indeed, nothing that
follows would follow.

The Queen's practice on Cymbeline is evidently long-standing;
it presumably began when the Queen—'a widow / That late he
married'—first sighted the possibility of making her own son king.
Significantly, we first see her true character through the heroine's
eyes. When the Queen has released the imprisoned Imogen and left
her with Posthumus, asserting that 'you shall not find me, daughter, /
After the slander of most step-mothers, / Evil-ey'd unto you', we
would have no cause to suspect trickery but for Imogen's exclamation:

Dissembling courtesy! How fine this tyrant
Can tickle where she wounds!

(Ibid. 84–85.)

249

Immediately, Shakespeare confirms Imogen's judgement with the
Queen's 'aside':

> Be brief, I pray you.
> If the King come, I shall incur I know not
> How much of his displeasure. (*Aside*.) Yet I'll move him
> To walk this way. I never do him wrong
> But he does buy my injuries, to be friends;
> Pays dear for my offences.
>
> (i. i. 101–6.)

So subtly has the Queen operated that Cymbeline has denounced
the paragon Posthumus as 'thou basest thing', preferred the brute
Cloten as Imogen's husband, and even turned against Imogen herself
with such bitter fury born of ignorance as Lear uses against
Cordelia:

> . . . let her languish
> A drop of blood a day; and, being aged,
> Die of this folly!
>
> (Ibid. 156–8.)

But though she has perpetrated the practice from which all follows,
and has given us an advantage over Cymbeline that is effective until
the denouement, the Queen herself occupies a level below ours: she
supposes that she has deceived Imogen, *who in fact first teaches us
what the Queen is*. At the end of the first scene, thus, like the
heroines of the romantic comedies, Imogen shares our vantage-
point. But, unlike her predecessors, she does not stay long with us.

In ii. ii, more baldly than we were informed of the Queen's
character, we are given the measure of Cloten. In a scene of forty-
three lines, a total of eight 'asides' are spoken by the Second Lord,
all to the purpose of making unmistakable the quality of this lesser
villain—lesser, not in brutish intent but because of brutish stupidity:
'That such a crafty devil as is his mother / Should yield the world
this ass!' Though not subtle the device by which we are shown
Cloten's nature is efficient and shrewd exposition, for even while we
are being warned of the danger from his bestiality we are invited to
laugh at his foolishness. At the opening of Act II the pattern of this
scene is repeated, the Second Lord again commenting in 'asides',
exploiting the ever-widening gap between Cloten's knowledge of
himself and our sense of him. A degree of variation in the second
scene is noteworthy. In the first, all of the comments of the Second
Lord by which we were shown Cloten's foolishness are in the form
of 'asides'. In the second, though he is this time given five 'asides',
the Second Lord can speak ironically, directly to Cloten's face—for

we have by this time been sufficiently advised of Cloten's quality to perceive the irony which Cloten misses:

Clo. Sayest thou?
2. Lord. It is not fit your lordship should undertake every companion that you give offence to.
Clo. No, I know that; but it is fit I should commit offence to my inferiors.
2. Lord. Ay, it is fit for your lordship only.   (Ibid. 27–33.)

Even now, however, we are not quite trusted to catch the irony unaided; in the next exchange the Second Lord remarks to Cloten —and then uses an 'aside' to make sure we have not missed:

Clo. Is it fit I went to look upon him? Is there no derogation in't?
2. Lord. You cannot derogate, my lord.
Clo. Not easily, I think.
2. Lord. (Aside.) You are a fool granted; therefore your issues, being foolish, do not derogate.   (Ibid. 46–51.)

Ignorant in both scenes that he is the Second Lord's butt, Cloten is a laughable monster. As suitor for a hand that is infinitely beyond him, he is in the line of Slender and Aguecheek; but he is not, like them, a humble worshipper. The line has dropped sharply, and he is what they have become, as the world of *Cymbeline* is what the world of romantic comedy has become. Though a logical extension of his predecessors into this new world, he is also a new thing for Shakespeare—a composite of fool and brute: though a fool, yet a brute; and though a brute, yet a fool. In the latter fact is offered a shred of comfort for us: encased in foolishness, brutishness may be less dangerous. One of the forces of evil in the play is thus partly blocked by its own shell.

The deeper source of evil is cut off also, but not before it has done initial harm that threatens to be irreparable. The Queen—'A mother hourly coining plots'—has already deceived Cymbeline and effected the separation of Imogen and Posthumus; so much evil is sown, whose consequence is to be reaped—and Shakespeare has given no cause for hope that it will not be bitter. But while that harvest waits, another is prevented. In this play of multiple secrets, the most important—aside from Iachimo's black one and Belarius's wonderful one—given us to hold throughout the action is that of the 'most poisonous compounds' ordered by the Queen of her physician-tutor, Cornelius. Possessed of such drugs, she would do permanent harm, and *Cymbeline* must then end tragically. Thus she speaks of Pisanio after presenting the box given her by Cornelius:

> I have given him that
> Which, if he take, shall quite unpeople her

Of liegers for her sweet, and which she after,
Except she bend her humour, shall be assur'd
To taste of too.

(I. v. 78–82.)

The presentation of what she believes to be 'Strange ling'ring poisons' is her second practice against Imogen and Posthumus, and its intent is even deadlier than the first, by which she separated husband and wife. But when Pisanio takes the box we know that it is harmless, having just heard Cornelius:

(*Aside*.) I do not like her. She doth think she has
Strange ling'ring poisons. I do know her spirit,
And will not trust one of her malice with
A drug of such damn'd nature. Those she has
Will stupefy and dull the sense a while . . .
. . . but there is
No danger in what show of death it makes.

(Ibid. 33–40.)

For the uses of our awareness no passage in *Cymbeline* is more significant. It offers the same kind—though not degree—of reassurance as does the appearance of Sebastian in *Twelfth Night*, while Viola remains distressed, thinking him dead; it is comparable to Dogberry's seizure of Hero's betrayers in *Much Ado about Nothing*; it is even comparable to the Duke's presence behind the curtain in the prison of *Measure for Measure*, while Claudio and Isabella weep and rage in their troubles.

But its effect falls far short of these. Sebastian's arrival, Dogberry's apprehension of the villains, and Vincentio's discovery of Angelo's evil proposition advise us unequivocally that though temporary afflictions will visit participants, all is ultimately well. But the Queen's box of 'most poisonous compounds' is only one of many sources of danger in the seemingly unprotected world of *Cymbeline*, and therefore, though comforting, our knowledge that the compounds are harmless cannot remove general anxiety. In showing us that Cloten is as much fool as monster and that the Queen's compounds are harmless, Shakespeare gives as much reassurance as he will give before the denouement—and it is precious little. For Cloten's foolishness does not make him entirely harmless, and a Queen who is hourly coining plots does not cease to be dangerous when one plot fails. Besides, these are only two of the sources of danger in this world.

The third is neither sealed off by its own stupidity nor recognized by its victims, but stealthily discharges its poison to infect all persons, all subsequent events, the very atmosphere. Iachimo is unique outside of tragedy—a villain whose vantage-point is above that of other participants, and over whom we ourselves have no advantage. In earlier plays some benevolent force has stood guard over villainy, eyeing its passes, ready to check it at need. The highest awareness has always belonged to good people. Don John of *Much Ado*, Shylock of *The Merchant of Venice*, Angelo of *Measure for Measure* are prevented not only from doing harm but even from appearing really dangerous; at last, because of Prospero, the monsters of *The Tempest* are pitiful even in their most swaggering moments. But no force—*to our knowledge while action continues*—watches Iachimo as Vincentio and Prospero watch Angelo and Caliban.

The scene (i. iv) of Posthumus and Iachimo's wager on Imogen's virtue gives us advantage over the heroine when she next appears; henceforth she is never again mistress of her situation and partner in our awareness. No heroine in the comedies is cast in such a role— kept unaware so long, ignorant of so many secrets, abused by so many practices, endangered from so many quarters. Only Isabella of *Measure for Measure* spends nearly as long in ignorance—but the cases are not comparable, for the fact unknown to Isabella is the most comforting in her world, the fact that her friendly 'friar' is the all-powerful Duke. Beside Imogen's, the unknowing moments of earlier heroines seem blessed, brief, trivial: those of Viola, unaware that Sebastian lives, and that the fierce duellist confronting her is a great booby who wants only to make peace or run away; of Hero, unaware that cruel denunciation waits at the altar—but unaware also that her name is already in process of being cleared; even of Marina—after she has escaped the assassin's blow—unaware that forces of her 'lasting storm' are converging on general reunion. If much that Imogen does not know is better than she supposes, yet much also is worse—and, worst of all, uncertain. 'I see before me, man,' she says ecstatically to Pisanio, setting off for Milford-Haven to meet her banished husband; 'nor here, nor here, / Nor what ensues, but have a fog in them / That I cannot look through.' But in truth she cannot see even straight ahead: not only will Posthumus not be at Milford-Haven, but he has ordered her to be murdered on the road.

But Imogen is a deeply unaware heroine only because she is cast into an uncertain universe, too large for its puny inhabitants, where a lasting storm whirs friend from friend and all events 'have a fog in them / That I cannot look through'. Her unawareness is itself a sign of the fearsome world; for Imogen is anything but naïve, anything but naturally incompetent. She has no trace of that congenital affliction of persons who need no deceiving to be deceived—

Bottom, Dogberry, Aguecheek, Malvolio: yet not even one of these remains so long ignorant of so much. The fact is that she is keen and capable. She looks through and through the Queen and Cloten, and her analysis of the situation in which we first find her and Posthumus is brilliant; so is her analysis of her circumstances after Posthumus has gone:

> A father cruel, and a step-dame false;
> A foolish suitor to a wedded lady
> That hath her husband banish'd. . . .
>
> (I. vi. 1–3.)

If she lacks the aggressive self-sufficiency of Rosalind, yet she would have had no difficulty managing Rosalind's world. She would have managed Viola's tangled affairs with far less than Viola's distress. She would have failed at Helena's task—but, then, she would never have wished to succeed at it! She is approximately as able as Marina, who talks brothel-keepers into giving her more congenial work, converts brothel habitués to church-goers, and so far transforms one of these as to make him a proper husband. Neither Imogen nor Marina shows a decline in heroinely competence; *they are lost in their worlds only because their worlds are as they are.* Isabella of *Measure for Measure*, whose perspective is less true than Imogen's and whose capability of dealing with life is inferior, is never so lost and abused as Imogen; but her wicked world has Vincentio, without whom she would have either to escape to the nunnery or be destroyed. Imogen strives alone in a world which has at least as dire a need for a Vincentio, and in which there seems to be none.

It is certainly not a sign of incompetence that Imogen falls victim to Iachimo's practice. She is quick to recognize and denounce his first attempt, when he makes a false report of Posthumus's behaviour in Rome and urges her to reciprocate:

> I dedicate myself to your sweet pleasure,
> More noble than that runagate to your bed,
> And will continue fast to your affection,
> Still close as sure.
>
> (Ibid. 136–9.)

'Away!' replies Imogen; 'I do condemn mine ears that have / So long attended thee.' Both her virtue and her rare acumen speak here. There was every cause for her to be taken in by Iachimo's report: she knows nothing of the wager; she has perfect faith in Iachimo, who comes introduced by Posthumus himself as 'one of the noblest note, to whose kindnesses I am most infinitely tied'; she has heard of such Italian temptations as might have overcome her own or any husband, as she shows later in referring to 'Some jay of Italy / Whose mother was her painting'.

But more than all is the reason of Iachimo himself, with his subtle persuasiveness, the representation of which excels the best of the kind that Shakespeare had achieved or would achieve again. Iachimo works like Iago, seeming preoccupied with his own musings while, as though unintentionally, he teases on the mind of the victim; thus, with an apparent disregard of Imogen, as though she should not hear, he debates with himself how Posthumus could ever have been induced to change mistresses:

> It cannot be i' th' eye, for apes and monkeys
> 'Twixt two such shes would chatter this way and
> Condemn with mows the other; nor i' th' judgement,
> For idiots in this case of favour would
> Be wisely definite; nor i' th' appetite;
> Sluttery to such neat excellence oppos'd
> Should make desire vomit emptiness,
> Not so allur'd to feed.
>
> (Ibid. 39–46.)

Not at all the meanest, Iachimo is the smoothest of Shakespeare's villains. Iago's front of a plain, blunt man is adequate to deceive Othello and everyone else in Venice and Cyprus; Iachimo's front is silken smooth, his persuasive charm irresistible. By all odds his is the finest language in the play. Shakespeare gives him the poet's tongue and the artist's eye: 'On her left breast, / A mole cinque-spotted, like the crimson drops / I' th' bottom of a cowslip.' The fifty lines he speaks while Imogen lies asleep, 'her sense but as a monument, / Thus in a chapel lying', have a hypnotic fascination beyond any other passage in Shakespeare. It does not at all diminish Imogen that she is briefly spell-bound by this villain's tongue; she is the more remarkable for having the strength to break the spell: 'Away! I do condemn mine ears that have / So long attended thee.'

Shakespeare does not with Iachimo, as with Iago, cause him to expose to us in advance the devices of his cunning mind—and there is reason. Imogen's intellectual prestige is thus further protected: when she consents to receive the trunk in her own chamber 'And pawn mine honour' for the safety of its contents, we, too, are ignorant that the contents will be Iachimo himself. Perhaps we may guess; but the dramatist gives us no help in guessing. When his first attempt has failed, we have no way of knowing that Iachimo will try again. Never shrewder in all his shrewd management of our awareness than now, the dramatist gives him no private word with us, but allows us to hear exactly what Imogen hears:

> *Iach.* I have spoke this to know if your affiance
> Were deeply rooted, and shall make your lord,
> That which he is, new o'er; and he is one
> The truest manner'd, such a holy witch
> That he enchants societies into him;
> Half all men's hearts are his.
> *Imo.*   You make amends.
> *Iach.* He sits 'mongst men like a descended god;
> He hath a kind of honour sets him off,
> More than a mortal seeming. Be not angry,
> Most mighty princess, that I have adventur'd
> To try your taking of a false report; which hath
> Honour'd with confirmation your great judgement
> In the election of a sir so rare,
> Which you know cannot err.
>
> (I. vi. 163–75.)

Iachimo is cunning past men's thought: though we know of the wager, whereas Imogen does not, we have no cause to doubt that he has forfeited. When he turns as with an afterthought—'I had almost forgot'—to the next piece of business, it is made to appear *to us as to Imogen* that his new request has no possible connexion with what has just passed. He does not immediately mention a trunk, but describes with fine circumstantial detail—not neglecting, as if incidentally, to lavish more praise on Posthumus—the occasion of his journey and the character of his purchase:

> 'Tis plate of rare device, and jewels
> Of rich and exquisite form, their values great;
> And I am something curious, being strange,
> To have them in safe stowage. May it please you
> To take them in protection?
>
> (Ibid. 189–93.)

'I will keep them / In my bedchamber', says Imogen, and then Iachimo: 'They are in a trunk, / Attended by my men.' There is no more discussion of the matter, the subject being suddenly changed to the question of Iachimo's return to Rome. Only at the tag end of the scene is the trunk mentioned again—and now without reference to the bedchamber. Thus, the last idea left in our minds is of no possible trick of Iachimo's, but of Imogen's responsibility to guard the plate and jewels: '. . . it shall safe be kept, / And truly yielded you.' If we have any anxious thought, it is only that she may somehow fail in this responsibility.

Since we are not to see Iachimo again until he emerges from the trunk beside Imogen's bed, we should ordinarily expect him to linger at the end of this scene in order to explain his intention. But he leaves with Imogen, without so much as a smirk for our advisement. The omission contradicts Shakespeare's method in every play until now. Usually we would have been advised explicitly even earlier—when Iachimo seemed to give up his hope of winning the wager—that he would shift from an honest test of Imogen's virtue to some treacherous device; next, as he continued to talk with Imogen about the plate and the jewels, the outline of his device would have taken definite shape in our minds; next, at the conclusion of the scene with Imogen, he would have remained for a moment to tell us plainly that he would enter the bedchamber in the trunk. There would have been even more: the bedchamber scene would not open as it now does—Imogen reading in bed, attended by her maid, the trunk resting to one side—but with the trunk being brought in, the bearers leaving, Iachimo then lifting the lid to glance around and speak a word to us: all this before Imogen should enter and go to bed. There would have followed Imogen's conversation with the maid—probably with some ironic allusions to the trunk and its precious contents—and then sleep, and only thereafter the emergence of Iachimo.

As the scenes are actually devised, however, not only is the usual care to make assurance double sure omitted, but the least suggestion that Iachimo will enter in the trunk is avoided. We may have guessed the truth, of course, or even have worked it out by reasoning that Iachimo's story of his mission to France to buy a present for the Emperor must be false, since Posthumus, whom he mentions as one of the contributors, would not have joined a group with Iachimo as 'the factor for the rest'. Yet so finely detailed is Iachimo's account of the mission, the jewels, and the 'plate of rare device' that even after the incident is past we may wonder, at one level of consciousness, just where Iachimo temporarily hid these jewels and plate while he occupied their place in the trunk during the night!

The point, in any event, is that Shakespeare has not told us what to expect. He has not even told us that Iachimo is a villain; we cannot know that he is dishonourable until he emerges from the trunk. Though the wager he proposed to Posthumus was insulting, yet Posthumus accepted it—and Posthumus is a paragon. His first test of Imogen, though deceitful, is quite within the terms of the wager, hence no proof of villainy. When his first attempt fails, we have been given no reason to doubt that, finding Imogen's virtue so far incorruptible as to make further trial absurd, he simply abandons his attempt to win Posthumus's ring. We have been given no reason to know, therefore, while Imogen lies reading, attended by her maid, that the trunk beside the bed contains other than jewels and plate. We have been given no reason to suppose but that Iachimo lies in his own room, sleeping or contemplating his return to Rome and his admission of failure.

By denying us the usual advance notice, Shakespeare prevents our gaining advantage over his heroine during the part of the action which is most vital for what follows. We are less likely to think her naïve in being deceived by the trunk when we ourselves have been deceived. It is the perfection of Shakespeare's management of the awarenesses during this central incident that he has at once made it convincing that Iachimo's trick should succeed, and avoided dimming Imogen's heroinely lustre. Once Iachimo has gained access to the chamber, the problem of protecting Imogen from seeming too easily 'taken in' vanishes—for she is now asleep, 'her sense but as a monument, / Thus in a chapel lying', while Iachimo greedily—yet somehow worshipfully, with an aesthete's relish—stores his mind with the evidence of precise detail. In short, Imogen is a truly great person, as brilliant as Rosalind and Portia, even more than worthy of the paragon Posthumus, and Shakespeare has taken pains to keep us in that opinion of her. We gain advantage over her only when and because she is asleep.

We are thus, grievously, made partners in a villain's secret, remembrance of which affects our view of all following scenes. Most immediately it shadows the action of the next morning, when Cloten and his company meet, talk, and sing outside Imogen's chamber door. 'I am advised to give her music o' mornings; they say it will penetrate', says this brute whose villainous potentiality, beside the new menace of Iachimo, has dwindled. The mind is therefore less on Cloten in this scene than on the harm that has been wrought behind the door. We cannot know but that this harm is irreparable, having received no such comfort as, for example, in *Much Ado about Nothing*, when, even before it is soiled, we know that Hero's honour will be cleared. What has happened to Imogen as she slept has been a kind of rape; within our awareness, as within a dome, Cloten's triumphant morning song gathers a stunning resonance:

> Hark, hark! the lark at heaven's gate sings,
>   And Phoebus 'gins arise
> His steeds to water at those springs
>   On chalic'd flowers that lies;
> And winking Mary buds begin
>   To ope their golden eyes;
> With every thing that pretty is,
>   My lady sweet, arise,
>   Arise, arise.   (II. iii. 21–30.)

So glorious a hymn, within itself, would call up a response of pure joy. But the circumstances in which it is set prevent a simple response: it is sung at the behest of Cloten, a beast repugnant to Imogen; Imogen, though she will not immediately recognize the fact, has been undone during the night and cannot arise to the same world she left when she folded down the leaf of her book 'Where Philomel gave up'; and the trunk containing Iachimo and his black secret still stands beyond the door.

Our discomforting knowledge of the night's business conditions our view of participants and action throughout the long and complex scene. Briefly, the dramatist exploits both this secret and that of Cymbeline's deception by the Queen's character and devices; says Cymbeline, accounting for Imogen's coldness to Cloten:

> The exile of her minion is too new;
> She hath not yet forgot him.
> (Ibid. 46–47.)

Here the King occupies the lowermost depth, being ignorant both that the Queen, in greedy ambition, has blinded him to Posthumus's virtues and, of course, that a mortal blow has been struck during the night to the relationship of Posthumus and Imogen. The Queen stands above Cymbeline in having deceived him, but she, too, is ignorant, of course, of the circumstance most immediately relevant —Iachimo's treachery. Cloten is ignorant of the same circumstance, but he shares with his mother—as far as his wit can extend—an advantage over Cymbeline. When Imogen enters, midway in the scene, it is inevitably the gap between her awareness and ours that claims our whole attention, for it is she to whom our secret knowledge most pertains. On this gap, therefore, Shakespeare concentrates his exploitative skill.

It is in keeping with his art that in the entire course of the play Shakespeare does not again show his heroine so much the paragon as in the moments after she emerges from the chamber—where still lie the symbols of her undoing—to confront Cloten. In fifty lines of dialogue in which arch irony and humaneness are mixed she masters her detested suitor. Here above all she shows herself the perfection of Shakespeare's heroines, fusing Rosalind's aggressive capability with Viola's all-feminine compassion. Though the wall she sets between herself and Cloten is bedizened with barbs, she would avoid hurting even him if she could. Only when Cloten speaks ill of Posthumus does her nature express itself in queenly contempt:

> *Imo.* Wert thou the son of Jupiter and no more
> But what thou art besides, thou wert too base
> To be his groom.
> (Ibid. 130–2.)

Though her exhibition of personal greatness alone has dramatic power, experience of the full force of the interview requires use of our awareness—which the dramatist prods from time to time— that even as she defends Posthumus, defies Cloten, and shows herself as far above him as angel above beast, Imogen stands in a situation direr than that of any other non-tragic heroine: the trunk, with Iachimo, lies behind the door of the bedchamber. In her outcry on discovering the loss of the bracelet given her by Posthumus, we are shown a token of the despair that would be hers if she recognized, instead of remote possibility, the certainty that we know: 'Shrew me / If I would lose it for a revenue / Of any king's in Europe . . . / I hope it be not gone to tell my lord / That I kiss aught but he.'

From this view of Imogen we are carried as if instantly, so that memory cannot dim, to Posthumus, just reaffirming his faith:

> Fear it not, sir. I would I were so sure
> To win the King as I am bold her honour
> Will remain hers.
>
> (II. iv. 1–3.)

Though his faith itself is justified, yet he speaks in ignorance, for seeming proof of Imogen's guilt *has* been taken. As the scene proceeds he exchanges one condition of unawareness for another and deeper one, beginning certain that his faith in Imogen's purity will not be challenged and ending certain that she has no purity. He is not easily moved from the one error to the other, but rejects in swift succession Iachimo's mere assertion that the ring is won, his knowledge of the tapestry-hung walls of the bedchamber, the detailed evidence of the sculptured chimney-piece, 'Chaste Dian bathing', of the roof of the chamber, which 'With golden cherubins is fretted', and of the andirons, 'two winking Cupids / Of silver, each on one foot standing, nicely / Depending on their brands'. Here again, as when he showed Iachimo deceiving Imogen, Shakespeare draws villainy whose persuasive power is art, not craft. A moment before, Posthumus was confident that Iachimo had acquired his knowledge of the bedchamber at second hand—'this you might have heard of here, by me, / Or by some other'; but when the poet's tongue of the villain has recited the telling details which the artist's eye had observed, he has grown uneasy: 'Let it be granted you have seen all this—and praise / Be given to your remembrance—the description / Of what is in her chamber nothing saves / The wager you have laid.' In the space of fifty lines (45–95), using nothing more tangible than finely discriminated words and phrases, Iachimo has so shaken Posthumus's confidence that a bare glimpse of tangible proof must shatter it; says Iachimo:

> Then, if you can,
>> (*Showing the bracelet.*)
> Be pale. I beg but leave to air this jewel; see!
> And now 'tis up again.
>> (Ibid. 95–97.)

What further struggle Posthumus's mind makes against belief merely tightens its hold. The evidence of the cinque-spotted mole —much too fine a touch to be omitted by the artist Iachimo—is superfluous; Posthumous would now reject Iachimo's oath if he swore that all the evidence was false:

> If you will swear you have not done 't, you lie;
> And I will kill thee if thou dost deny
> Thou'st made me cuckold.   (Ibid. 144–6.)

The completeness of Iachimo's triumph is marked in the final scene of Act II, when Posthumus utters perhaps the most remarkable of all speeches in Shakespeare made by persons utterly mistaken in their situations. This is one of several occasions in *Cymbeline* of Shakespeare's surpassing the finest work he had done with scenes that demand simultaneous, mutually contradictory responses. The function of the hero's soliloquy here contrasts with the typical soliloquy's function, which is to advise us. For here we know everything and the speaker nothing of the situation he describes, so that the soliloquy exists not to inform us but solely to exploit the chasm opened by Iachimo's dagger tongue between us and Posthumus. In itself, heard without interpretation by our superior awareness, the speech would be a devastating diatribe against woman, the more potent because earnest passion invests each syllable and image with the sound of truth. Shakespeare writes, indeed, as if we must be made at any cost to accept Posthumus's view. Starting with his 'proof' that Imogen, the nonpareil of womankind, is false, Posthumus generalizes to all women, to his own mother, 'the Dian of that time', and ultimately even to 'the woman's part in me', which he would destroy if he could isolate it. Moreover, he generalizes not only from her who has sinned to all other women, but from the one sin she has committed to all sins that are committed under the sun:

> For there's no motion
> That tends to vice in man, but I affirm
> It is the woman's part: be it lying, note it,
> The woman's flattering, hers deceiving, hers;
> Lust and rank thought, hers, hers; revenges, hers;
> Ambitions, covetings, change of prides, disdain,
> Nice longing, slanders, mutability,
> All faults that may be nam'd, nay, that hell knows,
> Why, hers, in part or all; but rather, all.
>> (II. v. 20–28.)

But since the initial premise is quite false, all that follows is false: Imogen is indeed the nonpareil of this world; undoubtedly Posthumus's mother was truly the Dian of her time; woman and the woman's part in man are not, therefore, the source of 'All faults that may be nam'd, nay, that hell knows'. Upon what appears an irrefutably reasoned indictment of womankind, our superior awareness executes a reversal. The powerful diatribe, translated by the mind's ear, becomes a eulogy of womankind.

When Iachimo has done his work upon both Imogen and Posthumus, he is removed from the action until v. ii. It is in part because of his long absence that the world of *Cymbeline* is dark and comfortless. During three acts the evil sown by him has wild growth, while we bear alone and helplessly the secret of its origin. But one glimpse of our wicked secret-sharer during this period would give hope that ultimately all might be well—for Iachimo holds the only usable key to the doors that lock the paragons in darkness. We are permitted no glimpse. The ubiquitous presence of Iago in *Othello*, telling all, doing his deviltry in full view, is not so terrifying as the long absence of Iachimo—who may, for all we know, have vanished from the earth. Shakespeare's dramatic art was never more cruel to our awareness.

In *Cymbeline* error spawns error at nightmarish rate. Ignorance is cumulative: as action continues, participants struggle under mounting layers of misapprehension. The compounding of errors takes its first spurt with Pisanio's receipt of Posthumus's letter ordering Imogen's murder. His head being level as well as loyal, Pisanio perceives that his master has been abused:

> O master! what a strange infection
> Is fall'n into thy ear! What false Italian,
> As poisonous-tongu'd as handed, hath prevail'd
> On thy too ready hearing?
>
> (III. ii. 3–6.)

Pisanio's quick perception of the truth might make his master seem gullible. But in fact Posthumus's hearing was not 'too ready'. Highly circumspect, Posthumus fell victim because Iachimo's evidence was undeniable. Not blinded by Iachimo's dazzling art, Pisanio can perceive the truth, and, perceiving it, knows that Imogen must not be slain. Hence he, too, is driven to perpetrate a practice that adds to the mounting error: 'I am ignorant in what I am commanded', he says as Imogen enters—and proceeds to deceive both master and mistress.

Though she has only begun, Imogen is even here involved in deeper error than was any earlier heroine. She is ignorant that her husband wagered on her virtue; that Iachimo took 'proofs' from her; that Posthumus was abused by these proofs; that he has ordered Pisanio to murder her; and that Pisanio's head, just now, is buzzing with a conflict of duties. She is thus victim of three practisers: of Iachimo; of Posthumus, by his letter directing her to Milford-Haven but in reality intending her murder on the road; and of Pisanio, by his present silence about his own letter from Posthumus which orders the murder. Thus because Iachimo was a practiser, Posthumus and Pisanio have become practisers; and almost immediately afterwards Imogen, the victim of multiple practisers, herself turns practiser. And starting it all, of course, was the Queen's practice that separated husband and wife.

When she has read her husband's letter, Imogen's ecstatic speech, all breathless haste and tumbling words, reminiscent of Juliet's as she awaits night and Romeo ('Gallop apace, you fiery-footed steeds'), achieves one of the play's many surpassing exploitations of discrepant awarenesses:

> O, for a horse with wings! Hear'st thou, Pisanio?
> He is at Milford-Haven. Read, and tell me
> How far 'tis thither. If one of mean affairs
> May plod in a week, why may not I
> Glide thither in a day?
>
> (Ibid. 50–54.)

While Juliet speaks, Romeo, banished, half crazed, sobs on the floor of Friar Laurence's cell; while Imogen speaks, Posthumus, in Rome, awaits word that her murder has been accomplished. The tragic heroine's situation was less dire than this. Imogen's ecstatic words demand joyous response; but preventing this response is our awareness, full of painful facts—of Iachimo, of Posthumus's order, of Pisanio; and less immediately, of the abused Cymbeline, of the cunning Queen, of the bestial Cloten—who, though momentarily they have receded, nevertheless contribute to the painful setting for Imogen's rhapsodical utterance. This setting is nearly but not quite all dark and comfortless. Just before Imogen speaks we have heard Pisanio:

> How? that I should murder her?
> Upon the love and truth and vows which I
> Have made to thy command? I, her? Her blood?
> If it be so to do good service, never
> Let me be counted serviceable.
>
> (Ibid. 11–15.)

A small part of the total environment—weak indeed beside the usual strong comfort with which Shakespeare provides us—

Pisanio's comment at least qualifies the despair which must otherwise be our response to Imogen's ecstasy.

To this point the action has been moved by six distinct practices: the Queen's on Cymbeline, Posthumus, and Imogen, which effected the separation; the Queen's on Pisanio, with the bottle of 'poisonous compounds'; Cornelius's on the Queen, substituting less potent compounds; Posthumus and Iachimo's joint practice, the wager, on Imogen; Iachimo's on Imogen and Posthumus, in obtaining and using false proofs; Posthumus's on Imogen, with the enticement of Milford-Haven. In the comedies many practices are devised, exploited, and then left behind as a new cycle starts. But in *Cymbeline* the effect of every practice abides. The force is cumulative, building in our awareness the sense neither of certain catastrophe nor of certain joy, but of uncertainty. Long ago, in *The Comedy of Errors*, we were left with a spot of anxiety for Aegeon while the farcical scenes were presented; in *Cymbeline* what is originally a spot of anxiety grows until it overwhelms the consciousness. As error mounts on error, practice on practice, the dread grows that truth, being buried ever deeper, can never be recovered by the participants, *and that we alone will be left aware of it at the end*—as at the end of *Romeo and Juliet*, despite Friar Laurence's efforts, we are left holding untellable and unbearable secrets. The absence of Iachimo, our secret-sharer and lone hope, contributes much to the sense of anxiety; but the steady piling of new error atop the old contributes also.

Practices breed ignorance, and out of ignorance are born new practices. Thus Imogen undertakes her first masquerade:

> Go bid my woman feign a sickness, say
> She'll home to her father; and provide me presently
> A riding-suit, no costlier than would fit
> A franklin's housewife.
>
> (III. ii. 76–79.)

No earlier heroine donned disguise to deceive others while so abused herself. Knowing nothing of Iachimo's trick with the trunk, of Posthumus's order for her murder, supposing that she need only reach Milford-Haven where Posthumus awaits her, she sets off joyously, brushing aside Pisanio's mild but profoundly meaningful admonition, 'Madam, you're best consider'. One layer of her error is removed as they approach Milford-Haven, when Pisanio, distracted, shows Posthumus's letter ordering her death. But the error removed is the one that had made her joy possible—the belief that Posthumus awaited her. That joyous misapprehension is now instantly replaced by an agonizing one: ignorant of Iachimo's trick

which she herself unknowingly aided, she imagines that her husband
is false, betrayed by 'Some jay of Italy, / Whose mother was her
painting', and has ordered her death to be rid of her. Here her
speech parallels that of Posthumus when, supposing Imogen false,
he castigated womankind:

> —O,
> Men's vows are women's traitors! All good seeming,
> By thy revolt, O husband, shall be thought
> Put on for villainy; not born where't grows,
> But worn a bait for ladies.
>
> (III. iv. 55–59.)

Royal in her birth, a paragon in mind, will, and character, gifted as
the finest of Shakespeare's best-endowed heroines, Imogen, paradoxically, unlike her predecessors, is rarely allowed more than an
unfocused glimpse of a small segment of the circle of her situation:
besides all else of which she is ignorant, she wrongly supposes that
Pisanio truly intends to murder her. The servant has great difficulty
in persuading her otherwise.

The scene of mixed amazement, fury, grief, and bitterness into
which Imogen is precipitated by reading her death order is the
varied parallel of that in which she became ecstatic on reading the
letter reporting her husband's presence at Milford-Haven. Our
awareness reverses the effects of each scene. In the earlier one we
know that Imogen's ecstasy is in fact baseless—hence its exhibition
is painful. In the present we know that Posthumus has been abused
by Iachimo, not seduced by an Italian jay—hence exhibition of
Imogen's mistaken grief is, if not pleasant, at least not so painful as
was that of her mistaken joy. In the earlier scene the truth is far
worse than she supposes; here, it is infinitely better. In both scenes
the demands on us are so complex and mutually contradictory that
it would seem impossible to respond adequately. The personal magnitude of Imogen, in either joy or grief, itself intensifies the demands
of these scenes—and, lest it lapse, our sense of her greatness is re-
freshed by every line she is given to speak. But her stature is only
one factor in the totality that crowds awareness nearly to bursting
before the scene is done.

And then, near the end of the scene, atop compounded practices,
multiple secrets, discrepant awarenesses, and layer on layer of consciousness, Shakespeare piles yet more, to make the burden staggering. First Imogen, earlier transformed from princess to franklin's
housewife in order to flee the palace, adopts a profounder masquerade, with doublet, hat, and hose supplied by Pisanio, in which
she will change 'Woman it pretty self'—

—into a waggish courage;
Ready in gibes, quick-answer'd, saucy, and
As quarrelous as the weasel. . . .

(III. iv. 160-2.)

And finally, at the very end—as though awareness might hold yet
a little without bursting—the dramatist revives and gives terrible
immediacy to an old threat which has continued to trouble only a
corner of the mind; says Pisanio, remembering the Queen's gift:

Here is a box—I had it from the Queen—
What's in 't is precious. If you are sick at sea,
Or stomach-qualm'd at land, a dram of this
Will drive away distemper.

(Ibid. 191-4.)

'I thank thee', says Imogen, and accepts the drugs with the character
Pisanio has given them. But for us they have two deeper associa-
tions—the Queen's false opinion that they are poisons; and Cornelius's true one that they are a harmless but powerful sleeping potion.

By accepting this box Imogen opens new gaps between her
understanding and ours—and complicates an already difficult problem of response. Considering all circles of circumstance that surround the heroine as she parts from Pisanio in this wild place and
strikes out alone toward Milford-Haven, have we greater cause for
comfort, or for dismay? Since these drugs are not the elixir that
Imogen supposes, the truth is worse than she supposes; but since
they are not the poisons that the Queen intended, it is much better
than it might have been. Imogen's acceptance of the box is only one
part of a fantastically complex, fantastically exploitable total situation. It is not the last occasion in *Cymbeline* that heavier demands
for response are made than, perhaps, we are capable of answering.
As action proceeds after Imogen takes up her second masquerade,
the difficulty of managing adequate responses increases. From the
middle of Act III until the denouement, hardly a person speaks who
truly understands more than his own identity—and the rural princes
are mistaken even in that. And as errors mount, the truths for which
our awareness is made responsible mount also, until the accumulation reaches gigantic proportions. Actions and utterances represented to eye and ear serve as stimuli to the bustling drama going on
in our heads, and everything requires drastic reinterpretation by
the mind's eye and ear.

Act III, v bristles with such stimuli when, after the interview with
the Roman ambassador, Cymbeline and the Queen discover that
Imogen is gone. 'Where is our daughter?' asks the King:

266

She looks us like
A thing more made of malice than of duty;
We have noted it. Call her before us, for
We have been too slight in sufferance.
(III. v. 32–35.)

Cymbeline is far behind the action: he remains ignorant even of the old practice by which the Queen moved his hatred of Posthumus; of the wedge of misunderstanding which Iachimo has driven; of the fact that Imogen has fled the palace; and of the whole pattern of perverse causes of her flight. Says the Queen:

Royal sir,
Since the exile of Posthumus, most retir'd
Hath her life been; the cure whereof, my lord,
'Tis time must do. Beseech your Majesty,
Forbear sharp speeches to her; she's a lady
So tender of rebukes that words are strokes
And strokes death to her.
(Ibid. 35–41.)

When knocking at Imogen's chamber brings no answer, Cymbeline is alarmed: 'Grant, heavens, that which I fear / Prove false!'—but he knows far too little to fear as he should if he knew all. Left alone the Queen soliloquizes:

He [Pisanio] hath a drug of mine; I pray his absence
Proceed by swallowing that, for he believes
It is a thing most precious. But for her,
Where is she gone?
(Ibid. 57–60.)

The speech compels the mind through a gymnastic course of correcting what it hears and then correcting the corrections: '. . . for he believes,' says the Queen, 'It is a thing most precious'; so Pisanio does believe, but he has not swallowed the drug and died, as the Queen hopes. He has given it to his mistress, who, if she should take it, would neither die, as the Queen thinks, nor be cured of sickness, as Pisanio and Imogen think, but would only sleep. The Queen continues: '. . . wing'd with fervour of her love, she's flown / To her desir'd Posthumus'; so Imogen did intend, but she fled under a misapprehension as deep as the Queen's and is now lost in Wales. And, finally, says the Queen:

She being down,
I have the placing of the British crown.
(Ibid. 64–65.)

It is on this expectation that she has fashioned all her practices; but in the opening scene of the play the First Gentleman told us of

267

Cymbeline's stolen sons, and in III. iii, shortly before the Queen makes this boast, *we saw them*. Though ignorant of their claim, they exist; hence Cloten's way to the throne would not be assured even if Imogen were 'down'.

The climactic portion of *Cymbeline* begins with Imogen's appearance in boy's clothes before Belarius's cave in III. vi and ends with IV. ii. Though these scenes are divided by brief expository scenes (III. vii and IV. i), they form in effect a single, strongly unified moment in the drama. Nor is this portion the peak only of *Cymbeline*: *judged for its artistry in the management of many highly exploitable discrepancies to produce multiple effects, it stands as the tallest peak in Shakespeare.*

The process of laying the base for this peak was begun in the opening scene, in Shakespeare's characteristic way, with the devising of practices. By the time Imogen adopted disguise, as housewife and then as boy, seven practices, some for good, some for ill, all interwoven, had been set in motion. The eighth practice, introduced in III. iii, is that of Belarius on the sons of Cymbeline—and, therefore, on Cymbeline and all Britain—in keeping them ignorant of themselves. Though revealed only now, this is in fact the longest-standing practice of all, since it began when these young men were 'three and two' years. The ninth, tenth, and eleventh practices are introduced in swift succession—hurried in just before we are to be shown Imogen at the cave's entrance. First is Pisanio's twisted, merciful-cruel practice on Posthumus:

> (*Aside.*) I'll write to my lord she's dead. O, Imogen,
> Safe mayst thou wander, safe return again!
> (III. v. 104–5.)

Next is Pisanio's practice on Cloten, when, in seeming friendliness, he provides the brute with Posthumus's suit and the information that Imogen has gone to Milford to meet her husband, but—

> To Milford go,
> And find not her whom thou pursuest. Flow, flow,
> You heavenly blessings, on her! This fool's speed
> Be cross'd with slowness; labour be his meed!
> (Ibid. 165–8.)

And finally is Cloten's practice on Imogen and Posthumus, in setting off dressed in Posthumus's suit: 'With that suit upon my back will I ravish her,—first kill him, and in her eyes. . . .' For the most part we share knowledge of each of these eleven practices with a practiser alone or with a practiser and one other person: thus, for

example, we share only with Cornelius one of the three most important of all secrets, that of the nature of the drugs carried by Imogen;
we share the secret of the princes' identities only with Belarius—and
this also is one of the three; and we share the deepest secret of all
only with Iachimo—who has vanished.

At this crucial moment, the beginning of the climactic portion,
we can have no confidence either that all is well or that all is ill, for
the facts that have been packed into our minds are in remarkable
balance: Pisanio's loyalty and wisdom, Cornelius's integrity and
foresight, the survival of Cymbeline's sons, whose innate royalty is
ready to burst their homespun garments—all these are reassuring
signs; but they are countered by Iachimo's disappearance, Cloten's
bestial new enterprise, the Queen's continuing domination of Cymbeline's mind, the deepening darkness in which all the participants
move, and, finally, above all, by the fact that we have had no hint
that any benevolent outside force watches over this world—not
even such a hint as the extraordinary billow reported by an obscure
bystander in *Pericles*.

These are only specimens from the catalogue of items that our
minds have been made to hold in preparation for the towering
moment of Imogen's appearance, 'alone, in boy's clothes', before
the cave of Belarius. All that happens or is said in the scenes that
next follow requires reinterpretation, in the light of many related
facts held in our minds—which are necessarily busied constantly
with making bridges between appearance and reality; and, especially in these scenes, lest our minds be lazy and cause us to miss
some edge of a complex effect, the dramatist repeatedly goads remembrance. Thus—as a simple example—at the opening, while the
outer eye sees only the approach of a boy to a cave's entrance, the
harried inner eye marks the approach of a disguised, multiple-
troubled princess to the wild home of her two royal brothers, and
must also apprehend the disposition of awarenesses among these
participants: the princess cannot recognize her brothers, nor they
her—for they do not truly recognize themselves. So much before
a word is spoken; when Imogen does speak it is to prod alive a nest
of facts lying near the surface of consciousness:

> I have tir'd myself, and for two nights together
> Have made the ground my bed. I should be sick. . . .
> (III. vi. 2–3.)

'Sick'? The mind's eye is prompted to look far back, to the Queen:

> Now, master doctor, have you brought those drugs?
> (I. v. 4.)

And to Cornelius:

> She doth think she has
> Strange ling'ring poisons. I do know her spirit,
> And will not trust one of her malice with
> A drug of such damn'd nature. Those she has
> Will stupefy and dull the sense a while. . . .
>
> (I. v. 33–37.)

And finally to Pisanio:

> Here is a box—I had it from the Queen—
> What's in't is precious. If you are sick at sea,
> Or stomach-qualm'd at land, a dram of this
> Will drive away distemper.
>
> (III. iv. 191–4).

Imogen's appearance before the cave, together with her first spoken lines, thus calls into play our sense of three profound secrets, each complex, each bound up with others: that of her own identity, that of the identity of the cave's occupants, and that of the drug. Continuing, her words stir the most painful secret our mind holds—that of Iachimo's treachery and the intricate pattern of misapprehensions by which the heroine has been brought to this spot at this moment:

> . . . falsehood
> Is worse in kings than beggars. My dear lord!
> Thou art one o' th' false ones.
>
> (III. vi. 13–15.)

From Imogen's initial soliloquy of twenty-five lines we learn nothing new; but through it the vital spots of our awareness all are alerted for what follows. The soliloquy thus fits like a cap over the climactic scenes, in which all gaps between participants' varied awarenesses and ours are exploited—sometimes boldly, sometimes subtly, but always flawlessly. For the most part the exploitation of Imogen's and the mountain youths' mutual ignorance of kinship is handled boldly, producing gaudy double flashes at each utterance; says Guiderius:

> Were you a woman, youth,
> I should woo hard but be your groom.
> (Ibid. 69–70.)

She *is* a woman, and he a prince; says Arviragus:

> I'll make't my comfort
> He is a man; I'll love him as my brother.
> (Ibid. 71–72.)

Finally—irony upon irony, and flash within flash within flash—

Imogen speaks an 'aside'—as if to advise us, who know more than she, in confidence:

> Would it had been so, that they
> Had been my father's sons! Then had my prize
> Been less, and so more equal ballasting
> To thee, Posthumus.
>
> (Ibid. 76–79.)

Such lines strike flashes that suddenly illuminate to the inner eye all the secrets of the play—and never before did Shakespeare spread out so many for the eye to sweep at once.

The brothers' unawareness has four depths: they are ignorant that 'Fidele' is a woman, that she is a princess, that she is their sister, that they are themselves royal. Exploitation is concentrated less on their multifold ignorance, however, than on their unsuspecting hits upon truth: the mountain youths possess an intuition that characterizes disguised royalty in romance, a sense of innate qualities which all but enables them to perceive what they are. Thus exploitation becomes flirtation with truth, and each near hit produces a flash of irony. Such toying with the secret of royalty, barely hidden, shining amid unlikely circumstances, Shakespeare briefly tried in *Pericles*, particularly when the disguised prince sits 'too melancholy' at Simonides' feast and his inner quality gleams through the garb of 'The mean knight' to attract the King and Thaisa. But in *Pericles* Shakespeare could exploit the situation from only one side —for Pericles knows his own royalty. In *Cymbeline* the possibilities are multiplied, the rustic princes themselves being ignorant of their identities. What is much more, not only are they as well as Imogen ignorant of their royalty, but all are ignorant also of the brother-sister relationship. Add to this the brothers' ignorance even that 'Fidele' is a woman, and it is evident that the potentialities of exploitation in *Pericles* were meagre in comparison. In this complex situation any word spoken must strike flash on flash; thus Imogen, closing the scene with an 'aside'—again as if she could possibly advise us of the situation—casts light, unwittingly, upon each spot where a secret lies buried:

> Great men
> That had a court no bigger than this cave,
> That did attend themselves and had the virtue
> Which their own conscience seal'd them, laying by
> That nothing-gift of differing multitudes,
> Could not out-peer these twain. Pardon me, gods!
> I'd change my sex to be companion with them,
> Since Leonatus false.
>
> (Ibid. 82–89.)

But this scene is only a preliminary. In the second phase of the climactic portion, IV. ii, the same accumulated discrepancies continue—but with additions that make the scene more elaborate than the first and more elaborate than any other in Shakespeare. Nor is it merely complex: its many movements and myriad cross-plays about the facts that awareness holds are flawlessly executed; its effects are the most daring and dazzling that the dramatist had achieved; its demands for responses of mind and emotion are varied, boldly conflicting, irresistible—and perhaps beyond our capacity to meet. Considered from the point of view of its uses of awareness, *Cymbeline*, IV. ii, is, beyond question, Shakespeare's finest dramatic achievement.

Of the six persons—Imogen, Belarius, Guiderius, Arviragus, Cloten, and Lucius—who take part, none perceives more than a segment of the complete circle, and most perceive only what is false. Occupying the lowest level are the rustic youths, mistaken in everything, including their own identities. Above them, Imogen, Belarius, and Cloten stand approximately on a level, each holding a special advantage as proprietor of a private practice: Imogen as 'Fidele'; Belarius as 'father' of the two boys; Cloten as 'Posthumus'. At the same time each is victim of others' practices—Imogen of multiple devices and of errors grown from these; Belarius of Imogen's disguise; Cloten of Pisanio's misinformation. To Lucius, coming from outside into such a situation, where the active participants are all mistaken, everything is quite other than it seems.

Throughout the scene, one by one, two by two, even three by three, the secrets in our awareness are struck and rung like bells by the words of 'knowing' speakers. Thus the first lines exploit at once the brothers' ignorance of themselves and of their guest's sex, and the mutual ignorance of kinship:

> *Arv.* (*To Imogen.*)   Brother, stay here.
> Are we not brothers?
> *Imo.*   So man and man should be;
> But clay and clay differs in dignity,
> Whose dust is both alike. I am very sick.
> *Gui.* Go you to hunting; I'll abide with him.
> *Imo.* So sick I am not, yet I am not well;
> But not so citizen a wanton as
> To seem to die ere sick. . . .
> *Gui.* I love thee; I have spoke it;
> How much the quantity, the weight as much,
> As I do love my father.
>
> (IV. ii. 3–18.)

While they flirt with the truths of royalty and kinship, these lines also prepare for exploitation of the second great secret, that of the drug; says Imogen:

> I am sick still, heart-sick. Pisanio,
> I'll now taste of thy drug.
> (Ibid. 37–38.)

These lines force the mind again through swift review of the tortuous history of the drugs: the Queen, intending murder, demanded poison; Cornelius, knowing the Queen, gave a sleeping potion instead; the Queen, at once knowingly and unknowingly, practised on Pisanio, giving him a drug she thought poisonous; Pisanio quite unknowingly practised on Imogen, giving her what he thought to be an elixir. Now, in taking the potion, Imogen unknowingly practises on the brothers and old Belarius—for the consequence is seeming-death which they mistake for very death. The secret of the drugs does not lose force, therefore, with Imogen's swallowing them: that is at once an end and a beginning. It creates an important new secret—of 'Fidele's' survival—which endures until the last moments of the play. Thus the history of the drug spans the whole action, from I. v to v. v. But most immediately swallowing the drug precipitates a situation in the treatment of which Shakespeare's long career of exploiting discrepancies in awareness attains its zenith.

The sequence which starts with the appearance of Arviragus at the cave's entrance, bearing 'Fidele' in his arms, and ends with Imogen's departure with Lucius is the very tip of the peak. It is composed of two distinct incidents: the 'funeral' of 'Fidele', and Imogen's soliloquy over 'Posthumus's' body. In the first of these the spectacle is set amid Shakespeare's most elaborate arrangement of exploitable discrepancies; in the second, that extraordinary boldness which distinguishes Shakespeare's dramatic manner throughout his career, and is most conspicuous in his management of awarenesses, is carried to its furthest limit.

The force of the dirge recited by Arviragus and Guiderius over Imogen's still form rises not only from qualities of the song itself, but, once more, from the frame that encloses it. What appears to the outer eye is only an adopted brother's funeral ceremony conducted by a pair of rustic lads, who lay the body beside their mother's grave and recite the song they had sung at their mother's burial. Accompanied by such words as are spoken here, the spectacle would be impressive if it were no more than it seems:

> *Arv.* And let us, Polydore, though now our voices
> Have got the mannish crack, sing him to th' ground,
> As once our mother; use like note and words,
> Save that Euriphile must be Fidele.

Gui. Cadwal,
    I cannot sing. I'll weep, and word it with thee;
    For notes of sorrow out of tune are worse
    Than priests and fanes that lie.
Arv.   We'll speak it, then.
                                   (IV. ii. 235–42.)

There follows the dirge itself, potent alone, without a setting; but its luminosity is enhanced by the richest context that Shakespeare ever constructed in our minds to embellish one moment: *for these lads are not Cadwal and Polydore, mountain rustics, but Arviragus and Guiderius, princes royal; Euriphile, whose funeral they remember and whose dirge they repeat, was not their mother, but their nurse; the youth Fidele is not a boy, but a girl; not only a girl, but a princess; not only a princess, but their sister; and, on top of all, not dead.*

What response is adequate in such a case, when all is at once far better and far worse than it seems? The grief of the princes, genuine and deep, would be deeper if they truly knew for whom they weep; yet this grief would not be at all if they knew that she only sleeps. Perhaps Shakespeare never made the grief of death more poignant than on this occasion—when, as we alone know, none is needed. Because this is borne as though Imogen were dead in fact, the pain of the princes demands pain in return; yet our knowledge that she is not dead contradicts the demand. But our awareness brings no joy, for Imogen, whose senses are for the moment sunk in total blackness, will wake to the same bleak, hopeless world that enclosed her before she slept. In the confusion of demands the emotions are not free to respond in any one way—and, struggling to be free, are more engaged.

From this perplexity the emotions are caught up, in the next instant, in a new ambivalence, the tensions of which are yet more urgent. All circumstances considered, the spectacle of Imogen sobbing over Cloten's headless body, dressed in Posthumus's suit, is Shakespeare's boldest exploitation of discrepant awarenesses, the ultimate to which long devotion to the method carried him. A moment before, while the 'rustics' wept over the 'body' of 'Fidele', the battle of responses raged between grief and joy; now, as Imogen sobs over the body of 'Posthumus', the war is between convulsive grief and raucous laughter.

As when the bewitched fairy queen Titania doted on the shallowest thickskin, Bottom, the situation is grotesque; both scenes depict incongruity in the utmost degree—the fairy doting on Bottom in an ass's head, the princess crying over Cloten in no head at all—and such gross incongruity must have gross laughter. Headless and dead, Cloten perpetrates the practice he undertook when he required Posthumus's garments of Pisanio; for though the practice has taken a turn he had not intended, it is unmistakably he who is the practiser here, and Imogen the victim. She had once scorned this Caliban–Cloten, contrasting him with Posthumus, and remarking most pointedly, for the present situation,

> His meanest garment
> That ever hath but clipp'd his body, is dearer
> In my respect than all the hairs above thee,
> Were they all made such men.
> (II. iii. 138–41.)

Shakespeare places no other heroine in a predicament which invites such gross laughter; Imogen's is the ludicrous situation of the unsuspecting fine lady with a louse on her bonnet. It is also a predicament which the heroine seems fairly to have brought upon herself by having earlier declared Posthumus's 'meanest garment' worth more than Cloten—thereby suggesting his masquerade in Posthumus's garments. Having wrought such a monstrous situation, the dramatist might still have handled it so delicately that the scene would forbid laughter—as, for example, he had handled Olivia's protestations of love for perplexed Viola. He does not handle it so, however, but boldly strikes exactly that which is supremely grotesque in the situation:

> The garments of Posthumus!
> I know the shape of 's leg; this is his hand,
> His foot Mercurial, his Martial thigh,
> The brawns of Hercules; but his Jovial face—
> Murder in heaven?—How!—'Tis gone.
> (IV. ii. 308–12.)

The Bottom–Titania performance demanded only laughter; hence, though complex, the scene is simple beside this. The Cloten–Imogen spectacle, equally grotesque, demanding the same sort of laughter, also demands grief in proportion to Imogen's grief. For at the same time he exploits boldly what is comic in the situation, Shakespeare keeps us aware of what this heroine and her estate are: Imogen's is a towering grief, which comes from no beggar under a bush but from a paragon of princesses, reduced to her present extremity by intolerable blows in an intolerable world.

It is certain that Shakespeare had prepared no such occasion as this before, and possibly he never wrote better than for his most abused heroine here (ll. 209–308), when, emerging from her death-like sleep and rising through a jumble of delirium to full consciousness, she discovers herself with a bloody bedfellow, sharing a covering of wild flowers. Though full consciousness finally returns, it does not bring awareness of her true situation; on the contrary, except that she correctly identifies the garments of her husband on the headless body, all that she thinks true is false. She wakes, that is to say, to the same misunderstandings that were hers before she slept. As her anguished soliloquy continues, each line requires correction by reference to the appropriate fact stored in our minds for this gigantic moment. Ignorant that she has just been the subject of a funeral ceremony conducted by persons as mistaken about everything as she herself, she exposes her misunderstanding of every old and every new shape within her view. Her blunder in mistaking Cloten's body for her husband's is of course the most immediate subject of exploitation. But after this she errs in her condemnation of Pisanio:

> Pisanio,
> All curses madded Hecuba gave the Greeks,
> And mine to boot, be darted on thee! Thou,
> Conspir'd with that irregulous devil, Cloten,
> Hath here cut off my lord.
> (IV. ii. 312–16.)

Ignorant of the treachery by which Posthumus was abused, she now rejects the lone truth which she had formerly accepted—that Posthumus had ordered her death:

> To write and read
> Be henceforth treacherous! Damn'd Pisanio
> Hath with his forged letters,—damn'd Pisanio—
> From this most bravest vessel of the world
> Struck the main-top!
> (Ibid. 316–20.)

She is quite mistaken about the drug, and the expression of her error requires the mind to flash once again over the history of the little box, back to Cornelius and the Queen:

> The drug he gave me, which he said was precious
> And cordial to me, have I not found it
> Murd'rous to the senses? That confirms it home.
> (Ibid. 326–8.)

She is wrong at every point—but often with an ironical rightness within the frame of wrongness, as when she imagines that Pisanio and Cloten conspired to kill Posthumus:

> Pisanio might have kill'd thee at the heart
> And left this head on. How should this be? Pisanio?
> 'Tis he and Cloten.
> (Ibid. 322–4.)

Indeed, Pisanio and Cloten collaborated to furnish this bloody sight
—Pisanio supplying Posthumus's suit, Cloten the body.

Deep, genuine, movingly presented, the grief of a paragon for a
paragon, Imogen's anguish demands anguish. Yet simultaneously
we are made to remember that the object of this anguish is the body
of the detested clot-clod, Cloten. Posthumus is alive. Pisanio is true.
Imogen's bitterest queries, striking against our awareness, demand
a shout of laughter: 'Where is thy head? Where's that? Ay me!
where's that?'—for we know that the brute's head has by now
sailed down the creek to the sea, to 'tell the fishes he's the Queen's
son'. Thus the manner of exploitation compels simultaneous tears
and laughter, and at the same time we know that some cause for
comfort surrounds the struggle: for Posthumus is yet living and, if
he were not the victim of Iachimo's practice, would be as loving as
before. But enveloping this seeming comfort that envelops the
conflict of laughter and tears remains our sense of the comfortless
world of the lasting storm—careless, uncontrolled, giving no sign
that all can ever be well again.

For where is Iachimo? From nothing that Shakespeare has told,
shown, or hinted since ii. iv can we think other than that the partner in our black secret has vanished from the earth, leaving no
means by which truth can be exposed.

In the final incident of this extraordinary scene, Imogen, multiple practiser and victim of multiple practices, deceives the Roman
Lucius by continuing to hide her sex and her identity; moreover
she seeks also to hide even what she herself does not know—the
identity of the headless body; once again we have an 'aside' which,
instead of informing us, exploits the unawareness of the speaker:

> *Luc.* Say his name, good friend.
> *Imo.* Richard du Champ. (*Aside.*) If I do lie and do
> No harm by it, though the gods hear, I hope
> They'll pardon it.
> (Ibid. 376-9.)

At once deceiver and deceived, she gets Lucius to bury the body,
and the great scene closes in a flash that illuminates the appalling
depth which hides truths that must somehow be uncovered if
happiness is ever to be restored; says Lucius:

> The boy hath taught us manly duties. Let us
> Find out the prettiest daisied plot we can,
> And make him with our pikes and partisans
> A grave. Come, arm him. Boy, he is preferr'd
> By thee to us. . . .
> (Ibid. 397-401.)

This is Imogen's darkest moment. Her decision to follow Lucius is born of despair that sees no purpose. In a remarkable parallel she has been reduced to the same aimlessness of the defeated Pericles, after learning of Marina's death, *and just before the winds carried him surely to Mytilene and reconciliation.* She has cut herself off from court; Pisanio is false, has tried to kill her, and has killed her husband; Posthumus is just now being laid in his grave. More than ever her pain demands pain of us.

And yet none of it is so: our facts contradict her beliefs at every point. Moreover—again as in *Pericles*—it is in this darkest moment just at the ending of Imogen's soliloquy—

> O!
> Give colour to my pale cheek with thy blood,
> That we the horrider may seem to those
> Which chance to find us. O, my lord, my lord!
> *(Falls on the body.)*
> (IV. ii. 329–32.)

that we catch our first glimpse of dawn through a sudden sign of a kind that has been denied until now. Says the First Captain to Lucius, as they approach the spot where Imogen lies with headless Cloten:

> . . . gentlemen of Italy, most willing spirits
> That promise noble service; and they come
> Under the conduct of bold Iachimo. . . .
> (Ibid. 338–40.)

'Bold Iachimo': the bare mention is nearly worth actual sight. While Iachimo was lost in silence an element indispensable to the clearing of multiple errors was missing; notification of his return from oblivion is notification that all can yet be well. This hint of hope comes just after Imogen, in a gesture marking total defeat, has fallen upon the headless body and daubed her face with its blood.

From Imogen and her darkest moment, in which we are shown light, we go abruptly to the court, to Cymbeline and his darkest moment—in which we are also shown light. To Cymbeline all is quite bleak: his queen is dying, his daughter has vanished, his stepson has vanished, and the Romans have landed on British soil. But for us the first lines have significance like that of the naming of Iachimo just before. Says the King:

> Again, and bring me word how 'tis with her.
> A fever with the absence of her son,
> A madness, of which her life's in danger.
> (IV. iii. 1–3.)

The Queen is a wicked thing, from whose practices sprang all these ills; news of her impending death, in these circumstances, is good news. In other ways also the truth is far better than Cymbeline knows: Imogen—'The great part of my comfort'—who narrowly missed being poisoned by the Queen and raped by Cloten —is, though absent and despairing, safe enough, and Cymbeline cannot imagine by what margin she escaped disaster; if Cloten's disappearance means a loss of support— 'So needful for this present'—yet in our perspective his death removes a source of danger. Moreover, as we learn in the scene that immediately follows, the loss of Cloten's support in the wars is more than compensated by the gain of Belarius and his two lads. At the end of Act IV the evil that the King trusted as good—the Queen and Cloten—is dead or dying; and the true good—his lost sons—of which he is quite ignorant, is rising.

From Cymbeline and his darkness lightened by our knowledge, we go next to Posthumus and his darkness. Here Posthumus holds the bloody cloth sent by Pisanio as proof of Imogen's death, and his soliloquy parallels the heroine's when she awoke to find the body of 'Posthumus' beside her. Though Imogen, abused by Iachimo's trick, had believed Posthumus false, his 'death' blotted memory of her former anger and left only grief; so Posthumus, also abused by Iachimo, now, in grief, pardons her supposed unfaithfulness:

> Gods! if you
> Should have ta'en vengeance on my faults, I never
> Had liv'd to put on this; so had you sav'd
> The noble Imogen to repent, and struck
> Me, wretch, more worth your vengeance.
>
> (v. i. 7–11.)

Mistaken in everything in his darkest moment, as was Imogen, being victim of Iachimo's false proofs of Imogen's infidelity and Pisanio's of her death, Posthumus himself now devises a practice— his first, but the twelfth of the play:

> I'll disrobe me
> Of these Italian weeds and suit myself
> As does a Briton peasant; so I'll fight
> Against the part I come with.
>
> (Ibid. 22–25.)

His donning of disguise and setting off to die in the wars—'For thee, O Imogen, even for whom my life / Is every breath a death' —completes a parallel with Imogen's scene that ended with her aimless departure with Lucius, in the character of a boy who has lost his master.

The paragons, thus, have reached the same depth: each seeks oblivion. While they form an artistic parallel, the two scenes also form a remarkable contrast. As we heard Imogen sobbing over the body of 'Posthumus', our only source of cheer was our knowledge that Cloten, not Posthumus, was dead; otherwise the world surrounding Imogen still was comfortless, the wall of misapprehension too dense to be pierced without an instrument—and Iachimo, the instrument, was not available. But as we hear Posthumus grieving over the bloody cloth standing for Imogen's 'death', not only have we cheer in our knowledge that Imogen is alive—but we have just heard news that has lightened the complexion of the environment: Iachimo is returning, and the Queen is dying. In short, we hear Posthumus's despairing soliloquy with some confidence that all can be well.

Immediately after this soliloquy the dramatist bolsters our assurance: as the opposing forces of Romans and Britons enter, we actually catch sight of Iachimo. It would seem paradoxical that the sight of a villain should be reassuring; ultimately, it is only the sight of omniscient, omnipotent benevolence that can be perfectly reassuring. But Iachimo is more frightening in his absence than in his presence. It is always disconcerting to share a villain's wicked secret while unsuspecting good people are endangered; but it is more so to hold it helplessly alone, the villain having vanished. The restoration of Iachimo is a welcome gift to our awareness, timed to release the mind from its deepest anxiety just as the skirmishes start, which announce the denouement.

The battle scenes of *Cymbeline*, though like earlier battle scenes in form, contrast with all others in Shakespeare in their significance. In the early history plays, and sometimes in the later, the prime purpose of such scenes is that of spectacle itself, when little knots of opposing soldiers, representing armies, meet, fight, go out fighting, return, and fight again, marking the ebb and flow of the general tide. Fortunes rise and fall, the tide turns and turns again, until at last, by a symbolic action involving principal persons, the dramatist represents victory and defeat. The action itself—the sight of men in arms, flights, pursuits, the sound of sword on sword—is the main purpose and significance of these scenes. In the tragedies the mere action of the skirmishes, though often—as in *King Lear* and *Macbeth*—as spectacular as in the histories, is not its only excuse for being; the significance lies in the meaning of the outcome for the protagonist's fate: so especially in *Julius Caesar*, *Macbeth*, *Antony and Cleopatra*, where defeat means personal catastrophe for Brutus, Macbeth, and Antony. But in the skirmishes of *Cymbeline* our attention is directed neither to the spectacle as spectacle nor to the meaning of victory or defeat for the protagonists: whether Romans defeat Britons or Britons Romans is all one to us. Rather, Shakespeare uses these battle scenes as he has used all scenes in the play: as occasions for persons to brush against one another in ignorance. They are only incidentally battle scenes. The dramatic character of *Cymbeline* is implied in the fact that here even the battle skirmish, one of Shakespeare's staples, becomes a device for exploiting discrepancies in awareness.

Thus, the first short scene (v. ii): along with Imogen's funeral scene and her soliloquy over the headless body, this contains some of the most potent exploitation of discrepant awarenesses in all Shakespeare. Says Lucius, '. . . the disorder's such / As war were hoodwinked', and the effects of the scene rise from our recognition that all eight participants, each in his special ways, are hoodwinked. Thus the first incident:

. . . enter again, in skirmish, Iachimo and Posthumus: he vanquisheth and disarmeth Iachimo, and then leaves him.

Says Iachimo privately from his vantage-point just below ours:

> I have belied a lady,
> The Princess of this country, and the air on 't
> Revengingly enfeebles me; or could this carl,
> A very drudge of Nature's, have subdu'd me
> In my profession?
>
> (v. ii. 2–6.)

Our awareness must supply all the meaning of this meeting; what is actually staged is only a means of prompting the real drama in our heads. Deceived by Posthumus's masquerade as a common soldier, Iachimo is ignorant that he has in fact been vanquished by a nobleman, a paragon—what is more, by the very man he had wronged and whose wrong the 'enfeebling air' of the island now truly revenges: this irony goes 'beyond beyond'. Posthumus, recognizing Iachimo and not himself recognized, thereby holds advantage. Yet in seeing and striking Iachimo only as an impersonal enemy, a member of the Roman forces, he does not really see him at all. Iachimo's advantage over Posthumus is thus far greater than Posthumus's over Iachimo: Posthumus's recognition of Iachimo is surrounded by irony while he remains ignorant of how the villain betrayed him.

The second incident also stages a little action that sets a gigantic one going in our heads:

Cymbeline is taken: then enter, to his rescue, Belarius, Guiderius, and Arviragus.

And, a moment later: '*Re-enter Posthumus, and seconds the Britons.*' Belarius, Guiderius, Arviragus, and Posthumus evidently know the King. But in recognizing and rescuing him as King, the mountain youths miss the real point; for us the meaning lies in the fact that he is their father. Belarius, aware of this relationship, occupies the level nearest ours; but he is ignorant of Posthumus's identity. Cymbeline, with his unknown, unknowing sons, occupies the lowest level. Posthumus, unknown son-in-law and unknown and unknowing brother-in-law, stands just above Cymbeline. In any other play of Shakespeare's the event itself—the rescue of the King, signifying British victory—would carry the essential meaning of the scene; but here the event merely provides occasion for exploitation of an extraordinary accumulation of discrepant awarenesses. Battle spectacle here shows only a fragment of the greater matter visible to the mind's eye.

The third and final incident completes the swift review which this scene requires the mind to make of almost every secret in the play: '*Then re-enter Lucius, Iachimo, and Imogen.*' Says Lucius to 'the Princess of this country': 'Away, boy, from the troops, and save thyself.' To Lucius, who knows simply nothing, the action is just a battle between Romans and Britons. Our awareness shrinks that aspect of it to nothing. The entrance of Imogen, disguised British princess, with the Roman army, and in the company of Iachimo, is packed with substance for the mind's eye. The incident parallels the earlier entrance of Posthumus and his encounter with Iachimo: like Posthumus, Imogen is sole proprietor of a special secret, that of her identity, hence knows Iachimo without being known; but Iachimo, though ignorant of Imogen's identity, still holds the greater advantage, for in recognizing Iachimo only, and not his black secret, Imogen recognizes only what is insignificant.

In sum, this scene of but eighteen lines and three brief skirmishes has a rare potency: minute in itself, it forces the mind to review all major lines of action—secrets, practices, errors, and compounded consequences—up to this moment of convergence. Its dramatic potency is to be measured by its effectiveness in activating knowledge stored in our minds, and so measured it must stand with the funeral ceremony for 'Fidele' and Imogen's scene with headless 'Posthumus'. Like these incidents it forces the mind through a course of intricate gymnastics; unlike them it does so through spectacle—battle skirmishes—almost without words. In this way its accomplishment is truly unique.

In the twelfth practice of the play, Posthumus suited himself 'As does a Briton peasant' and in this role aided the mountain youths

and Belarius—'A narrow lane, an old man, and two boys!'—in
rescuing Cymbeline and winning the battle. Now, in the thirteenth
and final practice, he is 'No more a Briton', but has 'resum'd
again / The part I came in'. To drop one's masquerade and return
to one's proper identity would not normally constitute a practice;
but this case is unusual: by taking up his Italian identity again
Posthumus hides the identity of one of the heroes of the narrow
lane and thus creates a mystery that must be cleared. The 'Briton
peasant' was itself, of course, a fiction; Posthumus's return to
'the part I came in' thus draws a second wrap around an identity
already once cloaked. Though the secret of the 'Briton peasant' is
the last to be opened in the scene of the denouement, the dramatist
does not wait to exploit it; we have barely seen Posthumus clothed
again in his Italian suit when two British captains enter:

> *1. Cap.* Great Jupiter be prais'd! Lucius is taken.
>   'Tis thought the old man and his sons were angels.
> *2. Cap.* There was a fourth man, in a silly habit,
>   That gave the affront with them.
>
>   (v. iii. 84–87.)

Having spoken these words they see Posthumus and take him
prisoner: 'Lay hands on him, a dog!' This scene ends in action
which silently exploits immense discrepancies:

> *Enter Cymbeline, Belarius, Guiderius, Arviragus, Pisanio . . . and Roman
> Captives. The Captains present Posthumus to Cymbeline, who delivers him
> over to a Gaoler.*

Excepting the Queen and Cornelius, the play's aggregate of practisers and their victims, of secret-holders and those whom the
secrets most concern, are here brought together: for the first time
since errors began to be compounded, all persons needed for the
recovery of truth and happiness are together before us. And
though the father knows not the sons, the sons either the father or
themselves, the husband the wife, or the wife the husband, the
loyal servant either his master or his mistress—though all present
are deeply submerged in error, yet the very fact of their being
together gives good reason to believe that all can be well.

*But, then, will it have been made well by chance, or by inten-
tion?* It is a fact that until v. iv Shakespeare has exhibited only an
uncontrolled universe the character of which is summed up by
Pisanio's statement in the last line of iv. iii: 'Fortune brings in
some boats that are not steer'd.' By the time of this summation we
have been shown some inconclusive signs that the drift of events

may be toward a happy ending: the death of Cloten; the mention of the imminent arrival in Britain of Iachimo; the report of the Queen's illness. Finally, the summation is itself reassuring, for surely, no matter what force or lack of force brings them in, it is better that boats come in than that they be lost.

But though these signs are reassuring, *they are only signs of favourable chance.* There has been no hint of existence of any directing force: indeed, Pisanio's summation argues that there is none. So far as our awareness was advised, the world of *Pericles*, too, until Act III, lacked a controlling force; then the dramatist—plainly dissatisfied with Gower's whim-directed universe—introduced the extraordinary billow that brought Thaisa's body to Cerimon, and from that point on, by various means, implied the existence of a benevolent intelligence behind the erstwhile seemingly unruled winds and waves. Gower's world of the first two acts of *Pericles* is extended through the first four and a half acts of *Cymbeline*—with nothing even so inconclusive as an extraordinary billow to suggest that any force is in control. Though we finally perceive an auspicious drift, yet we do so with the sense that things might as easily go ill as well. Nevertheless, v. iii makes it plain that *Cymbeline* could now end happily without the services of a controlling force, for all the persons needed to disentangle truth are assembled. The denouement of v. v, that is to say, could follow immediately after v. iii, without v. iv.

But a chance ending, for artistic if not philosophical reasons, was manifestly intolerable to Shakespeare: always, everywhere, he must have a divinity—either within or without man—that shapes the ends of action. Hence in v. iv Jupiter advises us of what we could not have guessed during the first four and a half acts—that the world of *Cymbeline* has been under control all the while; says Jupiter to the spirits of the four Leonati, Posthumus's kin:

> Be not with mortal accidents opprest;
> No care of yours it is; you know 'tis ours.
> Whom best I love I cross; to make my gift,
> The more delay'd, delighted. Be content;
> Your low-laid son our godhead will uplift.
> (v. iv. 99–103.)

This is more than a promise that all will be well: *it is an assertion that all has been well all the while.* During those four and a half acts when we feared that nobody knew the troubles we saw, the action lay in fact in Jupiter's palm—as that of *Measure for Measure* in Vincentio's and that of *The Tempest* in Prospero's.

But the difference is vast: we knew at once about Vincentio and

Prospero, and we were left ignorant of Jupiter. So far as the dramatic effect during the first four and a half acts is concerned, Jupiter had as well not have been, since he was not in our awareness. Yet on the evidence of Shakespeare's usual method, the reason for his introduction of Jupiter is apparent: he would not tolerate action that stumbles to one ending but could have stumbled to another. His means of avoiding an accidental ending is always some controlling force, mortal or immortal: a fairy king, a brilliant heroine in disguise, an all-powerful duke—or a Jupiter. The great question, then, is not why he introduced Jupiter, but why he left us unaware of him until the denouement.

A possible answer is that both *Pericles* and *Cymbeline* are deliberate experiments with the dramatic effects of uncertainty. This answer would make it appear that the dramatist toys with us during the first four and a half acts just as Jupiter toyed with Imogen and Posthumus, and for the same reason: 'Whom best I love I cross; to make my gift, / The more delay'd, delighted.' One formula, at least, is common to *Pericles* and *Cymbeline*: it is to make good people—Pericles, Thaisa, Marina; Cymbeline, Imogen, Posthumus—believe at first that they have suffered irreparable loss in an indifferent universe, and then to restore all. Applied to our own awareness, the formula is not quite so severe in these plays: though we are long denied the comforting knowledge that the world is benevolently controlled and are therefore subjected to the anxiety that comes of uncertainty, we are not made to believe that anyone has suffered irrecoverable loss. We know that death has not claimed Pericles' Thaisa and Marina, Imogen's Posthumus, or Posthumus's Imogen. But in the third romance, *The Winter's Tale*, as will be seen, the dramatist, *progressively deepening our anxiety* in the plays of the lasting storm, applies the same formula to our awareness as to that of Leontes: we, too, are made to believe that Hermione is dead. After reaching this extremity, Shakespeare returns to his old, habitual way: we are advised of Prospero immediately after the opening scene of *The Tempest*, and thereafter misgivings are impossible. If, therefore, the withholding of reassurance was a deliberate experiment, it was followed by quick, absolute repudiation. There are some objections to regarding it so, however, and there are other possible answers; but these must wait on the evidence of *The Winter's Tale* and *The Tempest*.

In any event, the introduction of Jupiter, however belated, serves unqualified notice that all now not only will but must be, and in fact always has been, well. It thus prevents the appearance of adventitious action running to adventitious ending. It enables us to watch the tortuous denouement with minds free from anxiety. From this point of view it is an artistic masterstroke.

But it is also an artistic fraud. The fact is that at the end of v. iii all lines of action have converged and all elements needed for a happy ending have been assembled; but more, it is a fact that to the denouement of v. v the eagle-borne Jupiter of v. iv actually contributes nothing but a riddling prophecy for the Soothsayer to interpret—and even this comes late, after all the secrets have been opened, and serves only to seem to prove Jupiter's earlier claim that he knew and controlled all, all the while. It is not Jupiter—nor is it Posthumus, to whom Jupiter appeared and on whose breast the prophetic tablet was laid—*but the bright-eyed heroine herself* who, having glimpsed a ring on the captive Iachimo's finger, finds her way up through mountains of error to the truth. So Jupiter is an artistic fraud—but perhaps the shrewdest in the plays. For while he gives the look of intention to what would otherwise seem accident, he actually does nothing, but leaves the participants to find their own way. As *deus ex machina* he is thus at once indispensable and superfluous.

The denouement, then, runs from v. iii to the end, with Jupiter serving only as a reassuring illusion. This is Shakespeare's longest final scene, and all but the very first and very last lines bustle with the exposure of secrets—for the preceding acts have buried more truths more deeply than in any other play. The opening of no other final scene finds our awareness so laden with secrets; no other finds the vision of so many participants so limited to small corners and pockets. The *King* is ignorant (1) that the Queen contrived the separation of Imogen and Posthumus for her own and Cloten's gain; (2) that Imogen lives and is present as the Roman page; (3) that the heroes who rescued him are his sons and his old servant; (4) that the prisoner he has handed over to the gaoler is Posthumus; (5) that this same prisoner was the fourth hero of the narrow lane. *Imogen* is ignorant (1) that both she and Posthumus were abused by Iachimo; (2) that Posthumus lives and is present; (3) that Pisanio was and is loyal; (4) that the rustics are her brothers; (5) that the drug given her by Pisanio was intended by the Queen to be fatal; (6) that she escaped death only by virtue of the physician's counter-practice. *Posthumus* is ignorant (1) that he and Imogen were abused by Iachimo; (2) that Pisanio deceived him with a false token of Imogen's death; (3) that Imogen is present as the Roman page; (4) that the mountaineers with whom he saved the kingdom are his brothers-in-law. *Arviragus* and *Guiderius* are ignorant (1) that they are princes; (2) that 'Fidele' was their sister;

(3) that she yet lives and is present as the Roman page; (4) that their heroic assistant in the battle of the narrow lane was their brother-in-law and that he is present now in Roman dress. *Belarius* is ignorant (1) that 'Fidele' was sister to the King's sons; (2) that she is alive and present as the Roman page. *Iachimo* is ignorant that both his victims are present. *Lucius* is ignorant that his page is Cymbeline's daughter—and of all that led to her final masquerade. *Pisanio* is ignorant (1) that the drug given him by the Queen was meant to kill him; (2) that both his master and his mistress are present.

At the same time that each is ignorant of others' secrets, most participants are also either proprietors of current practices or secret-sharers of past practices that contributed to the present condition. Only Cymbeline and Lucius are denied the privilege of holding any secrets. *Cornelius* alone knows that the Queen—whose death and true character are quickly reported—intended murder, and that the drug with which he provided her was capable of producing only the appearance of death. *Iachimo* alone bears the secret of the 'proofs' of Imogen's infidelity. *Pisanio* alone holds the secret of his deception of Posthumus in Imogen's 'death', and of Cloten's practice in dressing himself as Posthumus. *Imogen* holds the secret of her own identity and of her former role as 'Fidele'. *Posthumus* holds the secret of his double masquerade—as the heroic Briton, and, just now, as the Roman prisoner. *Belarius* alone holds the secret of the rustic youths' identities. *Arviragus* and *Guiderius*, with Belarius, hold the secret of Cloten's disappearance. Such is the general disposition of awarenesses at the opening of the most elaborate final scene in Shakespeare. What is most remarkable is that, though the strands are many and marvellously intertwined, nothing snarls, and no loose end remains at last.

Jupiter being absent, no participant knows all that we know, but each fact of ours is known to some participant. Our vantage-point is perfect; as usual the denouement has nothing to expose to us. For us, then, the experience of the closing scene is that of witnessing the revelation of secrets that have been locked in our minds, and of observing the effects of their revelation upon the persons who have been ignorant of them and to whom they are of most concern: of being at hand when Imogen learns that Posthumus lives, when Posthumus learns that Imogen lives and is chaste, when Cymbeline learns that the heroes who saved his kingdom are his own sons and his son-in-law. The process of making everything known is extended and exploited as nowhere else in Shakespeare. The release of each secret accomplishes a welcome reduction, degree by degree, of the pressure that has been mounting in our minds since error first began to pile on error; one effect of the scene, thus, is the relief of overmuch understanding, painful because it has been unsharable.

From the first comedies Shakespeare has concentrated exploitative efforts upon two great moments: *that in which ignorance has achieved greatest depth and universality, and that in which persons who have acted in ignorance learn of their errors.* *Cymbeline* surpasses all other plays in the celebration of these contrasting moments—the first, already examined, 'Fidele's' funeral and Imogen's soliloquy over 'Posthumus's' body; and the second, now, the explosion of secrets in the closing scene. Never one to surrender a secret until he has exhausted its potentiality, Shakespeare relieves pressures on our awareness only after a last intensification which raises them to the bursting-point. Thus when Iachimo has told how he destroyed Posthumus's faith in Imogen, the hero advances, identifies himself, curses Iachimo, and falls to berating himself for the Imogen he supposes dead. There is wilful cruelty to us in this last-minute exploitation of the space between Posthumus's ignorance and our awareness that Imogen stands within arm's length! Posthumus's speech raises the pressure to where the pain of the unsharable becomes excruciating. But Shakespeare is not yet through with us. Since the pressure can be raised no further by verbal exploitation, he raises it by physical action to the level of bursting:

> *Post.*   Imogen,
>   Imogen, Imogen!
> *Imo.*   Peace, my lord; hear, hear—
> *Post.* Shall's have a play of this? Thou scornful page,
>   There lie thy part.   (*Striking her; she falls.*)
>   (v. v. 226–9.)

This is a final turn of the screw. The physical blow, the ultimate expression of Posthumus's unawareness, is followed instantly by relief, with Pisanio's 'O, my Lord Posthumus! / You ne'er kill'd Imogen till now.'

This effective, if cruel, formula the dramatist repeats in yielding the last great secret. Guiderius grandly announces that it was he who slew Cloten: 'I have spoke it, and I did it.' Cymbeline, who earlier had knighted Belarius and the unknown youths for their heroic stand that saved his kingdom, now condemns Guiderius: 'Thou'rt dead.' Through forty lines, from Guiderius's confession until Belarius makes known the youths' royalty, Shakespeare sustains the painful pressure of our awareness by exploiting the King's unawareness that he has condemned his own son. Though no blow like that which felled Imogen is struck, yet physical action again pushes pressure to the bursting-point when Guiderius is roughly seized by guards. This time it is Belarius whose word releases the pressure: 'Let his arms alone; / They were not born for bondage.'

Thus it is throughout: the periods between successive revelations are busy with last-moment exploitation which intensifies pressure just before it is released. Though the method itself is not new, it differs both in extent of use and in purpose from Shakespeare's practice in the comedies. In these, through *Twelfth Night*, it was usually for a last laugh that secrets were given a final squeeze before surrender. After *Twelfth Night* final exploitation aims less at laughter, more at emotional thrill that edges on pain. In *Measure for Measure*, where physical violence is first used to reach the bursting-point, the effect is mixed emotional thrill and laughter when the 'friar' is seized, and Lucio snatches off his hood. Then, in *Pericles*, when Pericles, angry at the universe, spitefully thrusts his daughter aside, the comic is quite absent. *Cymbeline* simply goes further in the same direction, when Posthumus strikes Imogen to the ground. The total denouement is thus a spectacle of controlled violence, with pent-up pressures bursting as gaps between participants' awarenesses and ours are suddenly closed: pain rushes out as joy rushes in—and the final effect is that of calm after great storm. 'The fingers of the powers above', says Jupiter's accomplice, the Soothsayer, hastily reasserting his master's highly dubious claim to have brought about this happy ending,

> The fingers of the powers above do tune
> The harmony of this peace.

3. *The Winter's Tale*

When skill in the total management of complex dispositions of awareness is principally considered, no play of Shakespeare's could succeed *Cymbeline* without appearing anti-climactic. Yet *The Winter's Tale*—which does succeed it—is not lacking in features of unusual interest when it is similarly considered; and some of these features are even unique.

The Winter's Tale presents the next-to-final world of the lasting storm; but it presents the last in which we are made to think that the storm is uncontrolled. In this respect, moreover, it outdoes its predecessors. The worlds of the preceding romances are dangerous-seeming; their inhabitants stumble about in darkness and express

dismay at the enveloping adversity, while we are denied certainty
that they will either find their own salvation or be guided to it by
some external intelligence. But though comfort is denied us until it
begins to glimmer through hints in Act III of *Pericles* and through
signs of apparently accidentally converging lines of action at the
end of Act IV in *Cymbeline*, still in these plays Shakespeare never
actually tells us that comfort is impossible: he merely withholds it.
But in III. ii of *The Winter's Tale* he tells us flatly that we can have
no true comfort, because what has happened is beyond remedy: '*I
say she's dead; I'll swear it.*'

Always before we have at least shared the best-informed participant's awareness, and often ours has transcended his. Uniquely in
The Winter's Tale, we are not even allowed to know who *is* the
best-informed person. Aside from this crippling 'defect—which
both denies us comfort and prevents the dramatist from establishing
what might have been the play's most exploitable discrepancy—our
vision is unimpaired. Within the new and comfortless frame remain
the old familiar patterns of practisers, practices, and practisees, of
secrets and secret-holders, and of discrepancies that are exploitable
because we have a superior vantage-point. In all, we hold advantage
over one or more participants in twelve of fifteen scenes—a high
proportion, exceeded in few plays. We hold advantage also, at some
time, over every named person—even over Paulina during portions
of those very acts in which we are ignorant that her secret is more
momentous than all of ours together.

Though the total machinery used in creating, maintaining, and
exploiting discrepancies is simpler and the number of discrepancies
accordingly much reduced, the gaps that are opened between the
participants' awareness and ours are managed in ways very like
those of *Cymbeline*. With less elaborateness, here are the same
developments of conditions of unawareness within conditions of
unawareness, the same accumulations of error, the same graftings of
new misapprehensions on old, central ones. But even while the
familiar business of exploitation is going on before what we suppose
to be our all-seeing eyes, we are prevented from seeing the crucial
fact. It is therein that *The Winter's Tale* differs from all other plays
of Shakespeare.

Among the unique features of the management of awarenesses in
The Winter's Tale, the first is the means by which the initial discrepancy is created. Says Leontes, watching his wife and Polixenes:

> (*Aside.*) Too hot, too hot!
> To mingle friendship far is mingling bloods.
> I have *tremor cordis* on me; my heart dances,

But not for joy; not joy. This entertainment
May a free face put on, derive a liberty
From heartiness, from bounty, fertile bosom,
And well become the agent; 't may, I grant;
But to be paddling palms and pinching fingers,
As now they are, and making practis'd smiles,
As in a looking-glass; and then to sigh, as 'twere
The mort o' th' deer;—O, that is entertainment
My bosom likes not, nor my brows!
(I. ii. 108–19.)

This is the seed from which all grows, as in *Cymbeline* the prolifera-
tion of mishap and error rises from the Queen's practice which
causes the King to separate Imogen and Posthumus. But Cymbeline
is deceived by the device of a cunning practiser—and Leontes is
self-deceived. It is a surprising fact, in view of his large number of
deceived persons, that Leontes is Shakespeare's lone example of
unqualified self-deception. Most deceived persons in the plays are
fooled by a practice known to us—as Orlando by Rosalind's disguise, Claudio by Don John's scene at Hero's window, Claudius by
Hamlet's antic disposition, Brutus by Cassius's anonymous letters,
Macbeth by the witches' prophecies, Othello by Iago's machinations: the list is almost endless. A smaller number of persons are so
susceptible to deception and so simple as to *seem* self-deceived, and
with some of these self-deception takes control after their weak-
nesses have been first abused by an external practice. Sir Andrew
Aguecheek is highly susceptible to deception, but, like Bottom, is
congenitally unaware rather than self-deceived, and is deceived
only by Sir Toby's practices. The Falstaff of *The Merry Wives of
Windsor*, though overripe and ready to fall, nevertheless does not
fall, but is plucked: everyone deceives him, but he is not self-
deceived. These cases are nearer to Leontes than even Macbeth and
Othello, yet one cannot say that they are examples of pure self-
deception, or that self-deception rather than external practice is the
starting-point of the final error. Of course the nearest of all to
Leontes is Olivia's steward, whose day-dreams of 'Count Malvolio'
precede his finding the letter that is Maria's practice on him; but
Malvolio would unmistakably live on and on in his dreams, as he has
been living for some time, and would never cross over the line and
expose himself but for Maria. He is not truly self-deceived, because
until he finds the forged letter he does not truly believe.

But no one practices on Leontes: his error is initiated and fed
wholly from within. The conduct of Hermione and Polixenes at the
moment his *tremor cordis* begins would not upset a balanced mind,
and their talk is as chaste as their conduct:

291

Pol.　　　　　　　We were, fair Queen,
　　　Two lads that thought there was no more behind
　　　But such a day to-morrow as to-day,
　　　And to be boy eternal.
Her.　　　　　　　　　Was not my lord
　　　The verier wag o' th' two?
Pol.　　We were as twinn'd lambs that did frisk i' th' sun,
　　　And bleat the one at th' other. What we chang'd
　　　Was innocence for innocence; we knew not
　　　The doctrine of ill-doing, no, nor dream'd
　　　That any did.
　　　　　　　　　　　　　　　　　(I. ii. 62–71.)

'Is he won yet?' asks Leontes. 'He'll stay, my lord', replies Hermione. And Leontes: 'At my request he would not.' With this first sign of doubt in Leontes' mind, a rift begins to divide our awareness and his. In the next moment, when Hermione gives Polixenes her hand, *tremor cordis* strikes Leontes, and the rift is a gulf. Leontes' un-awareness is more precisely false awareness, and in this respect is identical to that of Posthumus when he believes Imogen unfaithful. But the sources of their common error are quite different—the one lying entirely within, the other entirely without. Posthumus is confronted with seemingly irrefutable proofs and deceived in spite of himself; but Leontes' own mind generates its initial suspicion and thereafter clings to what is false despite strong contrary evidence.

As the action proceeds, Leontes' condition is called variously a 'diseas'd opinion', a 'weak-hing'd fancy'. It is said that 'The root of his opinion . . . is rotten / As ever oak or stone was sound'. He is 'in rebellion with himself', possessed with 'dangerous unsafe lunes'. His condition gives the dramatist an angle of exploitation different from any earlier used, even in the case of Posthumus's false belief. Whereas Posthumus laments for and resists what seems truth forced on him, Leontes gloats on his own perspicacity, having perceived what no one else can see:

　　　　　　　　There have been,
　　　Or I am much deceived, cuckolds ere now;
　　　And many a man there is, even at this present,
　　　Now while I speak this, holds his wife by th' arm,
　　　That little thinks she has been sluic'd in's absence
　　　And his pond fish'd by his next neighbour, by
　　　Sir Smile, his neighbour.
　　　　　　　　　　　　　　　　(Ibid. 190–6.)

Posthumus, confronted with irrefutable proofs, would snatch any shred of contrary evidence; Leontes, having no proofs, spurns truth's attempts to penetrate his senses. Exploitation, thus, is concentrated on repeated exposures of Leontes' determination to be-

lieve what is false, to resist truth—that is to say, to be self-deceived.
In his determination he differs notably even from Othello, whose
situation much resembles this. It is noteworthy that Iago avoids the
risk of allowing Othello's mind to rest, feeding it poison incessantly.
But Camillo, Antigonus, other lords, Paulina, and Hermione herself
strive desperately to force truth into the sealed mind of Leontes.
Says Antigonus:

> You are abus'd, and by some putter-on
> That will be damn'd for't; would I knew the villain,
> I would land-damn him.
>
> (Ibid. 141–3.)

Antigonus is at once right and wrong; the King is abused, but by no
'putter-on' except his own fancy; he has no Iago, Iachimo, or Don
John. At great risk to herself Paulina descends on him like a fury,
carrying the new-born Perdita:

> I'll not call you tyrant;
> But this most cruel usage of your queen,
> Not able to produce more accusation
> Than your own weak-hing'd fancy, something savours
> Of tyranny, and will ignoble make you,
> Yea, scandalous to the world.
>
> (II. iii. 116–21.)

Even this effort fails, and Leontes proceeds with Hermione's 'trial'.

The primary, nearly sole, source of dramatic effect during the
long period from the first sign of 'diseas'd opinion' in I. ii ('At my
request he would not') until the abrupt recovery of sanity in III. ii
('I have too much believ'd mine own suspicion') is the exploitable
gap between Leontes' error and our truth. During part of this
period a secondary gap exists also—for other participants are at first
ignorant that error has seized Leontes. In succession Mamillius,
Hermione and Polixenes, Camillo, Polixenes again, and finally Hermione again are shown to stand below Leontes' level—even while
he labours under error and they do not. First is Mamillius, with a
child's innocence of what has infected his father's brain to make
him talk so wildly. Next are Hermione and Polixenes, on first
hearing Leontes' suddenly wild and whirling words:

> Pol. What means Sicilia?
> Her. He something seems unsettled.
> (I. ii. 146–7.)

Camillo's ignorance that the King is obsessed is the subject of exploitation during a hundred lines. When finally Leontes accuses
Hermione, Camillo instantly perceives the error: 'Good my lord, be

cur'd / Of this diseas'd opinion, and betimes; / For 'tis most dangerous.' Hermione, to whom it matters most, remains longest oblivious
to what has happened, and the dramatist makes exquisite use of her
ignorance in her conversation with Mamillius at the opening of
Act II, when neither dreams what storm is about to burst. Elsewhere most often complex and, especially in the earlier works,
aimed at creation of great flares of irony, exploitation here is subtle,
seeming almost to *avoid* exploitation; its force lies in its simplicity,
especially at the end of the conversation, when the child's chatter
gathers giant resonance from the dome of our awareness:

> *Her.*   Pray you, sit by us,
> And tell's a tale.
> *Mam.*   Merry or sad shall't be?
> *Her.* As merry as you will.
> *Mam.* A sad tale's best for winter. I have one
> Of sprites and goblins.
> *Her.*   Let's have that, good sir.
> Come on, sit down; come on, and do your best
> To fright me with your sprites; you're powerful at it.
> *Mam.* There was a man—
> *Her.*   Nay, come, sit down; then on.
> *Mam.* Dwelt by a churchyard. I will tell it softly;
> Yond crickets shall not hear it.
> *Her.*   Come on, then,
> And give't me in mine ear.
>   (II. i. 22–32.)

It is with the last line that the storm breaks: Leontes enters, and the
winter's tale has begun.

When Claudio of *Much Ado about Nothing* denounces Hero at
the altar, we find cheer in our knowledge that her defamers are
already captured and that all will be well. When Claudio of *Measure
for Measure* hears of Angelo's impossible terms for sparing his life,
we know that the mighty Duke hears them also. But during the
terrible period from I. ii, when lunacy first claims Leontes, until
III. ii, when it abruptly releases its hold—during the period, that is,
when the mad King turns tyrant, rejects the brave lords who dare
to argue with him, condemns Hermione, orders the prison-born
infant abandoned in 'some remote and desert place', and, in general,
stands for evil against good—we know of no possible source whence
comfort can come to oppose the swelling discomfort. Suddenly put
on trial for life and honour, Hermione utters a cry that raises the
crucial question:

> If powers divine
> Behold our human actions, as they do,

> I doubt not then but innocence shall make
> False accusation blush, and tyranny
> Tremble at patience.
>
> (III. ii. 29–33.)

'If ... as they do'—but we have been advised of no power that can check Leontes, as Vincentio could check Angelo. Even in the bleak world of *Pericles* we have a first hint in III. ii that intelligence lies behind the storm. In *The Winter's Tale* we have no such sign. True, we have heard Jove's name mentioned, and messengers have been sent to Apollo's temple:

> Yet, for a greater confirmation,
> For in an act of this importance 'twere
> Most piteous to be wild, I have dispatch'd in post
> To sacred Delphos, to Apollo's temple,
> Cleomenes and Dion, whom you know
> Of stuff'd sufficiency.
>
> (Ibid. 180–5.)

But though we can assume that the oracles will reveal truth and that the messengers will return in time, Shakespeare has portrayed a Leontes so crazed that we cannot imagine he will believe oracles any more than his own counsellors—who,

> ... or stupefied
> Or seeming so in skill, cannot or will not
> Relish a truth like us. ...
>
> (Ibid. 165–7.)

In his 'dangerous unsafe lunes' he will deny the oracle as he has denied Camillo, Antigonus, and Paulina: the representation of the King's mind seems calculated to forbid hope that he will do otherwise.

Moreover, at the opening of Act III, when the messengers are shown returning from Delphos, Shakespeare alters his usual method of making one scene cast special light on the next. Though we learn that the messengers have returned safely with word from Delphos, they do not themselves know what the word is. Knowing Hermione innocent and assuming that an oracle would know as much as we, we cannot doubt what the sealed package holds. But ordinarily this scene would have been used to make the point unmistakable: the messengers would know what word of 'Apollo's great divine' they are carrying, and would tell us. We would then go to Hermione's trial positive, at least, that the oracle had spoken true; as it is, we go without confirmation that it has told truth—and of course doubtful that Leontes would believe, in any event. Preparation for the trial

295

scene thus runs counter to Shakespeare's typical method. Instead of reassuring us he has avoided obvious means of reassurance.

With respect to the management of awarenesses, Leontes' uncompromised self-deception is the first unique feature of *The Winter's Tale*. The second is the deliberate deception of ourselves. Whereas in comedy before *Pericles* and *Cymbeline* he took great care to give us comfort during the participants' worst moments, and whereas in the first romances he merely withheld information that would have given comfort, but told us no lies, in *The Winter's Tale* Shakespeare wilfully serves us false information with the clear intent that we believe it:

> O lords,
> When I have said, cry 'Woe!'—the Queen, the Queen,
> The sweet'st, dear'st creature's dead, and vengeance for't
> Not dropp'd down yet.

1. Lord.   The higher pow'rs forbid!

Paul.   I say she's dead; I'll swear't. If word nor oath
> Prevail not, go and see. If you can bring
> Tincture or lustre in her lip, her eye,
> Heat outwardly or breath within, I'll serve you
> As I would do the gods.

> (III. ii. 200–8.)

Neither word nor tone hints that the information is false. On the contrary, all is designed to show it true. We know Paulina, our informant, as an outspoken, strong-willed woman—'When she will take the rein I let her run'—whose characterization has suggested that she would be the last person to invent a practice of any kind: she is not a secretive sort, but always speaks right out, even to an angry king. Moreover—if more were needed—the *true* report of Mamillius's death, brought in just before the false one of Hermione's, contributes to the supposition that the latter is to be accepted also; indeed, it appears even that Mamillius is introduced into the play so that report of his death will help to deceive us about Hermione's. Next, just as the scene ends, Leontes, deceived like us, removes any possible doubt by referring to the dead bodies and his future plans:

> Prithee, bring me
> To the dead bodies of my queen and son.
> One grave shall be for both; upon them shall
> The causes of their death appear, unto
> Our shame perpetual. Once a day I'll visit
> The chapel where they lie, and tears shed there
> Shall be my recreation.

> (Ibid. 235–41.)

And finally, at the opening of the following scene, Antigonus, *who had left the court for the shores of Bohemia before Hermione's death was reported*, recounts his dream of her ghostly visit, and he concludes: 'I do believe Hermione hath suffer'd death.' This is proof beyond proof: should any doubt have lingered in our minds, the supernatural evidence is infallible. Hermione is dead. Shakespeare has used his best means to tell us so.

At the end of III. ii, then, one play, the tragedy of Leontes, ends: Mamillius is dead; Hermione is dead; the new-born child has been taken 'to some place / Where chance may nurse or end it'. The King's tragic flow of jealousy has destroyed all his family and left him only a living death.

Our advantage over participants has ended also: it is a third unique feature of *The Winter's Tale* that at this point, when in the comedies the greatest accumulation of ignorances is being exploited most actively, we know no secrets. Leontes' eyes have been opened, not by the word from Apollo but by the word of Mamillius's death, which he takes as a judgement: 'Apollo's angry; and the heavens themselves / Do strike at my injustice.' Cured of his lunacy by shock, he stands even with us again, and the scene is left without an exploitable discrepancy for nearly a hundred lines—an unprecedented occurrence in Shakespeare at the end of the third act.

But most unusual of all is our lack at this point of any advantage that gives us comfort. The situation contrasts, in this respect, not only with that which exists in the middle of the comedies, but even with that which exists in the middle of the preceding romances. Pericles supposes Thaisa dead, but we know her to be alive. Posthumus supposes Imogen first false and later dead, and Imogen supposes Posthumus first false and later dead, but we know that both live true. Accordingly, though at these points in *Pericles* and *Cymbeline* we lack assurance that all will be well, *we know that there is at least a chance it may be*—for death has not sealed off the possibility. But in *The Winter's Tale* death has struck. The situation and the tone of the final 100 lines of III. ii are comparable only to the last moments of tragedy. Two of the family of Leontes are dead, the third cast forth to crows; Leontes looks ahead only to grief and death.

The fire that seems thus to have died entirely is saved, *as it chances*, by a surviving spark; the formal link between the two parts of the drama is III. iii, in which Antigonus lays down the infant Perdita on the sea-coast of Bohemia—observing to the letter Leontes' order to leave it 'Where chance may nurse or end it'. More precisely, the first half of this scene, ending with Antigonus's flight with a bear in pursuit, belongs with the first part of the play: it is the post-catastrophe—the final confirmation of the tragedy of Leontes.

Knowing, while he does not, that Leontes, his lunacy cured, would no longer wish his baby left to perish in this savage place, we hold a fearful advantage over Antigonus as he puts Perdita down. The effect which comes of our advantage is not comparable to any in comedy, but most resembles that when Romeo poisons himself, believing Juliet dead, when in fact the blood is just returning to her cheeks, or that created when Othello smothers his innocent wife. In the comedies the effect is typically the converse of this, as when Claudio of *Much Ado about Nothing* denounces Hero, while we have assurance that all is well. Here we have no assurance, but watch Antigonus perform an act that might be as irrevocable as Romeo's and Othello's. It might be—or it might not.

The moment during which all attention is concentrated on the infant Perdita, lying alone on the wild shore after Antigonus has fled with the bear at his heels and before the Shepherd enters, is the crucial one of *The Winter's Tale*. Along with Gower's image of the ship bobbing like a duck on the seas of *Pericles*, it is a telling symbol of the way of the world in the first three romances: a world which does not appear to be run, but only to run; a huge world, quite indifferent to its puny inhabitants. While Perdita lies alone, the bear may return, and all will end. It may return—or it may not: the instant is precariously suspended between past and future.

By chance, before the bear returns or a wolf comes, a Shepherd, *going angrily about business quite unconnected with the affairs of Leontes*, hunting two sheep that have been scared away from the flock by the hunting-horns of irresponsible youth—'these boil'd brains of nineteen and two-and-twenty'—finds the child instead: 'I'll take it up for pity.' By so thin a thread old action passes over to the new. 'Thou met'st with things dying', says the Shepherd to the Clown, who has described the shipwreck and the bear's feast: 'Thou met'st with things dying, I with things new-born.'

Of the Sicilians who carried Perdita to Bohemia, none escapes to tell Leontes of the fate of the child and the others on this wild coast 'famous for the creatures / Of prey that keep upon't'. The mariners are drowned, and Antigonus devoured: '. . . how the poor souls roared, and the sea mock'd them; and how the poor gentleman roared and the bear mock'd him'. So far as participants' knowledge is concerned, then, the break with the past is complete, and we are left alone with the full secret of Perdita's identity. Never before—even in *Cymbeline*, where only a villain who vanishes for two acts shares the truth with us—has an indispensable key been placed so precariously as in the hands of the two people who share a portion of our secret: the doddering, greedy, but good-hearted Shepherd, and his clown son, whose 'innocence . . . seems much'. Not only are they ignorant of the true significance of the papers which contain the 'character' of Perdita—'look thee, a bearing cloth for a squire's child!'—but they intend to hide what they do know: 'Up with 't, keep it close. Home, home, the next way. We are lucky, boy; and to be so still requires nothing but secrecy.'

It is another unique feature of the disposition of awarenesses in *The Winter's Tale* that the heroine herself, being an infant, is ignorant of her identity. In the comedies their identities were the heroines' best secrets: Julia, Rosalind, Portia, Viola, and Helena thus held a leverage that meant, in varying degree, control of their worlds. In the first two romances, even in their worst trials—Marina in the brothel and Imogen crying over Cloten's body—the heroines at least knew themselves when others did not know them. From Rosalind, who masqueraded for the joy of the game, to Perdita, who is ignorant that she masquerades at all, is a long way for heroines down the scale of awareness and control. Born in prison and abandoned to chance on the savage coast of an alien land, where wind, sea, bears, and wolves roar 'A lullaby too rough', the lost one begins her career amid less auspicious circumstances than did any predecessor—and with considerably less competence to deal with life. Earlier heroines, self-sufficient in their easier worlds, had relatively minor difficulties from which they extricated themselves with strength to spare; Perdita, quite helpless, survives her initial peril only because the Shepherd happens to arrive before the bear returns. The beginning is prophetic: in all that follows she takes her place with Miranda of *The Tempest* as one whose affairs must be managed by others' stronger hands. Having survived the initial danger, however, she is never again in quite such danger. As in *Pericles* the winds subside after the third tempest, so in *The Winter's Tale* the world brightens after Perdita has survived her perilous moment on the seashore.

Our possession of the secret of Perdita's royalty gives us advantage, then, over her and all other participants during the last two acts. The resultant gap, though single, is rich, and Shakespeare begins at once to exploit it. Old Time prepares us to recognize Perdita in Act IV as a maid of sixteen, 'now grown in grace / Equal with wond'ring'. We hold instant advantage over Camillo and Polixenes, therefore, when they speak of Florizel's mysterious absences from court and his visits to a shepherd's house; says Camillo:

· I have heard, sir, of such a man, who hath a daughter of most rare note. The report of her is extended more than can be thought to begin from such a cottage. (IV. ii. 47–50.)

Our advantage continues while Polixenes devises a practice:

Thou shalt accompany us to the place; where we will, not appearing what we are, have some question with the shepherd; from whose simplicity I think it not uneasy to get the cause of my son's resort thither. (Ibid. 52–56.)

Until this point *The Winter's Tale* has lacked its quota of practices. The initial error resulted from Leontes' self-deception rather than from practice; soon thereafter Leontes tried unsuccessfully to involve Camillo in a fatal practice, a poison plot against Polixenes; Camillo then counter-practised by aiding Polixenes' flight. Neither practice made a discrepancy available for exploitation. When Polixenes and Camillo don disguise to visit the Shepherd's cottage, then, the discrepancy created is the first that results from a practice.

From the point of view of the management of awarenesses, the most complex and most effective scene in *The Winter's Tale* is IV. iv—the sheep-shearing. Bedecked with rural trappings, alive with shepherds and shepherdesses, seeming-shepherds and seeming-shepherdesses, bright with costumery, spectacular to the eye, resonant with music, song, and the babble of voices, a feast for eye and ear—this is a pastoral scene like no other. The sparkling lyrics of Autolycus—'inkles, caddises, cambrics, lawns. Why, he sings 'em over as they were gods or goddesses'—the general holiday spirit, the dance of the twelve Satyrs: all this would be abundance if there were nothing more. But even at first, and certainly in the middle and last stages of his career, there was never enough for Shakespeare in such things alone. While there is rich spectacle for the eye and fine sound for the ear, there must always be that also which busies the mind's eye and the mind's ear.

At the sheep-shearing the pastoral is only a setting: the drama goes on in our heads, where enforced, incessant activity is the price we pay for possessing our two great secrets—the identities of Perdita and King Polixenes. The advantages we hold are alerted and set at their complex tasks of interpretation and adjustment by the first passages of the scene. The 'Shepherdess' Perdita appears, dressed like royalty. It is a brilliant new use of an old device: the masquerader unknowingly masquerading as what she is in fact, while the dialogue reminds that she, with all Bohemia, is ignorant what she is. The next lines exploit the same difference between our awareness and hers and also, by touching what we learned in the preceding scene from Camillo and the King, exploit the second gap:

Even now I tremble
To think your father, by some accident,
Should pass this way as you did. O, the Fates!
How would he look to see his work, so noble,
Vilely bound up?

(IV. iv. 18–22.)

Thus from its opening Shakespeare's sheep-shearing is more than
pastoral spectacle. Within the ornamental trappings moves complex dramatic machinery, as dialogue and action busy the mind
with attention to its two great secrets. Autolycus's lyrics and the
Satyrs' dance are bright incidents set within an elaborate frame of
awareness—not so elaborate but otherwise like that which encloses,
and enhances, the rustics' dirge for Fidele in *Cymbeline*. Throughout the scene exploitation alternately strikes the two principal
dramatic facts—and sometimes both together, as when the disguised
King and the unknowing Princess masquerading as royalty, brought
face to face, speak with a profundity that neither recognizes:

Pol.   Wherefore, gentle maiden,
       Do you neglect them?
Per.   For I have heard it said
       There is an art which in their piedness shares
       With great creating Nature.
Pol.   Say there be;
       Yet Nature is made better by no mean
       But Nature makes that mean; so, over that art
       Which you say adds to Nature, is an art
       That Nature makes. You see, sweet maid, we marry
       A gentle scion to the wildest stock,
       And make conceive a bark of baser kind
       By bud of nobler race. This is an art
       Which does mend Nature, change it rather, but
       The art itself is Nature.

(Ibid. 85–97.)

In ignorance Polixenes touches truth—for the festive queenliness of
Perdita is also real; and Perdita, in her turn, touches it also:

       Methinks I play as I have seen them do
       In Whitsun pastorals. Sure this robe of mine
       Does change my disposition.

(Ibid. 133–5.)

'I will begin / The fashion: less without and more within', said Post-
humus of *Cymbeline*, donning a peasant's garb: with Guiderius and
Arviragus in their cave, with Imogen in page's garb, with absolute
Marina in the brothel, and with Pericles in the rusty armour of 'the

301

mean knight', the inner royalty shines through the humble covering.
Perdita wears hers with a difference: royalty shines through the
'prank'd up' queenliness; says Polixenes:

> Nothing she does or seems
> But smacks of something greater than herself,
> Too noble for this place.
>
> (IV. iv. 157–9.)

All the exploitable secrets of the scene concern identities.
Polixenes recognizes his son, but takes Perdita for a shepherd's
daughter. Florizel misses his disguised father's identity—and of
course has never known Perdita's. Perdita also mistakes both the
King and herself. The old Shepherd stands in one sense below and
in another above the others with respect to these secrets. He knows
half a truth, that Perdita is not his own daughter, and he talks
knowingly to Polixenes of her heritage:

> If young Doricles
> Do light upon her, she shall bring him that
> Which he not dreams of.
>
> (Ibid. 178–80.)

But though, in knowing that Perdita is not his own, he knows more
than the others, he, too, misses the deep secret: he is ignorant that
she is a princess. Aside from his half truth he knows nothing. When
he talks with the King it becomes apparent that even Florizel's true
identity is unknown to him:

> *Pol.* Pray, good shepherd, what fair swain is this
> Which dances with your daughter?
> *Shep.* They call him Doricles; and boasts himself
> To have a worthy feeding; but I have it
> Upon his own report, and I believe it.
> He looks like sooth.
>
> (Ibid. 166–71.)

The Shepherd is thus the only one ignorant of the identities of all
three persons with and of whom he talks.

During this busy cross-play between discrepant awarenesses, the
main effects of exploitation are comic, and they harmonize with the
music, song, and dance that make festive gaiety. But after the Satyrs'
dance the scene darkens abruptly: ''Tis time to part them', says
Polixenes. Florizel and Perdita have sworn undying devotion to
each other, and the Shepherd—his words prodding us to remember
the King's, Perdita's, and Florizel's real identities—announces their
betrothal:

Take hands, a bargain!
And, friends unknown, you shall bear witness to 't:
I give my daughter to him, and will make
Her portion equal his.

(Ibid. 393–6.)

Sharp-edged strokes of irony, ominous rather than comic now,
illuminate the gap between Polixenes' and Florizel's awarenesses as
the King interrupts:

Pol.   Soft, swain, a while, beseech you.
     Have you a father?
Flo.   I have; but.what of him?
Pol. Knows he of this?
Flo.   He neither does nor shall.

(Ibid. 401–3.)

Two secrets, their exploitable potential used up, are opened when
Polixenes reveals himself: 'Mark your divorce, young sir, / Whom
son I dare not call.' Perdita, Florizel, and the old Shepherd now
know the King, and the Shepherd learns the identity of his 'daughter's' suitor. But the central secret remains for exploitation—and
with the comments, in succession, of the King, Perdita herself,
the Shepherd, and Florizel it fairly explodes in showers of sparks
that we alone perceive. Thus Polixenes unknowingly abuses and
threatens the daughter of his old friend of Sicilia:

. . . . if ever henceforth thou
These rural latches to his entrance open,
Or hoop his body more with thy embraces,
I will devise a death as cruel for thee
As thou art tender to 't.

(Ibid. 447–51.)

And Perdita, equally ignorant who she is:

This dream of mine,—
Being now awake, I'll queen it no inch farther,
But milk my ewes and weep.

(Ibid. 458–60.)

The Shepherd, with an eye to his own safety, adds his reproaches
for Perdita's presumption:

O cursed wretch,
That knew'st this was the Prince, and wouldst adventure
To mingle faith with him! Undone! undone!

(Ibid. 468–70.)

Florizel, in his ignorance, remains valiantly true to his 'shepherdess':

> Not for Bohemia, nor the pomp that may
> Be thereat gleaned, for all the sun sees or
> The close earth wombs or the profound seas hides
> In unknown fathoms, will I break my oath
> To this my fair belov'd. . . .
>
> (iv. iv. 498–502.)

The closing 350 lines of this second-longest scene in Shakespeare —from Camillo's 'Now were I happy if / His going I could frame to serve my turn' to the end—are the liveliest of the play in the coining of practices. But the management of this portion is markedly inferior to that in *Cymbeline*, *Twelfth Night*, *The Merry Wives*— and indeed in any of the mature works—at those moments of suddenly burgeoning complexity when the dramatist needs his best art to prevent repetition in our own minds of the participants' confusion. In *Cymbeline*, which best shows Shakespeare's mastery in this kind, many strands woven into intricate designs remain individually distinct, and the total pattern never blurs to the mind's eye. In contrast, though the pattern is less complex in *The Winter's Tale*, there is indefiniteness in the motives and means of practices. The relation of one practice to another is less certain, and the whole design becomes somewhat tangled.

At the start the design is clear enough. The enveloping practice remains Perdita's masquerade, of which even she is unaware. Next is Florizel's simple device, explained to Camillo:

> This you may know
> And so deliver: I am put to sea
> With her who here I cannot hold on shore.
>
> (Ibid. 507–9.)

An inexperienced practiser, Florizel has no purpose but to escape Polixenes, hence would drift aimlessly on the seas:

> . . . as th' unthought-on-accident is guilty
> To what we wildly do, so we profess
> Ourselves to be the slaves of chance, and flies
> Of every wind that blows.
>
> (Ibid. 548–51.)

Helpless children beside any of their predecessor heroes and heroines, neither is practical or ingenious: Perdita, indeed, contributes no idea—what a fall is here from Rosalind!—but stands silent while Florizel, with stout heart but no competence, does his best to plan. To his poor device, Camillo—the older generation, guiding this helpless younger one—adds detail and destination:

> ... make for Sicilia,
> And there present yourself and your fair princess,
> For so I see she must be, 'fore Leontes.
> She shall be habited as it becomes
> The partner of your bed.   (Ibid. 553–7.)

Camillo is a practised practiser: long ago he had feigned to plot with Leontes to poison Polixenes, but then, deceiving Leontes, had devised means to escape with Polixenes. 'What colour for my visitation shall I / Hold up before him?' asks Florizel, with a child's need to be told each step. 'Sent by the King your father,' replies Camillo,

> To greet him and to give him comforts. Sir,
> The manner of your bearing towards him, with
> What you as from your father shall deliver,
> Things known betwixt us three, I'll write you down;
> The which shall point you forth at every sitting
> What you must say. . . .
>
> (Ibid. 566–72.)

'Camillo, / Preserver of my father, now of me, / The medicine of our house, how shall we do?' When he was himself younger Shakespeare took a different view of the competence of youth; the helplessness of Florizel and Perdita in such crises as arise in these worsened worlds of the romances reflects a changed attitude. *But also it contributes much to the predominance of anxiety over assurance in our awareness*: not only is the world of *The Winter's Tale* more hazardous than the worlds of the comedies, but its lovers are less able than their predecessors to look out for themselves.

In devising for those who cannot solve their problem unaided, Camillo serves as a minor Prospero—but one who is ignorant of the deep secret which must be revealed before their problem can really be solved. Moreover, he is a Prospero who devises for others incidentally, for himself primarily: 'Now were I happy, if / His going I could frame to serve my turn.' Having designed a practice for the lovers on both Leontes and Polixenes, even superintending their disguise—'disliken / The truth of your own seeming'—he invents a private practice which envelops the other:

> What I do next shall be to tell the King
> Of this escape and whither they are bound;
> Wherein my hope is I shall so prevail
> To force him after; in whose company
> I shall re-view Sicilia, for whose sight
> I have a woman's longing.
>
> (Ibid. 675–80.)

Camillo's devising, too, suggests the world's way in *The Winter's Tale*: for though here it appears that the lines of action have begun to turn back toward the beginning, bringing the first hint that Perdita's buried identity may somehow be recovered, yet the reversal of direction has occurred irrelevantly. If Florizel and Perdita should visit Sicilia only because of Camillo's private purpose, and if, once they reach Leontes' court, Perdita's secret should somehow come out—then it must be said of *The Winter's Tale* that its action has stumbled accidentally upon a happy ending and might as easily have stumbled on another.

At this point in *Pericles* and *Cymbeline*, when action which had been running without apparent control began to turn back by chance or for reasons irrelevant to the main issue, and threatened to end by accident, Shakespeare introduced an external power representing purposeful, benevolent intelligence in the universe. This power conferred a look of intention upon the way of events—and thus, barely in time, prevented what must otherwise have been for the dramatist's art a fate worse than death— a happy ending reached by chance. In *Pericles* Neptune (and Diana) and in *Cymbeline* Jupiter performed this timely service. In *The Winter's Tale* it is performed, after a fashion, by a lesser light: '*My father nam'd me Autolycus . . . litter'd under Mercury.*' Intertwined with Camillo's, which already envelop Florizel's, the practices of this artfully masquerading rogue further complicate an already complex pattern. At the same time, they solve Perdita's problem—and Shakespeare's.

The seas of *Pericles* were an abstraction whose purposeful intelligence could only be hinted through a metonymy of occasional signs; they did not make a wholly satisfactory or wholly Shakespearian solution to the problem. The eagle-borne Jupiter of *Cymbeline*, anything but abstract, went too far in the opposite direction and was too gross to be credible—hence was also unsatisfactory. Each of these drastic expedients was thus in its own way an inadequate substitute for the brilliant heroines whose wills pervaded the worlds of the comedies and brought things right at last; for Oberon, who, though an immortal spirit, was every bit as credible as Bottom; and for Duke Vincentio, who, though mortal, effectively suggested divine power. In abandoning these earlier forms of control in order to represent worlds which seemed to run wild, but for which some kind of control must finally be asserted to prevent an accidental ending, Shakespeare had created a dilemma. Autolycus is the third, last, and most successful attempt to solve the artistic problem that was solved imperfectly in *Pericles* and *Cymbeline*.

Autolycus is a rogue with more than ample evidence of mortality about him; hence he is credible in the human setting, whereas

Jupiter on an eagle's back looked preposterous in it. At the same time, this rogue carries enough implication of divinity to give a look of authority to the ending. Less obtrusively, he plays a far more active part in bringing about the ending than did Jupiter—who claimed whole credit but actually did nothing. Drastically different from Neptune and Jupiter in form and behaviour, Autolycus suggests Shakespeare's dissatisfaction with these entirely external machines. He links Vincentio of *Measure for Measure* with Prospero of *The Tempest*, those two bustling master practisers who are nothing if not credible. But while these are mortals whose working in mysterious ways suggests more than mortal power, Autolycus, with the implication of divinity in his name, his birth, and his mercurial profession of hustling, strives so hard to seem only a mortal that he emerges as a credible god.

The Winter's Tale is Shakespeare's only play in which all participants are ignorant of the central secret. In *Cymbeline* the villain disappeared, taking the main secret with him and increasing our fears that nothing could ever be right again; yet even a vanished, villainous secret-sharer offers more of comfort than no secret-sharer at all. Besides, when Imogen, disguised, is captured with the Roman forces and taken to her father's palace, she need only speak to make herself known. But Perdita cannot reveal an identity that she does not know; hence Florizel and Camillo's decision to take her to her father's court is an imperfect plan which leaves the discovery to accident. Besides being ignorant who she is, Perdita differs otherwise also from the earlier sharp-eyed heroines, who actively aided— indeed, in most cases, devised and operated—the machinery of solution. Perdita contributes nothing to the counsels of Camillo and Florizel—in fact, is not consulted. She stands by during the activity that leads to her identification and reunion with her royal parents, exercising no more control over her fate than when, sixteen years earlier, she lay on the Bohemian shore at the mercy of whatever beast should first happen by.

Though the action has turned back toward Perdita's home, then, the turning is a blind one that denies us even such reassurance as was provided in *Pericles* and *Cymbeline* at the same point. Not only is Camillo's purpose private and unrelated to that of discovering Perdita's secret, and Perdita unable to help herself, but the proofs of her identity are held by 'a blind one, a mole', the old Shepherd *who* —besides being eighty-three years of age, doddering, and so frightened by Polixenes' threat that he seems likely to die within the hour, as he wishes to do—*does not himself know their significance.* Hurrying off with the Clown for Polixenes' court—'Pray heartily he be at palace'—with the precious 'fardel' containing 'those secret things' that require eyes more knowing than his to recognize, the Shepherd aims only to prove, in the Clown's words, that 'She being none of your flesh and blood, your flesh and blood has not offended the King; and so your flesh and blood is not to be punish'd by him.' Like Camillo's, thus, his purpose is selfish and tangential.

But more than this: it would not aid the identification of Perdita if Shepherd and Clown reached Polixenes' palace—for by the time they should arrive the King and Camillo would be aboard ship for Sicilia. *The Shepherd must get to Sicilia's court, not Bohemia's*; it is as necessary for him to do so as for Perdita herself. At this point, then—with Perdita and Florizel fleeing to Sicilia to escape Polixenes, with Polixenes and Camillo pursuing them for reasons unrelated to the identification of Perdita, and with the Shepherd and the Clown, afraid for their lives, starting off for Bohemia's court, it is evident that if the action continued undirected Perdita's identity would be found only by some great accident or not at all.

Here is therefore the exact place for another eagle-borne Jupiter. But instead of calling him down again or inventing something similarly gross, Shakespeare sets Autolycus in the Shepherd's path: 'Aside, aside; here is more matter for a hot brain. Every lane's end, every shop, church, session, hanging, yields a careful man work.'

Unlike Jupiter, Autolycus makes no large claims; his only pretension is that he is a mortal rogue with 'an open ear, a quick eye, and a nimble hand'. He is the only truly professional practiser in *The Winter's Tale*. Before this crucial encounter with the Shepherd and the Clown, he has practised on them twice, first posing as an unfortunate who has been robbed and beaten by a certain rogue—'some call him Autolycus'—and contriving to pick the Clown's pocket when he is helped to his feet; next at the sheep-shearing, where, unrecognized by the Clown, he has picked and cut purses at will among the shepherds whom he has enchanted with song: 'You might have pinched a placket, it was senseless; 'twas nothing to geld a codpiece of a purse; I would have fil'd keys off that hung in chains.' Thereafter he has discovered the escape plot of Florizel, Perdita, and Camillo—'I understand the business, I hear it'—and aided it by exchanging garments with Florizel, thus effecting their mutual disguise. Now, in the Prince's coat, his third masquerade, he deceives the Clown and the Shepherd, masters all of Perdita's secret that they themselves know, and finally perpetrates his fourth practice by taking them aboard the Prince's ship when they suppose it is the King's: 'He was provided', says the Shepherd, with profound unconscious wisdom, 'to do us good.'

308

At the end of Act IV, thus, because of Florizel and Perdita's desire to escape, Camillo's desire to revisit Sicilia, the Shepherd's fear of the King's threats, and Autolycus's stated ambition—'gold and a means to do the Prince my master good; which who knows how that may turn back to my advancement?'—all indispensable elements have been assembled, and for the first time we can hold assurance that so far as the heroine's problem is concerned all will now be well.

But well by virtue of a happy conjunction of accidents, or by intention? 'Be not with mortal accidents opprest; / No care of yours it is; you know 'tis ours', said Jupiter in *Cymbeline*, insisting that beginning and end were in his mind while we ourselves could see only the middle. Jupiter is a god who acts very godlike; Autolycus, the master-practiser and catalyst of disparate elements in *The Winter's Tale*, acts very like a rogue. He is certainly not a rogue trying to seem a god; but at the same time there is an air about him that makes his very mortality suspect. If not a rogue seeming to be a god, he must be a god seeming to be a rogue: such, at least, is the suggestion, made boldly enough to give authority for the solution of the problem, without being so outright as to invite disbelief. Autolycus is a shrewd improvement upon Jupiter, whose *deus ex* machinations with thunderbolt, lightning, eagle, and pompous claims were too evidently fraudulent.

But although Autolycus insinuates into our minds the comforting idea of a controlling force and actually brings the affair of Perdita so near an end that we know it must now end well, full comfort is still denied us. When Pericles supposes Thaisa and Marina dead, we have seen both escape death. When Cymbeline, Posthumus, and the mountain youths suppose Imogen–Fidele dead, we know that she lives; when Imogen sobs on the dead body of 'Posthumus', we know that Posthumus lives. During these blackest moments, though we cannot know that the seemingly uncontrolled world will not whirl on to catastrophe, we do know that catastrophe has not yet struck, hence that the chance of a happy ending remains. But in *The Winter's Tale* we know that catastrophe has struck: Hermione is dead.

Structurally, the affair of Perdita–Florizel is only an incident which interrupts the affair of Hermione–Leontes; hence, though all may be well for Perdita, nothing can be finally well. Even though a causal relationship had been established between the happy ending of Perdita's affair and Hermione's, so that we should expect the latter to follow in due course, yet here that course is blocked by the plain fact that Hermione is dead. And in any event, Perdita's recovery has not been made a condition of Hermione's. Apollo's oracle fore-told that Leontes should live 'without an heir, if that which is lost be not found'. Immediately thereafter Mamillius was reported dead. Now that Perdita is found, the oracle's words would obviously apply to herself as the 'heir' of Leontes; possibly, at second thought, they might suggest that Mamillius has miraculously been preserved. But the oracle's prophecy raises no thought of Hermione.

We are thus left, at the end of Act IV, with two certainties: that the affair of Perdita will be joyously concluded, and that, though the restoration of his daughter will kindle some joy in Leontes and provide him with an heir, the tale to which it is incidental has itself already ended in catastrophe.

Having reached this point, Shakespeare had three choices: to con-tinue on the line of these certainties, restoring some joy to Leontes through Perdita but leaving him inwardly destroyed by the loss of Hermione; to bring about the death of Leontes, and finally close, after Perdita's return, the enveloping tragedy; or—prospect least likely on the record of his whole career—to recall Hermione to life. Any one of these solutions would be artistically imperfect. The first, though it alone would not betray our expectation, would be a bastard issue, neither comic nor tragic: tragic but that the pro-tagonist is left alive, comic but for the bloody stump. The second would make Act IV—indeed, the whole history of Perdita, in-cluding Apollo's prophecy and the intervention of Autolycus—irrelevant: if it were to be tragedy, the story should have ended with Act III—the proper time both psychologically and artistically for Leontes to die. The third, though it would both give the envelop-ing story a happy ending and give Perdita's story artistic relevance to the happy ending of Hermione's, would mean violation of a prin-ciple that the dramatist had never before violated: though he had sometimes withheld vital information, as in *Pericles* and *Cymbeline*, he had never abused our awareness with a lie: 'I say she's dead; I'll swear't.'

Early in Act V the dramatist begins to hint at his choice; says Leontes, on the question of taking a new wife:

> One worse,
> And better us'd, would make her sainted spirit
> Again possess her corpse....
>
> (v. i. 56–58.)

Again:

> Cleo. You tempt him over-much
> Paul.   Unless another,
> As like Hermione as is her picture,
> Affront his eye.   (Ibid. 73–75.)

Again, Paulina:

> She shall not be so young
> As was your former; but she shall be such
> As, walk'd your first queen's ghost, it should take joy
> To see her in your arms.
>
> (Ibid. 78–81.)

And again:

> Leon.   My true Paulina,
> We shall not marry till thou bid'st us.
> Paul.   That
> Shall be when your first queen's again in breath;
> Never till then.
>
> (Ibid. 81–84.)

Whether these hints are meant to advise us fully that the dramatist has taken the third of three bad choices is impossible to be sure. The haste with which they are introduced in the beginning of Act V and the emphasis that comes of their quick repetition do suggest that Shakespeare aims to make amends for the bad treatment given our awareness in earlier acts: *very soon hereafter we are to be surprised, but we are to be shrewdly prepared for our surprise—so very shrewdly, indeed, that perhaps we may be deceived into imagining that we knew all along about Hermione's survival!*

In the interval between these hints and the revelation itself are set the final exploitation and denouement of Perdita's secret. The meeting of Florizel and Perdita with Leontes is brightly lighted by our knowledge that—thanks to Autolycus—the old Shepherd with his fardel of proofs is close behind. The exploitation is brief. At the first all participants are doubly ignorant: Leontes, that Florizel's 'princess' is his own child, left sixteen years before 'Where chance may nurse or end it', and that the Prince is just now deceiving him in seeming to have come with Polixenes' blessing and, absurdly, with a bride of Libya, daughter of 'warlike Smalus'; Florizel and Perdita, that this 'bride' is truly a princess and daughter of Leontes, and that their practice on Leontes is immediately to be exposed by means of Camillo's practice on them in bringing Polixenes to Sicilia. They are ignorant also, of course, of the significance for them of Autolycus's mysterious purpose in bringing the Shepherd aboard their ship. The total complex of secrets and practices is struck at its centre with Perdita's needlessly despairing cry on learning that Polixenes, rushing to Sicilia's court from the ship, has encountered the Shepherd and his son. If any anxiety has remained in our minds since Autolycus first took over in the affair of Perdita, the report of the arrival of Polixenes and Camillo and their meeting with the

Shepherd must dispel it. 'I now go toward him; therefore follow me', Leontes commands the lovers at the end of the scene—and the happy end of Perdita's affair is a foregone conclusion.

That the end itself is merely reported may be disappointing, but reasons for the dramatist's decision are not difficult to perceive, and then the decision appears the better of two hard choices. As at the end of *Pericles* Shakespeare had two reunions—of father with daughter and husband with wife—to manage. In *Pericles*, since Marina more than Thaisa had claimed our interest—and since this reunion offered an especially rich potential of effect—he chose to exploit the meeting of father and daughter and to scant that of husband and wife. This decision, too, was undoubtedly the better choice, even though it left the latter reunion hanging unimpressively. In *Cymbeline*, by adroit management of a fantastic number of elements, all lines were made to converge so that multiple reunions of approximately equal dramatic importance—father with daughter, father with sons, brothers with sister, wife with husband, Britain with Rome—could be shown in one scene without diminishing any. In *The Winter's Tale*, to have represented the father-daughter reunion would have been to give emphasis to what is in fact incidental. An anti-climactic ending for *The Winter's Tale* would have been intolerable: for not only is the husband–wife reunion the principal matter—but it is also a surprise. To have ended with both surprise and anti-climax would have been to make a bad situation worse.

Had the denouement of Perdita's secret offered richer potentials for exploitation, possibly Shakespeare would have represented it even at the risk of an anti-climactic Leontes–Hermione reunion. But the fact is that the best in Perdita's affair was exploited before the fleeing lovers first reached Leontes' court; what remained offered only spectacle, which could as well be reduced to report.

Toward the end of the report that Perdita's affair has been happily concluded, we are given a stronger hint that Hermione's will end happily also; says the Third Gentleman:

The Princess hearing of her mother's statue, which is in the keeping of Paulina,—a piece many years in doing and now newly perform'd by that rare Italian master. . . . He so near to Hermione hath done Hermione that they say one would speak to her and stand in hope of an answer. (v. ii. 102–10.)

From this we are presumably expected to gain advantage over Leontes before the curtain opens to show Hermione 'standing like a statue'. In any case, it is doubtless meant that we should recognize the truth as soon as we see the 'statue' itself. At the least, therefore,

Shakespeare has one truly exciting discrepancy to exploit during a period of nearly 100 lines, from the opening of the curtain until Hermione breaks her pose and comes down. Our advantage during this time is over all the participants—Leontes, Perdita, Polixenes, Florizel, Camillo, and several lords—excepting Paulina and, of course, Hermione herself. Exploitation concentrates upon Leontes' reactions, in his ignorance that the 'statue' is Hermione herself, with Paulina functioning in a gentler version of the harpy role she has played since Leontes first accused his queen of infidelity. Paulina is here the dramatist's exploitative instrument, used to strike the sparks that illuminate the discrepancy. A shrewd practiser, she conducts her personally staged scene towards its climax, while Leontes remains quite deceived:

> Paul. I'll make the statue move indeed, descend
> And take you by the hand; but then you'll think—
> Which I protest against—I am assisted
> By wicked powers.
> Leon. What you can make her do,
> I am content to look on; what to speak,
> I am content to hear; for 'tis as easy
> To make her speak as move.
> Paul. It is requir'd
> You do awake your faith. Then all stand still;
> Or those that think it is unlawful business
> I am about, let them depart.
> Leon. Proceed;
> No foot shall stir.
> Paul. Music, awake her; strike!
> (v. iii. 88–98.)

Though it uses no final act of physical violence, as do *Pericles* and *Cymbeline*, this denouement achieves comparable effect with Hermione's movement as she breaks her pose.

For us, certainly, the denouement came earlier—at the first glimpse of Hermione's statue. During nearly 100 lines from then until the participants' recognition, therefore, we have occupied the position that has always been ours in Shakespeare's denouements and have enjoyed our usual privilege—that of knowing observers during last-moment exploitation of participants' ignorance and final discovery of the truth. The fact raises one of the great questions of *The Winter's Tale*: since he would thus at last avoid surprise, advising us just in time to make possible the usual kind of denouement, why did Shakespeare deceive us about Hermione in the first place? Why did he not do as, for example, in *Much Ado about Nothing*, when, after the swooning Hero has been carried from the altar, the Friar suggests that Leonato spread 'The supposition of the lady's

death'? Through a brief scene with Hermione and Paulina, set between the present III. ii and III. iii, we could have been shown the
truth just before the scene shifts from Sicilia to Bohemia. Shakespeare would then not have needed first to abuse our awareness, next
to risk a bad surprise, and finally to disabuse us just in time to create
an exploitable discrepancy for use in the denouement. By telling us
flatly that Hermione was dead at the end of Act III, he placed himself in his most precarious dramatic position, with, as we have seen,
three imperfect choices: to restore Perdita, say nothing more of
Hermione, and let Leontes live on miserably; to let Leontes die after
Perdita's return, and thus complete a tragedy which properly ended
with Act III; or to restore Hermione. Doubtless the choice made
was the best of the three—*but why did Shakespeare not simply tell
us at the end of Act III that Hermione was alive, and thus avoid the
need to make any of them?*

It is of course possible that at the end of Act III he had not yet
made up his mind; he may have expected to follow his source and
end with Leontes' death.

It is also possible, there being no extant proof but that of the Folio,
that a crucial expository scene with Paulina and Hermione, at the
end of Act III, is lost.

It is even possible that, complying with a current fashion for
dramatic surprises, he intended originally to carry our deception to
the last moment and then to strike *us* with the same astonishment
with which he strikes Leontes and other participants. If this was
his intention, then evidently his long-standing preference for an
exploitable discrepancy between the participants' awareness and
ours won out at the last moment, and he hurriedly provided hints
to give us our usual advantage in the denouement.

Any one of these possibilities may represent the fact. But in view
of the direction of Shakespeare's recent experimentation with our
awareness in *Pericles* and *Cymbeline* it appears more likely that
*both our deception in Hermione's 'death' and our readvisement in
time to observe the denouement from our usual high vantage-point
were plotted from the beginning.* In the preceding romances Shakespeare evidently wished us to experience something of the participants' sense of an indifferent universe running wild. Therefore he
left us ignorant of a benevolent power's existence until late, and then
—as best he could—avoided the appearance of an accidental ending
by asserting that the world had been under control all the while.

But in neither of these romances did he actually tell us a lie in
order to have us share the participants' sense of a hazardous world.
And perhaps we do *not* truly experience the participants' sense in

Pericles and *Cymbeline*, because we know that despite the tempests and the brutes of those worlds, *nothing fatal and therefore irremediable has actually occurred.* In *The Winter's Tale*, to prevent our escape from the participants' sense, he confronts us with the naked finality: 'I say she's dead; I'll swear't.' And thereafter—having forced us to share the participants' sense during two acts—he begins stealthily to prepare our minds for Hermione's restoration.

Perhaps, even, he prepares us so effectively as to make us forget that we truly believed Hermione dead; we may thus be deceived twice without realizing that we have been once. By the time the denouement is done, he has made us share the participants' sense of an irresponsible universe; has avoided, by means of a 'prepared surprise', the fault of a real one, at the same time giving us something of the participants' thrill of surprise; and still has had his customary use of a richly exploitable discrepancy between the participants' awareness and ours. It hardly requires argument that this is very shrewd dramatic practice—like eating one's cake and having it too, but even more like eating it two or three times and having it too.

CHAPTER VIII

The Mask and the Mantle

LATE in *Measure for Measure,* needing a handy explanation, Shakespeare has Duke Vincentio thus justify his lie to Isabella about Claudio's survival:

> . . . I will make her ignorant of her good,
> To make her heavenly comforts of despair,
> When it is least expected.
>
> (IV. iii. 113–15.)

This possibly marks the origin in the dramatist's mind—and certainly it is his first expression—of a psychological principle underlying the management of awarenesses in the romances of the lasting storm: the idea of first making it *seem* that participants have suffered or will suffer irreparable losses in a hostile or indifferent universe, and then, in the end, of restoring all losses and putting a sudden face of benignity on the universe. 'O you gods,' cries Pericles when Thaisa dies in childbirth, 'Why do you make us love your goodly gifts / And snatch them straight away?' Afterwards, the buffeted Prince gains the first of his 'heavenly comforts' on finding Marina, whom he had thought dead:

> O Helicanus, strike me, honour'd sir;
> Give me a gash, put me to present pain,
> Lest this great sea of joys rushing upon me
> O'erbear the shores of my mortality
> And drown me with their sweetness.
>
> (*Per.,* v. i. 192–6.)

And he gains the rest with the recovery of 'dead' Thaisa:

> No more, you gods! Your present kindness
> Makes my past miseries sports.
>
> (Ibid. v. iii. 40–41.)

In *Cymbeline,* in similar perplexity about universal purposes, Posthumus's ghostly father berates the gods:

> *Sici.* Why did you suffer Iachimo,
> Slight thing of Italy,

To taint his nobler heart and brain
With needless jealousy,
And to become the geck and scorn
O' th' other's villainy?
(v. iv. 63–68.)

Jupiter's answer restates Duke Vincentio's argument:

Whom best I love I cross; to make my gift,
The more delay'd, delighted.
(Ibid. 101–2.)

Leontes of *The Winter's Tale*, bereft of Hermione during sixteen
penitent years, at length overflows with joy at the prospect merely
of continuing to imagine that her statue is alive:

O sweet Paulina,
Make me to think so twenty years together!
No settled senses of the world can match
The pleasure of that madness.
(v. iii. 70–73.)

'Go together,' says Paulina when parents, children, and old friends
have all received 'heavenly comforts' in abundance: 'You precious
winners all; your exultation / Partake to every one.'

But the uses to which this basic idea is put in *Measure for Measure*
and in the three romances are very different. In the former a participant applies it to another: Vincentio makes Isabella think Claudio
dead—but the dramatist tells us that he is alive. *In the romances,
with rising insistence, the dramatist applies it to us.* In *Pericles* and
Cymbeline, though we are kept informed of the survival of Marina
and Thaisa, Posthumus and Imogen, when their loved ones think
them dead, we are made anxious lest husbands, wives, sons, and
daughters, displaced and lost in an unruled and careless universe,
may never find their way together again—and it is only after our
own fears have been well exploited that we are shown their reunion
and are assured that gods Neptune and Jupiter have kept their welfare in mind all the while. In *The Winter's Tale*, going further with
the principle of making us 'heavenly comforts of despair, / When it
is least expected', the dramatist first flatly says that Hermione is
dead, leaves us long in this belief—and then blesses us with her
recovery.

The psychologically cruel way of the lasting storm endures
through only one scene of *The Tempest*, when it is renounced in no
uncertain terms: 'Tell your piteous heart / There's no harm done.'

The old way of the comedies which had culminated in *Measure
for Measure* is thus reasserted—and, as the whole play makes apparent, reasserted with unequivocal force. Though royalty has been

317

cast down and isolated with none but inhuman creatures, though
Alonso is made to think his son dead and Ferdinand his father dead,
and though brutal murder is mounted against all of the innocents
who exist in this world—yet we are prevented from experiencing
even momentary anxiety. Prospero keeps Ferdinand and Miranda
ignorant of their good—'this swift business / I must uneasy make'
—in order to make them heavenly comforts at last; but Shakespeare
permits us no fears for them. Thus although *The Tempest* resembles
the earlier romances in obvious and significant ways, it is not at all
like them in the most fundamental way of giving us absolute assurance that all is and must be well.

   To say so much is not, however, to suggest that the world of *The
Tempest* is in nature better than that of *Pericles*, *Cymbeline*, or *The
Winter's Tale*; on the contrary, in itself it must appear the worst of
Shakespeare's worlds, for it exposes depths of bestiality beneath any
shown elsewhere, even in the tragedies. In the bloody environment
of *Titus Andronicus*, hands, heads, and tongues are at least cleanly
lopped; even there, or in *King Lear*, where eyes are gouged, nothing
matches the sheer brutality of Caliban's plan for killing Prospero:

> ... 'tis a custom with him,
> I' th' afternoon to sleep. There thou mayst brain him,
> Having first seiz'd his books, or with a log
> Batter his skull, or paunch him with a stake,
> Or cut his wezand with thy knife.
>
> (III. ii. 95-99.)

Hubert of *King John* melts with pity; Clarence's murderers in
Richard III 'scarcely have the hearts' to tell their purpose, and the
murderers of the royal babes in the same play, Dighton and Forrest,
'Albeit they were flesh'd villains, bloody dogs, / ... Wept like two
children in their death's sad story'; Iago is always proving to himself that his wrongs deserve the revenge he plots; the minds of
Claudius and Macbeth are filled with scorpions. But thus speak two
of the typically bestial inhabitants of the world of *The Tempest*, as
they prepare to murder two sleeping men, one a king and a brother,
the other a golden-hearted old counsellor:

> *Seb.* But, for your conscience?
> *Ant.* Ay, sir, where lies that? If 'twere a kibe,
> 'Twould put me to my slipper; but I feel not
> This deity in my bosom.
>
> (II. i. 275-8.)

Mere unfeeling brutishness, more appalling than the impassioned,
sometimes grand villainy that threatened goodness in earlier plays,

is the force that would overwhelm the world of *The Tempest*; says
Antonio, eyeing the sleeping King:

> We all were sea-swallow'd, though some cast again,
> And by that destiny to perform an act
> Whereof what's past is prologue, what to come
> In yours and my discharge.
>
> (Ibid. 251-4.)

The callous brutality of Sebastian and Antonio is matched by the
clownish brutality of Stephano and Trinculo, also symbols of the
force that would dominate this world: 'Trinculo, the King and all
our company else being drown'd, we will inherit here.' And Caliban
—beside whose animality all Shakespeare's previous representatives
of base villainy are sophisticates—speaks thus of his old master to his
new: 'I'll yield him thee asleep, / Where thou mayst knock a nail
into his head.' The threat of conquest and rule by this order of
bestiality is a potential of deeper horror than any previously
imagined by Shakespeare. To keep in check a world that has such
monsters in it, he needed either another Jupiter or a mortal more
capable than any required before.

Considered as dramatic implementation, the mantle, staff, and
book of Prospero are ultimate expressions of lowlier means by
which his predecessors held advantage. Simple disguise gave Julia
of *The Two Gentlemen of Verona* the edge in awareness and control of her situation. Disguise also, along with rare qualities of mind
and spirit, raised Portia, Rosalind, and Viola above others in their
worlds and gave each a degree of control which she used according
to her nature. Helena of *All's Well that Ends Well*, with disguise
and a deadly singleness of purpose, handily mastered her worsening
world. But she was the last heroine to do so: in *Measure for Measure*
Isabella's only means of advantage, her chastity, is more liability
than asset in lustful Vienna, and, lacking the Duke's protection, she
could only have hidden it in the convent. Vincentio, taking over
a world grown too vicious for heroines to control, requires disguise, resourceful activity, and the authority of his title to keep
wickedness in check.

These, from Julia to Vincentio, are among the notable practisers
who, having a superior vantage-point and exercising various degrees
of control, prefigure Prospero. They are not the only ones: all
earlier practisers are related by their functions to Prospero. Biron
sitting in the sky, overpeering his friends in *Love's Labour's Lost*;
Lucentio masked as tutor but busy as suitor in *The Taming of the
Shrew*; nearly every inhabitant of Messina in *Much Ado about
Nothing*; Mistress Quickly plying her multiple sharp practices that

touch all persons in *The Merry Wives of Windsor*: all, variously endowed and diversely purposed, have a share in the eventual Prospero. Certain figures, of course, look more prophetic of him than others in their manner of working, or in the suggestion that something more than mortal lies behind their power. In some ways Oberon of *A Midsummer-Night's Dream* is nearest to Prospero; but his is a truly supernatural power, rather than mortal magic leagued with and dominating immortal spirits. Certain heroines, too, carry a hint of this 'something more': Portia, bringing to the workaday court of Venice the air of fabulous Belmont; Rosalind—though she invents the story—claiming to have been taught by 'a great magician / Obscured in the circle of this forest'—and in fact miraculously supplying Hymen to bless four marriages; Helena, leaving Rousillon for Paris with medicine to cure the King's fistula, darkly commenting that 'There's something in't / More than my father's skill', and prefacing her treatment with a chant that hints of witchery. In *Pericles*, for one brief scene, the magical healer Cerimon is closer than any other to Prospero, and, even more briefly, Simonides also comes close. In the same play Neptune and in *Cymbeline* Jupiter, though theirs is supreme power, like Prospero's, stand quite apart from the line; they are external controllers. In *The Winter's Tale* Prospero's function is widely distributed among a doddering shepherd of eighty-three; Camillo, a practiser whose private purposes serve main purposes incidentally; Paulina, a cunning manipulator who hides her devices even from us; Apollo's oracle, fronting presumably for the god himself; and Autolycus, whose obvious efforts to seem as ungodlike as possible imply a kinship with divinity.

Though we have seen him thus prefigured many times by parts, we have not before seen a whole Prospero. In the comedies through *Measure for Measure* no controlling force is so potent. Duke Vincentio, the most powerful mortal before him, keeps his wicked world secure, but by such ungodlike devices as disguise and eavesdropping; and, finally, his whole authority lies in his title. Though his power is absolute among the citizens of Vienna, it does not touch elemental forces of land, ocean, and air; no immortal agents obey him. Prospero requires neither disguise nor eavesdropping: his is not a mere masked identity, but a masked existence, for he wears the mantle of invisibility. An immortal spirit at his command—indeed, at his thought—keeps watch, discovers, reports, performs any task required on land or sea, working his master's will on mortals and elements alike. His authority, thus, is not, like titular authority, limited to creatures that respect titles. His omniscience extends both backward and forward in time and does not depend upon spying: 'My master,' says Ariel, preventing the murder of Alonso and Gonzalo, 'through his art foresees the danger / That you, his friend, are in.' He is not only able to create strange shapes and unearthly noises, induce sleep, and charm ordinary mortals to instant immobility, but capable even of willing things to be: 'It goes on, I see, / As my soul prompts it.' He is not only omniscient and omnipotent, but, with Ariel's aid, omnipresent.

Less powerful than Prospero, but adequate for their worlds, the controllers of the comedies were always credible human beings who could be introduced early in the action and given active roles. On the other hand, though possessed of infinite power, the gods of the romances lacked credibility and were kept hidden until the end of action. In Prospero Shakespeare sought to combine the credibility of the former with the supreme power of the latter. As has been suggested, he knew the need for controlling forces: his art required a controlled world. *Troilus and Cressida*, whose world alone lacks control, alone fails to become a whole work of art. Hence he did introduce them, and when the world became too rough for the usual human control he experimented with other forms. The invisible, implied intelligence behind the winds and seas of *Pericles* proved a nebulous solution, unacceptable in the company of the dramatist's usual fully dimensioned figures that can be seen, heard, and all but touched. On the other hand, eagle-borne Jupiter of *Cymbeline*, emerging abruptly from a sky which until then had looked quite empty, was too, too solid.

Neither force was at home in the worlds of *Pericles* and *Cymbeline*, for—romances or no—these are plays remarkable for a vivid and often terrible realism. If little comes alive in the first two acts of *Pericles*, yet thereafter the scene before Thaisa's body is cast overboard—

> A terrible childbed hast thou had, my dear;
> No light, no fire. Th' unfriendly elements
> Forgot thee utterly; nor have I time
> To give thee hallow'd to thy grave, but straight
> Must cast thee, scarcely coffin'd, in the ooze;
> Where, for a monument upon thy bones
> And aye-remaining lamps, the belching whale
> And humming water must o'erwhelm thy corpse
> Lying with simple shells.
>
> (III. i. 57-65.)

—the amazing but undeniable reality of Cerimon's swift, bustling art in restoring Thaisa; the sea-shore scene in which we first see

Marina, under Leonine's sword, bereft of parents, deceived by the Queen, and finally seized by pirates; the brothel scenes; the quarrel of Cleon and Dionyza after the 'murder' of Marina; the long, painfully detailed ordeal of recognition and reunion: all these have a peculiar quality of immediacy, sharper than mere credibility. In *Cymbeline* scenes having the same strange immediacy are too numerous to list; but, especially, the inhabitants of this world have a psychological imminence that is often startling—and these include not only obvious examples like Cloten and Iachimo, who fairly burst the frame of art, but others who, from the nature of their roles, might easily have been presented as bloodless idealizations: the paragons Posthumus and Imogen, and the rustic princes. If the remote origins of Dionyza of *Pericles* and the Queen of *Cymbeline* are in the wicked stepmother of fairy tale, yet in the dramatic representation they are realized with a terrifying immediacy that makes them quite at home with the other inhabitants of their worlds.

Hence Jupiter, suddenly dropping from the void hurling thunderbolts from an eagle's back, can look only out of place. Yet in the world of Shakespeare's vision after *Measure for Measure*, and after the tragedies in which the human will, vainly striving, had wrought catastrophe, *a force of Jupiter's magnitude was necessary to enable good to prevail.* The credible mortals of the comedies lacked power to master such a world, even as the powerful Neptune and Jupiter lacked credibility. Autolycus came nearer to satisfying than either of these—but perhaps only because ambiguity in his presentation deceives us into accepting a certain duality in his make-up: if he were all rogue he would fail to confer the look of authority on the ending; if all divinity he might look as far from home as Jupiter.

The crowning accomplishment of *The Tempest* is that, with Prospero, it restores control to man—not to *a* man, to be sure, but to *man*. In Prospero are combined the special virtues of the two earlier lines: he is a mortal, as credible as the heroines of comedy, one whose humanity is fully demonstrated and who fits without jarring into a world composed of such specimens of undeniable mortality as the Boatswain, Gonzalo, Stephano, and Trinculo; and at the same time, possessed of 'so potent art' that it can control the very elements, he has a god's power.

The casting of a mortal able to hold the world in the hollow of his hand in the role formerly given to the unassimilable gods of *Pericles* and *Cymbeline* marks, then, one profound distinction between *The Tempest* and the preceding romances. To establish in our awareness an abiding sense of Prospero's power—indeed, *to render this power so persuasively that the question of credibility will not occur*—Shakespeare proceeded with what was possibly his most exacting expository care. All of Act I but the final portion consists of steps designed and placed to accomplish this purpose. The opening scene itself, when we watch the spectacle of the shipwreck before we know of Prospero's existence, is the first calculated step. The howling winds and the crashing seas, the screams and curses, the 'confused noise' of the final splitting: these signify that we are again confronted with just such savage forces as those that buffeted Pericles and made Marina find the world a lasting storm. 'What cares these roarers for the name of king?' demands the angry Boatswain. 'You are a counsellor; if you can command these elements to silence, and work the peace of the present, we will not hand a rope more; use your authority.' Immediately after this ironical suggestion that a poor mortal try to allay the storm, the ship splits.

Had he written *The Tempest* in the year of *Measure for Measure*, or of *Twelfth Night*, Shakespeare would possibly have introduced Prospero before he showed us the shipwreck. To have done so, of course, would have been to sacrifice the excitement of one of his most spectacular scenes. But, more unfortunately, it would also have meant giving up the advantage of establishing Prospero's credit with us *even before we suspect that there is a Prospero*. By the present arrangement this first evidence of his power is slipped into our consciousness while we are unaware that the storm is other than natural. Immediately after we have seen it, what we have seen is recapitulated by Miranda, who has viewed the wreck from a point farther off, and our first-hand estimate of the scope and fury of the storm is substantiated by her testimony. Our own direct experience of the storm, Miranda's nearly hysterical account of the shipwreck, her loaded expression of a wish to have been 'any god of power' that could have halted the catastrophe—these steps invite us not just to accept but actually to *expect* what would otherwise seem an incredible announcement. After our conditioning that announcement comes almost as matter-of-fact narration:

> Wipe thine eyes; have comfort.
> The direful spectacle of the wreck, which touch'd
> The very virtue of compassion in thee,
> I have with such provision in mine art
> So safely ordered that there is no soul—
> No, not so much perdition as an hair
> Betid to any creature in the vessel
> Which thou heardst cry, which thou saw'st sink.
>
> (I. ii. 25–32.)

Finally, it is noteworthy that here, when we are first told of Prospero's power, our attention is fixed not on the speaker but on Miranda in her tears, and thus the revelation is made obliquely; the great secret which is the primary source of our dramatic satisfaction during subsequent action is insinuated into our consciousness while our main attention is on a father's efforts to cheer his weeping daughter—and in effect with our connivance, for we have been invited to share Miranda's wish for 'some god of power' who could indeed reassure this compassionate heart. In these calculated circumstances it is all but inevitable that we should let belief take hold of us. All told, the first scenes of *The Tempest* represent Shakespeare's most determined bid to have us accept a world of his artistic creation.

The replacement of incredible gods with a credible mortal of godlike power marks, then, one profound distinction between the way of *The Tempest* and the way of the previous romances. Another, made possible by this, is the introduction of this force to our awareness not, as in *Pericles* and *Cymbeline*, at the end of the action but at its beginning. By advising us initially that a benevolent, omniscient, omnipotent force exists, Shakespeare recovered for his use and our satisfaction the same eminently exploitable gap that had served him well in the comedies—that between the participants' ignorance and our knowledge that all is well. By doing so he restored the climate of comedy, lacking since *Measure for Measure*, and thus made possible, in the worst of his worlds, the enjoyment of comic effects like those that sparkled in the comfortable, bright world of the comedies but were dampened by anxiety in the romances. Monsters can be comic when we know that they can do no harm.

This main exploitable gap between awarenesses is opened a little by the first syllables of the second scene, which we hear and which the participants who have suffered shipwreck do not hear. 'If by your art, my dearest father', begins Miranda: 'If by your art . . . you have / Put the wild waters in this roar . . .'; and it is then widened with Prospero's initial words:

> Be collected;
> No more amazement. Tell your piteous heart
> There's no harm done.
>
> (I. ii. 13–15.)

The gap remains until the end of the final scene, when it is closed only with a promise:

Pros.   Sir, my liege,
Do not infest your mind with beating on
The strangeness of this business. At pick'd leisure,
Which shall be shortly, single I'll resolve you,
Which to you shall seem probable, of every
These happen'd accidents; till when, be cheerful
And think of each thing well.
                                    (v. i. 245-50.)

Within the main discrepancy numerous secondary gaps serve immediate uses of exploitation also. Some of these are opened by special practices, some otherwise. The limited vision of Miranda— a result of her isolation and a source of her unique charm—and the groping but unpromising intellect of Caliban—limited by his bestial nature—are conditions which create exploitable differences without need of practices devised to create them. Special practices within the frame of Prospero's encompassing one include Prospero's deception of Ferdinand and Miranda in causing them to believe that he is hostile to their love; Sebastian and Antonio's murderous plot against Gonzalo and Alonso; Caliban's unpremeditated deception of Trinculo, when he spreads himself flat and is mistaken for a merely human—if somewhat odd—islander stunned by a thunderbolt; Trinculo's similarly unintended practice on Stephano, when, hiding beneath Caliban's 'gaberdine', he appears to be part of a four-legged monster with two voices; and the abortive rebellion of Caliban and his drunken masters against the life and rule of Prospero. Invisible Ariel's various devices, though they must more properly be considered as implementation of Prospero's encompassing practice, also have the effect of creating momentarily exploitable discrepancies.

But though the secondary devices are numerous and contribute greatly to the movement and the effects of the play, it is mainly because we know of Prospero and his power that we stand above most participants during eight of the nine scenes—a very high proportion—and at some time above all except Prospero and Ariel. On the other hand, though the main gulf between participants and us is uncommonly wide and constant, and though exploitation produces an uninterrupted flow of varied, spectacular effects, yet the structural disposition of awarenesses is never elaborate, but is in fact the simplest in all the comedies and romances. Even *The Comedy of Errors* and *The Two Gentlemen of Verona* occasionally develop greater complexity. In this respect, then, *The Tempest* stands at the opposite pole to *Cymbeline*.

Exploitation of the great gap does not begin until we have been well prepared to appreciate the reactions of the first uninformed visitor to the island. From the participants' level in the opening scene, we are first lifted to share a god's vantage-point by Prospero's declaration that he himself raised the tempest and that, whatever the appearance, 'There's no harm done'. Through the storm itself, which demonstrates it, and through the successive, calculated interviews of Prospero with Miranda, Ariel, and Caliban, Prospero's omnipotence is rendered undeniable. These multiple-purposed interviews—ostensibly existing to inform Miranda and remind Ariel and Caliban—serve in fact to advise us of Prospero's history to the present moment. But they do much more than advise us: they are so managed that, in the guise of merely reporting history, *they persuade us to adopt the point of view of residents of the island*—to become, in effect, residents ourselves. When, therefore, Ferdinand, the first visitor, drawn along by invisible Ariel's music, enters our range of vision, we are already at home. It is noteworthy that Shakespeare never has us look on Prospero with the eyes of visitors, but with the eyes of residents. We do not approach with Ferdinand, staring incredulously, but are standing with Prospero when he arrives. Exploitation of the main gap between the participants' understanding and ours is managed thus throughout the action: the point of view of residents is always ours, no matter which visitors are before us. Our attention is fixed not on Prospero, but on those who are ignorant of the secret of the island—our secret. 'This is no mortal business,' says Ferdinand, 'nor no sound / That the earth owes.' Standing with Prospero, we have better opportunity than ever before to enjoy the effects of exploitation of a difference in awarenesses. The dramatist's 'so potent art' enables us to share a god's satisfaction; and who would disbelieve that in which he himself shares?

Before this scene is over Prospero initiates his special practice on Ferdinand and Miranda. Reminiscent of Simonides' fond fatherly deception of Pericles and Thaisa in pretending hostility to their quick affection, Prospero's practice seems hardly more honestly motivated than his predecessor's—but it serves multiple purposes for the dramatist. Like Simonides, Prospero first makes clear to us that he is delighted with the match: 'It goes on, I see, / As my soul prompts it. Spirit, fine spirit! I'll free thee / Within two days for this.' His own reason for the practice is first offered us privately:

> They are both in either's power; but this swift business
> I must uneasy make, lest too light winning
> Make the prize light.
>
> (v. i. 450-2.)

Later, when the log-bearing ordeal is over, he justifies it to the lovers very much as Jupiter justified his trial of Posthumus and Imogen in *Cymbeline*:

> All thy vexations
> Were but my trials of thy love, and thou
> Hast strangely stood the test.
>
> (IV. i. 5–7.)

But Jupiter spoke as a remote, pompous god, whereas Prospero speaks as a father, and such remarks, liberally sprinkled throughout the play, sustain our sense of him as a human being even while his godlike power is being demonstrated. For the sake of credibility, then, the device performs indispensable service. Further, the deception and 'trial' of Ferdinand and Miranda provide a much-needed, highly exploitable secondary gap between awarenesses. But its most salutary service is toward the cause of dramatic conflict. In an action devoid of actual conflict—in which, indeed, not only the winning of Miranda by Ferdinand, but even the all-encompassing purpose of Prospero promises to be too easy—whatever device can 'uneasy make' the road, or can be made to seem to do so, is a precious addition. Of this it will be necessary to speak more.

By making the courtship an 'ordeal', then, Shakespeare gains exploitable matter for three central scenes. Both ignorant that Prospero blesses their love—in fact, has willed it and wrought the tempest to make it possible—Ferdinand and Miranda hold a common level of awareness in the immediate situation. Their understandings of the enveloping situation are also even, but from different causes. Though only she knows that her father raised the tempest and that all the voyagers are safe, including the father for whose death the prince grieves, yet Miranda's vision is otherwise more limited than Ferdinand's. Lacking experience of any other world, she cannot judge what is remarkable in this one. Although she sees that her father controls all things, she does not see anything extraordinary in the fact. The invisible force that suddenly immobilizes and astonishes Ferdinand, she simply takes for granted—*as, indeed, having been conditioned, do we.* Spirits are the commonplaces of her experience; she marvels at first sight of Ferdinand, then sinks in disappointment: 'But 'tis a spirit.' Earlier, her utter lack of surprise on being told that Prospero had raised the sea storm helped to insinuate belief in his powers into our minds. Like Prospero himself, and like Caliban, Miranda is the ultimate figure of a line, the final result of a tendency. Even Perdita of *The Winter's Tale*, the least capable of her heroinely predecessors, could dispute ably with disguised King Polixenes about gillyflowers, and, in the one scene, evinced some competence to deal with life. Miranda could never

THE MASK AND THE MANTLE

deal with life: 'I have done nothing but in care / Of thee, my dear one, thee, my daughter, who / Art ignorant of what thou art', says Prospero—without whom this defenceless innocent could not survive at all in such a world.

In their youth and freshness, in the swiftness and intensity of their love, in the eagerness of each to sacrifice for the other, Ferdinand and Miranda are a new Romeo and Juliet. They are also like the tragic lovers in being quite helpless within their situation; both couples are pawns of an absolute power whose attention is centred on them. But the light in which we view them makes their conditions otherwise quite unlike: the love of Romeo and Juliet is doomed by Fate; that of Ferdinand and Miranda is blessed by Prospero. In the first balcony scene the shining joy of the star-crossed lovers is darkened by our knowledge that they are truly destroyed already; exploitation of the gap between their unawareness and our knowledge has the effect of intensifying our pain in contemplating their condition. But the ordeal of Ferdinand's labour and Miranda's misery for his sake is brightened by our awareness that they are blessed, and exploitation of the difference between their understanding and ours inspires in us a glow of paternal satisfaction like Prospero's; says Prospero, watching unseen while Miranda supposes him hard at study and 'safe for these three hours':

> So glad of this as they I cannot be,
> Who are surpris'd withal; but my rejoicing
> At nothing can be more.
>
> (III. i. 92–94.)

Throughout its course exploitation of the gap between the lovers' awareness and ours aims at this effect of satisfaction.

The affair of Ferdinand and Miranda, moving according to a rigid schedule that, in their misery, they dream not of, forms an idyllic portion of Prospero's total design. Less charming, but subject to the same absolute control, is the other portion—the affair of his enemies. Ignorant that their slightest action is known and their thought itself anticipated, the members of the King's party—except Gonzalo, the lone good man among them—are still oblivious rather than amazed when, in their turn, like Ferdinand before them, they first enter our residents'-eye view at the opening of Act II. Gonzalo alone remarks 'the miracle' of their salvation and marvels that 'our garments are now as fresh as when we put them on first in Afric'. The natures of Sebastian and Antonio, scoffing and vicious, are insensitive to wonder; and Alonso, sure that his son is drowned, is too distraught to be astonished by his own survival. During this scene our sense of the relation of these men to the supreme power of the island—a sense that is ever alerted anew by the comments of busy Ariel—functions variously. It provides, first of all, a warm assurance that no harm can come to the good Gonzalo, and thus contributes to that comfortable satisfaction which—as in the knowledge that the love of Ferdinand and Miranda is blessed—is the predominant effect of *The Tempest*. It is also an effect that can be achieved only because this brutal world is provided with a controlling force of uncompromised authority whose point of view we accept as our own.

Immediately, also, our awareness of Prospero provides assurance that no harm will befall Alonso, who, though formerly wicked, is just now being put by Prospero's art to the purgation of deep grief. Our knowledge that Ferdinand is both saved and enriched by a rare love is like a blessing held over the King's head, beyond his reach and out of his sight. It is in exploitation of the gap between Alonso's understanding and ours that Shakespeare creates effects of richer emotional force and complexity than elsewhere in *The Tempest*— for unlike the great comedies and the preceding romances, *The Tempest* rarely demands simultaneous conflicting responses. While Alonso suffers, our knowledge that all is well enables an experience that at once embraces satisfaction because justice is being served for past crime, and pity because his grief is profound and—Ferdinand being safe—needless. Especially upon Alonso Shakespeare requires that we look as from a great height, with the eyes of a god both severe and compassionate.

It is in the effects created by exploitation of Alonso's suffering that the contrast in the essential terms of *The Tempest* and the previous romances is most pronounced. There, when bereaved persons bewailed their losses and dreaded the hostile countenance of the universe, our own awareness, holding nothing to contradict their impressions, gave us no final comfort. Thus while Pericles grieved during the sea-storm in which Thaisa died in childbirth and was cast overboard, we had no evidence that the universe was kindlier than it seemed to him, no proof that there was any purpose in the heavens. But in *The Tempest*, immediately before Alonso cries 'My son is lost. . . . O thou mine heir / Of Naples and of Milan, what strange fish / Hath made his meal on thee?' we heard Ferdinand, happier than before he reached the island, proclaim that all trials 'are but light to me / Might I but through my prison once a day / Behold this maid'.

With respect to the trials of Gonzalo and Alonso, then, the chief effect of our advantage is satisfaction that they are safe; this is rather a steady, continuous, single effect than a series of sharp, showy effects. And it is a truly distinctive characteristic of *The Tempest* that the predominant result of exploitation is a steady and pervasive experience rather than explosive and sudden effects, as in earlier plays, when the purpose was to strike quick flashes of irony to light the discrepancy and then vanish.

With respect to Sebastian and Antonio the prevailing effect of our advantage is also warm satisfaction—but satisfaction born of knowledge that they can do no harm. These are beyond doubt the worst men of Shakespeare's invention. Callous, insensitive, checked by no thread of inner feeling, *they would be terrifying in any other world*: only our knowledge that a Prospero exists lets us see their antics as comic. Having just survived an experience that should have left them prayerful, they are instead quite unaffected; they scoff at Gonzalo as if nothing remarkable had happened, and the malice of their souls shows even in their jests. When invisible Ariel's music puts Gonzalo and Alonso suddenly to sleep, they squander only a moment on the marvel of it. Giving no more time to awe, Antonio sounds Sebastian on the question of fratricide-regicide, to be accompanied with an inconsequential detail, the ordinary murder of good Gonzalo—'This ancient morsel, this Sir Prudence, who / Should not upbraid our course.' There is a meeting of minds without need of persuasion: says Sebastian: '. . . as thou got'st Milan, / I'll come by Naples. Draw thy sword. One stroke / Shall free thee from the tribute which thou payest, / And I the King shall love thee.'

But in Prospero's world such brutes are harmless; though their swords are raised to strike, we cannot fear for Gonzalo and Alonso. Inevitably, before the blows can fall, ubiquitous Ariel comes: 'My master through his art foresees the danger / That you, his friend, are in; and sends me forth— / For else his project dies—to keep them living.'

Antonio and Sebastian, Stephano and Trinculo: such are the brutes who would rule Shakespeare's final world if there were no Prospero. The scenes which show the second pair occasion the same basic satisfaction, with added ludicrous effects. Like Sebastian and Antonio they are oblivious when they should be awe-struck. The first thought of each on discovering Caliban is to carry him back to civilization so as to gain money by exhibiting him; the second thought, to seize the opportunity offered by the shipwreck and loss of their superiors: 'Trinculo, the King and all our company else being drown'd, we will inherit here.' But though, like the other pair, they are uninhibited by anything like conscience, they too are helpless to do harm. Therefore it is possible to laugh freely at their antics. Joining with Caliban to invade Prospero's cell, kill him, and seize Miranda—'His daughter and I will be king and queen'—these specimens of human bestiality sound fierce indeed, and in another world their threat would be appalling. Here, however, Prospero's invisible instrument is with them, as with the other pair, at each critical moment:

> *Cal.* Within this half hour will he be asleep.
>   Wilt thou destroy him then?
> *Ste.*   Ay, on mine honour.
> *Ari.* This will I tell my master.
>
>   (III. ii. 122–4.)

But the Ferdinand–Miranda scenes, when we know and the lovers do not that Prospero blesses and brought about their meeting; the scenes of the former usurpers of Prospero's dukedom, ending with their guilt-maddened flight when the very thunder 'pronounc'd / The name of Prosper'; and the scenes of the clownish brutes, murder-bent but led astray, bewitched by invisible Ariel's tabor: these scenes—which consume three-fifths of the total action and carry the main dramatic burden until the climactic masque of Act IV—evince both the fundamental dramatic dilemma of *The Tempest* and Shakespeare's effort to solve it.

For unmistakably, in order to regain the rich resource of an exploitable discrepancy of richer potential than any before it, Shakespeare also raised a dramatic problem like none he had faced before. In order to recreate in the harsh world of *The Tempest* the old climate of comedy, with its warm assurance that all is well, he introduced at the outset of action a benevolent force *of such enormous power that it denied the possibility of true dramatic conflict as a source of dramatic interest.* In the preceding romances the problem was the converse of this. There, since we were kept ignorant that a benevolent force controlled the world, the effects of conflict were strong, and aroused genuine anxiety—but at the end rose the problem of achieving the appearance of designed, as opposed to chance-wrought, ending for action that had seemed to run without design. Shakespeare 'solved' this problem by asserting at last that external powers of planetary proportions had always been in control: 'Be not with mortal accidents opprest,' / said Jupiter; 'No care of yours it is; you know 'tis ours.' Had we known at first in *Pericles* and *Cymbeline* that benign gods were directing human affairs, the excitement of dramatic conflict would certainly have been diminished or altogether eliminated—unless, like Homer, Shakespeare had left room for uncertainty by showing discord in the heavens.

In the comedies through *Measure for Measure*, though beginnings

often made endings predictable and though regularly some participant was included who as a means of control foreshadowed the
ultimate Prospero, yet always also ample space was left for conflict: *no controlling person ever had such power as to make the idea
of struggle incompatible with the idea of his power*. Oberon of *A
Midsummer-Night's Dream* is served by a fallible and mischievous
sprite, whose error fills the woods with night-long jangling. Portia
of *The Merchant of Venice*, though marvellously capable, is not
so strong that the tension of the court scene is destroyed by her
arrival; on the contrary, her arrival tightens a contest which until
then had been slack, Shylock having no effective opposition. Duke
Vincentio of *Measure for Measure* is the most potent force employed in the comedies against the swelling evil, and it is undeniable
that, acting as Duke, he could resolve instantly and easily the difficulties raised by Angelo. But our knowledge that he could do so
does not destroy the dramatic tension, because it is not as Duke but
as Friar that he seeks to win justice and mercy—and to win as Friar
requires hard struggle, bustling activity, and great inventiveness:
indeed, it requires more than the Friar can do. In any event, even in
Measure for Measure, where the benevolent force comes nearest
the absoluteness of Prospero, space is left for struggle and for the
dramatic effects that struggle of the mightiest opposites, vice and
virtue, can produce. The fact is that in *Measure for Measure*, with
the Duke doubling as the Friar, Shakespeare enjoyed the luxury of
two rich sources of dramatic interest: that of conflict, in the 'friar's'
struggle to make truth prevail against great odds; and that of exploitation of the gap which always lies between the participants'
ignorance and our awareness of the mighty Duke's presence.

But in *The Tempest* Shakespeare is denied, or denies himself, both
of these sources. Prospero does not assume a humble character and
strive to win against odds. Prospero is always Prospero, whose godlike power is so conclusively demonstrated in the first scene and so
firmly consolidated in our minds by means of the successive interviews with Miranda, Ariel, and Caliban as to make it inconceivable
thereafter that any design of his could fail or that any creature in
his world could get out of hand. All that is and all that is to be must
be by his will, alone and uncontested. The world represented in the
play, like the art which represents it, is so tightly controlled that
such dramatic conflict as had always been one of Shakespeare's
staples becomes impossible. The dramatist's art in the opening scenes
fixes the idea that every movement occurs by Prospero's sufferance,
represents part of a design already complete in his mind, and falls
into place according to an exact time schedule. The 'ordeal' of

Ferdinand and Miranda, the attempts of Sebastian and Antonio
on the lives of Alonso and Gonzalo, the conspiracy of Caliban,
Stephano, and Trinculo against Prospero himself: these major incidents of the action, during which the active exploitation of discrepant awarenesses occurs, in fact only mark time within a stationary
pattern that was finished on the instant that the voyagers' ship
entered Prospero's waters. For Prospero all is easy: it can be accomplished with a thought, leaving him not even breathed by the strain.

Perhaps, in reaction from the way of the first three romances,
when he afflicted us with the participants' own anxieties, Shakespeare went too far in *The Tempest* and provided us with too great
assurance too soon. In exceeding the degree of awareness and control given Vincentio in *Measure for Measure*, he truly paid a heavy
price in the forfeiture of such dramatic interest as in earlier plays
came easily from the exhibition of conflict. The dramatic dilemma
of *The Tempest*, to state it finally, is an ironic one: *that here, where
the extreme opposition of brutes and innocents holds a potentiality
of uncommonly exciting struggle, there exists also a power of such
magnitude that even the common effects of conflict are eliminated.*

The dilemma was unquestionably one of deliberate choice. It is
not likely that Shakespeare forgot in *The Tempest* what he had
known in *Henry VI* and practised without deviation for more than
twenty years in comedy, history, and tragedy. He could have
avoided the dilemma in any of several obvious ways. He could have
imposed some special limitation on Prospero's power—or raised
that of his enemies nearer to equality. But he neither gives Prospero
an Achilles' heel nor suggests that his opponents are other than impotent. 'They all enter the circle which Prospero had made, and
there stand charmed': thus, the relation of the 'opposites' throughout the action. He could have involved Prospero in conflict with
gods. But he does not make this isle an Olympus; only one god is
mentioned, and he, by Caliban's own testimony, could not match
Prospero, whose

> . . . art is of such power
> It would control my dam's god, Setebos,
> And make a vassal of him.
>
> (I. ii. 372–4.)

He could have represented Prospero in conflict with himself—
but he rejects the possibility at the opening of Act V, when Ariel
raises the question of punishment or forgiveness for the enemies
helpless at Prospero's feet. Clearly, this question could have been
made the cause of great inner struggle for Prospero, and had *The
Tempest* centred on it dramatic tension would have been assured.

But nowhere is Prospero's nature evinced with more finality than in the announcement of his intention—which suggests no struggle, but only that struggle might have been had he been less than he is:

> *Ari.*   Your charm so strongly works 'em
> That if you now beheld them, your affections
> Would become tender.
> *Pros.*   Dost thou think so, spirit?
> *Ari.* Mine would, sir, were I human.
> *Pros.*   And mine shall.
> Hast thou, which art but air, a touch, a feeling
> Of their afflictions, and shall not myself,
> One of their kind, that relish all as sharply,
> Passion as they, be kindlier moved than thou art?
> Though with their high wrongs I am struck to the quick,
> Yet with my nobler reason 'gainst my fury
> Do I take part: the rarer action is
> In virtue than in vengeance: they being penitent,
> The sole drift of my purpose doth extend
> Not a frown further.
>
>   (v. i. 17–30.)

Though until this statement we have ourselves not known Prospero's plans for his old enemies, we have not been made to suppose either that he was himself uncertain or that he had at first intended vengeance rather than forgiveness. Neither the announcement nor anything earlier suggests inner struggle before the decision is reached. Prospero is not a Lear, who has to learn his lesson in human sympathy; whatever *The Tempest* is, it is not an account of Prospero's struggle with and final triumph over baser elements in himself.

Finally, had he wished to give the interest of conflict its usual large place, Shakespeare could have taken the way of the preceding romances, denying us acquaintance with Prospero and his power until the denouement. We should then, perhaps, have seen him first at the end of Act IV, emerging from his cell like Jupiter from the sky. But it is precisely this way that Shakespeare renounces with greatest emphasis, stamping the idea of the absoluteness of Prospero on our awareness in the first hundred lines of Act I and thus preparing a return to the old way of the comedies in providing us with assurance through our superior awareness.

Evidently, then, Shakespeare deliberately denied himself the use of conflict as a major source of dramatic interest. Nevertheless, occasionally, to the extent that he can do so without compromising Prospero's absoluteness, he stirs up an illusion of struggle: he would not be Shakespeare if, having made it impossible to use conflict, he did not then manage to use it a little. The most notable occasion is the ending of the masque, when Prospero 'starts suddenly', and the actor-spirits 'heavily vanish' with a 'strange, hollow, and confused noise'. In this climactic moment, perhaps, there is excitement, since it is made to appear that something has gone wrong, or has nearly done so—for of course nothing can really go wrong. Says Prospero aside:

> I had forgot that foul conspiracy
> Of the beast Caliban and his confederates
> Against my life: the minute of their plot
> Is almost come.
>
> (IV. i. 139-42.)

'Your father's in some passion / That works him strongly', says Ferdinand; and Miranda: 'Never till this day / Saw I him touch'd with anger so distemper'd.' A moment later he expresses vexation for his failure to reform the brute Caliban: 'A devil, a born devil, on whose nature / Nurture can never stick; on whom my pains, / Humanely taken, all, all lost, quite lost.'

An element of conflict is suggested also by Ariel's periodic demands for his freedom, and if it had been emphasized the threat of desertion by Prospero's chief instrument might have created considerable tension. But it is not emphasized; both the spirit and the brute are quite subdued, and no conflict of enough intensity to generate more than the bare appearance of it is gained from them. If Prospero's control of these two, and of other assorted 'shapes' of the island, is not so utterly easy as his domination of mortal enemies, yet neither is his power taxed in managing them. On the other hand, it seems unlikely that Shakespeare meant something of profound philosophical significance in representing Ariel as clamouring to be free and Caliban as incapable of redemption: these 'tests' of Prospero's power are dramatic devices which simulate conflict in a drama that really has none. And as for the 'vexation' moment at the end of the masque, it occurs just where the climactic peak normally stands in the comedies and the earlier romances. Perhaps Shakespeare may be excused for cheating just a little here: suggesting the excitement of climax in an action that, having no struggle, can have no climax is a difficult feat.

In spite of all, thus, Shakespeare contrives to create an occasional effect of conflict without compromising Prospero's absoluteness. But it is undeniable that *The Tempest* contains no genuine conflict. Prospero's human enemies are already defeated and helpless when the action starts; the non-human creatures, from brute to spirit, though vigilance is required to keep them in order, are quite incapable of breaking loose; and Prospero's own nature contains no rebellious elements. No real dramatic excitement can be engendered by his 'struggle' to regain and triumph in regaining his dukedom; not only is the task easy for him, but a dukedom is a small prize beside what he already enjoys: Prospero as god is more than Prospero as duke. Except for Miranda, he would not bother to return at all.

Interests other than the interest of struggle, certainly, *The Tempest* provides in profusion: there is the interest of poetry, which here achieves such accents as even Shakespeare had not touched before, poetry in which music, imagery, and matter combine to work a magic spell as potent as Prospero's own; there is the interest of spectacle: *The Tempest* offers Shakespeare's most extravagant assortment of strange and wonderful shapes, movements, poses, and settings; and there is the interest of character, exhibited in a range from the brute beast in whom the human is barely discernible up to the pure spirit touched with human sympathies, and to Prospero himself, who without making an issue of the matter simply prefers virtue to vengeance. But though the aggregate of these features is something rich and strange, their sum does not equal the dramatic interest that in other plays arises from representation of conflict; nor can this sum of interests adequately substitute for dramatic interest derived from conflict.

The forfeiture of conflict as a major source places virtually the whole responsibility for dramatic interest upon exploitation of discrepancies in awareness. The evident deliberateness with which Shakespeare refused to compromise an absolute power the knowledge of whose existence, held in our minds, made this exploitation possible at the expense of conflict is a final affirmation of faith in a dramatic method that had served him throughout his career.

Plainly, in *The Tempest* Shakespeare did not seek to represent struggle itself, but to proffer its fruits. Prospero's struggle is all past when this action commences—his struggle first to survive and then to acquire the power which is an accomplished fact when first we meet him and which renders further struggle unnecessary and impossible. The past struggle was long and hard. Its significance as underlying the action that we witness is implied by Prospero's heavy insistence that Miranda—and we too of course, for this is oblique exposition—heed well his account of it; eight times in their first brief scene he tells her to stay awake and mark the story. The interviews with Ariel and Caliban, immediately following, complete the account of his struggle to attain the place he now holds and contribute to our sense of the past struggle, the fierceness of which is suggested by the tones used to describe it.

Sharing the point of view of a god who is as mortal as ourselves, we are privileged to savour with him the fruits of this past struggle. Such is the dramatic satisfaction which in *The Tempest* largely replaces the excitement of dramatic conflict and which justifies Shakespeare's choosing, in spite of serious disadvantages, to introduce his god in Act I: it is the satisfaction of certainty that such innocents as Ferdinand and Miranda are protected in this world; the satisfaction of perceiving that such virtues as Gonzalo's do not go unnoticed; the basic satisfaction of seeing evil utterly helpless in the grasp of good.

These satisfactions, replacing the more dazzling cross-plays of the comedies, are the last benefits yielded by exploitation of the discrepancy between the participants' ignorance and our Olympian vision. They have a final, closing effect. It is difficult to imagine to what farther frontier Shakespeare could have pushed the use of his favourite dramatic condition.